C000253801

The Courage of Truth

Also in this series:

Forthcoming in this series:

MICHEL FOUCAULT

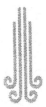

The Courage of Truth
(The Government of Self and Others II)
LECTURES AT THE COLLÈGE DE FRANCE
1983-1984

Edited by Frédéric Gros
General Editors: François Ewald and Alessandro Fontana

English Series Editor: Arnold I. Davidson

TRANSLATED BY GRAHAM BURCHELL

Liberté • Égalité • Fraternité
RÉPUBLIQUE FRANÇAISE

This book is supported by the
French Ministry of Foreign Affairs,
as part of the Burgess programme
run by the Cultural Department of
the French Embassy in London.
(www.frenchbooknews.com)

palgrave
macmillan

THE COURAGE OF TRUTH

© Éditions du Seuil/Gallimard 2008, Edition established under the direction of François Ewald and Alessandro Fontana, by Frédéric Gros. Translation © Graham Burchell 2011.
Softcover reprint of the hardcover 1st edition 2011 978-1-4039-8668-9

All rights reserved. No reproduction, copy or transmission of this publication may be made without written permission.

No portion of this publication may be reproduced, copied or transmitted save with written permission or in accordance with the provisions of the Copyright, Designs and Patents Act 1988, or under the terms of any licence permitting limited copying issued by the Copyright Licensing Agency, Saffron House, 6-10 Kirby Street, London EC 1N 8TS.

Any person who does any unauthorised act in relation to this publication may be liable to criminal prosecution and civil claims for damages.

The author has asserted his right to be identified as the author of this work in accordance with the Copyright, Designs and Patents Act 1988.

First published 2011 by
PALGRAVE MACMILLAN

Palgrave Macmillan in the UK is an imprint of Macmillan Publishers Limited, registered in England, company number 785998, of Houndmills, Basingstoke, Hampshire RG21 6XS.

Palgrave Macmillan in the US is a division of St Martin's Press LLC, 175 Fifth Avenue, New York, NY 10010.

Palgrave Macmillan is the global academic imprint of the above companies and has companies and representatives throughout the world.

Palgrave® and Macmillan® are registered trademarks in the United States, the United Kingdom, Europe and other countries

ISBN 978-1-4039-8669-6   ISBN 978-0-230-30910-4 (eBook)
DOI 10.1057/9780230309104

A catalogue record for this book is available from the British Library.

A catalog record for this book is available from the Library of Congress.

10 9 8 7 6 5 4 3 2 1
20 19 18 17 16 15 14 13 12 11

Transferred to Digital Printing in 2014

CONTENTS

FOREWORD

MICHEL FOUCAULT TAUGHT AT the Collège de France from January 1971 until his death in June 1984 (with the exception of 1977 when he took a sabbatical year). The title of his chair was "The History of Systems of Thought."

On the proposal of Jules Vuillemin, the chair was created on 30 November 1969 by the general assembly of the professors of the Collège de France and replaced that of "The History of Philosophical Thought" held by Jean Hyppolite until his death. The same assembly elected Michel Foucault to the new chair on 12 April 1970.[1] He was 43 years old.

Michel Foucault's inaugural lecture was delivered on 2 December 1970.[2] Teaching at the Collège de France is governed by particular rules. Professors must provide 26 hours of teaching a year (with the possibility of a maximum of half this total being given in the form of seminars[3]). Each year they must present their original research and this obliges them to change the content of their teaching for each course. Courses and seminars are completely open; no enrolment or qualification is required and the professors do not award any qualifications.[4] In the terminology of the Collège de France, the professors do not have students but only auditors.

Michel Foucault's courses were held every Wednesday from January to March. The huge audience made up of students, teachers, researchers and the curious, including many who came from outside France, required two amphitheatres of the Collège de France. Foucault often complained about the distance between himself and his "public" and of how few exchanges the course made possible.[5] He would have liked a seminar in which real collective work could take place and made a number of attempts to bring this about. In the final years he devoted a long period to answering his auditors' questions at the end of each course.

This is how Gérard Petitjean, a journalist from *Le Nouvel Observateur*, described the atmosphere at Foucault's lectures in 1975:

> When Foucault enters the amphitheater, brisk and dynamic like someone who plunges into the water, he steps over bodies to reach his chair, pushes away the cassette recorders so he can put down his papers, removes his jacket, lights a lamp and sets off at full speed. His voice is strong and effective, amplified by the loudspeakers that are the only concession to modernism in a hall that is barely lit by light spread from stucco bowls. The hall has three hundred places and there are five hundred people packed together, filling the smallest free space...There is no oratorical effect. It is clear and terribly effective. There is absolutely no concession to improvisation. Foucault has twelve hours each year to explain in a public course the direction taken by his research in the year just ended. So everything is concentrated and he fills the margins like correspondents who have too much to say for the space available to them. At 19.15 Foucault stops. The students rush towards his desk; not to speak to him, but to stop their cassette recorders. There are no questions. In the pushing and shoving Foucault is alone. Foucault remarks: "It should be possible to discuss what I have put forward. Sometimes, when it has not been a good lecture, it would need very little, just one question, to put everything straight. However, this question never comes. The group effect in France makes any genuine discussion impossible. And as there is no feedback, the course is theatricalized. My relationship with the people there is like that of an actor or an acrobat. And when I have finished speaking, a sensation of total solitude..."[6]

Foucault approached his teaching as a researcher: explorations for a future book as well as the opening up of fields of problematization were formulated as an invitation to possible future researchers. This is why the courses at the Collège de France do not duplicate the published books. They are not sketches for the books even though both books and courses share certain themes. They have their own status. They arise from a specific discursive regime within the set of Foucault's "philosophical activities." In particular they set out the program for a genealogy of knowledge/power relations, which are the terms in which he thinks of his work from the beginning of the 1970s, as opposed to the program of an archeology of discursive formations that previously orientated his work.[7]

The course also performed a role in contemporary reality. Those who followed his courses were not only held in thrall by the narrative that unfolded week by week and seduced by the rigorous exposition, they also found a perspective on contemporary reality. Michel Foucault's art consisted in using history to cut diagonally through contemporary reality. He could speak of Nietzsche or Aristotle, of expert psychiatric opinion or the Christian pastoral, but those who attended his lectures always took from what he said a perspective on the present and contemporary events. Foucault's specific strength in his courses was the subtle interplay between learned erudition, personal commitment, and work on the event.

✤

With their development and refinement in the 1970s, Foucault's desk was quickly invaded by cassette recorders. The courses—and some seminars—have thus been preserved.

This edition is based on the words delivered in public by Foucault. It gives a transcription of these words that is as literal as possible.[8] We would have liked to present it as such. However, the transition from an oral to a written presentation calls for editorial intervention: at the very least it requires the introduction of punctuation and division into paragraphs. Our principle has been always to remain as close as possible to the course actually delivered.

Summaries and repetitions have been removed whenever it seemed to be absolutely necessary. Interrupted sentences have been restored and faulty constructions corrected. Suspension points indicate that the recording is inaudible. When a sentence is obscure there is a conjectural integration or an addition between square brackets. An asterisk directing the reader to the bottom of the page indicates a significant divergence between the notes used by Foucault and the words actually uttered. Quotations have been checked and references to the texts used are indicated. The critical apparatus is limited to the elucidation of obscure points, the explanation of some allusions and the clarification of critical points. To make the lectures easier to read, each lecture is preceded by a brief summary that indicates its principal articulations.

The text of the course is followed by the summary published by the *Annuaire du Collège de France*. Foucault usually wrote these in June, some time after the end of the course. It was an opportunity for him to pick out retrospectively the intention and objectives of the course. It constitutes the best introduction to the course.*

Each volume ends with a "context" for which the course editors are responsible. It seeks to provide the reader with elements of the biographical, ideological, and political context, situating the course within the published work and providing indications concerning its place within the corpus used in order to facilitate understanding and to avoid misinterpretations that might arise from a neglect of the circumstances in which each course was developed and delivered.

The Courage of the Truth (The Government of Self and Others II) the course delivered in 1984, is edited by Frédéric Gros.

A new aspect of Michel Foucault's "œuvre" is published with this edition of the Collège de France courses.

Strictly speaking it is not a matter of unpublished work, since this edition reproduces words uttered publicly by Foucault, excluding the often highly developed written material he used to support his lectures. Daniel Defert possesses Michel Foucault's notes and he is to be warmly thanked for allowing the editors to consult them.

---

* [There are, however, no summaries for the lectures given in 1983 and 1984; G.B.]

This edition of the Collège de France courses was authorized by Michel Foucault's heirs who wanted to be able to satisfy the strong demand for their publication, in France as elsewhere, and to do this under indisputably responsible conditions. The editors have tried to be equal to the degree of confidence placed in them.

FRANÇOIS EWALD AND ALESSANDRO FONTANA

1. Michel Foucualt concluded a short document drawn up in support of his candidacy with these words: "We should undertake the history of systems of thought." "Titres et travaux," in *Dits et Écrits, 1954-1988*, four volumes, eds. Daniel Defert and François Ewald (Paris: Gallimard, 1994) vol. 1, p. 846; English translation by Robert Hurley, "Candidacy Presentation: Collège de France" in *The Essential Works of Michel Foucault, 1954-1984, vol. 1: Ethics: Subjectivity and Truth*, ed. Paul Rabinow (New York: The New Press, 1997) p. 9.
2. It was published by Gallimard in May 1971 with the title *L'Ordre du discours*, Paris, 1971. English translation by Rupert Swyer, "The Order of Discourse," appendix to M. Foucault, *The Archeology of Knowledge* (New York: Pantheon, 1972).
3. This was Foucault's practice until the start of the 1980s.
4. Within the framework of the Collège de France.
5. In 1976, in the vain hope of reducing the size of the audience, Michel Foucault changed the time of his course from 17.45 to 9.00. See the beginning of the first lecture (7 January 1976) of *"Il faut défendre la société." Cours au Collège de France, 1976* (Paris: Gallimard/Seuil, 1997); English translation by David Macey, *"Society Must be Defended." Lectures at the Collège de France 1975-1976* (New York: Picador, 2003).
6. Gérard Petitjean, "Les Grands Prêtres de l'université française," *Le Nouvel Observateur*, 7 April 1975.
7. See especially, "Nietzsche, la généalogie, l'histoire," in *Dits et Écrits*, vol. 2, p. 137; English translation by Donald F. Brouchard and Sherry Simon, "Nietzsche, Genealogy, History" in *The Essential Works of Michel Foucault 1954-1984, vol. 2: Aesthetics, Method, and Epistemology*, ed. James Faubion (New York: The New Press, 1998) pp. 369-392.
8. We have made use of the recordings made by Gilbert Burlet and Jacques Lagrange in particular. These are deposited in the Collège de France and the Institut Mémoires de l'Édition Contemporaine.

one

1 FEBRUARY 1984

First hour

Epistemological structures and alethurgic forms. ∽ *Genealogy of the study of* parrhēsia: *practices of truth-telling about oneself.* ∽ *The master of existence in the domain of the care of self.* ∽ *Its main defining feature:* parrhēsia. ∽ *Reminder of the political origin of the notion.* ∽ *Double value of* parrhēsia. ∽ *Structural features: truth, commitment, and risk.* ∽ *The parrhesiastic pact.* ∽ Parrhēsia *versus rhetoric.* ∽ Parrhēsia *as a specific modality of truth-telling.* ∽ *Differential study of two other kinds of truth-telling in ancient culture: prophecy and wisdom.* ∽ *Heraclitus and Socrates.*

[...*] THIS YEAR I WOULD like continue with the theme of *parrhēsia*, truth-telling, that I began to talk about last year. The lectures I would like to give will no doubt be somewhat disjointed because they deal

---

* The lecture begins with the following statements:
  - I was not able to start my lectures as usual at the beginning of January. I was ill, really ill. There were rumors saying that changing the dates was a way for me to get rid of some of my auditors. Not at all, I was really ill. And so I ask you to accept my apologies. I see moreover that it has not solved the problem of the number of places. Is the other room not open? You have asked? The answer was categorical?
  [answer from the public] - Oh yes.
  - It will not be open?
  - Yes, if we make a request.
  - If we make a request... Then I am all the more sorry because I thought it would automatically be open. Would it bother you to see if it isn't possible to have it opened now or possibly for the next hour? I hate having you come here to be left in these dreadful material conditions.

with things that I would like to have done with, as it were, in order
to return, after this several years long Greco-Latin *"trip,"*[*][1] to some
contemporary problems which I will deal with either in the second
part of the course, or possibly in the form of a working seminar.

Well then, I shall remind you of something. You know that the rules
are that the lectures of the Collège are and must be public. So it is quite
right that anyone, French citizens or otherwise, has the right to come
and listen to them. The Collège professors are obliged to report regularly on their research in these public lectures. However, this principle
poses problems and raises a number of difficulties, because the work,
the research one may undertake—especially [with regard to] questions
like those I dealt with previously [and] to which I would now like to
return, that is to say the analysis of certain practices and institutions in
modern society—increasingly involves collective work which, of course,
can only be pursued in the form of a closed seminar, and not in a room
like this and with such a large public.[2] I am not going to hide from you
the fact that I shall raise the problem of whether it is possible, whether
it may be institutionally acceptable to divide the work I am doing here
between public lectures—which, once again, are part of the job and of
your rights—and lectures which would be restricted to small working
groups with some students or researchers who have a more specialized
interest in the question being studied. The public lectures would be, as
it were, the exoteric version of the somewhat more esoteric work in a
group. In any case, I don't know how many public lectures I will give or
for how long. So, if you like, let's get going and then we'll see.

This year I would like to continue the study of free-spokenness
(*franc-parler*), of *parrhēsia* as modality of truth-telling. I will restate
the general idea for those of you who were not here last year. It is
absolutely true that the analysis of the specific structures of those discourses which claim to be and are accepted as true discourse is both
interesting and important. Broadly speaking, we could call the analysis of these structures an epistemological analysis. On the other hand,
it seemed to me that it would be equally interesting to analyze the
conditions and forms of the type of act by which the subject *manifests*
himself when speaking the truth, by which I mean, thinks of himself

---

* In English in original.

and is recognized by others as speaking the truth. Rather than analyzing the forms by which a discourse is recognized as true, this would
involve analyzing the form in which, in his act of telling the truth, the
individual constitutes himself and is constituted by others as a subject of a discourse of truth, the form in which he presents himself to
himself and to others as someone who tells the truth, the form of the
subject telling the truth. In contrast with the study of epistemological structures, the analysis of this domain could be called the study of
"alethurgic" forms. I am using here a word which I commented on last
year or two years ago. Etymologically, alethurgy would be the production of truth, the act by which truth is manifested.[3] So, let's leave the
kind of analysis which focuses on "epistemological structure" to one
side and begin to analyze "alethurgic forms." This is the framework in
which I am studying the notion and practice of *parrhēsia*, but for those
of you who were not here I would like to recall how I arrived at this
problem. I came to it from the old, traditional question, which is at the
very heart of Western philosophy, of the relations between subject and
truth, a question which I posed, which I took up first of all in classical, usual, and traditional terms, that is to say: on the basis of what
practices and through what types of discourse have we tried to tell the
truth about the subject? Thus: on the basis of what practices, through
what types of discourse have we tried to tell the truth about the mad
subject or the delinquent subject?[4] On the basis of what discursive
practices was the speaking, laboring, and living subject constituted as
a possible object of knowledge (*savoir*)?[5] This was the field of study that
I tried to cover for a period.

And then I tried to envisage this same question of subject/truth
relations in another form: not that of the discourse of truth in which
the truth about the subject can be told, but that of the discourse of
truth which the subject is likely and able to speak about himself, which
may be, for example, avowal, confession, or examination of conscience.
This was the analysis of the subject's true discourse about himself, and
it was easy to see the importance of this discourse for penal practices
or in the domain of the experience of sexuality.[6]

This theme, this problem led me, in previous years' lectures, to
[attempt] the historical analysis of practices of telling the truth about
oneself. In undertaking this analysis I noticed something completely

unexpected. To be more precise, I shall say that it is easy to note the great importance of the principle that one should tell the truth about oneself in all of ancient morality and in Greek and Roman culture. In support and as illustration of the importance of this principle in ancient culture, we can cite such frequently, constantly, continually recommended practices [as] the examination of conscience prescribed by the Pythagoreans or Stoics, of which Seneca provides such elaborate examples, and which are found again in Marcus Aurelius.[7] We can also cite practices like correspondence, the exchange of moral, spiritual letters, examples of which can be found in Seneca, Pliny the Younger, Fronto, and Marcus Aurelius.[8] We can also cite, again as illustration of this principle "one should tell the truth about oneself," other, perhaps less well-known practices which have left fewer traces, like the notebooks, the kinds of journals which people were recommended to keep about themselves, either for the recollection and meditation of things one has experienced or read, or to record one's dreams when waking up.[9]

So it is quite easy to locate a very clear and solid set of practices in ancient culture which involve telling the truth about oneself. These practices are certainly not unknown and I make no claim to having discovered them; that is not my intention. But I think there is a consistent tendency to analyze these forms of practices of telling the truth about oneself by relating them, as it were, to a central axis which is, of course—and entirely legitimately—the Socratic principle of "know yourself": they are then seen as the illustration, the implementation, the concrete exemplification of the principle of *gnōthi seauton*. But I think it would be interesting to situate these practices in a broader context defined by a principle of which the *gnōthi seauton* is itself only an implication. This principle—I think I tried to bring this out in the lectures I gave two years ago—is that of *epimeleia heautou* (care of self, application to oneself).[10] This precept, which is so archaic, so ancient in Greek and Roman culture, and which in Platonic texts, and [more] precisely in the Socratic dialogues, is regularly associated with the *gnōthi seauton*, this principle (*epimelē seautō*: take care of yourself) gave rise, I think, to the development of what could be called a "culture of self"[11] in which a whole set of practices of self are formulated, developed, worked out, and transmitted. Studying these practices of self as the historical framework in which the injunction "one should tell the truth about oneself" developed, I saw a figure emerge who was constantly present as the indispensable partner, at any rate the almost necessary helper in this obligation to tell the truth about oneself. To put it more clearly and concretely, I shall say: we do not have to wait until Christianity, until the institutionalization of the confession at the start of the thirteenth century,[12] until the organization and installation of a pastoral power,[13] for the practice of telling the truth about oneself to rely upon and appeal to the presence of the other person who listens and enjoins one to speak, and who speaks himself. In ancient culture, and therefore well before Christianity, telling the truth about oneself was an activity involving several people, an activity with other people, and even more precisely an activity with one other person, a practice for two. And it was this other person who is present, and necessarily present in the practice of telling the truth about oneself, which caught and held my attention.

The status and presence of this other person who is so necessary for me to be able to tell the truth about myself obviously poses some problems. It is not so easy to analyze, for if it is true that we are relatively familiar with the other who is necessary for telling the truth about oneself in Christian culture, in which he takes the institutional form of the confessor or spiritual director, and if it is fairly easy to spot this other person in modern culture, whose status and functions should no doubt be analyzed more precisely—this other person who is indispensable for me to be able to tell the truth about myself, whether in the role of doctor, psychiatrist, psychologist, or psychoanalyst—on the other hand, in ancient culture, where this role is nevertheless well attested, we have to acknowledge that its status is much more variable, vague, much less clear cut and institutionalized. In ancient culture this other who is necessary for me to be able to tell the truth about myself might be a professional philosopher, but he could be anybody. You recall, for example, the passage in Galen on the cure of errors and passions, in which he says that to tell the truth about oneself and to know oneself we need someone else whom we can pick up almost anywhere, so long as he is old enough and serious.[14] This person may be a professional philosopher, or he may be just anybody. He may be a teacher who is more or less part of an institutionalized pedagogical structure

(Epictetus directed a school),[15] but he may be a personal friend, or a lover. He may be a provisional guide for a young man who is not yet fully mature, who has not yet made his basic choices in life, who is not yet the full master of himself, but he may also be a permanent adviser who will accompany someone throughout his life and guide him until death. You recall, for example, the Cynic Demetrius who was the counselor of Thrasea Paetus, an important figure in Roman political life in the middle of the first century, and who served him as counselor until the day of his death, until his suicide—since Demetrius was present at the suicide of Thrasea Paetus and conversed with him until his last breath about the immortality of the soul, naturally in the manner of the Socratic dialogue.[16]

The status of this other person is variable therefore. Nor is it any easier to isolate and define his role, his practice, since in one respect it is connected with and leans on pedagogy, but it is also guidance of the soul. It may also be a sort of political advice. But equally the role may be presented metaphorically and even manifest itself and take shape as a sort medical practice, since it is a question of taking care of the soul[17] and of fixing a regimen of life, which includes, of course, the regimen of passions, but also the dietary regimen,[18] and the mode of life in all its aspects.

However, even if the role of this other person who is indispensable for telling the truth about oneself is uncertain or, if you like, polyvalent, even if it appears with a number of different aspects and profiles—medical, political, and pedagogical—which mean that it is not always easy to grasp exactly what his role is, even so, whatever his role, status, function, and profile may be, this other has, or rather should have a particular kind of qualification in order to be the real and effective partner of truth-telling about self. And this qualification, unlike the confessor's or spiritual director's in Christian culture, is not given by an institution and does not refer to the possession and exercise of specific spiritual powers. Nor is it, as in modern culture, an institutional qualification guaranteeing a psychological, psychiatric, or psychoanalytic knowledge. The qualification required by this uncertain, rather vague, and variable character is a practice, a certain way of speaking which is called, precisely, *parrhēsia* (free-spokenness).

To be sure, it has now become quite difficult for us to recapture this notion of *parrhēsia*, of speaking out freely, constitutive of the figure of this other person who is indispensable for me to be able to tell the truth about myself. But it has nonetheless left many traces in the Latin and Greek texts. In the first place, it has obviously left traces in the fairly frequent use of the word, and then also through references to the notion even when the word itself is not used. We find many examples, in Seneca in particular, where the practice of *parrhēsia* is very clearly picked out in descriptions and characterizations, practically without the word being used, if only because of the difficulties the Latins had translating the word *parrhēsia* itself.[19] Apart from these occurrences of the word or references to the notion, there are also some texts which are more or less wholly devoted to the notion of *parrhēsia*. From the first century before Jesus Christ, there is the text of the Epicurean Philodemus, who wrote a *Peri parrhēsia*, a large part of which is sadly lost.[20] But there is also Plutarch's treatise, *How to Distinguish the Flatterer from the Friend*, which is entirely taken up with an analysis of *parrhēsia*, or rather of the two opposed, conflicting practices of flattery, on the one hand, and *parrhēsia* (free-spokenness) on the other.[21] There is Galen's text, which I referred to a moment ago, on the cure of errors and passions, in which a whole section is devoted to *parrhēsia* and to the choice of the person who is rightly qualified as being able and having to use this free-spokenness so that the individual can, in turn, tell the truth about himself and constitute himself as subject telling the truth about himself.[22] So this is how I was led to focus on this notion of *parrhēsia* as a constitutive component of truth-telling about self or, more precisely, as the element which qualifies the other person who is necessary in the game and obligation of speaking the truth about self.

You may recall that last year I undertook the analysis of this free-spokenness, of the practice of *parrhēsia*, and of the character able to employ *parrhēsia*, who is called the parrhesiast (*parrhēsiastēs*)—the word appears later. The study of *parrhēsia* and of the *parrhēsiastēs* in the culture of self in Antiquity is obviously a sort of prehistory of those practices which are organized and developed later around some famous couples: the penitent and the confessor, the person being guided and the spiritual director, the sick person and the psychiatrist, the patient and the psychoanalyst. It was, in a sense, this prehistory that I was trying to write.

Only then, while studying this parrhesiastic practice in this perspective, as the prehistory of these famous couples, I became aware again of something which rather surprised me and which I had not foreseen. Although *parrhēsia* is an important notion in the domain of spiritual direction, spiritual guidance, or soul counseling, and however important it may be in Hellenistic and Roman literature in particular, it is important to recognize that its origin lies elsewhere, that it is not essentially, fundamentally, or primarily in the practice of spiritual guidance that it emerges.

Last year I tried to show you that the notion of *parrhēsia* was first of all and fundamentally a political notion. And this analysis of *parrhēsia* as a political notion, as a political concept, clearly took me away somewhat from my immediate project: the ancient history of practices of telling the truth about oneself. However, on the other hand, this drawback was compensated for by the fact that by taking up again or undertaking the analysis of *parrhēsia* in the field of political practices, I drew a bit closer to a theme which, after all, has always been present in my analysis of the relations between the subject and truth: that of relations of power and their role in the interplay between the subject and truth. With the notion of *parrhēsia*, originally rooted in political practice and the problematization of democracy, then later diverging towards the sphere of personal ethics and the formation of the moral subject,[23] with this notion with political roots and its divergence into morality, we have, to put things very schematically—and this is what interested me, why I stopped to look at this and am still focusing on it—the possibility of posing the question of the subject and truth from the point of view of the practice of what could be called the government of oneself and others. And thus we come back to the theme of government which I studied some years ago.[24] It seems to me that by examining the notion of *parrhēsia* we can see how the analysis of modes of veridiction, the study of techniques of governmentality, and the identification of forms of practice of self interweave. Connecting together modes of veridiction, techniques of governmentality, and practices of the self is basically what I have always been trying to do.[25]

And to the extent that this involves the analysis of relations between modes of veridiction, techniques of governmentality, and forms of practice of self, you can see that to depict this kind of research as an attempt to reduce knowledge (*savoir*) to power, to make it the mask of power in structures, where there is no place for a subject, is purely and simply

a caricature. What is involved, rather, is the analysis of complex relations between three distinct elements none of which can be reduced to
or absorbed by the others, but whose relations are constitutive of each
other. These three elements are: forms of knowledge (*savoirs*), studied
in terms of their specific modes of veridiction; relations of power, not
studied as an emanation of a substantial and invasive power, but in
the procedures by which people's conduct is governed; and finally the
modes of formation of the subject through practices of self. It seems to
me that by carrying out this triple theoretical shift—from the theme of
acquired knowledge to that of veridiction, from the theme of domination to that of governmentality, and from the theme of the individual
to that of the practices of self—we can study the relations between
truth, power, and subject without ever reducing each of them to the
others.[26]

Now, having recalled this general trajectory, I would like [to men-
tion] briefly some of the essential elements which characterize *parrhēsia*
and the parrhesiastic role. Very briefly, for a few minutes, and once
again [for the benefit of] those who were not here, I shall go back over
some things I have already said (I apologize to those who will be hearing this again), and then I would like, as quickly as possible, to move
on to another way of envisaging the same notion of *parrhēsia*.

You recall that, etymologically, *parrhēsia* is the activity that consists in saying everything: *pan rēma*. *Parrhēsiazesthai* is "telling all." The
parrhēsiastēs is the person who says everything.[27] Thus, as an example,
in his discourse *On the Embassy*, Demosthenes says: It is necessary to
speak with *parrhēsia*, without holding back at anything, without concealing anything.[28] Similarly, in the *First Philippic* he takes up exactly
the same term and says: I will tell you what I think without concealing
anything.[29] The parrhesiast is the person who tells all.

But we should immediately add the clarification that this word *parrhēsia* may be employed with two values. I think we find it used in a
pejorative sense, first in Aristophanes, and afterwards very commonly,
even in Christian literature. Used in a pejorative sense, *parrhēsia* does
indeed consist in saying everything, but in the sense of saying anything (anything that comes to mind, anything that serves the cause one
is defending, anything that serves the passion or interest driving the
person who is speaking). The parrhesiast then becomes and appears as

the impenitent chatterbox, someone who cannot restrain himself or, at any rate, someone who cannot index-link his discourse to a principle of rationality and truth. There is an example of this use of the term *parrhēsia* in a pejorative sense (saying everything, saying anything, saying whatever comes to mind without reference to any principle of reason or truth) in Isocrates, in the discourse entitled *Busiris*, in which Isocrates says that, unlike the poets who ascribe everything and anything, absolutely every and any qualities and defects to the gods, one should not say everything about them.[30] Similarly, in Book VIII of *The Republic* (I will give you the exact reference shortly because I will come back to this text) there is the description of the bad democratic city, which is all motley, fragmented, and dispersed between different interests, passions, and individuals who do not agree with each other. This bad democratic city practices *parrhēsia*: anyone can say anything.[31]

But the word *parrhēsia* is also employed in a positive sense, and then *parrhēsia* consists in telling the truth without concealment, reserve, empty manner of speech, or rhetorical ornament which might encode or hide it. "Telling all" is then: telling the truth without hiding any part of it, without hiding it behind anything. In the *Second Philippic*, Demosthenes thus says that, unlike bad parrhesiasts who say anything and do not index their discourses to reason, he, Demosthenes, does not want to speak without reason, he does not want to "resort to insults" and "exchange blow for blow"[32] (you know, those infamous disputes in which anything is said so long as it may harm the adversary and be useful to one's own cause). He does not want to do this, but rather he wants to tell the truth (*ta alethē*: things that are true) with *parrhēsia* (*meta parrhēsias*). Moreover, he adds: I will conceal nothing (*oukh apokhrupsōmai*).[33] To hide nothing and say what is true is to practice *parrhēsia*. *Parrhēsia* is therefore "telling all," but tied to the truth: telling the whole truth, hiding nothing of the truth, telling the truth without hiding it behind anything.

However, I don't think this suffices as a description and definition of this notion of *parrhēsia*. In fact—leaving aside the negative senses of the term for the moment—in addition to the rule of telling all and the rule of truth, two supplementary conditions are required for us to be able to speak of *parrhēsia* in the positive sense of the term. Not only must this truth really be the personal opinion of the person who is speaking,

but he must say it as being what he thinks, [and not] reluctantly*—
and this is what makes him a parrhesiast. The parrhesiast gives his
opinion, he says what he thinks, he personally signs, as it were, the
truth he states, he binds himself to this truth, and he is consequently
bound to it and by it. But this is not enough. For after all, a teacher, a
grammarian or a geometer, may say something true about the grammar
or geometry they teach, a truth which they believe, which they think.
And yet we will not call this *parrhēsia*. We will not say that the geometer and grammarian are parrhesiasts when they teach truths which
they believe. For there to be *parrhēsia*, you recall—I stressed this last
year—the subject must be taking some kind of risk [in speaking] this
truth which he signs as his opinion, his thought, his belief, a risk which
concerns his relationship with the person to whom he is speaking. For
there to be *parrhēsia*, in speaking the truth one must open up, establish,
and confront the risk of offending the other person, of irritating him,
of making him angry and provoking him to conduct which may even
be extremely violent. So it is the truth subject to risk of violence. For
example, in the *First Philippic*, after having said that he is speaking *meta
parrhēsias* (with frankness), Demosthenes [adds]: I am well aware that,
by employing this frankness, I do not know what the consequences will
be for me of the things I have just said.[34]

In short, *parrhēsia*, the act of truth, requires: first, the manifestation
of a fundamental bond between the truth spoken and the thought of
the person who spoke it; [second], a challenge to the bond between the
two interlocutors (the person who speaks the truth and the person to
whom this truth is addressed). Hence this new feature of *parrhēsia*: it
involves some form of courage, the minimal form of which consists in
the parrhesiast taking the risk of breaking and ending the relationship
to the other person which was precisely what made his discourse possible. In a way, the parrhesiast always risks undermining that relationship which is the condition of possibility of his discourse. This is very
clear in *parrhēsia* as spiritual guidance, for example, which can only
exist if there is friendship, and where the employment of truth in this
spiritual guidance is precisely in danger of bringing into question and

---

* Reconstruction of the meaning. M.F. says:...not only that he happens to speak the truth or
that he speaks it reluctantly, but he must speak it as what he thinks.

breaking the relationship of friendship which made this discourse of truth possible.

But in some cases this courage may also take a maximal form when one has to accept that, if one is to tell the truth, not only may one's personal, friendly relationship with the person to whom one is speaking be brought into question, but one may even be risking one's life. When Plato goes to see Dionysius the Elder—this is recounted in Plutarch—he tells him truths which so offend the tyrant that he conceives the plan, which in fact he does not put into execution, of killing Plato. But Plato fundamentally knew and accepted this risk.[35] *Parrhēsia* therefore not only puts the relationship between the person who speaks and the person to whom he addresses the truth at risk, but it may go so far as to put the very life of the person who speaks at risk, at least if his interlocutor has power over him and cannot bear being told the truth. In the *Nicomachean Ethics*, Aristotle lays stress on the connection between *parrhēsia* and courage when he links what he calls *megalopsukhia* (greatness of soul) to the practice of *parrhēsia*.[36]

Only—and this is the last feature I would like to recall briefly— *parrhēsia* may be organized, developed, and stabilized in what could be called a parrhesiastic game. For if the parrhesiast is someone who, by telling the truth, the whole truth, regardless of any other consideration, risks bringing his relationship to the other into question, and even risks his life, on the other hand, the person to whom this truth is told—whether this is the assembled people deliberating on the best decisions to take, or the Prince, the tyrant or king to whom advice must be given, or the friend one is guiding—this person (people, king, friend), if he wants to play the role proposed to him by the parrhesiast in telling him the truth, must accept the truth, however much it may hurt generally accepted opinion in the Assembly, the Prince's passions or interests, or the individual's ignorance or blindness. The people, the Prince, and the individual must accept the game of *parrhēsia*; they must play it themselves and recognize that they have to listen to the person who takes the risk of telling them the truth. Thus the true game of *parrhēsia* will be established on the basis of this kind of pact which means that if the parrhesiast demonstrates his courage by telling the truth despite and regardless of everything, the person to whom this *parrhēsia* is addressed will have to demonstrate his greatness of soul by accepting being told the truth. This kind of pact, between the person who takes the risk of telling the truth and the person who agrees to listen to it, is at the heart of what could be called the parrhesiastic game.

So, in two words, *parrhēsia* is the courage of truth in the person who speaks and who, regardless of everything, takes the risk of telling the whole truth that he thinks, but it is also the interlocutor's courage in agreeing to accept the hurtful truth that he hears.

You can see then how the practice of *parrhēsia* is opposed to the art of rhetoric in every respect. Very schematically, we can say that rhetoric, as it was defined and practiced in Antiquity, is basically a technique concerning the way that things are said, but does not in any way determine the relations between the person who speaks and what he says. Rhetoric is an art, a technique, a set of processes which enable the person speaking to say something which may not be what he thinks at all, but whose effect will be to produce convictions, induce certain conducts, or instill certain beliefs in the person [to whom he speaks].* In other words, rhetoric does not involve any bond of belief between the person speaking and what he [states]. The good rhetorician, the good rhetor is the man who may well say, and who is perfectly capable of saying, something completely different from what he knows, believes, and thinks, but of saying it in such a way that, in the final analysis, what he says—which is not what he believes, thinks, or knows—becomes what those he has spoken to think, believe, and think they know. The connection between the person speaking and what he says is broken in rhetoric, but the effect of rhetoric is to establish a constraining bond between what is said and the person or persons to whom it is said. You can see that from this point of view rhetoric is the exact opposite of *parrhēsia*, [which entails on the contrary a] strong, manifest, evident foundation between the person speaking and what he says, since he must openly express his thought, and you can see that in *parrhēsia* there is no question of saying anything other than what one thinks. *Parrhēsia* therefore establishes a strong, necessary, and constitutive bond between the person speaking and what he says, but it exposes to risk the bond between the person speaking and the person to whom he speaks. For, after all, it is always possible that the person to whom one is speaking

---

* M.F. says: the person who speaks

will not welcome what one says. He may take offence at what one says, he may reject it and even punish or take revenge on the person who has told him the truth. So rhetoric does not entail any bond between the person speaking and what is said, but aims to establish a constraining bond, a bond of power between what is said and the person to whom it is said. *Parrhēsia*, on the other hand, involves a strong and constitutive bond between the person speaking and what he says, and, through the effect of the truth, of the injuries of truth, it opens up the possibility of the bond between the person speaking and the person to whom he has spoken being broken. Let's say, very schematically, that the rhetorician is, or at any rate may well be an effective liar who constrains others. The parrhesiast, on the contrary, is the courageous teller of a truth by which he puts himself and his relationship with the other at risk.

These are all things which I spoke to you about last year. I would like now to move on a bit and note straightaway that we should not think of *parrhēsia* as a sort of well-defined technique in a counter-balancing and symmetrical relation to rhetoric. We should not think that in Antiquity, facing the rhetorician who was a professional, a technician, and facing rhetoric, which was a technique and required an apprenticeship, there was a parrhesiast and a *parrhēsia* which would also be [...*].

The parrhesiast is not a professional. And *parrhēsia* is after all something other than a technique or a skill, although it has technical aspects. *Parrhēsia* is not a skill; it is something which is harder to define. It is a stance, a way of being which is akin to a virtue, a mode of action. *Parrhēsia* involves ways of acting, means brought together with a view to an end, and in this respect it has, of course, something to do with technique, but it is also a role which is useful, valuable, and indispensable for the city and for individuals. *Parrhēsia* should be regarded as a modality of truth-telling, rather than [as a] technique [like] rhetoric. To arrive at a better definition we can contrast it with other basic modalities of truth-telling found in Antiquity, and which will no doubt be found, in displaced and different guises and forms,

---

* Michel Foucault is interrupted at this point by pop music from one of the cassette recorders. We hear a member of the audience rush to their machine.
M.F.: "I think you are mistaken. It is at least Michael Jackson? Too bad."

in other societies, as well as our own. Basing ourselves on the clear understandings which Antiquity has left us about these things, we may define four basic modalities of truth-telling.*

First, the truth-telling of prophecy. I will not try here to analyze what the prophets said, (the structures, as it were, of what was said by prophets), but rather the way in which the prophet constitutes himself and is recognized by others as a subject speaking the truth. Evidently, the prophet, like the parrhesiast, is someone who tells the truth. But I think that what fundamentally characterizes the prophet's truth-telling, his veridiction, is that the prophet's posture is one of mediation. The prophet, by definition, does not speak in his own name. He speaks for another voice; his mouth serves as intermediary for a voice which speaks from elsewhere. The prophet, usually, transmits the word of God. The discourse he articulates and utters is not his own. He addresses a truth to men which comes from elsewhere. The prophet's position is intermediary in another sense in that he is between the present and the future. The second characteristic of the prophet's intermediary position is that he reveals what time conceals from humans, what no human gaze could see and no human ear could hear without him. Prophetic truth-telling is also intermediary in that, in one way of course, the prophet reveals, shows, or sheds light on what is hidden from men, but in another way, or rather at the same time, he does not reveal without being obscure, and he does not disclose without enveloping what he says in the form of the riddle. Hence prophecy basically never gives any univocal and clear prescription. It does not bluntly speak the pure, transparent truth. Even when the prophet says what is to be done, one still has to ask oneself whether one has really understood, whether one may not still be blind; one still has to question, hesitate, and interpret.

Now *parrhēsia* contrasts with these different characteristics of prophetic truth-telling in each of these precise respects. You can see then that the parrhesiast is the opposite of the prophet in that the prophet does not speak for himself, but in the name of someone else, and he articulates a voice which is not his own. In contrast, the parrhesiast,

---

* [*Parrhēsia* has just been introduced as one "modality of truth-telling"; Foucault now goes on to discuss the other three; G.B.]

by definition, speaks in his own name. It is essential that he expresses his own opinion, thought, and conviction. He must put his name to his words; this is the price of his frankness. The prophet does not have to be frank, even when he tells the truth. Second, the parrhesiast does not foretell the future. Certainly, he reveals and discloses what people's blindness prevents them from seeing, but he does not unveil the future. He unveils what is. The parrhesiast does not help people somehow to step beyond some threshold in the ontological structure of the human being and of time which separates them from their future. He helps them in their blindness, but their blindness about what they are, about themselves, and so not the blindness due to an ontological structure, but due to some moral fault, distraction, or lack of discipline, the consequence of inattention, laxity, or weakness. It is in this interplay between human beings and their blindness due to inattention, complacency, weakness, and moral distraction that the parrhesiast performs his role, which, as you can see, is consequently a revelatory role very different from that of the prophet, who stands at the point where human finitude and the structure of time are conjoined. Third, the parrhesiast, again by definition, and unlike the prophet, does not speak in riddles. On the contrary, he says things as clearly and directly as possible, without any disguise or rhetorical embellishment, so that his words may immediately be given their prescriptive value. The parrhesiast leaves nothing to interpretation. Certainly, he leaves something to be done: he leaves the person he addresses with the tough task of having the courage to accept this truth, to recognize it, and to make it a principle of conduct. He leaves this moral task, but, unlike the prophet, he does not leave the difficult duty of interpretation.

Second, I think we can also contrast parrhesiastic truth-telling with another mode of truth-telling which was very important in Antiquity, doubtless even more important for ancient philosophy than prophetic truth-telling: the truth-telling of wisdom. As you know, the sage—and in this he is unlike the prophet we have just been talking about—speaks in his own name. And even if this wisdom may have been inspired by a god, or passed on to him by a tradition, by a more or less esoteric teaching, the sage is nevertheless present in what he says, present in his truth-telling. The wisdom he expresses really is his own wisdom. The sage manifests his mode of being wise in what he says and, to that extent, although he has a certain intermediary function between timeless, traditional wisdom and the person he addresses, unlike the prophet, he is not just a mouthpiece. He is himself wise, a sage, and his mode of being wise as his personal mode of being qualifies him as a sage, and qualifies him to speak the discourse of wisdom. To that extent, insofar as he is present in his wise discourse and manifests his mode of being wise in his wise discourse, he is much closer to the parrhesiast than to the prophet. But the sage—and this is what characterizes him, at least through some of the traits that we can find in the ancient literature—keeps his wisdom in a state of essential withdrawal, or at least reserve. Basically, the sage is wise in and for himself, and does not need to speak. He is not forced to speak, nothing obliges him to share his wisdom, to teach it, or demonstrate it. This accounts for what might be termed his structural silence. And if he speaks, it is only because he is appealed to by someone's questions, or by an urgent situation of the city. This also explains why his answers—and then in this respect he may well be like the prophet and often imitate and speak like him—may well be enigmatic and leave those he addresses ignorant or uncertain about what he has actually said. Another characteristic of the truth-telling of wisdom is that wisdom says what is, unlike prophecy where what is said is what will be. The sage says what is, that is to say, he tells of the being of the world and of things. And if this telling the truth of the being of the world and of things has prescriptive value, it is not [in] the form of advice linked to a conjuncture, but in the form of a general principle of conduct.

These characteristics of the sage can be read and rediscovered in the text in which Diogenes Laertius portrays Heraclitus; it is a late text, but one of the richest in various kinds of information. First, Heraclitus lived in an essential withdrawal. He lived in silence. And Diogenes Laertius recalls the moment at which and why the break took place between Heraclitus and the Ephesians. The Ephesians had exiled his friend, Hermodorus, precisely because he was wise and better than them. They said: We want "there to be no one among us who is better than us."[37] And if there is someone who is better than us, let him go and live elsewhere. The Ephesians could not bear the superiority of precisely someone who tells the truth. They drove out the parrhesiast. They drove out Hermodorus, who was obliged to leave, forced into the exile with which they punished the person capable of telling the truth. Heraclitus, for his part, responded with voluntary withdrawal. Since the Ephesians have punished the best among them with exile, well, he says, all the others, who are less worthy, should be put to death. And since they are not put to death, I will be the one to leave. And from that time on, when asked to give laws to the city, he refused. Because, he says, the city is already dominated by a *ponēra politeia* (a bad mode of political life). So he withdraws himself and—in a famous image—plays knucklebones with children. To those who are indignant at him playing knucklebones with children, he replies: "Why are you surprised, rascals, isn't this more worthwhile than administering the republic with you [*met'humōn politeuesthai*: than conducting political life with you; M.F.]?"[38] He retires to the mountains, practicing contempt of men (*misanthropōn*).[39] And when asked why he remained silent, he replied: "I keep quiet so that you may chatter."[40] Diogenes Laertius relates that in this retirement Heraclitus wrote his Poem in deliberately obscure terms so that only those who were capable could read it and so that he, Heraclitus, could not be despised for being read by all and sundry.[41]

The figure and characteristics of the parrhesiast stand in contrast with this role, this characterization of the sage, who basically remains silent, only speaks when he really wants to, and [only] in riddles. The parrhesiast is not someone who is fundamentally reserved. On the contrary, it is his duty, obligation, responsibility, and task to speak, and he has no right to shirk this task. We will see this precisely with Socrates, who recalls it frequently in the *Apology*: the god has given him this office of stopping men, taking them aside, and questioning them. And he will never abandon this office. Even under the threat of death, he will carry out his task until the end, until his final breath.[42] Whereas the sage keeps silent and responds only sparingly, as little as possible, to the questions he may be asked, the parrhesiast is the unlimited, permanent, unbearable questioner. Second, whereas the sage is the person who, against the background of an essential silence, speaks in riddles, the parrhesiast must speak, and he must speak as clearly as possible. And finally, whereas the sage says what is, but in the form of the very being of things and of the world, the parrhesiast intervenes, says what is, but in terms of the singularity of individuals, situations, and conjunctures. His specific role is not to tell of the being of nature and things. In the analysis of *parrhēsia* we will constantly find this opposition between useless knowledge which speaks of the being of things and the world, on the one hand, and on the other the parrhesiast's truth-telling which is always applied, questions, and is directed to individuals and situations in order to say what they are in reality, to tell individuals the truth of themselves hidden from their own eyes, to reveal to them their present situation, their character, failings, the value of their conduct, and the possible consequences of their decisions. The parrhesiast does not reveal what is to his interlocutor; he discloses or helps him to recognize what he is.

Finally, the third modality of truth-telling which can be contrasted with the parrhesiast's truth-telling is that of the professor, the technician, [the teacher]. The prophet, the sage, the person who teaches.*

---

* So, if you like, because maybe some of you are a bit weary from listening and others from not hearing, some from sitting down and others from standing, and me at any rate from speaking, we will stop for five or ten minutes. And then we will meet again shortly, OK? I will try to finish around 11.15. Thank you.

1. Foucault's lectures at the Collège de France became devoted to ancient thought from January 1981, with "Subjectivité et Vérité." See the course summary in *Dits et Écrits, 1954-1988*, eds. D. Defert and F. Ewald (Paris: Gallimard, 1994) vol. 4, pp. 213-218; English translation by Robert Hurley, "Subjectivity and Truth" in *The Essential Works of Michel Foucault, 1954-1984, vol. 1: Ethics: Subjectivity and Truth*, ed. Paul Rabinow (New York: The New Press, 1997) pp. 87-92.

2. Already in the previous year, faced with the same difficulty, Foucault had called for the formation, in parallel with the main course, of a small working group which would be made up exclusively of researchers working on closely related themes. See *Le Gouvernement de soi et des autres. Cours au Collège de France, 1982-1983*, ed. Frédéric Gros (Paris: Gallimard-Le Seuil, 2008) p. 3 (lecture of 5 January 1983, first hour) and p. 68 (lecture of 12 January 1983, second hour); English translation by Graham Burchell, *The Government of Self and Others. Lectures at the Collège de France, 1982-1983*, ed. Frédéric Gros, English series editor Arnold I. Davidson (London: Palgrave Macmillan, 2010) p. 1 and p. 70.

3. On the concept of alethurgy, see the Collège de France lectures of 23 and 30 January 1980: "by creating the fictional word *alēthourgia* from *alēthourgēs*, we could call 'alethurgy' (manifestation of truth) the set of possible procedures, verbal or otherwise, by which one brings to light what is posited as true, as opposed to the false, the hidden, the unspeakable, the unforeseeable, or the forgotten. We could call 'alethurgy' that set of procedures and say that there is no exercise of power without something like an alethurgy" (lecture of 23 January).

4. M. Foucault, *Histoire de la folie à l'âge classique* (Paris: Plon, 1961; Gallimard, 1972); English translation by Jonathan Murphy and and Jean Khalfa as *History of Madness* (London: Routledge, 2005); M. Foucault, *Surveiller et Punir* (Paris: Gallimard, 1975); English translation by Alan Sheridan as *Discipline and Punish: Birth of the Prison* (London: Allen Lane and New York: Pantheon, 1977, reprinted Harmondsworth: Peregrine, 1979).

5. M. Foucault, *Les Mots et les Choses* (Paris: Gallimard, 1966); English translation by Alan Sheridan as *The Order of Things* (London: Tavistock, and New York: Pantheon, 1970). For a similar presentation of the analysis of the "speaking, laboring, living subject," see the notice "Foucault" in *Dits et Écrits*, vol. IV, p. 633; English translation by Robert Hurley as "Foucault" in *The Essential Works of Foucault, 1954-1984, vol. 2: Aesthetics, Method, and Epistemology*, ed. James D. Faubion (New York: The New Press, 1998) p. 460.

6. The same systematic presentation of his œuvre in the form of a triptych is found in the first lecture of 1983, *Le Gouvernement de soi et des autres*, pp. 4-7; *The Government of Self and Others*, pp. 2-5.

7. On the examination of conscience as spiritual exercise, see the lecture of 24 March 1982, second hour, in M. Foucault, *L'Herméneutique du sujet. Cours au Collège de France, 1981-1982*, ed. Frédéric Gros (Paris: Gallimard-Le Seuil, 2001) pp. 460-464, as well as the lectures of 20 and 27 January 1982, ibid. pp. 86-87, 146-149, and 151-157; English translation by Graham Burchell as *The Hermeneutics of the Subject. Lectures at the Collège de France, 1981-1982*, English series editor Arnold I. Davidson (New York: Palgrave Macmillan, 2001) pp. 480-485, and pp. 89-90, 151-154, and 157-163.

8. On correspondence as spiritual exercise, see the lectures of 20 and 27 January 1982, ibid., Fr. pp. 86-87, 146-149, and 151-157; Eng. pp. 89-90, 151-154, and 157-163.

9. On the *hupomnēmata* and other writing exercises, see the lecture of 3 March 1982 in ibid., Fr. pp 341-345; Eng. pp. 358-362, as well as "L'écriture de soi" in *Dits et Écrits*, vol. IV, pp. 415-430; English translation by Robert Hurley as "Self Writing" in *The Essential Works of Foucault, Vol. I*, pp. 207-222.

10. See, *L'Herméneutique du sujet; The Hermeneutics of the Subject*, all the lectures of January 1982.

11. On this concept, see the lecture of 3 February 1982, ibid., Fr. pp. 172-173; Eng. pp. 179-180. One could also consult the article by Pierre Hadot in *Michel Foucault philosophe* [Rencontre internationale Paris, 9-11 January 1988] ed. l'Association pour le Centre Michel Foucault (Paris: Le Seuil, 1989); English translation by Timothy J. Armstrong in *Michel Foucault Philosopher* (Hemel Hempstead: Harvester Wheatsheaf, 1992).

12. On this history see the lecture of 19 February 1975 in M. Foucault, *Les Anormaux. Cours au Collège de France, 1974-1975*, ed. Valerio Marchetti and Antonella Salomoni (Paris:

Gallimard-Le Seuil, 1999) pp. 161-171; English translation by Graham Burchell as *Abnormal. Lectures at the Collège de France, 1974-1975*, English series editor Arnold I. Davidson (New York: Picador, 2003) pp. 174-184. See also, M. Foucault, *La Volonté de Savoir* (Paris: Gallimard, 1976) the chapter "L'incitation aux discours"; English translation by Robert Hurley as *The History of Sexuality, vol. 1: An Introduction* (New York: Pantheon, 1978 and Harmondsworth: Penguin, 1984), "The Incitement to Discourse."

13. On this concept see the lecture of 22 February 1978 in M. Foucault, *Security, Territory, Population. Lectures at the Collège de France, 1977-1978*, ed. Michel Senellart (Paris: Gallimard-Le Seuil, 2004); English translation by Graham Burchell as *Security, Territory, Population. Lectures at the Collège de France, 1977-1978*, English series editor Arnold I. Davidson (Basingstoke: Palgrave Macmillan, 2007). See also, "*Omnes et singulatim*" trans. P.E. Dauzat, in *Dits et Écrits*, vol. IV, pp. 136-147; Original English version, "'*Omnes et singulatim*': Toward a Critique of Political Reason" in *The Essential Works of Foucault, 1954-1984, vol. 3: Power*, ed. James D. Faubion (New York: New Press, 2000) pp. 300-315.

14. Galien, *Traité des passions de l'âme et des erreurs*, trans. R. Van der Elst (Paris: Delagrave, 1914); English translation by P.W. Harkins as, Galen, *On the Passions and Errors of the Soul* (Columbus, Ohio: Ohio State University Press, 1963). For Foucault's analysis of this text, see *L'Herméneutique du sujet*, pp. 378-382; *The Hermeneutics of the Subject*, pp. 395-398; and lecture of 12 January 1983, first hour, in *Le Gouvernement de soi et des autres*, pp. 43-45; *The Government of Self and Others*, pp. 43-45.

15. On the organization of Epictetus' school, see the lecture of 27 January 1982, first hour, in *L'Herméneutique du sujet*, pp. 133-137; *The Hermeneutics of the Subject*, pp. 138-142.

16. On this figure see, ibid., Fr. pp. 137-138; Eng. pp. 142-144.

17. On this "medical" dimension of the care of the soul, see Foucault's clarifications in the lecture of 20 January 1982, first hour, ibid., Fr. pp. 93-96; Eng. pp. 97-100.

18. See the chapter "Du régime en général," in M. Foucault, *L'Usage des plaisirs* (Paris: Gallimard, 1984); English translation by Robert Hurley, "Regimen in General," *The Use of Pleasure* (New York: Random House, 1985, and Harmondsworth: Viking, 1986).

19. On *libertas* (the Latin translation of *parrhēsia*) in Seneca, see the lecture of 10 March 1982, second hour, in *L'Herméneutique du sujet*, pp. 382-388; *The Hermeneutics of the Subject*, pp. 398-405.

20. For a first analysis of the treatise by Philodemus, see ibid., Fr. pp. 370-374; Eng. pp. 387-391, and the lecture of 12 January 1983, first hour, *Le Gouvernement de soi et des autres*, pp. 45-46; *The Government of Self and Others*, pp. 41-59.

21. See on this text, *L'Herméneutique du sujet*, pp. 357-358; *The Hermeneutics of the Subject*, pp. 373-374, and the lecture of 2 March 1983 in *Le Gouvernement de soi et des autres*; *The Government of Self and Others*.

22. See above, note 14.

23. For the history of this "divergence," see the lecture of 2 March 1983, first hour, in *Le Gouvernement de soi et des autres*, pp. 277-282; *The Government of Self and Others*, pp. 299-323.

24. *Sécurité, Territoire, Population*; *Security, Territory, Population*.

25. For a similar presentation of *parrhēsia* as the node of the three major axes of research, see *Le Gouvernement de soi et des autres*, p. 42; *The Government of Self and Others*, p. 42.

26. For a "long version" of the presentation of his method, see the start of the lecture of 5 January 1983, ibid., Fr. pp. 3-8; Eng. pp. 1-6.

27. See the first definitions in March 1982, *L'Herméneutique du sujet*, p. 348; *The Hermeneutics of the Subject*, p. 366, and January 1983, *Le Gouvernement de soi et des autres*, pp. 42-43; *The Government of Self and Others*, pp. 42-43.

28. Démosthène, *Plaidoyers politiques*, vol. III, trans. G. Mathieu (Paris: Les Belles Lettres, 1972) p. 76, §237: "It is necessary, Athenians, to speak with frankness (*meta parrhēsias*) without holding back before anything"; English translation by Douglas M. MacDowell, in Demosthenes, *On the False Embassy (Oration 19)*, ed. Douglas M. MacDowell (Oxford: Oxford University Press, 2000) p. 157: "It's necessary to speak to them freely, men of Athens, without restraint."

29. Démosthène, *Première Philippique*, §50, in *Harangues*, vol. I, trans. M. Croiset (Paris: Les Belles Lettres, 1965) p. 49: "I have just stated my thought to you without concealing anything (*panth'haplōs ouden huposteilamenos, peparrhēsiasmai*)"; English translation by J.H. Vince,

Demosthenes, *First Phillipic* in *Demosthenes. Orations*, vol. I, §51 (Cambridge, Mass.: Harvard University Press, Loeb Classical Library, 1930) p. 99: "to-day, keeping nothing back, I have given free utterance to my plain sentiments."

30. Isocrate, *Busiris*, §40, in *Discours*, vol. I, trans. G. Mathieu and E. Brémond (Paris: Les Belles Lettres, 1972) p. 198: "We are not to say everything concerning the gods (*tēs d'eis tous theous parrhēsias oligōrēsomen*)"; English translation by Larue Van Hook, Isocrates, *Busiris*, in *Isocrates*, vol. III, (Cambridge, Mass.: Harvard University Press, Loeb Classical Library, 1945) p. 125: "we [shall] disregard loose-tongued vilification of the gods."

31. For a first analysis of this passage of *The Republic*, Book VIII, 557a-b et seq., see the lecture of 9 February 1983, first hour, in *Le Gouvernement de soi et des autres*, pp. 181-185; *The Government of Self and Others*, pp. 197-201.

32. Démosthène, *Seconde Philippique*, in *Harangues*, vol. II, trans. M. Croiset (Paris: Les Belles Lettres, 1965) §32, p. 34; English translation by J.H. Vince, Demosthenes, *The Second Phillipic*, in *Demosthenes. Orations*, vol. I, p. 141: "It is not that by descending to abuse I may lay myself open to retaliation in your presence."

33. Ibid., §31, Fr. p. 34: "Ah! I will speak to you with open heart, I call on the gods to witness it, I wish to conceal nothing (*egō nē tous theous talēthē meta parrhēsias erō pros humas kai ouk apokrupsōmai*)"; Eng. p. 141: "I vow that I shall boldly tell you the whole truth and keep nothing back."

34. *Première Philippique*, §51, p. 49: "In fact, I do not know what the consequences of my proposals will be for me"; *First Philippic*, p. 99: "in the uncertainty of what the result of my proposals may be for myself."

35. On this story and Foucault's analysis of it in terms of *parrhēsia*, see the lecture of 12 January 1983, first hour, *Le Gouvernement de soi et des autres*, pp. 47-52; *The Government of Self and Others*, pp. 47-52.

36. Aristotle, *Nicomachean Ethics*, trans. W.D. Ross, revised by J.O. Urmson, Book IV, 1124b, 26-29, in *The Complete Works of Aristotle. The Revised Oxford Translation*, Vol. 2, ed. Jonathan Barnes (Princeton: Princeton University Press, 1984) p. 1775: "He must also be open in his hate and in his love (for to conceal one's feelings is a mark of timidity), and he must care more for truth than for what people will think, and must speak and act openly; for he is free of speech because he is contemptuous, and he is given to telling the truth, except when he speaks in irony to the vulgar."

37. "Heraclitus" in Diogène Laërce, *Vie, doctrines et sentences des philosophes illustres*, vol. II, ed. and trans. R. Genaille (Paris: Garnier-Flammarion, 1965), p. 163; and Diogène Laërce, *Vie et doctrines des philosophes illustres*, ed. and trans. M.-O. Goulet-Cazé (Paris: Le Livre de poche, 1999) Book IX, §2, p. 1048; English translation by R.D. Hicks, "Heraclitus" in Diogenes Laertius, *Lives of Eminent Philosophers*, Vol. II, Book IX (Cambridge, Mass.: Harvard University Press, Loeb Classical Library, 1925) p. 411: "'We will have none who is worthiest among us.'"

38. Ibid.; Eng.: "'Why, you rascals,' he said, 'are you astonished? Is it not better to do this than to take part in your civil life?'"

39. Ibid.

40. Ibid., Fr. p. 165 (Goulet-Cazé trans. IX, 12, p. 1050); Eng. p. 419: "... when asked why he kept silence, he replied 'Why, to let you chatter.'"

41. Ibid., Fr. p. 165 (Goulet-Cazé trans. IX, 6, p. 1050); Eng. p. 413.

42. Platon, *Apologie de Socrate*, 30b, trans. M. Croiset (Paris: Les Belles Lettres, 1970) p. 157; English translation by Hugh Tredennick, *Socrates' Defence (Apology)*, in Plato, *The Collected Dialogues*, eds. Edith Hamilton and Huntington Cairns (Princeton: Princeton University Press, 1961) p. 16.

1 FEBRUARY 1984

Second hour

[...*] I HAVE TRIED THEN to pick out the relationships and differences between the parrhesiastic mode of truth-telling and, first, the prophetic mode of truth-telling, and then that of wisdom. And now I would like to indicate, very schematically and allusively, some of the relations between parrhesiastic veridiction and the veridiction of someone who teaches—I would prefer to say, basically, of the technician. These characters (the doctor, the musician, the shoemaker,

---

* M.F.: [beginning inaudible] ... and ambiguity of the always limited *parrhēsia* of institutions. In fact room 6 was not, is not, and will not be fitted with a public address system. You were told the truth when you were told that room 6 was not fitted with a public address system, but what you were not told, and what I was not told either, is that room 5 was. At any rate, it is now. So those of you who have had enough of standing up or sitting on the floor can find in room 5 a place where you will be able to sit down, read the newspaper, and chat peacefully. OK? There you are. So thanks and my apologies. So from now on, if I understand correctly, every Wednesday room 5 will be linked up with this room. It will no longer be rooms 8 and 6, but 8 and 5. That's it, my apologies for what has happened.

the carpenter, the teacher of armed combat, the gymnastics teacher), frequently mentioned by Plato in his Socratic and other dialogues, possess a knowledge characterized as *tekhnē*, know-how, that is to say, entailing particular items of knowledge, but taking shape in a practice and involving, for their apprenticeship, not only a theoretical knowledge, but a whole exercise (a whole *askēsis* or *meletē*).[1] They possess this knowledge, they profess it, and they are capable of teaching it to others. The technician, who possesses a *tekhnē*, has learned it, and is capable of teaching it, is someone obliged to speak the truth, or at any rate to formulate what he knows and pass it on to others; and, of course, this distinguishes him from the sage. After all, the technician has a certain duty to speak. He is obliged, in a way, to tell the knowledge he possesses and the truth he knows, because this knowledge and truth are linked to a whole weight of tradition. This man of *tekhnē* would not himself have been able to learn anything and today would know nothing at all, or very little, if there had not been, before him, a technician (*tekhnitēs*) like him, who had taught him, whose pupil he had been, and who had been his teacher. And just as he would not have learned anything if someone had not previously told him what they knew, so, in the same way, he will have to pass on his knowledge so that it does not die with him.

So, in this idea of someone with knowledge of *tekhnē*, someone who has received this knowledge and must pass it on, there is the principle of an obligation to speak which is not found in the sage but is found in the parrhesiast. But clearly, this teacher, this man of *tekhnē*, of expertise and teaching, does not take any risk in the truth-telling he has received and must pass on, and this is what distinguishes him from the parrhesiast. Everyone knows, and I know first of all, that you do not need courage to teach. On the contrary, the person who teaches establishes, or at any rate hopes or sometimes wants to establish a bond of shared knowledge, of heritage, of tradition, and possibly also of personal recognition or friendship, between himself and the person or persons who listen to him. Anyway, this truth-telling establishes a filiation in the domain of knowledge. Now we have seen that the parrhesiast, to the contrary, takes a risk. He risks the relationship he has with the person to whom he speaks. And in speaking the truth, far from establishing this positive bond of shared knowledge, heritage, filiation, gratitude, or friendship, he may instead provoke the other's anger, antagonize an enemy, he may arouse the hostility of the city, or, if he is speaking the truth to a bad and tyrannical sovereign, he may provoke vengeance and punishment. And he may go so far as to risk his life, since he may pay with his life for the truth he has told. Whereas, in the case of the technician's truth-telling, teaching ensures the survival of knowledge, the person who practices *parrhēsia* risks death. The technician's and teacher's truth-telling brings together and binds; the parrhesiast's truth-telling risks hostility, war, hatred, and death. And if the parrhesiast's truth may unite and reconcile, when it is accepted and the other person agrees to the pact and plays the game of *parrhēsia*, this is only after it has opened up an essential, fundamental, and structurally necessary moment of the possibility of hatred and a rupture.

We can say then, very schematically, that the parrhesiast is not the prophet who speaks the truth when he reveals fate enigmatically in the name of someone else. The parrhesiast is not a sage who, when he wants to and against the background of his silence, tells of being and nature (*phusis*) in the name of wisdom. The parrhesiast is not the professor or teacher, the expert who speaks of *tekhnē* in the name of a tradition. So he does not speak of fate, being, or *tekhnē*. Rather, inasmuch as he takes the risk of provoking war with others, rather than solidifying the traditional bond, like the teacher, by [speaking] in his own name and perfectly clearly, [unlike the] prophet who speaks in the name of someone else, [inasmuch as] finally [he tells] the truth of what is in the singular form of individuals and situations, and not the truth of being and the nature of things, the parrhesiast brings into play the true discourse of what the Greeks called *ēthos*.

Fate has a modality of veridiction which is found in prophecy. Being has a modality of veridiction found in the sage. *Tekhnē* has a modality of veridiction found in the technician, the professor, the teacher, the expert. And finally, *ēthos* has its veridiction in the speech of the parrhesiast and the game of *parrhēsia*. Prophecy, wisdom, teaching, and *parrhēsia* are, I think, four modes of veridiction which, [first], involve different personages, second, call for different modes of speech, and third, relate to different domains (fate, being, *tekhnē*, *ēthos*).

Actually, in this survey I am not essentially defining four historically distinct social types. I do not mean that there were four professions or four social types in ancient civilization: the prophet, the sage, the teacher, and the parrhesiast. Certainly, it may be that these four major modalities of truth-telling (prophetic, wise, technical, and ethical or parrhesiastic) correspond to quite distinct institutions, or practices, or personages. One of the reasons why the example of Antiquity is privileged is precisely that it enables us to separate out, as it were, these different [modalities] of truth-telling, these different modes of veridiction. Because, in Antiquity, they are fairly clearly distinguished and embodied, formulated, and almost institutionalized in different forms. There is the prophetic function, which was quite clearly defined and institutionalized. The character of the sage was also quite clearly picked out (see the portrait of Heraclitus). You see the teacher, the technician, the man of *tekhnē* appear very clearly in the Socratic dialogues (the Sophists were precisely these kinds of technicians and teachers who claimed to have a universal function). As for the parrhesiast, his specific profile appears very clearly—we will come back to this next week—with Socrates, and then with Diogenes and a series of other philosophers. However, as distinct as these roles may be, and even if at certain times, and in certain societies or civilizations, you see these four functions taken on, as it were, by very clearly distinct institutions or characters, it is important to note that fundamentally these are not social characters or roles. I insist on this; I would like to stress it: they are essentially modes of veridiction. It sometimes happens, and it will happen very often, even more often than not, that these modes of veridiction are combined with each other, and we find them in forms of discourse, types of institutions, and social characters which mix the modes of veridiction with each other.

Already you can see how Socrates puts together elements of prophecy, wisdom, teaching, and *parrhēsia*. Socrates is the parrhesiast.[2] But you recall: who gave him his function as parrhesiast, his mission to question people, to take them by the sleeve and tell them: Take some care of yourself? It was the Delphic god, the prophetic authority which returned this verdict. When asked who was the wisest man in Greece, it replied: Socrates. And it was in order to honor this prophecy, and also to honor the Delphic god laying down the principle of "know yourself," that Socrates undertook his mission.[3] His function as parrhesiast is not therefore unrelated to this prophetic function, from which he nevertheless maintains his distinctness. Equally, although a parrhesiast, Socrates has a relationship with wisdom. This is evident in several traits: his personal virtue, his self control, his abstention from all pleasures, his endurance in the face of all kinds of suffering, and his ability to detach himself from the world. You recall the famous scene in which Socrates becomes insensible, remaining immobile, impervious to the cold when he was a soldier at war.[4] We should also not forget that Socrates has that, in a sense even more important feature of wisdom, which is a particular kind of silence, regardless of everything. Because Socrates does not speak, he does not deliver speeches, he does not say spontaneously what he knows. On the contrary, he claims to be someone who does not know, and who, not knowing and knowing only that he does not know, will remain reserved and silent, confining himself to questioning. Questioning is, if you like, a particular way of combining the essential reserve of the sage, who remains silent, with the duty of *parrhēsia* (that is to say, the duty to challenge and speak). Except that the sage remains silent because he knows and has the right not to speak of his knowledge, whereas Socrates remains silent by saying that he does not know, and by questioning everyone and anyone in the manner of the parrhesiast. So here again you can see that the parrhesiastic feature combines with the features of wisdom. And finally, of course, there is the relationship with the technician, the teacher. The Socratic problem is how to teach the virtue and knowledge required to live well or also to govern the city properly. You recall the *Alcibiades*.[5] You recall too—we will come back to this next week—the end of the *Laches*, where Socrates agrees to teach the sons of Lysimachus and [Melesias] to take care of themselves.[6] So Socrates is the parrhesiast, but, once again, with a permanent, essential relationship to prophetic veridiction, the veridiction of wisdom, and the technical veridiction of teaching.

So, prophecy, wisdom, teaching, technique, and *parrhēsia* should be seen much more as fundamental modes of truth-telling than as characters. There is the modality which speaks enigmatically about that which is hidden from every human being. There is the modality of truth-telling which speaks apodictically about being, *phusis*, and the order of things. There is the veridiction which speaks demonstratively about kinds of knowledge and expertise. There is finally the veridiction which speaks polemically about individuals and situations. These four modes of truth-telling are, I believe, absolutely fundamental for the analysis of discourse to the extent that, in discourse, the subject who tells the truth is constituted for himself and for others. I think that since Greek culture, the subject who tells the truth takes these four possible forms: he is either prophet, or sage, or technician, or parrhesiast. It would be interesting to investigate how these four modalities, which, again, once and for all, are not identified with roles or characters, are combined in different cultures, societies, or civilizations in different modes of discursivity, in what could be called the different "regimes of truth" found in different societies.

It seems to me—at any rate, this is what I have tried to show you, however schematically—that in Greek culture at the end of the fifth and the beginning of the fourth century B.C.E. we can find these four major modes of veridiction distributed in a kind of rectangle: that of prophecy and fate, that of wisdom and being, that of teaching and *tekhnē*, and that of *parrhēsia* and *ēthos*. But if these four modalities are thus quite clearly decipherable, separable, and separated from each other at this time, one of the features of the history of ancient philosophy (and also no doubt of ancient culture generally) is that there is a tendency for the mode of truth-telling characteristic of wisdom and the mode of truth-telling characteristic of *parrhēsia* to come together, join together, to link up with each other in a sort of philosophical modality of truth-telling which is very different from prophetic truth-telling as well as from the teaching of *tekhnai*, of which rhetoric is an example. We will see a philosophical truth-telling separating off, or anyway the development of a philosophical truth-telling which will ever more insistently claim to speak of being or the nature of things only to the extent that this truth-telling concerns, is relevant for, is able to articulate and found a truth-telling about *ēthos* in the form of *parrhēsia*. And to that extent, we can say that, only up to a certain point, of course, wisdom and *parrhēsia* merge. Anyway, it is as though they are attracted to each other, that there is something like a phenomenon of gravitation of wisdom and *parrhēsia*, a gravitation which manifests itself in the famous characters of philosophers telling the truth of things, but above all telling their truth to men, throughout Hellenistic and Roman, or Greco-Roman culture. If you like, there is the possibility of an analysis of a history of the regime of truth concerning the relations between *parrhēsia* and wisdom.

If we take up again these four major fundamental modes I have been talking about, we could say that medieval Christianity produced other groupings. Greco-Roman philosophy brought together the modalities of *parrhēsia* and wisdom. It seems to me that in medieval Christianity we see another type of grouping bringing together the prophetic and parrhesiastic modalities. The two modalities of telling the truth about the future (about what is hidden from men by virtue of their finitude and the structure of time, about what awaits men and the imminence of the still hidden event), and then telling the truth to men about what they are, were brought together in a number of particular [types] of discourses, and also institutions. I am thinking of preaching and preachers, and especially of those preachers, starting with the Franciscans and Dominicans, who played an absolutely major role across the Western world and throughout the Middle Ages in the perpetuation, but also renewal and transformation [of] the experience of threat for the medieval world. These great preachers played the role of both prophet and parrhesiast in that society. Those who speak of the threatening imminence of the future, of the Kingdom of the Last Day, of the Final Judgment, or of approaching death, at the same time tell men what they are, and tell them frankly, with complete *parrhēsia*, what their faults and crimes are, and in what respects and how they must change their mode of being.

Counterposed to this, it seems to me that the same medieval society, the same medieval civilization tended to bring together the other two modes of veridiction: that of wisdom, which tells of the being of things and their nature, and that of teaching. Telling the truth of being and telling the truth of knowledge was the task of an institution which was as specific to the Middle Ages as was preaching: the University. Preaching and the University appear to me to be institutions specific to the Middle Ages, in which we see the functions I have spoken about grouping together, in pairs, and defining a regime of veridiction, a regime of truth-telling, which is very different from the regime we could find in the Hellenistic and Greco-Roman world, where instead it was *parrhēsia* and wisdom that were combined.

And what about the modern epoch, you may ask? I don't really know. It would no doubt have to be analyzed. We could say perhaps—but these are hypotheses, not even hypotheses: some almost incoherent remarks—that you find the prophetic modality of truth-telling in some political discourses, in revolutionary discourse. In modern society, revolutionary discourse, like all prophetic discourse, speaks in the name of someone else, speaks in order to tell of a future which, up to a point, already has the form of fate. The ontological modality of truth-telling, which speaks of the being of things, would no doubt be found in a certain modality of philosophical discourse. The technical modality of truth-telling is organized much more around science than teaching, or at any rate around a complex formed by scientific and research institutions and teaching institutions. And the parrhesiastic modality has, I believe, precisely disappeared as such, and we no longer find it except where it is grafted on or underpinned by one of these three modalities. Revolutionary discourse plays the role of parrhesiastic discourse when it takes the form of a critique of existing society. Philosophical discourse as analysis, as reflection on human finitude and criticism of everything which may exceed the limits of human finitude, whether in the realm of knowledge or the realm of morality, plays the role of *parrhēsia* to some extent. And when scientific discourse is deployed as criticism of prejudices, of existing forms of knowledge, of dominant institutions, of current ways of doing things—and it cannot avoid doing this, in its very development—it plays this parrhesiastic role. That's wanted I wanted to say to you.*

---

* M.F. continues: I intended to begin to speak to you of *parrhēsia* as I want to study it this year. But what would be the point? I would have five minutes and then it would be necessary to start again next week. So, if you like, we will go for a coffee. I could tell you: I do want to reply to your questions, but I fear that it does not have much meaning in lecture theaters...
[*reply to a question from the public concerning the closed seminar:*]
I have two things to say to you, this question and then another little thing. Concerning the seminar, once again, there is an institutional and legal problem. In principle, we do not have the right to have a closed seminar. And when I had a closed seminar—the one on Pierre Rivière, for example, some of you may recall it—there were complaints. And in fact, legally, we don't have the right to have a closed seminar. Only, I think that for certain kinds of work there is a contradiction between, [on the one hand] asking professors to give a public account of their research, and then, [on the other] preventing them from having a closed seminar where they can undertake research with some students. In other words, a professor can be asked to report on his research in public lectures, and nothing other than this, if he is doing research that he can undertake on his own. And, if you like, one of the purely technical reasons why, in fact, for some years I have lectured on ancient philosophy, is that, after all, it suffices to have the two hundred volumes of Budé available, and there you are. You don't need a working group. But if—as I would like to do—I want to study the practices, forms, and rationalities of government in modern society, I can only really do this in a group.

---

1. On these two notions and their difference, see *L'Herméneutique du sujet*, for example, pp. 301-306 and 436-437; *The Hermeneutics of the Subject*, pp. 315-321 and 454-456.

2. On this aspect of Socratic speech, see the lecture of 2 March 1983, first hour, in *Le Gouvernement de soi et des autres*, pp. 286-296; *The Government of Self and Others*, pp. 310-321.

3. Platon, *Apologie de Socrate*, 21a-e, pp. 145-146; Plato, *Socrates' Defence (Apology)*, pp. 7-8.

4. The scene is related by Alcibiades in the *Symposium* (220a-220d). See the reference to this scene in the 1982 lectures, *L'Herméneutique du sujet*, p. 49; *The Hermeneutics of the Subject*, pp. 49-50.

5. See the analysis of this dialogue in the lectures of 6 and 13 January 1982 in *L'Herméneutique du sujet*, pp. 3-77; *The Hermeneutics of the Subject*, pp. 1-79.

6. Platon, *Lachès*, 200e, trans. M. Croiset (Paris: Les Belles Lettres, 1965) p. 121; English translation by Benjamin Jowet, *Laches*, in Plato, *The Collected Dialogues*, p. 144.

Now you can well understand—it is not offending anyone here—that this audience won't be able to function as a team. So what I would like is the right to divide the teaching in two: a public teaching, which is statutory; but also a teaching or research in a closed group which is, I think, the condition for being able to carry out, or in any case replenish the public teaching we give. There is, I think, a contradiction in asking people to undertake research and public teaching if they are not given the institutional supports which make the research they have to do possible.

So second, a small thing, it is probable—you know that I never really know what I will be doing from one week to the next—that either next week or the following week I will give a lecture, [or] half a lecture, on one of Dumézil's last two books, the one, you know, on "the black monk in gray" which concerns Nostradamus and includes a second part on Socrates (the *Phaedo* and the *Crito*). So as it is a difficult text, if some of you wish or have the opportunity to read it before—obviously, there is no obligation, we are not in a closed seminar, you do as you like—I would very much like to talk about it, certainly in two weeks, or maybe next week.

[question from the public:] - In a seminar or in the lectures?

- The lectures. It's just that I am well aware that if I want to give a lecture on this, it presupposes to some degree that people have an idea of what is in the book. That's it, many thanks.

three

8 FEBRUARY 1984

First hour

[
Parrhēsia *in Euripides: a privilege of the well-born citizen.* ⌒
Criticism of democratic parrhēsia: *harmful for the city and dangerous for the person who exercises it.* ⌒ *Socrates' political reserve.*
⌒ *The blackmail-challenge of Demosthenes.* ⌒ *The impossibility of ethical differentiation in democracy: the example of the*
Constitution of the Athenians. ⌒ *Four principles of Greek political thought.* ⌒ *The Platonic reversal.* ⌒ *Aristotelian hesitation.* ⌒ *The problem of ostracism.*
]

[I WOULD LIKE TO take up this problem of] *parrhēsia* from where I left it last year, and try to present a somewhat simplified account of what I think was an important transformation in this history of *parrhēsia*, that is to say, the transition from a practice, right, obligation, and duty of veridiction defined in relation to the city, its institutions, and the status of the citizen, to a different type of veridiction, a different type of *parrhēsia*, which will be defined not in relation to the city (the *polis*) but to individuals' ways of doing things, being, and conducting themselves (*ēthos*), and also to their formation as moral subjects. And, through this transformation of a *parrhēsia* oriented towards and correlative to the *polis* into a *parrhēsia* oriented towards and correlative to *ēthos*, I would like to show you today how Western philosophy, at least in some of its fundamental features, may have been constituted as a form of practice of true discourse.

First, [a] brief reminder. Forgive me, this is schematic and repetitive [for] those who were here last year, but maybe indispensable in order to clarify things and reactualize the problem. You recall, last year we considered *parrhēsia* in the political field and in the framework of democratic institutions. The word *parrhēsia* is attested for the first time in the texts of Euripides, in which it referred to the right to speak, the right to take the floor and speak publicly, to have one's say, as it were, in order to express one's views in the realm of matters of interest to the city. The word *parrhēsia* designates the right to have one's say in the city's affairs. And several of Euripides' texts enabled us to see, first, that this *parrhēsia*, this right to have one's say, is not a right if one is not a citizen by birth. You recall that Ion did not want to return to Athens in the guise of the son of a father who was not a citizen of Athens and of an unknown mother.[1] He wanted to be able to exercise his *parrhēsia* as a birthright. Second, we also saw that one does not have this right of *parrhēsia* when one is exiled in a foreign city. You remember the dialogue between Iocasta and Polyneices in *The Phoenician Women*. Iocasta meets Polyneices returning from exile and asks him: But what is exile, is it something so hard? And Polyneices replies: Certainly, it is the hardest thing to bear, because in exile one does not have *parrhēsia*, one does not have the right to speak, and so one finds oneself the slave (*doulos*) of the masters, and one cannot even oppose their madness.[2] Finally, third, we saw that even when one is a citizen, living in one's own city, and possessing *parrhēsia* as a birthright, one may lose this right if one's family is in some way marked by a stain, dishonor, or shame. This is [*Hippolytus**], when Phaedra confesses her love and fears that her own confessed wrongdoing will deprive her children, her sons of *parrhēsia*.[3] So, *parrhēsia* appeared in these texts as a right and a privilege which was part of the well-born, honorable citizen's existence, giving him access to political life understood as the possibility of giving one's view and thereby contributing to collective decisions. *Parrhēsia* was a right to be preserved at any price, a right to be exercised to the fullest possible extent, and one of the forms in which the free existence of a free citizen manifested itself—[taking] the word "free" [in] its full and positive sense, that is to say: a freedom which gives one the right to exercise

---

* M.F. says "Phèdre," confusing Euripides' title with the title of Racine's play.

one's privileges in the midst of others, in relation to others, and over others.

Now—and this was the direction we were following when we stopped last year—in later texts, *parrhēsia* appeared in a somewhat different light. In the (mainly philosophical and political) texts at the end of the fourth and beginning of the fifth century, *parrhēsia* appears much less as a right to be exercised in full freedom than as a dangerous practice with ambiguous effects, and a right which is not to be exercised without caution or limits. From Plato to Demosthenes and including Isocrates, we saw the development of this mistrust of *parrhēsia*.[4] This crisis of *parrhēsia*, as it appears in the philosophical and political literature of the fourth century, and with which I would like to begin to structure this year's lectures, can be characterized by two major phenomena.

First: the criticism of democratic *parrhēsia*. Here I would like to try to show you how this criticism was carried out, how and why the possibility of democratic institutions allowing space for truth-telling came to be questioned in Greek philosophical and political thought from Plato to Aristotle. And if the democratic institutions are unable to make room for truth-telling and get *parrhēsia* to function as it should, it is because these democratic institutions lack something. And I will try to show you that this something is what could be called "ethical differentiation."

Let's be a bit more precise and exact. In the criticism of democratic *parrhēsia* that we see developing in philosophical and political texts of the fourth century, what is at issue is really the criticism of the traditional pretensions of democracy, of democratic institutions and the practices of democracy—claims such as are represented, allusively at least, in Euripides—to be the privileged site for the emergence of truth-telling. Athens, a democratic city-state proud of its institutions, claimed to be the city in which the right to speak, to give one's views, to tell the truth, and the possibility of accepting the courage of this truth-telling were actually better realized than elsewhere. This claim, of democracy in general and of Athenian democracy [in particular], is challenged. Values seem to be overturned and democracy appears instead as the place where *parrhēsia* (truth-telling, the right to express one's opinion, and the courage to go against the opinions of others)

increasingly becomes impossible, or at any rate dangerous. This criticism of the claim of democratic institutions to be the site of *parrhēsia*
has two aspects.

First, in democracy, *parrhēsia* is dangerous for the city. It is dangerous for the city because it is the freedom of everyone and anyone
to give their views. In democracy, indeed, the freedom to give one's
views is not exercised as the statutory privilege of those whose birth,
status, and position give them the ability to tell the truth and speak
usefully in the city. In democracy, *parrhēsia* gives scope for everyone to
express their opinion and say what is in accord with their private will
and with what will enable them to satisfy their interests or passions.
Consequently, democracy is not the place where *parrhēsia* will be exercised as a privilege-duty, but the place where *parrhēsia* will be exercised
as the freedom for everybody and anybody to say anything, that is to
say, to say whatever they like. You recall that this is how, in the *Republic*
(Book VIII, 557b),[5] Plato evokes the motley and diverse city in which
everyone gives their opinion, follows their own decisions, and governs
himself as he likes. In this city there are as many *politeiai* (constitu-
tions, governments) as there are individuals. Similarly, at the beginning of *On the Peace* (paragraph 13), Isocrates mentions the orators
who the Athenians like to listen to. Who are these people who get up,
speak, give their opinion, and are listened to? Well, they are drunks,
people who have lost their sense (*tous noun ouk ekhontas*: those who are
not reasonable), and those who share out public wealth and money
between themselves.[6] Thus, in this parrhesiastic freedom, understood
as freedom of speech given to everybody and anybody (to both good
and bad orators, to those pursuing their own interest as well as those
devoted to the city), true and false discourses, useful as well as bad or
harmful opinions, all become mixed up and intermingled in the game
of democracy. So we see that, in democracy, *parrhēsia* is dangerous for
the city. This was the first aspect. You remember that we found several
of these texts.

The second worrying aspect concerning democratic *parrhēsia*, or
democracy as the supposedly privileged place for *parrhēsia*, is that in
democracy *parrhēsia* is not only dangerous for the city itself, but also
for the individual who attempts to exercise it. In this case, a different
aspect of *parrhēsia* is considered. With the first danger, *parrhēsia* proved

to be the freedom granted to everybody to say anything. Now, *parrhēsia* appears dangerous inasmuch as it calls for courage on the part of whoever wishes to employ it in a democracy, a courage which may not be respected. In the hubbub of all the orators arguing with each other and trying to seduce the people and seize control of the helm—this is the image of the ship Plato gives in Book VI of the *Republic*[7]—who will be listened to, approved, followed, and loved? It will be those who please the people, say what they want to hear, and flatter them. The others, those who say or try to say what is true and good, and not what pleases the people, will not be listened to. Worse, they will provoke negative reactions, irritation, and anger. And their true discourse will expose them to vengeance or punishment. You recall that, in a precise passage in the *Apology*, Socrates refers to this danger for the individual speaking the truth in the democratic space. After having explained the mission entrusted to him by the god—which consisted in cross examining different citizens, one after another, stopping them in the street or calling on them in their workplaces and homes—Socrates puts the following objection to himself: Since I claim to be so useful to the city, why then have I not taken part in public life? Why have I never mounted the platform to state my opinion, express my views, and give advice to the city in general? And he replies: "If long ago I had devoted myself to politics, I would have lost my life long ago...Do not get angry [he says to his judges; M.F.] when you hear me tell you these truths: no man can escape death if, however nobly [*gnēsiōs*: for noble reasons], he should oppose you, or any other popular assembly, and endeavor to prevent injustice and illegality in his city."[8] Consequently, a man who speaks for noble reasons and, for these noble reasons opposes the will of all, Socrates says, risks death. The problem arises (we will come back to it either today or next week): why did Socrates, who did not fear exposing himself to the risk of death in the name of a particular practice of *parrhēsia* which he did not want to relinquish, nevertheless refuse to practice political and democratic *parrhēsia* before the Assembly? But this is another question.[9] Anyway, the danger of *parrhēsia* as truth-telling in democratic practice is clearly pointed out here, not as a danger for the city in general, but for the individual who, for noble reasons, wishes to oppose the will of the others.

Isocrates evokes the same kind of danger at the beginning of *On the Peace*, which I just referred to, when he says, for example: "I see that you do not give an equal hearing to the speakers, that you pay attention to some, while you cannot stand even the voice of others. Moreover, it is not at all surprising that you act in this way, for your custom is always to throw out speakers who do not agree with your desires."[10] I know, Isocrates concludes, that it is dangerous to oppose your views, because although we live in a democracy, there is no *parrhēsia*.[11]

So you see the notion of *parrhēsia* splitting. On one side it appears as the dangerous latitude given to everyone and anyone to say everything and anything. And then there is the good, courageous *parrhēsia* of someone who nobly tells the truth, even when the truth is disagreeable, and this *parrhēsia* is dangerous for the individual who employs it and there is no place for it in democracy. Either democracy makes room for *parrhēsia*, in which case it can only be a freedom which is dangerous for the city, or *parrhēsia* is a courageous attitude which consists in undertaking to tell the truth, in which case it has no place in democracy.

You also find many references to this crisis, this criticism, this denunciation of the inability of democracy to make room for the good *parrhēsia* in many of Demosthenes' discourses. For those who are interested, I refer you to *The Third Olynthiac*, for example, where he begins by making a serious accusation against his fellow citizens: You have been reduced to slavery and think yourselves happy because you are given money for entertainments.[12] After having uttered this truth, which is of course wounding for those to whom it is addressed, after telling this courageous truth, he immediately adds: But I know that after speaking to you in this way and having told you that you are people satisfied with the money given you for entertainments, "I would not be surprised if these words [that I have just uttered; M.F.] were to cost me more than it costs those [the bad orators; M.F.] for the harm they have done you. You do not tolerate frankness [speaking out freely, *parrhēsia* says the text; M.F.] on every subject, and what surprises me is that you have let me speak today."[13] A sort of parrhesiastic game unfolds here, which is fairly common in Demosthenes and the orators of this time, in which one attempts to force the listener to accept a truth which hurts him, in which one forces the people of Athens to agree to hearing it being said: You are a people who are satisfied with the money given to you for entertainments. One forces them to accept this hurtful truth by wounding them a second time with a further reproach. This new reproach consists in saying: In any case, you are not capable of accepting the truth. In the first place, you take money for entertainments, and are satisfied with it. Secondly, I know the risk I am taking in telling you this, and you will very likely punish me for having done so. It is a sort of challenge-blackmail so that room can be made for the true discourse. A century after Euripides, true discourse in democracy no longer appears as a privilege possessed by those who meet certain conditions. True discourse can only take place through an operation of challenge-blackmail: I am going to tell you the truth, and you are likely to punish me; but if I tell you in advance that you are likely to punish me, this will probably stop you from punishing me and enable me to tell the truth.

You find the same mechanism at the beginning of the *Third Philippic*, when Demosthenes refers to the uncontrolled distribution of the right to speak and the unlimited granting of this right in Athenian institutions. He emphasizes the pleasure with which the people listen to those who flatter them, he recalls the disappearance of *parrhēsia* as truth-telling—as a consequence, an effect of these institutions and the indulgence of flattery—and he stresses the risks he is taking in speaking as he does. Again he starts on this challenge-blackmail where he says: Either you give up listening only to flatterers and agree to listen to true *parrhēsia*, or else I will say nothing. There is this passage in the *Third Philippic*: "If I frankly tell you some truths, Athenians, I do not think you have cause to get angry. Think about it for a moment. On every other matter you want free-spokenness (*parrhēsia*) to be everyone's right in our city; you even grant it to foreigners, and, what is more, to slaves; and, in fact, there are many more servants among you who say whatever they want more freely than citizens in other cities."[14] Here then is *parrhēsia* in Athenian democracy: everybody, even servants and slaves, can speak freely. But you have driven *parrhēsia* (free-spokenness) in its positive sense, as courage to speak the truth, from the platform. When there is *parrhēsia* as freedom for everyone, there cannot be *parrhēsia* as courage to speak the truth. And what is the result of this? Well, says Demosthenes, the result is that, in the assemblies, you take delight in hearing yourself flattered by speeches which aim only to please you. But then your very safety is endangered by subsequent events. If—and this is the challenge-blackmail—that is how you feel now, I have nothing more to say to you, and all I can do is remain silent. If, on the other hand, you really want to listen to me and not punish me for the truth I am going to tell you, if you really want to listen to what requires your attention, without demanding to be flattered, then I am ready to speak.

This then is how this criticism of democratic *parrhēsia*, or rather this pointing out of a sort of impossibility of making a full and positive use of *parrhēsia* in democratic institutions, is expressed. But then, we may ask: what is the reason given for the failure of true discourse to prevail over false discourse in the democratic game? After all, how is it that a courageous speaker who tells the truth cannot get himself recognized? Or again, how is it that people are unable to hear, to listen to and recognize the speaker who tells the truth? For what reason, why and how is it not possible to distinguish between true and false discourse in democracy? I think that there is a fundamental problem here which we should try to grasp. What makes true discourse powerless in democracy? Is true discourse powerless in itself? Certainly not. There is, as it were, a contextual powerlessness. True discourse is powerless due to the institutional framework in which it emerges and tries to assert its truth. The powerlessness of true discourse in democracy is obviously not due to the true discourse, to the fact that the discourse is true. It is due to the very structure of democracy. Why will democracy not allow this triage of true and false discourse? Because in democracy one cannot distinguish between good and bad speakers, between discourse which speaks the truth and is useful to the city, and discourse which utters lies, flatters, and is harmful.

The theme that democracy cannot be the place of true discourse pervades this criticism that we see throughout the fourth century. And in order to recapture something of the central argument from which all these criticisms will spring, I think we can refer to what is, in a sense, its crudest, simplest, most schematic, forthright, and blunt, but also most revealing formulation. The principle that there cannot be any division between true and false discourse in democracy is expressed in a text which was for a long time attributed to Xenophon, [but] which actually comes from another source [and] was doubtless written at the turn of the fifth and fourth centuries. The text is called *Constitution of the Athenians (Politeia Athēnaiōn)*. It is in fact a pamphlet, obviously of aristocratic origin, which appears in the slightly twisted form of a paradoxical, false eulogy of Athenian democracy, an ironic hymn in its honor, which turns, of course, into harsh criticism. Under the pretext of highlighting all the merits of Athenian democracy, the author puts forward such derisory reasons, such dreadful motives in support of these merits that the eulogy is immediately recognized as a fundamental, radical criticism of Athenian institutions. All these modulations around the form of the eulogy were frequent in Greek literature of the fourth century.

In this paradoxical, critical, and farcical eulogy of Athenian democracy, there are some lines which are devoted precisely to *parrhēsia*. They are in the first chapter. In this passage, the author of the *Constitution of the Athenians* refers to certain cities where, he says, it is the most skillful (we would say, the most competent) who make the laws. Also, he says, in these cities it is the good citizens who chastise, keep a tight rein on, repress, and impose the necessary punishments on bad citizens. Finally, he says, in these cities it is the decent people (*khrēstoi*) who deliberate and take decisions, and instead of giving the insane, the mad (*hoi mainomenoi*: those who are not in their right mind) the right to speak, they are prevented from *bouleuein* (from taking part in the deliberative and decision making bodies which determine the city's policy). These people who are not in their right mind (the mad, the insane) are not allowed to take part in the deliberations of decision making bodies, or to give their views, and they have no voting rights. But that's not all. Not only are these people denied access to the *Boulē* (the Council) in these cities, they are not even allowed to speak (*legein*). And not only are they not allowed to speak, they are not even allowed *ekklēsiazein* (to come to the *Ekklēsia*, the Assembly). They do not have a place at the Assembly, or the right to speak, so *a fortiori* they have no right to give their views in the councils. And, the author says, with all these precautions, *eunomia* (the good constitution, the good regime) prevails in these cities.[15]

After defining the good regime in this way, that is to say, after having dealt himself some winning cards, the author of the feigned, ironic, paradoxical, and farcical eulogy of Athenian institutions goes on to say: The great merit of Athens is precisely that of not having given itself this luxury of *eunomia* and not having taken these precautions which prevent the mad from taking part in the Council, from speaking, and even from coming to the Assembly. Athens' great merit, he says, is that of avoiding this *eunomia* and not having accepted such restrictions. Why has Athens not accepted this regime of restricted speech, the good system of government, and the good constitution? These are the reasons he gives and, again you will see that the argument is interesting, despite their crude, sophistical, twisted character. It is for the following reason, he says. What happens in a city where only the best have the right to speak and are the ones to voice their opinions and make decisions? The best—precisely because they are the best—try to come to decisions in line with the city's good, interest, and utility. Now what is good and useful for the city is at the same time, by definition, what is good, useful, and advantageous for the city's best. So that, by encouraging the city to take decisions which are useful for it, they are only serving their own interests, the selfish interest of those who are the best.[16] Now what happens in democracy, in a true democracy like Athens? You have a regime in which decisions are not taken by the best, but by the many (*hoi polloi*). And what do they seek? Not to submit to anything. In a democracy the many (*hoi polloi*)[17] want above all to be free, not to be slaves (*douleuein*), not to serve.[18] What don't they want to serve? They do not want to serve the interests of the city any more than they want to serve the interests of the best. They want to command (*arkhein*) by themselves.[19] They will therefore pursue what is useful and good for them, since what is it to command? It is being able to decide and impose what is best for oneself. But since they are the most numerous (*hoi polloi*), they can no longer be the best, since the best are by definition fewer. Consequently, being the most numerous they are not the best; and not being the best, they are the worst. So what those who are the worst seek will be good for whom? For the worst in the city. Now what is bad for those who are bad in the city is also what is bad for the city. [The author] concludes that, in such a city, speech must indeed be given to everyone, to the many, and so to the worst.[20] Because, he says, what would happen if speech and deliberation were the exclusive privilege of decent, respectable people, if *parrhēsia* was only granted to the best? Being granted *parrhēsia*, the best would want to lay down the city's good, that is to say, their own good. And if they were to impose their own good, what is useful to them, this could only be to the advantage of these decent people, and to the disadvantage of the people.[21] Consequently, in a true democracy, like Athens, if you want what is said to be for the advantage of the people and the many, the right to speak should not be reserved for the best. The bad, the author says, must be able to get up and speak. And then he will express what is good for him, the evil person, and for those like him.[22]

I am not going to dwell any more on these, as you can see, somewhat sophistical arguments. But I think that these games are interesting and important. Because if their logic is obviously completely questionable, I think they put into practice, they apply, some principles that it is important to see were commonly accepted in the fourth century form of the criticism of democracy as the place of *parrhēsia*. Anyway, these few principles are found in much more serious forms of thought than this somewhat caricatural pamphlet.

The underlying principles of this and many other texts can be summarized in the following way—and it seems to me that, in a sense, they have been a permanent matrix and challenge for political thought in the Western world.

First, a principle which could be called the quantitative principle, or, if you like, the principle of opposition founded on a quantitative differentiation. The reasoning of the author of *Politeia Athēnaiōn*, in fact, accepts as self-evident—and hundreds of other texts would show that people who are infinitely more serious than him reason in the same way and invoke the same opposition—that individuals in a city are distinguished from each other as falling into two major groups characterized solely, but fundamentally, by the fact that one group contains more and the other less. On one side are the "masses," on the other the "few." It is this quantitative division between the *"hoi polloi"* and "the few" which basically organizes opposition in the city, the conflicts which may develop within it, and raises at the same time the problem of who should govern. So, quantitative opposition is the first principle; a principle of quantitative division of the city's unity.

Second, this opposition, this quantitative division between the many and the others coincides with the opposition between the best and the worst. The quantitative division between the many and the others traces the same line as that of the ethical division between the good and the bad. This could be called, if you like, the principle of (forgive the barbaric expression) ethico-quantitative isomorphism.

The third principle underlying this paradoxical text I have just cited is that this ethical distinction, between the best and the less good, corresponds to a political distinction. On one side, what is good for the best in the city is also what is good for the city: the good for the best is the city's good. On the other hand, what is good for the worse is evil for the city; good for the worse is the city's evil. This could be called, if you like, the principle of political transitivity. The will of the best, in seeking the good, is useful to the city. The will of the worse, in seeking their good, is bad for the city.

The consequence of this, and this is the fourth principle, is that the truth in the realm of political discourse—that is to say: what is good, useful, and healthy for the city—naturally cannot be told in the form of democracy understood as the right for everyone to speak. The truth can be told in a city and political structure only when an essential quantitative division between the good and bad is marked, maintained, and institutionalized. It is only to the extent that this essential ethical discrimination between the good and the bad has actually taken shape, found its place, and achieved definite manifestation within the political field that it will be possible for the truth to be told. And when the truth can be told, the city's good (that which is useful and healthy for it) will be able to take effect.

In other words, there has to be truth for the city to exist and for it to be saved. But the truth cannot be told in a political field defined by an absence of differentiation between the subjects speaking. The truth can be told only in a political field marked and organized by a division between the more and less numerous, which is also the ethical division between those who are good and those who are bad, between the better and the worse. That is why truth-telling cannot have its place in the democratic game, inasmuch as democracy is unable to recognize and cannot make room for the ethical division on the basis of which, and only on the basis of which, truth-telling is possible. So it would not be enough to say—as might be suggested by the first texts I cited, which take up those I referred to last year—that granting freedom of speech to everyone risks mixing up true and false, favoring flatterers, and exposing those who speak to personal dangers. All this is true, but it is only the effect of a more fundamental, structural impossibility. What is important to grasp in [the type] of analysis suggested by this paradoxical text is that by subjecting the better to the worse, by reversing the order of values, by installing this disorder, and by sustaining its absurdity, the very form of democracy cannot leave any place for truth-telling. It can only eliminate truth-telling by not listening to it when it is expressed or by suppressing it physically with death [...*]. This enables us to understand what could be called very schematically—forgive me, I am going to give a very rough overview—the Platonic reversal and the Aristotelian hesitation.

First of all, the Platonic reversal. If indeed it is true that one cannot find *parrhēsia* in democracy, due to the fact that it lacks the ethical sense of discrimination which is indispensable for truth-telling, then, Plato will say, true discourse, when it is established through philosophy and in the form of philosophy as the foundation of the *politeia*, can only eliminate and banish democracy. We could say, again very schematically, that there is this great struggle between democracy and truth-telling: on the one hand, when we look at democratic institutions, we see that they cannot tolerate truth-telling and that they cannot fail to eliminate it; [on the other hand], if we valorize truth-telling on the basis of the ethical choice characteristic of the philosopher and philosophy, then democracy cannot but be eliminated. Either democracy or truth-telling. After the criticism of democracy's inability to make room for truth-telling, the Platonic reversal consists in the validation of truth-telling as the defining principle of a *politeia* (of a political structure, a constitution, a type of regime) from which, precisely, democracy is carefully excluded. I refer you to what is [stated] in the *Republic*, Book VI, 488a-b—I have forgotten to provide you with the text, but you can read it yourselves. This is the passage I referred to earlier where Plato says: Listen, to make myself understood I will have to appeal to a comparison (a very classical, fundamental comparison which is a matrix in all Greek political thought). We should think of the city as like a boat, a ship, with a pilot who is a good man of

---

* After a break, only the end of the following phrase is heard: ... democratic, to make room for the truth, to listen to and tolerate it.

good will but a bit blind and unable to see beyond the end of his nose. This pilot is, of course, the people. And around him are the members of the crew who try to do only one thing—seize the helm and steer the ship in their interest. These are the demagogues. In order to take control of the helm, they flatter the pilot, seize the helm, and then, of course, steer, not according to any science of piloting, or of the sea, or sky, but according to their own interests. Democracy cannot appeal to true discourse. Contrasted with this will be the famous philosophers' descent back down into the cave, in Book VII, when, after having actually contemplated the truth, they are told: Whatever pleasure you have felt in contemplating this truth, and even though you have recognized it as your homeland, you know very well that you must go back down into the city and become those who govern.[23] You will impose your true discourse on all those who wish to govern the city according to the principles of flattery. After the criticism of democratic *parrhēsia*, which shows that in democracy there cannot be *parrhēsia* in the sense of courageous truth-telling, the Platonic reversal shows therefore that good government, a good *politeia*, must be founded on a true discourse, which will exclude democracy and demagogues.

All this is well known, but I would like to dwell a bit more on what could be called the Aristotelian hesitation which, notwithstanding Aristotle's much more "democratic" (in a thousand quotation marks) sentiments, is based on the same problematic, the same difficulty in admitting the existence of *parrhēsia*, of truth-telling in democratic institutions when democracy cannot make room for the ethical differentiation of speaking, deliberating, and decision-making subjects.

Of course, Aristotle considerably developed, modified, transformed, and up to a point refuted the schematic and crude principles which I have just referred to. The principle, for example, that the city is divided into two opposing groups (the many and the few). Aristotle asserts this principle, but at the same time he supplements it, modifies it, and questions it by bringing into play another form of opposition: the opposition between the rich and the poor. In a very interesting chapter in Book III of the *Politics*, [he] puts the question: Does the opposition between the many and the few correspond exactly to that between the poor and the rich?[24] For example, can we not envisage— and he considers it as a real possibility—a city in which the rich would be the many and the poor would be the few? In this case, assuming that power is given to the poor (that is to say, the few), could we speak of democracy? In other words, if we define democracy as a constitution in which power is given to the many, would there be democracy if the rich were the many? And if the poor are the few, can their power be called democracy, or should it be called an aristocracy? And—in an extremely interesting and fundamental answer, which to an extent might have shifted the whole basis of Greek political thought—Aristotle says: It is the power of the poor which characterizes democracy.[25] And even if there were a much smaller number of poor than rich, it would be enough that they exercise power for there to be a democracy. You can see that he hesitates here and, as it were, puts the rich/poor opposition to work on the many/few opposition, which was the fundamental, general, and relatively little developed framework found in other texts.

Second, Aristotle also questions the other principle I have just referred to, according to which the many are the least good, and the few are necessarily the best. This coincidence between the best/least good opposition and the few/many opposition, this ethical-quantitative isomorphism is again questioned and put in doubt by Aristotle. He does this again in Book III of the *Politics* where he says (4, 1276b-1277b): But, after all, what is "the best"? Should we not distinguish between the virtue of the citizen and the virtue of the good man? Is there not a specifically political virtue which means that the individual will not only be a good citizen who, of course, fulfills his duties as such, but also someone who really seeks the interest of the city and takes decisions which are for the good of the city?[26] He will be a good citizen therefore, and yet he may not necessarily be a virtuous man, in the sense that we say a good man is generally virtuous in every aspect of his life and conduct. May it not be that one can be a good citizen without actually being a good man? Aristotle gives a complex, rather than a simple answer. He distinguishes this relationship between the two virtues in the case of someone who is simply one of the governed, and in the case of someone who governs.[27] I don't want to go into all these details, but you can see how, here again, Aristotle cannot purely and simply accept, naively and crudely, this superimposition of the distinctions between the many and the few and between the worst and the best, which was accepted and fundamental for so long. He challenges this ethical-quantitative isomorphism.

Finally, third, Aristotle also questions what I have called the principle of political reversibility. That is to say, by pursuing their own interest, the best seek and find the city's interest, and by pursuing their own interest, the worst aim at and achieve—because they are the worst—what is harmful for the city. Again in Book III of the *Politics*, Aristotle questions this principle by asserting that there may well be two basic orientations in every type of government, be it a monarchy, an aristocracy, or the government of all.[28] There may be a monarchy in which, naturally, only one person commands. And this monarchy may have two forms. The monarch may well govern alone, pursuing his own rather than the city's interest. Or, alternatively, he may govern by himself, but basically, first and foremost, having the city's interest as the objective. The same goes for government by an aristocracy, whose objective may be its own or the city's interest. And the same goes for the government of all or of the greatest number. That is to say, Aristotle does not accept the principle that government by the few can only be government by the best, or that government by the best, in the interest of the best, [will mean] government in the interest of the city. Rather, he posits as a principle that, whatever the form of government, those who govern may do so either in their own or in the city's interest.

You see then that Aristotle challenges, questions, and works on these three principles that we saw at work, implicitly accepted, and roughly worked out in the Pseudo-Xenophon text. Granted this, even so we have to remark that, if, unlike Plato, Aristotle by no means concludes that a city should be founded only by true discourse, and that such a city, precisely inasmuch as it is established by true discourse, cannot be a democracy, with regard to the relations between true discourse and democracy his position is still neither very clear nor, above all, very conclusive.

To start with, I would like you to consider first of all this passage from [again] Book III of the *Politics* (7, 1279a-b), which is a famous passage on which commentators have dwelt for a long time without coming to a final solution, the more so as the reliability of the text itself is uncertain. Anyway, the passage is concerned with naming the different forms of government, and [Aristotle] contrasts or distinguishes

"monarchy" and what we translate as "kingship": kingship is a monarchical type of government "which considers the common interest."[29]
So, we have this regime, called "kingship," in which the objective of
the one who governs is not his own, but the city's interest. Second,
he says, we may call a government "aristocracy" when it is a form of
government by a few, but in which these few have the good of the city
and all its members in view. As for the third form of government, in
which it is the greatest number who govern, well, he says, it is very
difficult to give it a name, and I can only call it by the general name
of *politeia*. Why is there no specific name for that form of government
in which the many govern and where they pursue the city's interest
rather than their own, than that of the greatest number? Aristotle
explains by saying that if it is possible for one individual, or even a
small number of individuals, to surpass the rest in virtue, it is very
difficult for a larger number of men to "attain perfection in every kind
of virtue."[30] This is an enigmatic text which can only be understood, I
think, in the following way. If there are in fact two formal possibilities
for the three types of government—if it is true that, in a monarchy, the
monarch may be interested in either his own or the city's advantage;
if there may be a form of aristocracy that pursues the interests of the
aristocrats and the few, or the interests of the city—on the other hand,
when we come to the form of democracy in which the multitude rule,
can we really expect this multitude to pursue anything other than its
own interest? The text appears to say this: In the first two cases we
may concede that a king or a few may pursue the city's interest rather
than their own. Why is this conceivable? Well, he says, because it is
possible for a single individual, or a small number of individuals, to
excel in virtue. So it is their ethical choice, their ethical differentiation
from the others which will make possible and ensure that government
will be for all the others. On the other hand, he says, it is very difficult for a greater number of men to "attain perfection in every kind of
virtue." Which means that when we turn to a mass of people, even if
this mass governs the city, it is impossible, or very difficult, to find in
it that ethical differentiation, division, and singularity on the basis of
which truth-telling will be possible and the city's interests recognized
through this truth-telling. Consequently, there cannot be a specific
name for the type of democratic regime which would not be oriented

toward the interest of the greater number, but toward the interest of the city itself. It has no name, because, in all likelihood, it has no concrete existence. This is an enigmatic text which seems to suggest that a democracy in which the interest of everyone would be in command is a formal possibility, if we follow Aristotle's general schema, but it does not and cannot really exist because there is no ethical differentiation in a democracy. Certainly, you can see that this is not exactly the structural impossibility defined a moment ago on the basis of the Pseudo-Xenophon text, but it is nevertheless an inevitable impossibility.

You can also find (still in Book III of the *Politics*, 10, 11, 12, and 13) a discussion of this problem of ethical excellence, differentiation, and division, in short the problem of the best in democracy. With, as a result, the problem of whether there is a place and status for the best, for ethical differentiation within democratic institutions. And the very way in which Aristotle poses the problem, envisages the difficulties, and carefully analyzes them takes place on the basis of a democracy that is not so much defined as the power of the many over the others, as by the principle of alternation. A democratic *politeia* is a constitution in which the governed always have the possibility of becoming governors. The problem Aristotle poses is how ethical differentiation is possible given this principle of the rotation and alternation of governed/ governors.

And here I would just like to point out to you the very interesting passage—which is only one of the examples of the difficulties which Aristotle himself raises about his own line of argument—[concerning] ostracism (an utterly remarkable chapter).[31] Ostracism is the measure available to the Athenian city which permits the people to exile an individual, not so much because of an offense or crime he may have committed, but solely because his prestige, his excellence, and the personal qualities of which he has given proof raise him too far above other citizens. This measure of ostracism, of which a number of famous Athenians of high merit were the victims, honorable men but victims nevertheless, clearly raised a lot of problems. It was quite difficult to justify ostracism, and Aristotle [raises] the question: is ostracism, that is to say, the decision which enables the people to get rid of someone simply because he stands out rather too much above the others, a justifiable measure? He answers the question and says: of course, there are many objections to ostracism, and yet it is justifiable. It is justifiable not only against ambitious citizens, whose superiority gives them the chance, the temptation, and the desire to exercise single, absolute, tyrannical power, but also against citizens who, because of some qualities, would stand out above the others. Why does Aristotle justify ostracism of citizens who, because of some qualities, would stand out above the others? It is basically because the city should be likened to a picture or a statue.[32] We know very well that there may be a completely perfect detail in a picture. The painter has managed to render perfectly a hand, a finger, a toe, or an ear which are little masterpieces of painting or sculpture.[33] Nevertheless, it may still be that this detail is too much in the picture, and for the sake of the picture's beauty, perfection, and balance the painter may be led to suppress this detail, however excellent it may be in itself. The same goes for the city. For reasons at once of perfection of form, aesthetics, and political balance, one may have to part with a citizen who would too clearly stand out above the others through certain of his qualities.

But immediately after [these considerations], at the end of the chapter on ostracism, he [adds]: If someone is particularly exceptional through his virtue in the city, is it just to exile him, is it even just to want to subject him "to the common rule"?[34] An exceptional man, someone wholly exceptional for his virtue, should not be exiled or even subjected "to the common rule." Concerning this man, he says, the only alternative is to [adopt] the solution which is "in accordance with the nature of things."[35] What is this solution "in accordance with the nature of things"? It is that "everyone, every citizen should willingly obey such a man, so that those like him are ever kings in their cities."[36] You can see how, after all this discussion of the question of founding democracy on the principle of the rotation and alternation of governors and governed, in which Aristotle runs up against this very difficult, paradoxical problem, this real political challenge constituted by ostracism, after having said that ultimately ostracism can be justified, here, in the case of a particularly marked ethical difference in which certain individuals would truly surpass all the others in their ethical value, [asking himself] what place these individuals can be given in a democratic city, [Aristotle answers]: We cannot apply ostracism to them; we cannot even apply to them the laws which are valid for everyone else.

Even more, we have to submit to them, to obey them, and give them a place, and a place which, really, in its formulation, has Platonic echoes, since it involves giving the place of king in the city to those men who are wiser than others. The kingship of virtue, the monarchy of virtue, finds its place and asserts itself as soon as democracy tries to raise the question of moral excellence. In short, when, with Aristotle, an attempt is made to give the best possible justification for the laws and rules of democracy, we see that democracy can give only one place to moral excellence, a place which itself embodies the refusal of democracy. If there really is someone virtuous, let democracy disappear and let men obey this man of virtue, this man of ethical excellence, like a king.

These are just a few moments in the history of what could be called, somewhat pretentiously, the crisis of democratic *parrhēsia* in Greek thought of the fourth century. You see that straightaway this has led us, brought us up against, the problem of *ēthos* and ethical differentiation.

I will stop there, if you like, for five minutes. We will start again shortly, and I will then try to show you the other aspect of the elaboration of this problem of *parrhēsia* in fourth century Greek thought.

1. For the analysis of Euripides' tragedy, *Ion*, see the lectures of 19 and 26 January 1983 in *Le Gouvernement de soi et des autres*, pp. 71-136; *The Government of Self and Others*, pp. 74-147.
2. Euripide, *Les Phéniciennes*, 388-394, trans. H. Grégoire and L. Méridier (Paris: Les Belles Lettres, 1927) p. 170; English translation by Philip Vellacott, Euripides, *The Phoenician Women* in *Orestes and Other Plays* (London: Penguin Books, 1972) p. 248:
    "IOCASTA: What is an exile's life? Is it great misery?
    POLYNEICES: The greatest; worse in reality than in report.
    IOCASTA: Worse in what way? What chiefly galls an exile's heart?
    POLYNEICES: The worst is this: right of free speech does not exist.
    IOCASTA: That's a slave's life—to be forbidden to speak one's mind.
    POLYNEICES: One has to endure the idiocy of those who rule.
    IOCASTA: To join fools in their foolishness—that makes one sick."
3. Euripide, *Hippolyte*, 421-423, trans. L. Méridier (Paris: Les Belles Lettres, 1927) p. 45; English translation by Philip Vellacott, Euripides, *Hippolytus*, in *Three Plays* (Harmondsworth: Penguin Books, 1974) p. 96: "I want my two sons to go back and live/In glorious Athens, hold their heads high there, and speak/Their mind like free men." For the study of this text, see the lecture of 2 February 1983, first hour, in *Le Gouvernement de soi et des autres*, pp. 148-149; *The Government of Self and Others*, pp. 161-162.
4. On the development of this mistrust, using these three authors, see the lectures of 2 and 9 February 1983 in *Le Gouvernement de soi et des autres*, pp. 137-204; *The Government of Self and Others*, pp. 149-208. Demosthenes is only cited in passing (*The First Philippic*), but Isocrates (*On the Peace*) and Plato are discussed at length.
5. Platon, *La République*, Book VIII, 557b, trans. E. Chambry (Paris: Les Belles Lettres, 1934) p. 26: "Is it not true that in such a State one is first of all free, and that everywhere there is freedom (*eleutheria*), free-spokenness (*parrhēsia*), and the license to do as one likes?"; English translation by Paul Shorey, *Republic*, in Plato, *The Collected Dialogues*, p. 785: "To begin with are they not free? And is not the city chock-full of liberty and freedom of speech? And has not every man license to do as he likes?"
6. Isocrate, *Sur la paix*, §13, trans. G. Mathieu (Paris: Les Belles Lettres, 1942) p. 15: "You set to work the most vicious of those who take the floor, and you think you see better democrats among the drunks than among reasonable people, among those who share out the public fortune than among those who devote their personal resources to your service"; English translation by George Norlin, "On the Peace" in *Isocrates*, Vol. 2 (Cambridge and London: Harvard University Press, Loeb Classical Library, 1968), p. 15: "you ... cultivate ... the most depraved of the orators who come before you on this platform; and you prefer as being better friends of the people those who are drunk to those who are sober, those who are witless to those who are wise, and those who dole out the public money to those who perform public services at their own expense." See the analysis of this discourse of Isocrates in the lectures 2 February 1973, second hour and 9 February 1973, first hour, in *Le Gouvernement de soi et des autres*, pp. 165-166 and 174-175; *The Government of Self and Others*, pp. 181-182 and 190-191.
7. Platon, *La République*, Book VI, 488-489a, pp. 107-108; Plato, *Republic*, pp. 724-735.
8. Platon, *Apologie de Socrate*, 31d-e, pp. 159-160; *Socrates' Defence (Apology)*, p. 17: "... if I had tried gentlemen long ago to engage in politics, I should long ago have lost my life ... Please do not be offended if I tell you the truth. No man on earth who conscientiously opposes either you or any other organized democracy, and flatly prevents a great many wrongs and illegalities from taking place in the state to which he belongs, can possibly escape with his life."
9. For a first treatment of this question, see the lecture of 2 March 1983, first hour, in *Le Gouvernement de soi et des autres*, pp. 290-295; *The Government of Self and Others*, pp. 314-320.
10. Isocrate, *Sur la paix*, §3, p. 12; Isocrates, *On the Peace*, §3, pp. 7-9: "I observe ... that you do not hear with equal favor the speakers who address you, but that, while you give your attention to some, in the case of others you do not even suffer their voice to be heard. And it is not surprising that you do this; for in the past you have formed the habit of driving all the orators from the platform except those who support your desires." For a first analysis of this discourse, see the lectures of 2 February 1973, second hour and 9 February 1973, first

hour, in *Le Gouvernement de soi et des autres*, pp. 165-166 and 174-175; *The Government of Self and Others*, pp. 181-182 and 190-191.

11. Ibid., §14, Fr. p. 15: "For my part, I know that it is hard to oppose your state of mind, and that in full democracy there is no freedom of speech (*parrhēsia*)"; Eng. p. 15: "But I know that it is hazardous to oppose your views and that, although this is a free government, there exists no 'freedom of speech.'"

12. Démosthène, *Troisième Olynthienne*, §31 in *Harangues*, vol. I, trans. M. Croiset, p. 134; Demosthenes, *The Third Olynthiac*, §31, in *Orations*, vol. I, p. 61.

13. Ibid., §32, Fr. p. 134; Eng. p. 61: "I should not wonder if I got rougher treatment from you for pointing out these faults than the men who are responsible for them. For you do not allow liberty of speech on every subject, and indeed I am surprised that you have allowed it now."

14. Démosthène, *Troisième Philippique*, §31, in *Harangues*, vol. I, p. 93; Demosthenes, *Third Philippic*, §31, in *Orations*, vol. I, p. 227: "I claim for myself, Athenians, that if I utter some home-truths with freedom, I shall not thereby incur your displeasure. For look at it in this way. In other matters you think it so necessary to grant general freedom of speech to everyone in Athens that you even allow aliens and slaves to share in the privilege, and many menials may be observed among you speaking their minds with more liberty than citizens enjoy in other states."

15. [Pseudo-]Xénophon, *La République des Athéniens*, §9, trans. P. Chambry, in *Œuvres complètes*, vol. II (Paris: Garnier, 1967) p. 475: "If you are looking for a good government (*eunomian*), you will see first of all that the most skillful make the laws; then the good (*khrēstoi*) will punish the wicked (*ponērous*); decent people will deliberate on the city's affairs without allowing the mad to give a view, or to speak, or to gather together (*mainomenous anthropous bouleuein oude legein oude ekklēsiazein*)"; English translation by J.M. Moore, "The Constitution of the Athenians (ascribed to Xenophon the Orator)" in J.M. Moore, ed., *Aristotle and Xenophon on Democracy and Oligarchy* (London: Chatto and Windus, 1975) pp. 38-39: "If you are looking for an admirable code of laws, first you will find that the ablest draw them up in their own interest; secondly, the respectable will punish the masses, and will plan the city's affairs and will not allow men who are mad to take part in planning or discussion or even sit in the *Ekklesia*."

16. Ibid., §6, Fr. p. 474: "If speech and deliberation were the privilege of decent people (*khrēstoi*), they would use it to the advantage of members of their class and to the disadvantage of the people"; Eng. 38: "If none but the respectable spoke in the *Ekklesia* and the *Boule*, the result would benefit that class and harm the masses."

17. To describe the popular mass, the text speaks rather of the *ponēroi* (wicked), *penēntes* (poor), and *dēmotikoi* (common people). See, for example, ibid., §4, Fr. p. 474: "There are people who are surprised that on every occasion the Athenians favor the wicked (*ponērois*), the poor (*penēsi*), and men of the people (*dēmotikois*) more than the good; it is precisely in this that their skill in maintaining the popular State (*dēmokratian*) appears"; Eng. pp. 37-38: "Again, some people are surprised at the fact that in all fields they give more power to the masses, the poor and the common people than they do to the respectable elements of society, but it will become clear that they preserve the democracy by doing precisely this."

18. Ibid., §8, Fr. pp. 474-475: "What the people want is not a well governed State (*eunomoumenēs tēs poleōs*) in which they will be slaves (*autos douleuein*), but a State in which they will be free and in command (*all'eleutheros einai kai arkhein*)"; Eng. p. 38: "For the common people do not wish to be deprived of their rights in an admirably governed city, but to be free and to rule the city."

19. See previous note.

20. Ibid., §6, Fr. p. 374: "It is again a very wise measure to let even the wicked speak"; Eng. p. 38: "in this also they are acting in their own best interests by allowing the mob also a voice."

21. See above, note 16.

22. [Pseudo-]Xénophon, *La République des Athéniens*, §6, p. 374: "The bad man who wants to get up and speak discovers what is good for him and his kind"; *The Constitution of the Athenians*, p. 38: "anyone who wishes rises and speaks, and as a member of the mob he discovers what is to his own advantage and that of those like him."

23. Platon, *La République*, Book VII, 519c-521b, pp. 152-155; Plato, *Republic*, pp. 751-753.

24. Aristote, *Politique*, Book III, 8, 1279b-1280a, trans. J. Tricot (Paris: Vrin, 1962) pp. 201-202; English translation by B. Jowett, Aristotle, *Politics*, in *The Complete Works of Aristotle*, in two volumes, Vol. Two, ed. Jonathan Barnes (Princeton: Princeton University Press, 1984) pp. 2030-2031.

25. Ibid., Book III, 8, 1279b, Fr. p. 201: "We call democracy [the regime] in which it is rather the poor (*aporoi*) majority which governs"; Eng. p. 2031, "where the poor rule, that is democracy."

26. Ibid., Book III, 4, 1276b, Fr. pp. 178-181; Eng. pp. 2025-2026.

27. Ibid., 1277a, Fr. pp. 181-183; Eng. pp. 2026-2027.

28. Ibid., Book III, 7, 1279a, Fr. p. 199; Eng. p. 2030.

29. Ibid.; Eng: "which regards the common interest."

30. Ibid., 1279a-1279b, Fr. p. 200; Eng. p. 2030: "One man or a few may excel in excellence; but as the number increases it becomes more difficult for them to attain perfection in every kind of excellence."

31. Ibid., Book III, 13, 1284b, Fr. pp. 233-235; Eng. pp. 2038-2039.

32. Ibid., Fr. p. 233; Eng. p. 2038. Aristotle uses the examples of the painter, the ship-builder, and the chorus-master.

33. Ibid. Aristotle actually takes only the example of the foot.

34. Ibid., Fr. p. 234; Eng. p. 2038.

35. Ibid., Fr. p. 234; Eng. p. 2039: "according to what seems to be the order of nature."

36. Ibid.; Eng.: "all should happily obey such a ruler ... and that men like him should be kings in their state for life."

four

8 FEBRUARY 1984

Second hour

I SAID TO YOU, when starting, that the problematization of *parrhēsia* in the fourth century had two aspects. [The first was] a criticism of democracy's claim to be the political framework in which *parrhēsia* [can be] both possible and effective: democracy is not the privileged site of *parrhēsia*, but the place in which *parrhēsia* is most difficult to practice. I would now like to move on to another aspect of this problematization of *parrhēsia*, which is its complementary or positive side. If democracy is increasingly discredited as the possible, privileged site of *parrhēsia*, conversely another type of political structure, or rather, another type of relationship between true discourse and government increasingly appears as the privileged site of *parrhēsia*, or at any rate, as the site favorable for *parrhēsia* and truth-telling. And this other relation—I referred to this last year, and this was where we had got to—is that between the Prince and his counselor. It is no longer the assembly; it is the court, the Prince's court, the group of those to whom he is prepared to listen. It is within this framework, it is in this form that *parrhēsia* can and has to find its place.

Even so, we must be careful and not think that the relation to the Prince suddenly became the valued, sure, and guaranteed form of a political structure in which *parrhēsia* can assume its rights and meet with favorable effects. We must always keep in mind that the figure of the Prince, his personal and monarchical power, includes a danger, or dangers. And this or these dangers will never be forgotten or dispelled. Even if it is dim and somewhat blurred, there is always in the background, and always active, the image of the tyrant as someone who, exercising personal power, does not and cannot accept the truth, because he does and wants to do only what pleases him. In his desire to do only what pleases him, he is prepared to listen only to flatterers, who tell him precisely what pleases him. Even when he would like to hear the truth, no one dares tell him. This schema, this figure, this negative valuation of personal, monarchical, tyrannical power is a constant of Greek thought.

One of its most characteristic expressions is found in someone like Xenophon, even though he is in favor of a non-democratic (aristocratic or monarchical) power. I refer to the text called *Hiero*, where there is again a kind of paradoxical game. In this text, Simonides praises the tyrant's life and addresses his eulogy to Hiero. And to each of the reasons Simonides advances to hymn the tyrant's happiness and felicity, Hiero replies with a complaint. He complains of the tyrant's hard life. And, in the last chapter, Simonides simply gives the tyrant the formula for his personal and monarchical government to be able to have beneficial effects for both himself and the city. Anyway, the first chapters are devoted to this kind of game in which Simonides pretends to sing the praises of the tyrant, or rather of the tyrannical life, of tyrannical existence, to which Hiero replies with complaints. Thus, there is a paragraph devoted precisely to flattery and *parrhēsia*. Simonides congratulates the tyrant and says to him: Ah! You tyrants are lucky. "All those around you praise everything you say and do. And abuse, the most tiresome thing to hear, never reaches your ear, for no one would take the risk of rebuking a tyrant in his presence."[1] To which Hiero replies by complaining of the tyrant's situation and explaining how hard it is to be a tyrant: "How can you think that a tyrant is delighted not to hear anyone speak badly of him, when we know full well that these silent people only nourish evil plans against him. And what pleasure do you think the tyrant takes in hearing himself praised when he suspects that this praise is only ever dictated by flattery?"[2]

This representation of tyranny as a form of government which is incompatible with truth-telling, of tyranny as favoring silence and flattery, is a commonplace which is frequently found, modulated in different ways, in all Greek literature. I refer you to an interesting passage in Aristotle's *Politics* where he says that the tyrant sends out spies to inform him of what is really going on and what the citizens are really thinking.[3] Aristotle comments that for tyrants this endeavor to know the truth about what is going on in the town can only lead to a result which is the exact opposite of the one they are seeking. For when the citizens know that they are being spied on by people who will inform the tyrant of what they truly say or think, they will naturally hide what they say and think and the tyrant will not be able to discover the truth. You also find (again in Aristotle, *Politics*, V, 11, 1313b) the idea that the position of truth-telling in tyranny is just as difficult as in democracy or demagogy (the negative, bad expression of democracy). Flattery on the contrary, he says, is held in high esteem under these two forms of government. In democracies, the demagogue occupies the role of the flatterer, because he is a sort of "people's courtier." In tyrannies, "it is those who live in a demeaning familiarity with the master" who play the role of flatterers. This familiarity "is only flattery in action ... Tyrants enjoy being fawned upon, while the man of independent character would never give them this pleasure."[4]

But whatever the permanent dangers Greek thought recognized in tyrannical governments, whatever danger truth-telling may encounter in this form of government, it remains nonetheless that a place for parrhesiastic practice was recognized in the relationship between the Prince and the person who speaks the truth, between the Prince and his counselors. And the relationship between the Prince and his counselor is ultimately more favorable to *parrhēsia* than that between the people and orators.

That the sovereign may be open to the truth, and that there was a site, a place, a location for truth-telling in the relationship with the sovereign is recognized by some authors. Aristotle, in the *Constitution of Athens*, [provides] a very precise [illustration of this] with regard to Pisistratus, a tyrant certainly, but of whom he gives a positive portrait, saying that he governed Athens *metriōs* (with moderation) *kai mallon politikōs ē turannikōs* (and in a way which was more republican or democratic than tyrannical).[5] And he gives an example of *parrhēsia* in this government, which was more republican or democratic than tyrannical. Walking in the countryside, Pisistratus meets a peasant who is working. He asks him what work he is doing and what he thinks about the situation. The other replies: I would happily work if I did not have to give a tenth of my earnings to Pisistratus.[6] Of course, the peasant had not recognized Pisistratus, but the latter learned a good lesson from this kind of involuntary *parrhēsia* and exempted the peasant from his taxes. Plato cites Cyrus, the Persian sovereign, in the same way. In the *Laws*, for example, (Book III, 694a and seq.), he presents Cyrus as a sovereign open to *parrhēsia*. He gives the following picture of Cyrus' court: the lower orders had a share of freedom, and this ensured the soldiers' boldness and their friendship for their commanders. And because the king, without jealousy, authorized free-spokenness (*parrhēsia*) and honored those who could give advice on any matter, anyone who was prudent and had good advice to offer put his skill and capabilities at the service of all. So that in a short time everything thrived among the Persians, thanks to freedom, friendship, and community.[7] Consequently, a court in which freedom of speech reigns, and in which counselors can practice *parrhēsia*, is a factor which contributes to the unification of the city and the success of its undertakings.

So we have a series of texts which clearly valorize the relationship to the Prince as the site of *parrhēsia*. But—and this is the problem I want to look at now—we have to answer a question which is symmetrical to the question raised a short while ago concerning democracy. The question was: why is democracy such a difficult, improbable, and dangerous place for the emergence of truth-telling? We have seen the crucial and, as it were, structural reason for this: it was the impossibility of the political field of democracy making room for and giving rise to ethical differentiation.

Now, on the other hand, how can the relation to the Prince be this site, when the power the Prince exercises is, by definition, unlimited, often without laws, and consequently capable of every violence? The reason is—and it is symmetrical to and the opposite of what we found concerning democracy—that the chief's soul as such, and precisely to the extent that it is an individual soul (the *psukhē* of an individual), is capable of ethical differentiation, which is introduced, enhanced, formed, and made effective through a moral training and development which both makes him capable of grasping the truth, and, following from this, teaches him to limit his power. Truth-telling can have its place in the relationship to the leader, Prince, king, or monarch, quite simply—to put things bluntly and crudely—because they have a soul, and this soul can be persuaded and educated, and because, through true discourse, one can instill in it the *ēthos* which will make him capable of grasping the truth and of conducting himself in conformity with this truth.

This is in fact how Plato, you recall, conceived of, or at least retrospectively justified, the journeys he made to Sicily, and specifically his undertaking with Dionysius the Younger. In the famous Letter VII which we commented on last year,[8] Plato gives his justification in three stages. First, he says, he [went] to Sicily to undertake the education of Dionysius the Younger, because he had had a prior, favorable experience with a certain individual, Dion (Dionysius' uncle), who, through his ability to learn philosophy and translate it into good conduct, had shown that Plato's pedagogy could produce its effects in a soul, and in the soul of someone destined to govern. "Dion, very open to everything and especially to my discourse, understood me admirably, better than all the young people I had frequented until then. He decided [after having heard Plato's lessons; M.F.] to lead henceforth a different life than that of most Italians or Sicilians by attaching more importance to virtue than to a life of pleasure and sensuality."[9] The first reason therefore is success in this particular case. The second reason for going to Sicily is connected to the first and follows on from it. Dionysius the Younger has inherited power after the death of Dionysius the Elder. The "youth of Dionysius and his lively taste for *philosophia* (philosophy) and *paideia* (training, culture, education),"[10] and the readiness of his circle to adopt the doctrine (*logos*) and life (*bios*) recommended by Plato, was a second favorable element.[11] Finally, third, there was the particular fact that Dionysius, advised by his uncle Dion, and with his good disposition towards *philosophia* and *paideia*, had inherited from his father a personal and absolute power. And thanks to this personal power it would be possible, once one gained access to his soul, to gain access to the city, to the State, to the *politeia* that he ruled. Plato says: "As I reflected and hesitantly asked myself whether or not I should take to the road and yield to the appeals, what tipped the balance [and consequently made me decide to go to Sicily; M.F.] was the thought that if ever one could undertake the realization of my legislative and political plans [the Greek text says precisely: if one wishes to undertake the realization of the things I had thought on the subject of the laws and the republic; M.F.], this was the time to attempt it: it was only necessary to persuade one man (*hena monon*) and all would be won."[12]

It could no doubt be said, and the Letter VII shows this, that this great hope came to nothing and the whole enterprise ended in failure. But it is important to understand that Plato does not consider the failure he [met with] in Sicily, the episodes of which he describes in detail, to be a structural failure. Whereas democracy is structurally unable to make room for *parrhēsia*, Plato's truth-telling, his philosophical veridiction did not take hold of Dionysius the Younger and failed in Sicily for essentially historical and conjunctural reasons which he describes in detail: Dionysius' bad character, his bad circle, all the plots he had to counter at Dionysius' court, [and] finally, later, the murder of Dion. It is these particular, conjunctural, historical reasons which are invoked to explain the failure of Platonic *parrhēsia* in Sicily—and which give Letter VII its distinctive appearance, since it is basically an historical narrative (of all of Plato's texts, it is the only one, apart from Letter VIII, which is the detailed narrative of an historical chain of events). The principle itself is not questioned. The objective is still to give a philosophical training to those who rule. The failure of Platonic *parrhēsia* [in the case of] Dionysius is conjunctural; the failure, the impossibility of *parrhēsia* in a democratic constitution is structural.

The idea that *parrhēsia* is always risky with the Prince, may always fail, may always encounter unfavorable circumstances, but is not in itself impossible and is always worth a try is also found in a text of Isocrates, at the beginning of the discourse *To Nicocles*. If you like, Nicocles was not very different from Dionysius the Younger, in his political situation at least. He was the son of a tyrant, Evagoras. Evagoras dies. Nicocles inherits power or authority in his city, and it is at this point that Isocrates addresses him. He begins by referring to all those courtiers who bring various gifts of clothes and gold to those who reign, to kings (*tois basileusin*).[13] As for me, Isocrates says, I do not want to bring you this kind of gift. In my view, the gift I bring to you is "the finest": "... if I could determine the habits of life (*epitēdeumata*) you should pursue, and those you should avoid in order to direct your State and government according to the best method. Many factors contribute to the education of private individuals," but "sovereigns generally do not have anyone available to them" who is capable of giving them advice.[14] "Those [that is to say, kings and sovereigns; M.F.] who should receive a more carefully prepared education than others, as soon as they are installed in power, pursue their life without receiving any warning."[15] Now it is precisely this warning to the Prince that Isocrates wants to give. And he clearly distinguishes this role of the Prince's moral counselor, moral instructor, from the office of giving the Prince precise and conjunctural advice for this or that situation. He distinguishes the role of counselors who intervene and give their views "in every action to be undertaken (*kath'hēkastēn men oun tēn praxian*),"[16] from his, Isocrates' task as instructor of the Prince's soul, insofar as by speaking the truth he can ensure the Prince's ethical formation and ethical differentiation. [His task will consist in] prescribing the set of *epitēdeumata* (habits, ways of living) to which Nicocles should devote himself and his time (*diatribein*).[17] So there is a contrast between conjunctural advice for political action and moral counsel which trains the Prince in habits of life which he must preserve throughout his life in his activity as man and as someone who governs.

I am leaving aside a number of other texts which could be cited and which go in the same direction. We see that what makes truth-telling with the Prince possible, desirable, and even necessary is that the way in which he governs the city depends on his *ēthos* (on the way in which he, the individual, is formed as moral subject), and that this *ēthos* is formed and defined through the influence of the true discourse addressed to him. You see that, insofar as, on the one hand, the Prince's *ēthos* is accessible to true discourse and formed on the basis of the true discourse addressed to him, and, on the other hand, further down the line as it were, this *ēthos* is the principle and matrix of his way of governing, then this *ēthos* is the element which enables veridiction, *parrhēsia* to articulate its effects in the field of politics, in the field of the government of men, in how men are governed. In the case of a tyrant, a monarch, or a personal sovereign, *parrhēsia* can produce its political effects and benefits in the art of governing men through the Prince's individual *ēthos*. In the case of democracy, [on the other hand], the reason why *parrhēsia* was not welcomed or listened to, and why anyone who had the courage to employ *parrhēsia* was eliminated rather than honored, was precisely that the structure of democracy could not acknowledge or make room for ethical differentiation. The absence of a place for *ēthos* in democracy means that truth has no place and cannot be heard in democracy. On the other hand, it is because the Prince's *ēthos* is the principle and matrix of his government that *parrhēsia* is possible, precious, and useful in the case of [autocratic]* government. It really is the question of *ēthos*, you see, which emerges in both cases. It arises in one case because democracy is unable to make room for it. In the other case, and it is for this reason that *parrhēsia* with the Prince is possible and necessary, *ēthos* is the bond, the point of connection between truth-telling and governing well. I have retraced a path, maybe at too great a length, that, partially and insufficiently, I took last year, in order to bring out more clearly what is at stake in this analysis of *parrhēsia*, and to bring out also how the history of thought in the West, and not just political, but also philosophical thought, engages with this question for quite some time.

It is important to stress the following point. First, with this development—on the one hand, the criticism of democracy as site of *parrhēsia* and, on the other, the valorization of monarchy and personal power as site of *parrhēsia*—you see that *parrhēsia* is not just, as it was in Euripides,[18] a privilege, the exercise of which is inseparable from the honorable citizen's freedom. *Parrhēsia* now appears, not as a right possessed by a subject, but as a practice whose privileged correlate, its first point of application, is not the city or body of citizens which has to be persuaded and led by it, but something which is both a partner to which it is addressed and a domain in which it is effective. This partner to which *parrhēsia* is addressed, and this domain in which it is effective, is the individual's *psukhē* (soul). First thing: we move from the *polis* to the *psukhē* as the essential correlate of *parrhēsia*.

---

* M.F. says: democratic

Second, the objective of this truth-telling, of this parrhesiastic practice now oriented towards the *psukhē*, is now not so much useful advice in this or that particular circumstance, when the citizens are at a loss and are looking for a guide who may enable them to escape danger and be saved, as the formation of a certain way of being, a certain way of doing things, of conducting oneself as an individual. The objective of truth-telling is therefore less the city's salvation than the individual's *ēthos*.

Third, this double determination of the *psukhē* as correlate of truth-telling, and of *ēthos* as the objective of parrhesiastic practice, means that *parrhēsia*, while being organized around the principle of truth-telling, now takes shape in a set of operations which enable veridiction to induce transformations in the soul.

Singling out this transformation of a *parrhēsia* considered in terms of its democratic and political effects for the salvation of the city, into a *parrhēsia* which addresses the *psukhē* of individuals and aims at the formation of their *ēthos*, enables us to grasp two sets of consequences. First, (I will very quickly pass over this consequence, which is, as it were, somewhat retrospective), it seems to me that the analysis of this *parrhēsia* may shed a particular light, in a particular way, on the famous question—traditional in the history of Greek philosophy, at least since the end of the nineteenth century, let's say since Rohde,[19] with the works of Snell,[20] and Patočka[21]—of the formation of the Greek notion of *psukhē*, of the progressive delineation and definition of this reality of the *psukhē*. And if it is true that there were many different routes and tracks, many different practices which led to this emergence of the soul as a central problem for philosophy, politics, and morality in fifth century Greek culture, if it is true that many ways led to the emergence and definition of the *psukhē*, it seems to me that amongst all these practices we should accord a place to the exercise of *parrhēsia*, to the crisis and criticism of *parrhēsia*, and to the shift which redirected its practice from the political stage to the interplay of individual relationships.

But above all it seems to me that, in trying to recapture something of this transformation of *parrhēsia* and its shift from the institutional view of democracy to the perspective of the individual practice of the formation of *ēthos*, we can see something which has an important bearing on our understanding of some fundamental features of Greek philosophy, and so of Western philosophy. With these shifts and changes in *parrhēsia* we are confronted with basically three realities, or at any rate three poles: the pole of *alētheia* and truth-telling; the pole of *politeia* and government; and finally the pole of what, in late Greek texts, is called *ēthopoiēsis* (the formation of *ēthos* or of the subject).[22] Conditions for and forms of truth-telling on the one hand; structures and rules of the *politeia* (that is to say, of the organization of relations of power) on the other; and finally, modalities of formation of the *ēthos* in which the individual constitutes himself as moral subject of his conduct: these are the three poles which are both irreducible and irreducibly linked to each other. *Alētheia, politeia, ēthos*: the essential irreducibility of these three poles, their necessary and mutual relationship, and the structure of the reciprocal appeal of one to the other, has underpinned, I believe, the very existence of all philosophical discourse from Greece to the present.

Now what precisely makes philosophical discourse not just a scientific discourse, which [would be confined to] defining and implementing the conditions of truth-telling, what makes philosophical discourse, from Greece to the present, not just a political or institutional discourse, which would be confined to defining the best possible system of institutions, and what finally makes philosophical discourse not just a pure moral discourse prescribing principles and norms of conduct, is that with regard to each of these three questions it poses two others at the same time. Scientific discourse is a discourse whose rules and objectives can be defined in terms of the question: what is truth-telling, what are its forms, what are its rules, what are its conditions and structures? What makes a political discourse no more than a political discourse is that it confines itself to posing the question of the *politeia*, of the forms and structures of government. What makes a moral discourse no more than a moral discourse is that it confines itself to prescribing the principles and norms of conduct.

What makes a philosophical discourse something other than each of these three discourses is that it never poses the question of the truth without at the same time inquiring about the conditions of this truth-telling, [either from the side of] the ethical differentiation which opens up access to this truth for the individual, [or from the side] of the political structures within which this truth-telling will have the right, the freedom, and the duty to pronounce. What makes a discourse a philosophical discourse and not just a political discourse is that when it poses the question of the *politeia* (of the political institution, of the distribution and organization of relations of power), at the same time it poses the question of truth and true discourse on the basis of which these relations of power and their organization will be able to be defined, and it also poses the question of the *ēthos*, that is to say, of the ethical differentiation to which these political structures can and must give space. And finally, if philosophical discourse is not just a moral discourse, it is because it does not confine itself to wanting to form an *ēthos*, to being the pedagogy of a morality, the vehicle of a code. It never poses the question of *ēthos* without at the same time inquiring about the truth and the form of access to the truth which will be able to form this *ēthos*, and [about] the political structures within which this *ēthos* will be able to assert its singularity and difference. Philosophical discourse, from Greece to the present, exists precisely in the possibility, or rather the necessity, of this interplay: never posing the question of *alētheia* without at the same time taking up again, with regard to this truth, the question of *politeia* and the question of *ēthos*. The same goes for *politeia*, and for *ēthos*.

And now, if you want to return to the four modalities of truth-telling we referred to last week, when I tried to schematize the four major forms of truth-telling in Greek culture (the truth-telling of prophecy, wisdom, *tekhnē*, and *parrhēsia*), well, on the basis of these four modalities of truth-telling, we can define four basic philosophical attitudes which may combine with each other, or exclude each other, or argue with each other. We can find four ways of linking together the question of *alētheia*, the question of *politeia*, and the question of *ēthos*.

Or again, by defining philosophy as the discourse which never poses the question of truth without at the same time raising the question of the *politeia* and the question of *ēthos*, which never poses the question of *politeia* without raising the question of truth and the question of ethical differentiation, and which never poses the question of *ēthos* without raising the questions of truth and politics, we can say that there are four ways of linking these three questions together, in order to connect them to each other or to bring them together.

We could term prophetic the standpoint in philosophy which, beyond the limit of the present, promises and predicts the moment and form in which the production of truth (*alētheia*), the exercise of power (*politeia*), and moral formation (*ēthos*) will finally, exactly, and definitively coincide. The prophetic standpoint in philosophy speaks of the promised reconciliation of *alētheia*, *politeia*, and *ēthos*.

Second, the standpoint of wisdom in philosophy claims to speak, at the same time, in one and the same fundamental and single discourse, of the nature of truth, *politeia*, and *ēthos*. The attitude of wisdom in philosophy is the discourse which tries to think and express the founding unity of truth, *politeia*, and *ēthos*.

The technical standpoint, or the standpoint of teaching in philosophy, does not look for the point of coincidence between *alētheia*, *politeia*, and *ēthos* in a promised future, or in a fundamental unity, but seeks rather to define, in their irreducible specificity, their separation, and their incommensurability, the formal conditions of truth-telling (logic), the best forms of the exercise of power (political analysis), and the principles of moral conduct (quite simply, morality). We may say that this standpoint in philosophy is the discourse of the heterogeneity and separation of *alētheia*, *politeia*, and *ēthos*.

There is, I think, a fourth standpoint in philosophy. It is the parrhesiastic standpoint, which tries precisely, stubbornly, and always starting over again, to bring the question of truth back to the question of its political conditions and the ethical differentiation which gives access to it; which constantly and always brings the question of power back to the question of its relation to truth and knowledge on the one hand, and to ethical differentiation on the other; the standpoint, finally, which constantly brings the question of the moral subject back to the question of the true discourse in which this moral subject constitutes itself and to the question of the relations of power in which this subject is formed. This is the parrhesiastic discourse and standpoint in philosophy: it is the discourse of the irreducibility of truth, power, and *ēthos*, and at the same time the discourse of their necessary relationship, of the impossibility of thinking truth (*alētheia*), power (*politeia*), and *ēthos* without their essential, fundamental relationship to each other.

That's it, thanks. Next week I will try to analyze, or at any rate I will work from three texts. For those who would like to read them, they will be *Socrates' Apology*, of course; second, the *Laches*; and third, the end of the *Phaedo*. And in relation to this, I will try to say something about Dumézil's interpretation and analysis of this text in his book *Le Moyne noir en gris*.[23]

1. Xénophon, *Hiéron*, §1, in *Œuvres complètes*, I, trans. P. Chambry (Paris: Garnier-Flammarion, 1967) p. 399; English translation by Robin Waterfield as, Xenophon, *Hiero the Tyrant and Other Treatises* (London: Penguin Books, 1997) p. 9: "your courtiers never stop applauding every word you speak and every action you perform. And criticism, the harshest sound in the world, never reaches your ears, because no one is prepared to condemn a tyrant in his presence."

2. Ibid.; Eng: "'Do your really think,' Hiero replied, 'that the fact that people refrain from speaking ill of a tyrant can give him the slightest pleasure, when he knows for sure that for all their silence every one of them is *thinking* ill of him? Do you really think this praise gives pleasure, when it looks very much as though its purpose is flattery?'"

3. Aristotle, *Politics*, 1313b, V, 11, Fr. p. 407: "A tyrant should also endeavor not to be without information on what each of his subjects is saying or doing, but will employ *observers*, like the female spies, as they were called, at Syracuse, or the listeners Hiero sent wherever there was a meeting or assembly (because one expresses oneself less frankly when one fears the presence of indiscreet ears)"; Eng. p. 2085: "A tyrant should also endeavour to know what each of his subjects says or does, and should employ spies, like the 'female detectives' at Syracuse, and the eavesdroppers whom Hiero was in the habit of sending to any place of resort or meeting; for the fear of informers prevents people from speaking their minds."

4. Ibid., 1313b-1314a, Fr. p. 409; Eng. p. 2086: "For the people too would fain be a monarch, and therefore by them, as well as by the tyrant, the flatterer is held in honour; in democracies he is the demagogue; and the tyrant also has those who associate with him in a humble spirit, which is a work of flattery... Hence tyrants... love to be flattered, but no man who has the spirit of a freeman in him will lower himself by flattery."

5. Aristote, *Constitution d'Athènes*, XVI, 2, trans. G. Mathieu and B. Hassoulier (Paris: Les Belles Lettres, 1967) p. 16; English translation by F.G. Kenyon, Aristotle, *Constitution of Athens*, 16, in *The Complete Works of Aristotle*, vol. 2, ed. Jonathan Barnes, p. 2350: "His administration was temperate... and more like constitutional government than a tyranny."

6. Ibid., XVI, 6, Fr. p. 17; Eng. p. 2350.

7. Platon, *Les Lois*, Book III, 694a-b, trans. E. Des Places (Paris: Les Belles Lettres, 1965) p. 36: "It is a fact that the Persians, when, under Cyrus, they held to the middle course between servitude and freedom, began by being free, so to become later the masters of a great many other peoples: chiefs who gave to those under their command the gift of freedom and raised them to the same level as themselves; soldiers, who were rather friends of their generals, eager furthermore to face danger. And if one of them was intelligent and able to give good advice, the king, being free of any jealousy in his regard, and giving rather a full freedom of speech (*didontos de parrhēsian*) and honors to whoever could advise him, offered him the means to bring to light his intellectual capabilities in the interest of everyone. As a result, everything in them advanced in this time, thanks to freedom (*eleutherian*), friendship, and collaboration (*philian kai nou koinōnian*)." (Foucault prefers to read "friendship" rather than "collaboration"); English translation by A.E. Taylor, Plato, *Laws*, Book III, 694a-b, in Plato, *The Collected Dialogues*, p. 1288: "While the Persians steered a middle course between subjection and liberty, in the time of Cyrus, they began by winning their own freedom and went on to make themselves masters of numerous peoples. As a government they gave these subjects their share of liberty and placed them on equal terms with themselves; their soldiers thus grew attached to their commanders, and showed themselves forward in danger. Again, if a subject was a man of wisdom and a capable adviser, the king showed no jealousy of him, but permitted free speech and bestowed distinctions on such competent counselors, so that the gift of wisdom was freely placed at the disposal of the public service. Hence the combination of liberty with amity and generally diffused intelligence led, for the time, to all-round progress."

8. See the analyses of this letter in the lectures of 9, 16, and 23 February 1983 in *Le Gouvernement de soi et des autres*; *The Government of Self and Others*.

9. Platon, lettre VII, 327a-b, in *Lettres*, trans. J. Souilhé (Paris: Les Belles Lettres, 1977) p. 31; English translation by L.A. Post, Plato, *Letter VII*, in Plato, *The Collected Dialogues*, p. 1576: "At any rate Dion, who was very quick of apprehension and especially so in regard to my instruction on this occasion, responded to it more keenly and more enthusiastically than

any other young man I ever met, and resolved to live for the remainder of his life differently from most of the Greeks in Italy and Sicily, holding virtue dearer than pleasure or than luxury."

10. Ibid., 328a, Fr. p. 32. (Souilhé translates *paideia* as "science" in the Belles Lettres edition); Eng. p. 1577: "Dionysius young and interested, emphasizing his situation in respect of philosophy and education."

11. Ibid., Fr.: "His nephews and relatives, easy to win to the doctrine (*logos*) and life (*bios*) that I always preach"; Eng.: "Furthermore his own nephews and kindred might readily be won over to the doctrine and the way of life that I always preach, and they would be just the persons to help win over Dionysius."

12. Ibid., 328b-c, Fr. pp. 32-33; Eng. p. 1577: "Hence as I considered and debated whether I should hearken and go, or what I should do, the view nevertheless prevailed that I ought to go, and that if anyone were ever to attempt to realize my ideals in regard to laws and government, now was the time for the trial. If I were to convince but one man, that in itself would ensure complete success."

13. Isocrate, *Discours*, vol. II, trans. G. Mathieu and E. Brémond (Paris: Les Belles Lettres, 1938), §1, p. 97; English translation by George Norlin as, Isocrates, *To Nicocles*, in *Isocrates*, vol. I (Princeton: Harvard University Press, Loeb Classical Library, 1928) p. 41.

14. Ibid., §2, Fr. p. 98; Eng. pp. 41-43: "if I could prescribe what pursuits you should aspire to and from what you should abstain in order to govern to the best advantage of your state and kingdom. For when men are in private life, many things contribute to their education... Kings, however, have no such help."

15. Ibid., §4, Fr. p. 98; Eng. p. 43: "they, who more than other men should be thoroughly trained, live all their lives, from the time when thy are placed in authority, without admonition."

16. Ibid., §6, Fr. p. 99; Eng. p. 43: "each particular course of action."

17. Ibid., Fr.: "But for what concerns the conduct of life in general (*kath'holōn de tōn epitēdeumatōn*), I will strive, for my part, to examine in detail the practices you should adopt and which merit you devoting your time to (*peri ha dei diatribein*)"; Eng. p. 45: "but as regards a king's conduct in general, I shall attempt to set forth the objects at which he should aim and the pursuits to which he should devote himself."

18. On this point, see the lectures of 12, 19 January, and 2 February 1983 in *Les Gouvernement de soi et des autres*; *The Government of Self and Others*.

19. E. Rohde, *Psyche. Seelencult und Unsterblichkeitsglaube der Griechen* (Tübingen: J.C.B. Mohr, 1925); English translation by W.B. Hillis as *Psyche: The Cult of Souls and Belief in Immortality among the Ancient Greeks* (New York: Harcourt, Brace & Co., 1925).

20. B. Snell, *Die Entdeckung des Geistes. Studien zur Entstehung des Europaischen Denkens bei den Greichen* (Hamburg: Claassen & Goverts, 1946); English translation by R.G. Rosenmyer, *The Discovery of the Mind* (Cambridge, Mass.: Harvard University Press, 1953).

21. Jan Patočka, *Plato and Europe*, trans. Petr Lom (Stanford: Stanford University Press, 2002).

22. On this notion see the lecture of 10 February 1982, second hour, *L'Herméneutique du sujet*, pp. 227-228; *The Hermeneutics of the Subject*, pp. 237-238.

23. G. Dumézil, *"Le Moyne noir en gris dedans Varennes"* (Paris: Gallimard, 1984); English translation by Betsy Wing as *The Riddle of Nostradamus. A Critical Dialogue* (Baltimore and London: The Johns Hopkins University Press, 1999).

five

15 FEBRUARY 1984

First hour

[*The danger of forgetfulness of self.* ∿ *Socrates' refusal of political commitment.* ∿ *Solon confronting Pisistratus.* ∿ *The risk of death: the story of the Generals of the Arginusae and Leon of Salamis.* ∿ *The Delphic oracle.* ∿ *Socrates' response to the oracle: verification and inquiry.* ∿ *Object of the mission: the care of self.* ∿ *Irreducibility of Socratic veridiction.* ∿ *Emergence of a specifically ethical* parrhēsia. ∿ *The cycle of Socrates' death as ethical foundation of the care of self.*]

AFTER THE CRISIS OF political *parrhēsia*, or at least the crisis of political institutions as a possible site for *parrhēsia*, today I would like to begin the study of *parrhēsia*, of the practice of truth-telling in the field of ethics, and to do this I will obviously start again with Socrates as someone who is ready to face death rather than renounce truth-telling, but who does not practice this truth-telling by taking the floor in public and saying what he thinks, without disguise, before the people at the Assembly. Socrates has the courage to tell the truth, accepts the risk of death in order to tell the truth, but he does so by practicing the testing of souls in the game of ironic cross-examination.

To study this foundation of *parrhēsia* in the field of ethics, as opposed to political *parrhēsia*, or in a founding separation from political *parrhēsia*, I would like to comment on two texts. The first is in the *Apology*: it is the famous text in which Socrates says he did not play any political role in the city because if he had done so he would have put his life at risk.

[The] second text, which we will study in the second hour, [will be] Socrates' famous last words, in the *Phaedo*, asking his disciples to offer a cock to Asclepius as payment for a debt, urging them: Think about it, don't forget, don't be neglectful. None of the historians of philosophy or commentators who have pondered this text for two thousand years have managed to explain or interpret it. This is the text that Dumézil has analyzed, and to which I think he has found the solution, in the book which I recommended to you last week. Anyway, between these two texts (that of the *Apology* in which Socrates says: I have not, as we would say, "engaged in politics," I have not got up to speak publicly, because if I had done so I would now be dead; and the last text of Socrates happily agreeing to die and asking that some kind of debt be paid to the gods, in the form of a cock), there is the whole cycle of Socrates' death in its relation to truth-telling and the mortal risks truth-telling incurs. So that is what I would like to talk about now.

So first, the *Apology*. I will start with a remark which we will put to one side for the moment, leaving it for future use. This [concerns] the first lines of the *Apology*. Since it is a judicial type of discourse, Socrates' speech, at least as Plato reports it, begins, like every good judicial discourse, at any rate like many speeches for the defense, [with the claim]: My opponents are lying, but I am telling the truth.[1] One could hardly saying anything else, in fact, when countering one's accusers in court. My opponents lie, but I tell the truth. Second, Socrates says: My opponents are skillful speakers (*deinoi legein*), but I, he says, speak straightforwardly, directly, without skill or affectation.[2] This is again a traditional theme. And he adds as well, which is not unusual in this kind of discourse: They are skillful speakers, whereas I speak simply and directly. Moreover, they are so skilled at speaking that they would have you believe that I am the skillful speaker. But it is precisely in saying this that they lie: I am not a skillful speaker.[3] This maybe would not warrant a much more detailed commentary, if, in this rhetorical form, in this entirely traditional form of presentation of judicial discourse, Socrates had not introduced a variation in which he says: It is my opponents who lie, my opponents who are skillful speakers, but they are such skillful speakers that they have almost succeeded in getting me to "forget who I am." Through them (*hup'autōn*), I have almost lost my memory of myself (*emautou epelathomēn*).[4] So, I would like us to put this remark to one side, if you like, a bit like a squirrel's winter provisions, a little something stored away for future use, as tribute to the person we will talk about later. I would just like you to keep in mind that the skillful speech of the others, the opponents, may go so far as to cause one to forget oneself. So that, correspondingly and negatively, as it were, we may feel inclined towards the opposite proposition. If skillfulness in speech causes forgetfulness of self, then simplicity in speech, speech without affectation or embellishment, straightforwardly true speech, the speech of *parrhēsia* therefore, will lead us to the truth of ourselves.

Second, I would like to point out that what might be called the cycle of Socrates' death—the set of texts which we can group together comprising the *Apology* (the trial), the *Crito* (the discussion in prison between Socrates and Crito concerning a possible escape), and the *Phaedo* (the account of Socrates' last moments)—begins by evoking something which will be important throughout the cycle: the danger of forgetting oneself. The relationship between truth of self and forgetfulness of self is at issue throughout, from the start (they almost made me forget myself) to the final "don't forget," which is Socrates' last word (*mē amelēsēte*: don't be neglectful, don't forget),[5] which we will have to comment on. This is the key theme of Socrates' trial, his discussion of exile and possible rescue, and finally his death. We will leave it there for the moment; we will keep this comment for later.

I would like now to come to the text I was talking about, which is at 31c of the *Apology*, and concerns the question: should one engage in politics? Or rather: why did Socrates not engage in politics? Immediately before this passage Socrates has explained how he sought out the citizens of Athens, how he was concerned about them—we will come back to this below—how he cared for them ("acting like a father or an elder brother to each one").[6] He has thus taken care of the Athenians like a father or elder brother. Immediately after he has said this, he puts the following objection to himself. But then, "how come that, while I go round freely giving advice here and there to each individually and getting somewhat involved in their lives," I do not venture to present myself to the people publicly (*dēmosia*), to address the people ("*anaibainōn eis to plēthos*," in the strict sense: take the floor to address the people) and give advice to the city (*sumbouleuein tē polei*)?[7] Again, this is a technical term. *Sumbouleuein* means to take part in the Council, in the deliberative bodies of the city. Why then do I not venture, publicly, to come forward and take part in the decisions of the town, of the city?

Clearly, in this reference to a political role in which someone comes forward, gets up, speaks to the people, and takes part in the deliberations of the city, there is a reference to the democratic arena and the institutions which should have made room for *parrhēsia*. What Socrates is evoking is that possible figure of the parrhesiast politician who agrees to take the floor, regardless of dangers and threats, because it is in the city's interest. And, possibly risking death, he speaks the truth. We could recall here the anecdote of Solon's famous action, taking a stand, which is frequently recounted in Greek literature. The episode is reported in chapter 14 of Aristotle's *Constitution of Athens*,[8] in Plutarch's *Life of Solon*,[9] and also in Diogenes Laertius.[10] When Athens is about to lose its liberty because Pisistratus is asserting his personal authority, setting about exercising sovereignty over Athens in his own name, exercising what is called tyranny, the aged Solon, witnessing this rise of the young Pisistratus, decides to come to the Assembly. Pisistratus had demonstrated his desire to exercise tyranny by getting himself granted a personal bodyguard—this was the traditional way for a citizen to take power in Greek cities: surround yourself with a personal bodyguard. Seeing this event, Solon comes to the Assembly, and he comes as a simple citizen of Athens, but armed with breastplate and shield, thereby showing what is happening, namely that Pisistratus, by getting himself granted a personal bodyguard, considers the citizens as enemies against whom he may have to struggle. If the sovereign presents himself as exercising a military power, threatening the other citizens with armed force, it is natural for the citizens to arrive armed in turn. So Solon comes to the Assembly with breastplate and shield. To criticize the Assembly which has just authorized Pisistratus taking a personal bodyguard, he says to his fellow citizens: "I am wiser than those who have failed to understand the designs of Pisistratus, and I am more courageous than those who have understood but remain silent out of fear."[11] You see Solon's double *parrhēsia* here: *parrhēsia* with regard to Pisistratus, since by arriving at the Assembly with his breastplate and armed he shows what Pisistratus is up to. He discloses the truth of what is taking place and, at the same time, addresses a discourse of truth to the Assembly, criticizing those who do not understand, but also those who, although they understand, remain silent. He, however, will speak. And, after Solon's speech denouncing what is taking place and criticizing his fellow citizens, the Council replies that in fact Solon is going mad (*mainesthai*). To which Solon retorts: "You will soon know if I am mad... when the truth comes to light."[12] You have here, a very precise, typical example, constructed *a posteriori* of course, of the practice of *parrhēsia*.

It is precisely this practice of *parrhēsia* that Socrates does not want to adopt, this role he does not want to play. He does not venture to give advice to the city publicly by appearing before the people. Socrates will not be Solon. So the problem is how Socrates justifies not playing the role of Solon, not coming forward and speaking the truth *dēmosia* (publicly). His reason for not playing this role is well known. He has heard a sort of familiar, divine or daemonic voice, which makes itself heard from time to time, speaking in him and to him, and which never prescribes anything positive, never tells him what he must do, but occasionally makes itself heard in order to stop him doing something he was about to do or might have done.[13] And this is actually what is involved in this case. Why did the voice make itself heard? It did so in order to turn him away from politics. He, who cares for the citizens like a father or an elder brother, is turned away by this voice from caring for them in the form of politics. What does this ban mean? Why this sign? Why this voice which stops him from practicing political *parrhēsia* at the point when he could have given his true discourse this form, in this arena, and with this objective?

It is at this point that Socrates puts forward some considerations which, at first sight, might pass for the pure and simple explanation of this prohibition, or at any rate of this negative indication which the daemonic voice addressed to him. The apparent explanation is the bad functioning of democratic *parrhēsia*, or of political *parrhēsia* more generally; it is the impossibility of performing the parrhesiastic role properly, fully, and thoroughly when one is dealing with political institutions. Why should this be the case? Quite simply because of the risk incurred. This is the text on which I would like to focus: "If long ago I had devoted myself to politics, I would have lost my life long ago."[14] You remember, I read you this passage last week. And Socrates adds: "Don't be angry [he says to his judges; M.F.] when you hear me tell you these truths [the truth, that is: if I had engaged in politics I would be dead; M.F.]: there is no man who can escape death if, however nobly, he should oppose you, or any other popular assembly, and endeavor to prevent injustice and illegality in his city."[15] If we pass quickly over this text, things seem clear: Why have I not been involved in politics? Because if I were to have engaged in politics, if I had come forward to speak to you, to tell you the truth, you would have put me to death, along with all those who nobly wish to prevent injustice and illegality in their city. Only we should look a bit more closely, we should look especially at the examples and justifications Socrates gives. In fact, to support his assertion that one risks one's life when one addresses the people's Assembly in order to tell it the truth, or even when one just wants to concern oneself directly and generally with the city's interests, the examples he gives are both odd and paradoxical, because they are both examples and refutations.[16]

They are examples in that they are indeed cases in which we see the political institutions, whether democratic, tyrannical, or oligarchic, preventing or wanting to prevent those on the side of justice and legality from speaking the truth. But these examples are at the same time refutations, because we see here that, precisely in the two specific cases he cites, Socrates did not accept this blackmail and threat. He confronted them, and in both cases he accepted the risk of death. This is what was involved: the risk of death. Socrates gives a precise example, taken from his own experience and life, of the fact that one may risk death when one wants to tell the truth in the game of a democratic regime. The scene takes place around 406 when, as a result of the rotation of political responsibilities, Socrates was prytanis. This was not some kind of personal activity that he could choose to take up on his own behalf; it was up to his tribe to exercise the prytany. At this time a trial was being brought against the Athenian generals who were the victors in the Arginusae and who, for a number of reasons, had failed to retrieve the corpses after their battle and victory—which was both an impiety and a somewhat dubious political gesture, but let's leave that aside. So, there are people in the Assembly who have lodged a complaint against the Arginusae generals. So what does Socrates do? "I was the only prytanis to stand up to you in order to prevent you from violating the law; I was the only one to vote against your wishes."[17] In actual fact the Assembly did condemn the Arginusae generals and they were executed. Well, despite the fact that the whole Assembly was in favor of this condemnation, I, says Socrates, "voted against your wishes." "Although the orators [those supporting the condemnation of the generals; M.F.] were ready to bring a charge against me and have me arrested, and you invited them to do so with your shouts [Socrates says to the people of Athens; M.F.], I judged it my duty to brave the danger on the side of law and justice, rather than associate myself, out of fear of prison and death, with your desire for injustice."[18] We have here an example which proves that, in democracy, one risks death by wanting to speak the truth in favor of justice and the law. But at the same time as Socrates shows that one really does risk one's life, he also shows that in actual fact he did confront this danger and did indeed play the typical role of the political *parrhēsiaste*. It is true that *parrhēsia* is dangerous, but it is also true that Socrates had the courage to confront the risks of this *parrhēsia*. He had the courage to speak out. He had the courage to give a contrary opinion before an Assembly which sought to silence him, hound him, and possibly punish him.

After this paradoxical example (proof that *parrhēsia* is dangerous in democracy, but example of Socrates accepting the risk), Socrates gives another example, taken from another episode of Athenian history and a different form of political system. He refers to the short period at the end of the fifth century when Athens was under the authoritarian, bloody, oligarchic government of the Thirty. Here he shows that it is just as dangerous to tell the truth in an authoritarian and oligarchic government as it is in a democracy. But at the same time he shows how this was all the same to him and how he accepted the risk. He recalls the moment when the Thirty tyrants wanted to have an unjustly accused citizen called Leon of Salamis arrested. The Thirty asked four citizens to carry out the arrest, and Socrates was designated as one of these four. Now, while the three others did go to arrest Leon of Salamis, "on this occasion [Socrates reminds his accusers; M.F.] I demonstrated not by words but by actions (*ou logō all'ergō*) that I do not

care about death at all [*emoi thanatou melei oud'hotioun*: I draw your attention to the expression "*melei*" which we will come across frequently;
M.F.], but wish to do nothing unjust or impious, and that I care about
this above all else [and again: *toutou de to pan melei*; M.F.]."[19]

This is a symmetrical and opposite example. Opposite, since we are
in an aristocratic, oligarchic regime. Symmetrical, since *parrhēsia* is not
possible in this regime, but Socrates accepted the risk all the same. You
can see the problem. Socrates has just said: Why is it that, concerning
myself with citizens, I have never and do not want to concern myself
with them *dēmosia* (in public, by coming forward and speaking out)?
The reason is that, if I did so I would die. How can he say this and give,
as justification of his standpoint, examples which actually show that it
is dangerous, but that he had accepted the danger and death? Under
these conditions, can we say that the mortal dangers faced by the parrhesiast as a result of faulty politics, the death one risks by telling the
truth, were the true reasons why Socrates never committed himself on
the political stage and never spoke out before the people? On two occasions (in a democracy and under an oligarchy) he accepted the risk of
death in order to assert truth and justice, and precisely in his defense,
in the *Apology*, he explains, and explains throughout the text, that he
does not fear death, so how is it that in this defense he says: I have not
engaged in politics because if I had done so I would be dead? The question is this: can these dangers be the true reason for his abstention from
politics? The answer is both no and yes. Obviously no, and I stress this:
Socrates has not renounced politics out of fear of death and in order to
avoid it. And yet we may say: yes, he did abstain from politics because
of these dangers, not out of fear of death, but because if he had got
involved in politics he would be dead, and being dead he would have
been unable—as he says in the text—to be useful to himself and to the
Athenians.[20] So the reason Socrates did not want to tell the truth in
the form of political veridiction was not the fear of death, it was not
Socrates' personal relation to his own death. It is not that personal
relation but rather some kind of relation of utility, some kind of relation to himself and to the Athenians; this useful, positive, and beneficial relation is the reason why the threat hanging over the truth in
political systems prevented him from speaking this truth in the political form. What the daemonic voice recommended through this negative

sign, by calling out to stop him, was that he guard against dying. And this is not because dying is an evil to be avoided, but because death would have prevented Socrates from doing something positive. He would have been unable to establish with others and himself a particular kind of invaluable, useful, and beneficial relationship. So the effect and doubtless the function of the daemonic sign, which, when Socrates could have come forward before the Assembly, turned him away from mortal engagement in politics, was precisely to safeguard this positive task and responsibility he had been given.

This brings us back to the mission which the god had entrusted to Socrates and which needed to be protected against the pointless risks of politics. It should not be forgotten—we will have to return to this— that this cycle of Socrates' death is punctuated throughout by references to divine interventions. This is one of them. What positive, useful task does this divine intervention—which interrupts things at the point when political *parrhēsia* would have been possible for Socrates—save and protect? The whole of the *Apology*, or the first part at least, is devoted to defining and describing this useful task that needed to be protected against death. This task is a particular kind of exercise, a particular practice of truth-telling; it is the implementation of a particular mode of veridiction which is completely different from those which may take place on the political stage. The voice which addresses this injunction to Socrates, or rather turns him away from the possibility of speaking in the form of politics, signals the establishment of another truth-telling, converse to political truth-telling, which is that of philosophy: You will not be Solon, you must be Socrates. What is this other practice of truth-telling whose essential, fundamental, and founding difference in relation to political truth-telling is indicated by the divine voice? This is all in the first part of the *Apology*, and I think this other truth-telling made possible by the care Socrates takes not to die may be schematized by three moments.

The first moment of this veridiction is found in the relationship to the gods, to Apollo, to prophecy. Nor is this, you will see, insignificant. Socrates' friend, Chaerephon, went to ask the god of Delphi: What Greek is wiser than Socrates? And you know that the god's answer to this question, put not by Socrates but by one of his friends, was: No one is wiser than Socrates.[21] Of course, like all the god's answers, this is enigmatic, and the person to whom the god gives the answer is never really sure of understanding it. In fact, Socrates does not understand it. And he wonders, like all or almost all of those who have received the god's enigmatic words: *Ti pote legei ho theos*[22] (what is the god saying in veiled terms: *ainittetai*)?[23] Now we need to show straightaway that in asking this traditional question after the god's traditional enigmatic answer Socrates is not putting forward what could be called an interpretative method for discovering the meaning of what the god has said. He is not seeking to decipher the hidden meaning beneath the words; he is not seeking to divine what the god said. What Socrates explains with regard to what he did at this point is very interesting. He says: Having been given the answer to Chaerephon's question, and not understanding it, wondering what the god could really mean, I undertook a search. The verb used is *zētein* (you find the word *zētēsis*).[24] He undertook a search, and once again this does not consist in interpreting, in deciphering. It does not involve producing an exegesis of what the god might have wanted to say and might have hidden in an allegorical form or in a half truthful and half deceptive discourse. The investigation Socrates undertakes aims to find out if the oracle told the truth. Socrates wants to test what the oracle said. He is anxious to subject the oracle to verification. Significantly, he uses a characteristic word to designate the modality of this search (*zētēsis*). This is the word *elegkhein*,[25] which means: to reproach, to object, to question, to subject someone to cross-examination, to challenge what someone has said in order to find out whether or not it stands up. It is, in a way, to dispute it. So he will not interpret the oracle, but dispute it, subject it to discussion, to challenge, in order to find out if it is true. And in order to subject the oracle to this verification, and not to interpretation, Socrates undertakes a tour, a journey (what he calls a *planē*)[26] in order to arrive at knowledge of whether the prophecy may in actual fact become indisputable (*anelegktōs*)[27] and therefore established as true.

It is important really to grasp the singularity of Socrates' attitude. Certainly, like Chaerephon himself, he has reverence for the oracle, which means that he takes note of what it tells him and questions himself about it. But you see how far we are from the usual attitude towards prophecy and oracular speech. What is the usual attitude—the attitude we see constantly, and for a long time, and, you remember, we saw last year when we studied Euripides' *Ion* and the mother's and father's questioning of the oracle to find out what had become of their son, or if they would have a son?[28] First, it consists in trying to interpret what the oracle has said in order to understand it in the greatest detail, and then, either waiting to see if the oracle will actually be fulfilled in reality, or, if one understands it to be a danger or a misfortune, trying to avoid its realization. In other words: interpreting the oracle's words and waiting for or avoiding its effects in reality. This interplay between interpretation and expectation of realization characterizes the traditional, usual attitude towards oracular speech. Now the Socratic attitude is completely different. Rather than an interpretation, it involves an investigation in order to check the truth of the oracle. It involves disputing it. And this investigation takes the form of discussion, possible refutation, or proof in which the emphasis is not on the domain of a reality in which the oracle's words will in fact be effectuated, but on the domain of a truth in which one will be able to accept or reject the words as true *logos*. The usual attitude is interpretation and expectation in the domain of reality. Socrates' attitude towards prophecy is investigation and test in the game of truth. This is the first moment of the Socratic attitude, of Socratic veridiction and the mission Socrates has been given of telling the truth.

Second moment: what is the form in which Socrates carries out this verifying investigation? How, concretely, does he try to find out if the oracle has told the truth? How, instead of waiting for or avoiding its realization, does he undertake this discussion with the oracle, in relation to the oracle? He has said then that he makes a journey, an investigation (a *planē*: he will travel round trying to test the oracle). And he conducts this quest throughout the town and in different categories of individuals and citizens. First a politician, and then others; second stage: the poets; third stage, finally: the craftsmen. His journey, you see, is through the town, from top to bottom through the body of citizens. Socrates goes all over the town, from the politician, who is so important that he does not name him,[29] down to the least craftsman.[30] And he discovers increasingly sound forms of knowledge as he goes down among the citizens who make up the city. The first politician he visited was thought by many people, and especially by the politician himself, to be wise, but in actual fact he was not wise at all. On the other hand, he observes that the craftsmen [know] many things, and much more than Socrates himself knew. But all of them, ignorant politicians or knowledgeable craftsmen, share the belief that they know things that in reality they do not know, whereas Socrates knows that he does not know these things. No doubt he does not have the knowledge possessed by some of them (the craftsmen), but nor does he have their ignorance. It is this investigation, this challenging, questioning, and examination of others, comparing them with himself, that Socrates calls *exetasis* in this text.[31] *Exetazein* is to subject to examination.[32] And this examination is first of all a way of checking whether or not the oracle has told the truth. [Second], this way of checking whether the oracle has told the truth consists in testing souls, testing what they do and do not know about things, about their profession and their activity (be they politicians, poets, or craftsmen), but also about themselves (what they know that they know and what they do not know). And finally, this *exetasis* involves not only testing souls about what they do and do not know about things and themselves, but also comparing these souls with Socrates' soul. So Socrates, who modestly went to check whether the oracle really spoke the truth when it asserted that he, Socrates, was the wisest of men, and who tried to show, to emphasize his own ignorance before the supposed knowledge of others, finally appears as being in fact the person who knows more than others, at least in that he knows his own ignorance. And this is how Socrates' soul becomes the touchstone (*basanos*)[33] of the souls of others.

This is how this *exetasis* unfolds. So we have a first stage concerning the god's words: questioning oneself, searching (this is the *zētēsis*), and practicing verification through discussion (*elegkhos*). In the second stage verification takes the concrete form of the investigation (*planē*). He will go all over the town subjecting everyone to this *exetasis* which enables him to know what each person knows and does not know, what each person knows about things and about himself, and testing this knowledge and ignorance by comparing [each person's soul], by rubbing it against the touchstone of his own, Socrates' soul. The third moment of this cycle: these examinations, this *exetasis*, these verifications that Socrates practiced high and low throughout the city naturally earned him great hostility, and in particular the accusations of Meletus and Anytus, against which precisely he is now defending himself in the *Apology*.[34] And yet, despite these hostilities—which date from long before the accusations of Meletus and Anytus, these latter being, as it were, their last expression and final episode—Socrates was not held back by the dangers they might involve. Furthermore, he says this very clearly at this point: A man of any worth is not to "calculate his chances of life and death."[35] Now that we are in the cycle, the unfolding of this form of *parrhēsia* and veridiction, you can see that the risk of life and death, which a moment ago was a reason for not engaging in politics, is here, on the contrary, at the very heart of his enterprise. Whatever the dangers this form of *parrhēsia* may entail, he knows full well that as a man of "some worth" he must not weigh the importance of this *parrhēsia* against his own chances of life and death. "When a man of any worth acts he must consider solely whether or not what he is doing is just, whether he is conducting himself as a man of courage or as a coward."[36] Consequently he must not question the fact that he may die as a result of his actions.

With this form of truth-telling or veridiction we are dealing with a certain form of *parrhēsia*, if by *parrhēsia* we understand the courage of truth, the courage of truth-telling. We are dealing with a *parrhēsia* which, in its foundation and in the way it unfolds, is clearly very different from political *parrhēsia*. [Socrates] will practice this new, other *parrhēsia* in a very particular way. He defines it in its form as a mission, and a mission on which he insists, which he will never abandon, and which he will practice constantly to the very end. You can see that from this point of view he is not like the sage. He will not be like Solon, for example, who, at risk and danger to himself, intervened in the city to tell the truth, but who intervened only occasionally, the rest of the time remaining silent in his wisdom. The sage intervenes only when his intervention is called for as a matter of urgency. Apart from this he withdraws into the silence of his own wisdom. Socrates is someone with a mission, we could almost say a job; he has at any rate a responsibility. And it is significant that he does not compare himself to the sage, who intervenes occasionally, but to a soldier who is always at his post.[37] [Think of Solon], who previously was asked to give the city laws, and who, when he sees these laws corrupted and Pisistratus exercising his tyranny, dons soldier's clothing for the occasion, clasps his shield, puts on his armor, and then, and only then, presents himself at the Assembly in order to make the truth burst out. Contrast him with Socrates who, throughout his life always thought of himself as a sort of soldier among the citizens, having to struggle at every moment to defend himself and them.

Now what is the aim of this mission? What must he do in this mission which the god has given him and which the god has protected by telling him: Above all do not engage in politics, for you will die. The aim of this mission is, of course, to watch over the others continuously, to care for them as if he were their father or brother. But to what end? To encourage them to take care, not of their wealth, reputation, honors, and offices, but of themselves, that is to say, of their reason, of truth, and of their soul (*phronēsis, alētheia, psukhē*).[38] They must attend to themselves. This definition is crucial. Oneself in the relation of self to self, oneself in this relation of watching over oneself, is [first] defined by *phronēsis*,[39] that is to say, practical reason, as it were, reason in practice, the reason which enables good decisions to be taken and false opinions to be driven out. Second, oneself is also defined by *alētheia* inasmuch as this is what will in fact be the index of *phronēsis*, what it is pegged to, what it looks for, and what it obtains; but *alētheia* is also Being insofar as we are related to it, precisely in the form of the *psukhē* (the soul). If we can have *phronēsis* and take good decisions, this is because we have a particular relation to the truth which is founded ontologically in the nature of the soul. Such, then, is Socrates' mission which, you can see, is very different in the course of its development, its form, and its aim from political *parrhēsia*, from the political veridiction we have been talking about until now. It has a different form and a different aim. This other aim is in fact to see to it that people take care of themselves, that each individual attends to himself [as] a rational being having a relation to truth founded on the very being of his soul. And in this we now have a *parrhēsia* on the axis of ethics. What is at stake in this new form of *parrhēsia* is the foundation of *ēthos* as the principle on the basis of which conduct can be defined as rational conduct in accordance with the very being of the soul.

Zētēsis, exetasis, epimeleia. Zētēsis is the first moment of Socratic veridiction—the search. *Exetasis* is examination of the soul, comparison of the soul, and test of souls. *Epimeleia* is taking care of oneself. Socrates' investigation of the meaning to be given to the oracle's words has led to this activity of the test of souls by each other with the aim of encouraging each individual to take care of himself. Investigation, test, care. Investigation of what the god says, testing of souls against each other, care of souls as the aim of this search: you see that we have here an *ensemble* which defines Socratic *parrhēsia*, Socrates' courageous veridiction, as opposed to political veridiction, which is not practiced as an investigation, but manifests itself as someone's assertion that they are capable of telling the truth; which does not practice the examination and confrontation of souls, but is addressed courageously, on its own, to an Assembly or a tyrant who does not want to hear it; which does not aim at *epimeleia* (encouraging people to take care of themselves), but tells people what they have to do, and then, once it has told them, turns away, leaves, and lets them manage as best they can with themselves and the truth.

The famous daemonic ban which Socrates heard just before he might have come forward and spoken publicly, the famous daemonic ban which restrained him and prevented him from entering public life, actually traced a line of division and marked, I believe, the separation in Greek, and so Western thought, between a practice of [political] truth-telling, which has its danger, and another practice of truth-telling, formed entirely differently, obeying other formulae, having other aims, but—and the example and history of Socrates clearly proves it—just as dangerous. Two forms of courage of telling the truth, consequently, take shape and are distributed around this enigmatic line traced and marked by the daemonic voice which restrained Socrates.

I would now like to add the following two remarks. In the exposition of this other form of courageous veridiction, this other form of veridiction which is the raison d'être, underpins, and runs through the whole of the first part of the *Apology*, it is very easy to find references to other types of veridiction, and in particular to the three other major forms of veridiction I talked about last week and the week before (the veridiction of prophecy, the veridiction of wisdom, and the veridiction of teaching). I have tried to tell you, schematically and, as it were, synchronically, that four major forms of truth-telling could be found in Greek culture: the truth-telling of the prophet, of the sage, of the technician (the man of *tekhnē*), and then the veridiction of the parrhesiast. I think the three other forms of veridiction (prophecy, wisdom, and teaching) are present explicitly in the *Apology*. In trying to define the nature of his mission, Socrates quite explicitly marked the points of differentiation with the other forms of veridiction, and he showed how he marked out his way alongside [them].

First—we have just seen, we even started from this—with regard to prophetic veridiction, in actual fact Socrates set out on his mission of *parrhēsia* on the basis of the prophetic words of the god who had been consulted precisely at Delphi, the place where he delivers his prophetic discourse. So, in that sense—and he is anxious to underline this for a number of reasons—all of the new *parrhēsia* rests on the god's prophecy, which enables him to avoid the charge of impiety. But importantly, we have also seen that Socrates subjects this prophecy, or, if you like, the prophetic attitude and listening to the prophet's true discourse, to a number of inflections by subjecting the god's utterance to an investigation involving inquiry and truth. He transposed prophetic speech and its effects from the domain of the reality in which its effectuation is understood, to the game of truth in which what one wants to find out is whether this speech is in actual fact true. Consequently, there is a transposition of prophetic veridiction to a field of truth.

Second, there is also a very clear reference in the text to the truth-telling of wisdom, the truth-telling of the sage. It is found in the passage in which Socrates recalls the accusation made against him, which is a very old accusation, dating from well before the accusation of Anytus and Meletus. The accusation was that Socrates was impious, that he was guilty, that he had committed an offense (*adikein*), because he sought to know what happens in the sky and below the earth, making the weaker discourse stronger (a traditional formula for saying that he got the false taken for the true).[40] And the word used here is *zētein* (seeking), the same word used by Socrates. For precisely, Socrates wants to show that, contrary to the accusations made against him, what he does is completely different from the *zētēsis*, from the activity which consists in inquiring (*zētein*) into what may take place in the sky or below the earth. In 18d he in fact challenges anyone to find someone who has heard him speak in this way on these subjects. He has spoken neither of what takes place in the sky nor of what takes place below the earth, and furthermore, throughout the *Apology*, he shows that what he is striving for is not at all the being of things and the order of the world, which is in fact the object, the domain of the discourse of wisdom. He does not speak of the being of things or the order of the world; he speaks of the test of the soul. And Socratic *zētēsis* is contrasted with that of a sage, who seeks to tell of the being of things and the order of the world, inasmuch as the point at issue in the *zētēsis* (the search) of his soul is the soul and the truth of the soul. So, there is not only differentiation from prophetic truth-telling, but also differentiation from or contrast with the truth-telling of wisdom.

Finally, third, Socrates clearly marks the difference between his veridiction and the truth-telling of those who know, those with technical knowledge which they can teach. He also says this quite explicitly with regard to the accusation that he tried to teach (*didaskein*) the research he undertook. He again replies to this in two ways. An apposite and immediate way: by asserting forcefully that he is not like the Sophists Gorgias, Prodicus, and Hippias, who sell their knowledge for money and are traditional teachers.[41] And then, throughout the *Apology*, he also replies by bringing out his permanent ignorance and by showing that he is not like a teacher who, without taking risks, calmly conveys what he knows, or claims to know, or thinks he knows, to those who do not know. What he does, on the contrary, is courageously show others that they do not know and that they need to take care of themselves.

In short, if you like, Socrates establishes a search, an investigation with regard to the god's enigmatic words, whose aim is not to await or avoid its realization. He shifts their effects by embedding them in an investigation of truth. Second, he establishes the difference from the speech, the veridiction, the truth-telling of the sage by radically distinguishing his object. He does not speak of the same thing and his search is not pursued in the same domain. Finally, he establishes a difference in relation to the discourse of teaching by, if you like, reversal. Where the teacher says: I know, listen to me, Socrates will say: I know nothing, and if I care for you, this is not so as to pass on to you the knowledge you lack, it is so that through understanding that you know nothing you will learn to take care of yourselves.

So you see that in this text from the *Apology* Socrates basically does two things which I will summarize in the following way: first, he radically distinguishes his own truth-telling from the three other major [modalities of] truth-telling he meets with around him (prophecy, wisdom, teaching); second, as I was explaining, he shows how courage is necessary in this form of veridiction, of truth-telling. But this courage is not to be employed on the political stage where this mission cannot in fact be accomplished. This courage of truth must be exercised in the form of a non-political *parrhēsia*, a *parrhēsia* which will take place through the test of the soul. It will be an ethical *parrhēsia*.

In conclusion, I would like to say this. I think we see emerging here another *parrhēsia* which must not be exposed to the danger of politics, both because it has a completely different form, because it is incompatible with public speaking and the forms of rhetoric peculiar to political discourse, and, on the other hand, because it would risk being silenced if it tried to manifest itself in either a democracy or an oligarchy. [For all that], this *parrhēsia* which must be kept from the political risk is nonetheless useful to the city. And this is what Socrates repeats tirelessly throughout the *Apology*: By encouraging you to take care of yourselves I am useful to the whole city. And if I protect my life, it is precisely in the city's interest. It is in the city's interest to protect the true discourse, the courageous veridiction which encourages citizens to take care of themselves. Finally, philosophy—as courageous veridiction, as non-political *parrhēsia*, yet maintaining an essential relation with the city's utility—will be deployed throughout what could be called the great chain of cares and concerns. It is because the god cared about men that he called on Socrates as the wisest of men. The god cared about Socrates and constantly showed concern for him, by signaling to him that he was not to do this or that. And in response to this concern of the gods and the god, Socrates is concerned to know what the god meant. With the characteristic zeal of his concern, he will try to check what the god said. Through his concern about himself, this leads him to concern himself with others, but in such a way that he shows them that they in turn have to be concerned about themselves, about their *phronēsis*, about *alētheia*, and their *psukhē* (reason, truth, and the soul).

So that—and this is the last conclusion of this first hour—it seems that in all of this first part of the *Apology* we can see a coincidence between, on the one hand, the introduction of a discourse of truth different from prophecy, wisdom, and teaching, and, on the other, the definition of a philosophical *parrhēsia* distinct from political *parrhēsia*, but just as exposed to the risk of death and not foreign to the interest of each and all. What finally appears as the fundamental theme of this courageous and philosophical discourse, as the major objective of this *parrhēsia*, this philosophical and courageous truth-telling, is the care of self connected to the relation to the gods, the relation to truth, and the relation to others. So that, it seems to me, what runs through the whole cycle of the Socratic death is actually the establishment, the foundation, in its non-political specificity, of a form of discourse whose preoccupation, whose concern is the care of self.

After all—and here I return to my squirrel's hoard—is not the first sentence of *Apology* in fact: My enemies are liars, they are skillful speakers, and they are such skillful speakers that they are in danger of making me forget myself?[42] The theme of the care of self is indeed present, and it heralds as it were, as a kind of negative opening, everything that takes place afterwards in the *Apology* and the other texts [relating to] Socrates' death, that is to say the theme of the care of self. We may also recall Socrates' last words which conclude his little expression, his little entreaty to his followers: Remember to sacrifice a cock to Asclepius. Do it, don't forget, don't neglect it: *mē amelēsēte*.[43] You find, this same word "care," the noun that designates forgetting or not forgetting, negligence and non-negligence, all this series of expressions, throughout the *Apology*, the *Crito*, and the *Phaedo*. Only, of course, if from start to finish we do in fact find this same theme (don't forget, don't be neglectful, remember), it is important to note nonetheless that in Socrates' last words—don't be neglectful (*mē amelēsēte*)—it is clearly not, or at least apparently not the care of self that is at issue, since it is simply a matter of a ritual and religious prescription. A cock should be sacrificed to Asclepius, and this is what one must take care to do, what should not be neglected. After having encountered the theme of the care of self so often in the long cycle of Socrates' death, with all the words like *epimeleia*, *epimeleisthai*, *amalein*, and *melei moi*, my problem was why do we again, one last time, come across a word formed from the same root, and in which the point at issue is again this care, but applied no longer to the great reality of the soul, truth, and *phronēsis*, but simply to a cock to be offered to Asclepius? It is this peculiarity, this irony, this strangeness that I was unable to resolve. And then I read Dumézil's text. So, in the next hour I would like to analyze how Dumézil resolves the problem of the last thing Socrates' said, the meaning he [gives] to it, and how we can, I think, fairly easily connect his interpretation with the themes I have just been referring to.

1. Platon, *Apologie de Socrate*, 17a-b, p. 140: "They have not spoken a single true word. ... I, on the other hand, will speak only the truth"; Plato, *Socrates' Defense (Apology)*, p. 4: "scarcely a word of what they said was true ... but from me you shall hear the whole truth."

2. Ibid. The expression *deinos legein* is used twice, but in the malicious representation of Socrates by his accusers.

3. Ibid. Fr.: "What most astonished me is that they warned you to be on your guard and not let yourselves be deceived by me, representing me as a skillful speaker *(deinos legein)*"; Eng.: "I was especially astonished at one of their many misrepresentations; I mean when they told you that you must be careful not to let me deceive you—the implication being that I am a skillful speaker."

4. Ibid. Fr.: "Listening to them, I almost forgot who I am"; Eng.: "I was almost carried away by them—their argument was so convincing."

5. Platon, *Phédon*, 118a, trans. P. Vicaire (Paris: Les Belles Lettres, 1983) p. 110: "Crito, we owe a cock to Asclepius. Settle my debt, don't forget *(mē amelēsēte)*"; English translation by Hugh Tredennick, Plato, *Phaedo*, in *The Collected Dialogues*, p. 98: "Crito, we ought to offer a cock to Asclepius. See to it, and don't forget."

6. *Apologie*, 31b, p. 159; *Socrates' Defense*, p. 17: "going like a father or an elder brother to see each one of you privately."

7. Ibid., 31c, Fr. p. 159: "How come that, while I go round freely giving advice here and there to each individually and getting somewhat involved in their lives, I do not venture to act publicly *(dēmosia)*, speak to the people *(anaibainōn eis to plēthos)*, or give advice to the city *(sumbouleuein tē polei)*?"; Eng. p. 17: "It may seem curious that I should go round giving advice like this and busying myself in people's private affairs, and yet never venture publicly to address you as a whole and advise on matters of state."

8. Aristote, *Constitution d'Athènes*, §14, trans. G. Mathieu and B. Haussoulier (Paris: Les Belles Lettres, 1930) pp. 14-15; English translation by F.G. Kenyon, Aristotle, *Constitution of Athens*, 14, in *The Complete Works of Aristotle*, p. 2349.

9. Plutarque, "Vie de Solon," §30, in *Vies parallèles*, trans. B. Latzarus (Paris: Garnier Frères, 1950) pp. 105-106; English translation by Bernadotte Perrin, Plutarch, *Life of Solon*, in *Lives*, vol. I (Cambridge, Mass.: Harvard University Press, "Loeb Classical Library," 1967) pp. 497-499.

10. Diogène Laërce, *Vie, doctrines et sentences des philosophes illustres*, Book I, §49, trans. M.-O. Goulet-Cazé, p. 98; Diogenes Laertius, *Lives of Eminent Philosophers*, Vol. 1, Book I, p. 51.

11. *Vie, doctrines et sentences des philosophes illustres*, vol. 1, trans. R. Genaille, p. 61; *Lives of Eminent Philosophers*, Vol. I, Book I, p. 51: "'Men of Athens, I am wiser than some of you and more courageous than others: wiser than those who fail to understand the plot of Pisistratus, more courageous than those who, though they see through it, keep silence through fear.'"

12. Ibid.; Eng.: "A little while, and the event will show/To all the world if I be mad or no."

13. Platon, *Apologie de Socrate*, 31c-d, p. 159; Plato, *Socrates' Defense (Apology)*, p. 17.

14. Ibid., 31d, Fr. p. 159; Eng. p. 17: "... if I had tried gentlemen long ago to engage in politics, I should long ago have lost my life."

15. Ibid., 31d-e, Fr. pp. 159-160; Eng. p. 17: "Please do not be offended if I tell you the truth. No man on earth who conscientiously opposes either you or any other organized democracy, and flatly prevents a great many wrongs and illegalities from taking place in the state to which he belongs, can possibly escape with his life."

16. See a first analysis of these examples in the lecture of 2 March 1983, first hour, in *Le Gouvernement de soi et des autres*, pp. 291-295; *The Government of Self and Others*, pp. 315-319.

17. Platon, *Apologie de Socrate*, 32b, p. 160; Plato, *Socrates' Defense (Apology)*, p. 18: "I was the only member of the executive who insisted that you should not act unconstitutionally, and voted against the proposal."

18. Ibid., 32b-c, Fr. p. 160; Fr. p. 18: "although your leaders were all ready to denounce and arrest me, and you were all urging them on at the top of your voices, I thought that it was my duty to face it out on the side of law and justice rather than support you, through fear of prison or death, in your wrong decisions."

19. Ibid., 32c-d, Fr. p. 161; Eng. p. 18: "On this occasion, however, I again made it clear not by my words but by my actions that death did not matter to me at all—if that is not too strong an expression—but that it mattered all the world to me that I should do nothing wrong or wicked."

20. Ibid., 31e, Fr. p. 159; Eng. p. 17.
21. Ibid., 21a, Fr. p. 145; Eng. p. 7.
22. Ibid., 21b, Fr. p. 145; Eng. p. 7.
23. Ibid., Fr.: "Let's see, what do the god's words mean (*ti pote legei ho theos*), what meaning is hidden in them (*kai ti pote ainittetai*)?"; Eng.: "What does the god mean? Why does he not use plain language?"
24. Ibid., 21a, Fr. p. 145: "I decided to check it in the following way (*epi zētēsin autou toiautēn tina etrapomēn*)"; Eng. p. 7: "I set myself at last with considerable reluctance to check the truth of it in the following way."
25. Ibid, 21c, Fr. p. 145: "I went to find one of the men who are considered wise, certain that here if anywhere I would be able to check the oracle (*elegxōn to manteion*)"; Eng. p. 7: "I went to interview a man with a high reputation for wisdom, because I felt that here if anywhere I should succeed in disproving the oracle."
26. Ibid., 22a, Fr. p. 146: "I am obliged to recount to you this round of investigations (*tēn emēn planēn*)"; Eng. p. 18: "I want you to think of my adventures as a sort of pilgrimage."
27. Ibid., Fr.: "It was truly a cycle of works that I performed in order to check the oracle"; Eng.: "I want you to think of my adventures as a sort of pilgrimage undertaken to establish the truth of the oracle once and for all."
28. See the lecture of 19 January 1983 in *Le Gouvernement de soi et des autres*; *The Government of Self and Others*.
29. *Apologie de Socrate*, 21c, p. 145; *Socrates' Defense (Apology)*, p. 7.
30. Ibid., 21c-22e, Fr. pp. 145-146; Eng. pp. 7-8.
31. Ibid., 22e, Fr. p. 146: "Such was, Athenians, the investigation (*exetesaōs*) which has made me so many enemies"; Eng. p. 9: "The effect of these investigations of mine, gentlemen, has been to arouse against me a great deal of hostility."
32. Ibid., 23c, Fr. p. 148: "They take pleasure in seeing people subjected to this examination (*exetazomenoi*)"; Eng. p. 9: "they enjoy hearing other people cross-questioned."
33. See the lectures of 19 January 1983, *Le Gouvernment de soi et des autres*, pp. 71-104; *The Government of Self and Others*, pp. 75-111.
34. *Apologie de Socrate*, 23e, p. 148; *Socrates' Defense (Apology)*, p. 10.
35. Ibid., 28b, Fr. p. 155; Eng. p. 14: "You are mistaken, my friend, if you think that a man who is worth anything ought to spend his time weighing up the prospects of life and death."
36. Ibid.; Eng.: "a man who is worth anything... has only one thing to consider when performing any action—that is, whether he is acting rightly or wrongly, like a good man or a bad one."
37. Ibid., 28d, Fr. p. 155: "Whoever occupies a post—whether he has chosen it himself as the most honorable or has been placed there by a commander—has the duty, according to me, to stay firm, whatever the risk, taking no account of possible death or danger"; Eng. p. 15: "Where a man has once taken up his stand, either because it seems best to him or in obedience to his orders, there I believe he is bound to remain and face the danger, taking no account of death or anything else before dishonor."
38. Ibid., 29e, Fr. p. 155: "But you do not concern yourself with your reason, with truth, and with your soul and its improvement"; Eng. p. 16: "Are you not ashamed that you... give no attention or thought to truth and understanding and the perfection of your soul?"
39. On *phronēsis* (translated in Latin as *prudentia*), see the classical work of P. Aubenque, *La Prudence chez Aristote* (Paris: PUF, 1963).
40. Ibid., 19b, Fr. p. 142: "Socrates is guilty (*adikei*): he indiscreetly investigates (*zēton*) what takes place below the earth and in the sky, he wins acceptance for the bad cause (*ton hēttō logon kreittō poiōn*), and teaches others to follow his example (*kai allous ta auta tauta didaskōn*)"; Eng. p. 5: "Socrates is guilty of criminal meddling, in that he inquires into things below the earth and in the sky, and makes the weaker argument defeat the stronger, and teaches others to follow his example." These accusations are already mentioned by Socrates at 18b.
41. Ibid., 19e, Fr. p. 143; Eng. p. 6.
42. Ibid., 17a, Fr. p. 141; Eng. p. 4.
43. See above, note 5.

15 FEBRUARY 1984

Second hour

- HAVE ANY OF YOU read Dumézil's book? Yes?

- *[the public]* Not yet.

- Not yet? There is something that amuses me, which is the way the
papers talk about it. First of all, you will have noticed that the book
is in two parts. One is devoted to Nostradamus, the other to Plato.
So, I would like to make a few remarks about this juxtaposition and
confrontation of the two texts, but I won't do so straightaway because
it would be too much of an interruption of what I am telling you. I
think it is better to keep hold of the threads. So I will talk now about
the second of the texts Dumézil has brought together in *Le Moyne noir*,
the one devoted to Plato. And then, if I have time, either today or next
week I will try to tell you, from my personal point of view, which in
no way represents Dumézil's own opinion, what may be read, deci-
phered, made out, or perceived in the fact that these two texts have
been juxtaposed.

Let's confine ourselves now to the text on Plato. If you read the newspapers (which is not obligatory), you may have noticed that some of the more decent ones speak about another book by Dumézil, a study of mythology,[1] which appeared at the same time, and that they make do with noting at the end of this learned article devoted to this other book, that there is a book called *Le Moyne noir*, which is a secret garden, and that's all. And then there are those that do speak of this book and review it, but without speaking about the text on Plato, as if the whole book was devoted to Nostradamus. Paradoxically this means that if in fact part of the scientific establishment* experiences some difficulty in accepting that Dumézil talks about Nostradamus, there seems to be an even greater difficulty in accepting that he talks about Plato, or [rather], in accepting what he actually says about Plato. And, in fact—again, I will try to comment on this when we come to talk about Nostradamus—it is rather odd to see that this text (the last lines of the *Phaedo*, and precisely Socrates' last words reported by Plato) has always been a sort of blind spot, an enigmatic point, at any rate a small gap in the history of philosophy. God knows, Plato's texts [have been] commented on in every way; [nevertheless], it turns out that the last words of Socrates, of the person who founded Western philosophy, have remained, in their strange banality, unexplained.

You are familiar with this text. I will re-read it all the same: "Socrates then uncovered his face—for he had covered it—and said these words, the last [*ho dē teleutaion ephthegxato*: these are Socrates' last; M.F.]: 'Crito, we owe a cock to Asclepius. Pay my debt, don't forget' [*alla apodote kai mē amelēsēte*: pay *the* debt; the French translation says *my* debt...and Dumézil isn't happy with this; M.F.]."[2] Pay the debt/ don't forget: the positive/negative repetition—do this and don't do the contrary—is a traditional Greek rhetorical form. It remains however that, as is often the case with the Greeks, and very often in Plato, the use of a common rhetorical form may be surcharged with additional and sometimes crucial significations. Anyway, this text is the object of Dumézil's analysis. So, when Socrates is about to die, we have this recommendation to his disciples to offer a cock in sacrifice to Asclepius, which, for anyone familiar with Greek civilization, with the Greek

---

* [In English and italics in the original; G.B.]

rites, and with the significance of Asclepius, can only be interpreted in a certain way. Asclepius is in fact the god who does only one thing for humans, which is occasionally to cure them. Sacrificing a cock is the traditional act by which one thanks Asclepius when, Dumézil emphasizes, he has *in actual fact* cured someone, after the cure has been carried out.[3] This then is the starting point; this is what we know.

Now this text, formulated in this way, referring to this kind of practice, has been interpreted in a fairly standard way which Dumézil amuses himself by synthesizing with some lines from a poem by Lamartine. Socrates, then, would have a debt to pay to Asclepius who had cured him. Of what, then, would Socrates have been cured, thus being in debt to Asclepius and having to thank him? What is this debt for? Well, with his death Socrates would have been cured of the illness of living. The lines from Lamartine are these:

> "To the liberating gods," he said, "make sacrifice!
> They have cured me"—"Of what?" said Cebes,—
> "Of life!"

Then, faced with this interpretation, Dumézil gets annoyed and says: Socrates has nothing in common with his colleague in sophistry, Sakyamuni.[4] Socrates was not a Buddhist, and it is absolutely not a Greek idea, a Platonic, or a Socratic idea that life is an illness of which we are cured by death. So Dumézil symbolizes a whole interpretation with these lines from Lamartine.[5]

Actually this interpretation is neither Lamartinian nor Buddhist; it is a very traditional interpretation in the history of philosophy. I will just give a few examples. In the earlier Budé edition of the *Phaedo* there is a small note at this point in which Robin says: by sacrificing a cock to Asclepius, Socrates wanted to give thanks for his soul finally being cured of being joined to a body. Socrates' gratitude, explains Robin, "will therefore go to the god who restores health."[6] To live is to be ill; dying is therefore being restored to health. This then is the interpretation given by Robin, who was not exactly a Buddhist. In his commentary on the *Phaedo*,[7] Burnet says that Socrates hopes to wake up cured like those who recover their health through incubation in Asclepius' temple. The idea is the same, slightly modified, slightly different. Here, death is a sort of sleeping cure similar to that undergone by those who come to Asclepius' temple to ask him for a cure. They fall asleep and have a dream which indicates to them how they can be cured. Well, approaching death, Socrates hopes, wants his death to be a sort of sleep from which he will wake up cured. Burnet was not a Buddhist either. You also find this interpretation in Nietzsche. In paragraph 340, Book IV of *The Gay Science* you read the following: " 'O Crito, I owe Asclepius a rooster.' This ridiculous and terrible 'last word' means for those who have ears: 'O Crito, *life is a disease.*' "[8] So there is not just Lamartine, there is also Nietzsche. Maybe you will find that more convincing.

But even more grave and important, if we go back to late Antiquity we find the commentary of Olympiodorus, one of the great neo-Platonists, devoted to the *Phaedo* (paragraph 103).[9] Why the offer of a cock to Asclepius? In order, he says, that the soul be cured of what it has suffered *en tē genesei* (in becoming, in time). So, through death the soul will gain access to eternity, escaping *genesis* (becoming, its changes, and its corruption), and consequently by dying it will be cured of all the ills linked to *genesis*. This is not exactly the idea that life itself is a disease, but all these ideas have certain similarities and we can say that in fact, for almost two thousand years you have this interpretation of the last words of Socrates as recommending a sacrifice to thank the god who is present, watching over this death, for having freed Socrates from the disease of life.

Actually, several people have not been entirely satisfied with this interpretation. Two in particular, for the primary, fundamental, essential reason that the idea that life is a disease cured by death in no way goes together with, works with, coincides with, or fits into the whole of Socratic teaching. Nietzsche himself saw this (aphorism 340 of *The Gay Science*, entitled *The dying Socrates*), for if he said that the meaning of the phrase: "O Crito, I owe Asclepius a rooster," had to be: "O Crito, *life is a disease*," nevertheless in the same passage Nietzsche reformulates the traditional interpretation: "I admire the courage and wisdom of Socrates in everything he did, said—and did not say. This mocking and enamored monster and pied piper of Athens, who made the most overweening youths tremble and sob, was not only the wisest chatterer of all time: he was equally great in silence. I wish he had remained taciturn also at the last moment of his life; in that case he might belong to a still higher order of spirits. Whether it was death or the poison or piety or malice—something loosened his tongue at that moment and he said: 'O Crito, I owe Asclepius a rooster.' This ridiculous and terrible 'last word' means for those who have ears: 'O Crito, *life is a disease.*' Is it possible that a man like him, who had lived cheerfully and like a soldier in the sight of everyone, should have been a pessimist? He had merely kept a cheerful mien while concealing all his life long his ultimate judgment, his inmost feeling. Socrates, Socrates *suffered life!* And then he still revenged himself—with this veiled, gruesome, pious, and blasphemous saying. Did a Socrates need such revenge? Did his overrich virtue lack an ounce of magnanimity?—Alas, my friends, we must overcome even the Greeks."[10] So Nietzsche saw perfectly well that there was a contradiction between those words uttered at the final moment of Socrates' life and everything else he had said, done, and been throughout his life, a contradiction between those words and that life. And he resolves the contradiction by saying that, in short, he had broken down and revealed this secret, this obscure secret that he had never told, thus contradicting at the last moment everything he had said and done.

The same feeling of uneasiness leads Dumézil to completely different conclusions on the meaning of this text. Anyway, that the interpretation that "life is a disease" does not gel, does not work, and that we cannot simply accept it and see it as in keeping with, think it in the same breath as everything Socrates said previously and is saying now, can be established, it seems to me, by a number of texts—by many texts, for sure, in the whole of Plato's œuvre, but certain texts which are close to this one and from the *Phaedo* itself.

That life is not a disease, that it is not an evil in itself, is clearly stated, once again, not just in the rest of the Platonic œuvre, but precisely close to these words in the *Phaedo*. At 62b, for example: this is the famous text—the subject of many discussions moreover, maybe we will come back to it—in which Socrates cites a Pythagorean saying according to which "we are in the *phroura*,"[11]—which some translate as "prison," some as "enclosure" "day center," and others as "military guard post" (we are "on sentry duty"), according to whether *phroura* is given a passive or active sense.[12] No matter, what we should keep hold of, and what some commentators seem to forget entirely, is that after having quoted this Pythagorean "saying" Plato adds: Oh you know, in any case this is an obscure term and very difficult to decipher (*ou radiōs diidein*).[13] It is very difficult to know what it means; this is how I understand it: The gods look after us (*epimeleisthai*—take care of us, care about us, are concerned about us) and we are their *ktēmata* (their possessions or, more likely, their flock).[14]

In any case—leaving aside the problem of the *phroura*—it is pointed out here that in this world we are the objects of the gods' care and concern. This is why, I think, we cannot give this passage the meaning and signification of: we are in a prison supervised by the gods, because *epimeleia*, *epimeleisthai* always designate positive activities. *Epimeleia* is not the warder's supervision of his slaves; it is not the prison guard's supervision of his prisoners. It is the positive concern of a father for his children, of a shepherd for his flock, of a good sovereign for the citizens of his country. It is the concern of the gods for men. We are in the gods' care, and this is why, Plato says, we must not kill ourselves. We cannot escape, not from prison, but from this benevolence and solicitude of the gods. So it is not possible to get the idea of a life-disease from which we are freed by death to match up with the idea that, down here, we are in the custody and concern of the gods.

In 69d-e there is this short phrase, which passes by quickly, in which Socrates says: "I am convinced that there, just as here [there, that is, in the other world, just as here, that is in this world; M.F.] I will find good masters (*despotai*) and good companions."[15] The good masters are the gods—the gods already there and who, we have just learned, look after men. And there are good companions, even if at several points in the text Socrates evokes the trouble one may have in the city with boring citizens hounding you. So, we will find there—and consequently there is no reason to fear death—good masters and good companions, just as one does here. Which proves that there is a difference between here and there, and this will be that everything is better there than here. But this does not mean at all that we are here as patients who are seeking to be freed, liberated from, and cured of their illness.

Furthermore, we should remember that Socrates appears throughout the *Phaedo*, throughout the cycle of his death, and throughout the whole of Plato's œuvre, as the person who, by definition, leads the philosophical life, the pure life, the life untroubled by any passion, any desire, any unrestrained appetite, or any false opinion. And it is this life moreover—this life here, perfectly calm, pure, and in control of itself—that Socrates evokes in paragraph 67a when he says that the philosophical life consists in "carefully avoiding association and dealings with the body, except when unavoidable, without letting ourselves be contaminated by its nature and keeping ourselves purified of our contact with it until the divinity itself will have delivered us."[16] This is Socrates' representation of his own life. He does not renounce life; he renounces, in life, his body, which is obviously something completely different. But, until the gods give us a sign (that is, until we are dying) he envisages the possibility of living in this way, uncontaminated and pure. How could this uncontaminated and pure life, Socrates' life, be thought to be a disease?

To these texts I will limit myself to adding one from the *Apology* which in a way is even clearer, rejecting in the most decisive way, it seems to me, the idea that life could be a disease. In the third and last part of the *Apology*, Socrates recommends his judges to take note "of this truth, that no evil may befall the good man [that is to say, of course, Socrates; M.F.], either in this life or after, and that the gods are not indifferent to his fate [that of the good man; M.F.]."[17] So you see here the different themes I have referred to linked together very clearly. Actually, the phrase: "the gods are not indifferent to his fate" is the translation of the Greek: "*oude ameleitai hupo theōn ta toutou pragmata.*" That is to say: this man's affairs (*ta toutou pragmata*) are not neglected by the gods. We are dealing here with the theme of *epimeleia*, of *epimeleisthai* (taking care of), and *ameleisthai* (neglecting). So the gods take care of the wise man's affairs, and consequently no evil can befall him either in this life or in the other.

In the light of this set of texts (and of others in the *Apology* and the *Phaedo*), how could it be supposed that what is involved in the sacrifice to Asclepius is thanks to the god for having delivered Socrates from the disease of life? Socrates has lived such a wise life, so detached from the body, that no evil can befall him down here. So, at the point of death, at which he accepts death and is happy to die, Socrates does not say or think, did not say or think that life is a disease. So Socrates' last words are singularly enigmatic if we grant that, on the one hand, the offering to Asclepius puts us precisely within a ritual which refers to disease and that, on the other hand, for Socrates death cannot be considered in itself as a cure, because life cannot be in itself a disease. What then is this disease from which people have in actual fact been freed, calling for a sacrifice?

It is this difficulty moreover—obscurely felt, albeit rarely, if ever formulated before Dumézil—which has led some commentators to put forward other solutions. Nietzsche then, clearly sensing the discrepancy between Socrates' teaching and the interpretation "life is a disease," imagined that Socrates had broken down and revealed his secret at the last moment. There is one commentator who obviously had reasons for not following Nietzsche's suggestions, and this is Wiliamowitz.[18] Wiliamowitz, then, dodged the issue and said: If we have to accept that a disease is involved, since it is obviously not life as disease that is at issue, then it must be that Socrates had previously had a disease (we don't really know what disease) and then remembered it at the point of death.[19] Wiliamowitz is, after all, an eminent figure. There is also the solution offered by Frantz Cumont, who says in the *Compte rendu de l'Académie des Inscriptions et Belles Lettres* of 1943: Yes, for sure this sacrifice of the cock to Asclepius is a cure ritual, [a] response to a cure. But we should not forget that the cock in fact came from Persia, and in Persian mythology it is the animal which guides and protects souls on the journey to the underworld. And no doubt it is the echo, the evocation of this importation of the cock that we have at the moment of Socrates' death.[20] This amounts to asking Persian mythology to solve a problem which does not appear, to Cumont at least, entirely solvable in the terms of Greek thought.

Faced with all this, what does Dumézil do? First of all, he accepts, because he has to, that a disease is in fact involved. Asclepius = cock = disease.[21] Second, it cannot be some slight disease in the distant and forgotten past, as Wiliamowitz thought. It must be an important disease for these to be Socrates' last words, so solemnly introduced in the dialogue. And finally, we cannot go along with Nietzsche and accept that Socrates has broken down. He has not broken down but rather, at the last moment, said what for him was most essential and manifest in his teaching; he had only to repeat it. And you will see that he does in fact repeat it.

For what, then, must Asclepius be thanked; what is this disease, the cure of which calls for the final act of gratitude? Well, Dumézil brings in the dialogue of the *Crito* and the episode from which the dialogue takes off and in which Crito suggests to Socrates that he escape.[22] Why does Dumézil introduce this dialogue? He starts quite simply from a somewhat vague remark made by Frantz Cumont, but only half made, without drawing out its consequences. Dumézil notes that the demand to offer a sacrifice of a cock to Asclepius is addressed to Crito (*"Crito,* we owe a cock to Asclepius"). And Dumézil points out that is therefore Crito who is called upon, but that immediately after the debt is not designated as Crito's, but as a debt that *we* owe—at least Crito and Socrates, and maybe even Crito, Socrates, and the others, but in any case certainly at the least Socrates and Crito.[23] Now to what can this debt refer which they both would have incurred and of which Crito would be perfectly aware, since he is the person addressed? The solution to this problem must be sought in the only dialogue in which we see Crito and Plato alone together.

So Dumézil turns to the *Crito* for the reason I have just given, and what does he look for in this dialogue? You know that in this dialogue Crito proposes to help Socrates escape. His friends have worked out a plan of escape and it only needs Socrates to accept its grounds for it to be carried out immediately. In support of his proposal, and to provide Socrates with arguments for accepting it, Crito points out certain things. He tells Socrates that if were not to escape he would, first of all, betray himself;[24] secondly, if he were to accept death he would betray his own children and abandon them to a life in which he would be unable to do anything for them;[25] finally, it would bring dishonor to Socrates' friends in the eyes of other citizens and public opinion if they could be reproached for not having sought to do all that they could and not having tried every resort to save Socrates.[26] Thus Socrates and his friends would be in some way dishonored before and by public opinion.

This is precisely the point to which Socrates replies. It is on this problem of general opinion, of common, un-thought out opinion that Socrates constructs his reply to Crito by putting the question: Should we consider everybody's judgment? Should we consider the common opinion? Or are there people whose opinion we should take account of, and others whose opinion we may disregard? To answer this question Socrates takes an example designed to show the need to discriminate between opinions. Following a very common procedure in the Platonic dialogues, the example he gives is taken from the care and attention to be given to the body and to gymnastics. He says to Crito: But look, you can see that it is inconceivable that we should follow people's opinion blindly. You tell me that the opinion of the people will condemn me, and you, if I do not escape. But when it is a question of gymnastics, when it is a question of the care and attention to be given to the body, do we follow the opinion of everybody, or the opinion of those who know something about it? What would happen if we were to follow the opinion of everybody and anybody? We would follow a bad regimen and the body would suffer a thousand ills. It would be corrupted, ruined, destroyed (he uses the word *diephtarmenon*: destroyed, led to decay, deterioration).[27] If it is true, Socrates says, that in the realm of the body we should follow the opinion of those who know, the gymnastics masters who can give you a good regimen, without you suffering a thousand deaths, in the same way, don't you think that, not with regard to the body and what is useful or harmful to it, but with regard to good and bad, to the just and unjust, we should do the same thing? In following the opinions of those who do not know the difference between the just and the unjust, between good and bad, is there not the risk of "whatever part of ourselves it is to which justice and injustice are connected" being ruined, corrupted, and destroyed (*diephtarmenon*)?[28] That "part of ourselves to which justice and injustice are connected" is, of course, the soul. It is interesting that the soul is not named here. Its place is left empty, as it were. The demonstration of the soul's existence as immortal substance will be given in the *Phaedo*. For the moment, it exists; it is a part of us. So, well before the soul is founded metaphysically, it is the relation of self to self that is questioned here. The part of ourselves related to justice and injustice is in danger of being *diephtarmenon* (destroyed, corrupted: exactly the same word as for the body)[29] if we follow everybody's and anybody's opinion, and if we do not refer to the opinion of those who know.

So the conclusion of all this is: we should not "care about" (Socrates uses the verb *phrontizein*)[30] the opinion of everybody and anybody, but only about that opinion which enables us to decide what is just and unjust. And here he names the truth. It is the truth that determines what is just and unjust. So we should not follow the opinion of everybody, but if we wish to be concerned about ourselves, if we want to take care of "that part of ourselves, whatever it is" and avoid its destruction and corruption, what should we follow? It is necessary to follow the truth. You see that here again we find the elements I was talking about with regard to Socratic veridiction. In any case, this is how, by following the truth, we will avoid that ruin/destruction of the soul caused by the opinion of the crowd. On the basis of the comparison with the body, we have here the idea that the soul is corrupted, destroyed, ruined, reduced to a bad condition by opinions which have not been tried out and tested in terms of truth. And, of course, this disease is not to be treated by medical means. But if it is produced by false opinion, by the opinion of everybody and anybody, then it will be opinion armed by *alētheia*, rational *logos* (the *logos* precisely that characterizes *phronēsis*), which will be able to prevent this corruption or to restore the soul from a corrupt to a healthy condition.

We may well suppose therefore that the disease, for the cure of which a cock is owed to Asclepius, is precisely the disease of which Crito was cured when, in discussion with Socrates, he had been freed from the common opinion, from the opinion capable of corrupting souls, in order, on the contrary, to choose, resolve, and make up his mind through opinion founded on the relation of self to the truth. The comparison employed by Socrates between corruption of the body and the ruin of the soul by common opinions does seem to indicate at any rate that we are dealing with some sort of disease. And it could well be for the cure of this disease that thanks is due to Asclepius.

Only here I think we have to make an objection. And this objection was made by someone whose opinion I value, and who said to me: But even so, is it not a bit weak to say, [on the basis of] this comparison between the body and the soul, that the ruin of the body and the ruin of the soul refer to some sort of disease which would be precisely the object of a cure and so of the future sacrifice? When Dumézil says [that] in Socrates' logic a well-chosen comparison is as good as reason, we may wonder if this is not to establish something important on rather weak grounds. [Now] I do not think that the grounds are weak, for Dumézil establishes and strengthens the analogy between the ruin of the body and the ruin of the soul [by reference] to other texts, one of which is taken from Sophocles' *Antigone*, and the other from Euripides'

Agamemnon.[31] And we see here that an unsound, a false opinion is in actual fact designated by the noun *nosos* (disease). So that if, in actual fact, we cannot find in Plato's text the clear formulation of this corruption of the soul as disease, on the other hand, in texts which have more or less the same structure and refer to the same type of situation, it is indeed a matter of *nosos*.

But I think we could strengthen Dumézil's arguments and the citations he takes from Sophocles and Euripides by highlighting some texts from precisely the *Phaedo* itself. This would enable us, on the one hand, to reply to two objections. First: is it really a matter of a disease when false opinions are replaced by sound opinion? Second: is it actually this disease—the risk, the appearance of which we saw in the *Crito*—which is the object of the final sacrifice in the *Phaedo*? I think we may manage to get round the first, and also the second objection by focusing on two texts. These two texts, prior to Socrates' death and the final sacrifice, show, on the one hand, that a false, poorly grounded, unexamined opinion is an evil which must be cured and, on the other, that in his final moment Socrates actually echoes a whole debate with Crito, and also with his other interlocutors in the *Phaedo*.

This is what I mean. The *Phaedo* is a discussion concerning the immortality of the soul and of the valid arguments which can be advanced in favor of this immortality. You know that Socrates' (beloved, cherished, and close) disciples make two objections to the arguments advanced by Socrates: one is made by Cebes and the other by Simmias. Simmias says: But is not the soul simply a harmony, like the harmony of a lyre, for example? So that, just as when the lyre is broken, the harmony breaks up and no longer exists, so when the body breaks up and no longer exists, the soul may well die along with it, as the harmony dies with the broken musical instrument.[32] And Cebes' argument is this: It may well be that the soul really continues to exist after the body. But can we infer from this that the soul is immortal? May we not merely suppose that it lives longer than the body, that it successively makes use of several bodies, but that it is worn out after using a certain number of them? And we should think of the soul as rather like a living being which uses a number of costumes, clothes. But the wearing out of these clothes does not mean that the living being does not wear out too and one day dies.[33]

In 89a, after these two objections, which are precisely the false opinions Socrates has to refute, Phaedo, who recounts this final scene and who, up until this point, has recounted directly in the first person what took place, breaks off a little, and says to the interlocutor to whom he is reporting Socrates' last moments: Ah, if you knew how admirable Socrates was when he replied to these two objections. I admired the way in which he received them, perfectly aware of the effect they had on the listeners and how they ate into their souls, how they were ready to be convinced by them to the point that we wondered how Socrates was going to deal with these two terrible objections. I admired [...] the way in which he understood how close we were to being persuaded and the way in which he cured us all (*iasato*: he cured us).[34] So there really is a cure in the *Phaedo*, the cure carried out by Socrates on the disease which consists of a false opinion. And we find here, with regard to the immortality of the soul, a schema, a problem, and a cure which are the same as in the *Crito* when, invoking common opinion, Crito proposed that Socrates escape.

The second text is also in the *Phaedo*. It is found in 90e. Here it is a matter of a discussion concerning the *logos* and its dangers. Socrates wants to warn his disciples against hatred of reasoning, against the idea that all reasoning may be dangerous, false. He warns against misology. He says: We should not think that there is nothing "healthy" in reasoning (the French text translates the Greek word *hugies*, that is to say, organically healthy, concerning health); rather, we should think that it is we who are not well (*oupō hugiōs ekhomen*: we are not well, we are not healthy) and we should want to be well, you for the life you are going to have, me because of my death.[35] It is clear here, therefore, that Socrates says: Be careful! It may be that reasoning leads to errors, but it would be completely false to think that there is nothing sound, nothing healthy in reasoning. On the contrary, when reasoning looks like leading us to a result which is not good, in fact it is we who are not in good health, for we allowed ourselves to be seized by false reasoning. And we must become well, by reasoning properly; you for your future life, and me because of my death.

These two texts take up again, [on the one hand], the theme of the *Crito* that a badly formed opinion is like an ill which attacks the soul, corrupts it, destroys its health, and from which it is necessary to be cured, and, [on the other hand], the idea [which is also present] in the *Crito*, that the cure is obtained through *logos*, through good reasoning. You can also see that this idea of the cure by *logos*, the idea of false opinion as like a disease of the soul, is echoed in the *Phaedo*. And the texts I have quoted from the *Phaedo* link together the big risk of disease in the *Crito*, represented by Crito himself (when he allows himself to be influenced by opinion to the extent of proposing escape to Socrates), and then, in the *Phaedo*, the other errors, of Simmias and Cebes in particular. Crito was affected by a disease which caused him to believe that it was better for Socrates to live than die. Simmias and Cebes were affected by the disease which caused them to believe that if one dies one is not certain to release an immortal soul. And I think that we have here confirmation that it is for the cure of this kind of disease that a cock is owed to Asclepius. Dumézil's interpretation may be confirmed by the reading of the *Phaedo* itself in which we find the link between what happens in the *Crito* and what is said at the final moment.*

There remains a final difficulty which Dumézil resolves in his text. I will just summarize it.[36] If it is true that it is Crito who was affected by a disease, or if in addition, as I have just suggested, Cebes and Simmias were also sick due to their false opinion, why does Socrates say: Crito, *we* owe a cock to Asclepius? He should have said: Crito, *you* [*tu*] owe a cock to Asclepius, since you have been cured. Or, if we accept that the others have also been cured, he should have said: Crito, you who are something like the leader of my disciples, [they and you] *you* [*vous*] owe a cock to Asclepius. Now what he says is: *we* owe. Therefore he too has been cured. Dumézil replies to this question, on the one hand, by pointing out, quite legitimately I think, that there is, of course, a bond of sympathy and friendship between Socrates and his disciples such that when one of them is suffering from an illness, the others suffer too from this illness, and Socrates shares in this. On the other hand, Dumézil also points out, which is important, that no doubt Socrates— without, of course, having been the victim of temptation, it is not a question of that—might to some extent also have been by persuaded by Crito and could have decided to escape (after all, nothing but Socrates'

---

* M.F.: - Can I continue for five or ten more minutes, or ... ?
[*answers from the public;*] - Yes, yes!

personal courage and endurance in holding to the truth guarantees [the contrary]). Insofar as he is not completely dead, insofar as he has not arrived at the final moment of his life, the risk of being affected by a false opinion and of seeing the soul corrupted exists. That is why this sacrifice, which in one way could have been made at the time that Crito was cured of his disease, must be made not only in Crito's, but also Socrates' name, and can only be made at Socrates' last moment, at the point of death. It can only be Socrates' final action and his last recommendation since precisely only his courage, only his relation to himself and to the truth prevented him from listening to this false opinion and letting himself be seduced by it.

In any case, I think we could add the following to Dumézil's analysis: it is a feature which marks the dramatic art of all the Platonic dialogues that, whatever their subject, everyone ends up jointly committed to the undertaking of discussion. And on many occasions in other dialogues Socrates says: it is a defeat for all if the bad discourse triumphs, but everyone is the winner if the good discourse triumphs. Up to a point, the principle of *homologia*, which Socrates expresses so frequently in the dialogues, is found again here: having the same *logos* as those with whom one is discussing, that is to say, accepting that the same truth is valid for all, and signing, entering into that kind of pact according to which when a truth is discovered, everyone will recognize it.[37] There was this great enterprise of the discussion of opinions, this great battle of the *logos*, and there was this *elegkhos* which made it possible to check which opinion was good and which opinions were bad. And, in accordance with the principle of *homologia*, everyone was jointly committed to this operation. The healing operation is like a general form in which Socrates is caught up, even if he was actually the one who directed it. It is therefore quite normal for him to call on Crito, reminding him that there was indeed a disease, and a disease in him. But if Crito had won, then this disease would, after all, have been Socrates' disease as well. And everyone being jointly committed, the sacrifice in thanks for this cure must be made in the name of everyone.

So now I would like to get back to my subject and try to answer the question you are asking yourselves: why have I dwelt on this text and Dumézil's interpretation, which does not exactly appear to be on the same lines as what I was telling you a short while ago and last week.

We must pose the question: what is this curing, this activity by which both Socrates and his disciples have been cured with the help of the god who must be thanked? There is no sense in asking, as some may perhaps be tempted to do, whether this operation of cure is a medical activity, or if it is already something like psychiatry, whether or not the Greeks, and Socrates, really thought that this kind of error might be seen as a mental illness. We cannot discover what is at issue in this kind of anachronistic *a posteriori*. It makes more sense to try to situate this operation of cure, to which Socrates alludes several times, in the field of practices in which it could figure for the Greeks in general and for Socrates in particular. And this general field of practices is precisely all that is called "*epimeleia*." Caring for someone, looking after a flock, taking care of one's family, or, as is often found with regard to physicians, caring for a patient, are all called "*epimeleisthai*." The curing that Socrates speaks about here is part of all those activities by which one cares for someone, takes care of him if he is ill, sees to his diet so that he does not fall ill, prescribes the food he must eat or the exercises he must perform, and it is also part of those activities by which one points out to him the actions he should perform and those he should avoid, by which one helps him to discover the true opinions he should follow and the false opinions he should guard against, it is that activity by which one nourishes him with true discourse. All of this belongs to the *epimeleisthai*. Or we may say again that there are some cases in which this great many-sided activity of *epimeleia* (of the care of oneself and others, of the care of souls) may take on the most urgent, intense, and necessary form. These are the cases in which precisely a false opinion is in danger of ruining a soul and making it ill. It is important to remember that the whole cycle of Socrates' death which I tried to evoke in the previous hour, this great cycle which begins with the *Apology*, continues with the *Crito*, and ends with the *Phaedo* is permeated by this theme of *epimeleia*.

I tried to show you how, in his *Apology*, Socrates defined his *parrhēsia*, his courageous truth-telling, as a truth-telling whose final objective and constant concern was to teach men to take care of themselves. Socrates took care of men, but not in the political form: he wants to take care of them so that they learn to take care of themselves. The whole of the *Apology* is therefore underpinned by this theme of *epimeleia* and care.

You notice that this theme of care, of *epimeleia* is also present in the *Crito*. It is present in a small detail which is important because we will come across it again. It concerns Socrates' children. When Crito says to him: But what about your children, you won't be able to take care of them? How will you take care of them if you die?[38] Socrates will reply to this problem of *epimeleia* later on, precisely in the *Phaedo*. And then, apart from this little detail, more generally *epimeleia*, care, concern is the central theme in the *Crito*. You [encounter] it quite simply in the personification of the Laws.[39] Socrates brings in these laws [when he asks]: If I escape, don't you think that the Laws will rise up before me? They say to him: But who took care of your birth? Are you unhappy with the way in which marriages take place in your city? Who took care of you when you were a child, and who raised you? Who looks after what takes place in the city [...*]? The Laws are precisely the agent of *epimeleia*. And just as it will be said in the *Phaedo* that we must not escape from the world because we are watched over by the gods (*epimeleisthai*: the gods care for us),[40] similarly, in the *Crito*, the reason one must not escape from prison (that is to say, leave the city and go into exile), is that, like the gods who watch over the whole world, the city's Laws watch over the citizens, take care of them, are vigilant. They have concern. You find again this same theme of *epimeleia*.

Finally and especially, in the *Phaedo*, as death approaches, what does Socrates say to his disciples in his next to last words? The text here is absolutely clear. This is in 115b (Socrates is about to take, or has already taken the hemlock, I no longer know, at any rate at this point death is really close),[41] when Crito, leader of the group of Socrates' disciples, asks: What instructions do you give us regarding your children (they come back into the discussion here) or anything else? What do you ask us to do that will please you? It is Crito, who will be asked to do something at the end (sacrifice a cock), who asks: What would you have us do for your children? He thinks of the last will, the testament. And Socrates replies: "Do what I always tell you... Nothing new."[42] What is it that Socrates always says, which is nothing new, and which is the last wish that he will convey to his children, his circle, and his friends? "Take care of yourselves (*humōn autōn epimeloumenoi*)."[43]

---

* End of sentence inaudible.

This is Socrates' testament, his final wish. Furthermore, this final wish, so clearly expressed in the *Phaedo*, echoes what the *Apology* says at a symmetrical moment. There are three moments, three discourses in the *Apology*: the first discourse in which he defends himself; the second in which he proposes what his punishment should be; and the third in which he accepts, in which he registers the fact that he is condemned to death. In this final part of the *Apology* in which he registers and accepts his condemnation to death, [in his] final discourse, already doomed to death, Socrates says this in 41e: "When my children have grown up [another reference to the children; so we have three references to the children: in the *Apology*, after the condemnation; in the *Crito*, in Crito's objection; and in the *Phaedo*, in the passage I read to you; M.F.], Athenians, punish them by plaguing them as I myself have plagued you, if they appear to you to be more concerned (*epimeleisthai*) about money or anything else than about virtue."[44] *Epimeleisthai aretēs*: they must take care of their virtue. These are Socrates' last words in the *Apology*, the discourse he addresses to his judges. It is the last word Socrates utters to his friends when they ask him: What do you want us to do? His final wish expressed before the citizens; his final wish expressed to his circle of friends.

One further small detail on this problem of the care of self: in the last lines of the *Phaedo* there is the passage where Socrates' disciples ask: What do you want us to do about your burial? And he answers by going to take a bath, so that the women do not have to wash his body after his death. He takes care of himself, and even of his body.[45]

In any case, when he is asked: What do you want us to do for your children and what advice do you give to your friends? Socrates' last word, his final wish, is: What I have always said, "take care of yourselves," this is my final wish. But there is still a small supplement. This is precisely the mention of what is owed to Asclepius, reference to the sacrifice that must be made, the promise to Asclepius. In thanks for what? In thanks for the god's assistance, as healer, to all those, Socrates and his disciples, who have undertaken to care for themselves (*epimeleisthai*), look after themselves, take care of themselves, to, as Socrates often says, "*therapeuein*" (in the sense of looking after and curing). And Socrates' last word (after "give a cock to Asclepius"), the final word after which Socrates will never speak again, I have quoted it to you several times already, is: *mē amelēsēte* (don't be neglectful, no negligence). I have dwelt for a long time on the fact that this non-negligence recommended to his disciples concerns the sacrifice of the cock. In fact he refers explicitly, directly to the sacrifice of a cock, and so to some kind of disease. But one can be cured of this disease by oneself if one takes care of oneself, and being capable of this concern for oneself makes you know what your soul is and how it is linked to the truth. Etymologically, the word *"amelēsēte"* belongs to that family of words we have come across so often and which designate the different ways of caring about, taking care, and solicitude. Through the sacrifice to Asclepius you can see that this final word ("don't be neglectful") says that the sacrifice must not be neglected, but it is related indirectly, through this, to the care of self. Don't forget to make this sacrifice to the god, to the god who helps us to cure ourselves when we take care of ourselves. For we should not forget—on this we should refer to the different texts referred to on the gods who take care of men—that if we are concerned about ourselves, it is to the extent also that the gods have shown concern for us. It was precisely out of concern for us that they sent Socrates to teach us to take care of ourselves.

So you can see that Socrates' death, the practice of his *parrhēsia* which exposed him to the risk of death—and well and truly exposed him to this risk since he actually dies as a result of it—, the practice of his truth-telling, and finally this devotion to inducing others to take care of themselves just as he took care to take care of himself, all form a very closely woven ensemble whose threads intertwine throughout the series on Socrates' death (*Apology, Crito,* and *Phaedo*). All these threads running through these three texts come together one last time in Socrates' two final recommendations. First, manifestly, when he says: My final wish is that you take care of yourself. And a second time, symbolically, in the form of the sacrifice to Asclepius, no longer referring to the care men must take of themselves, but to the gods' care for men so that they take care of themselves. All these threads come together for the last time in the sacrifice of the cock. It is the mission concerning the care of oneself that leads Socrates to his death. It is the principle of "caring for oneself" that, beyond his death, he bequeaths to the others. And it is to the gods, favorable towards this care of oneself, that he addresses his last thought. I think that Socrates' death founds philosophy, in the reality of Greek thought and therefore in Western history, as a form of veridiction which is not that of prophecy, or wisdom, or *tekhnē*; a form of veridiction peculiar precisely to philosophical discourse, and the courage of which must be exercised until death as a test of the soul which cannot take place on the political platform. There you are. I apologize for keeping you for so long, thank you.

1. G. Dumézil, *La Courtisane et les seigneurs colorés, et autres essais. Esquisses de mythologie* (Paris: Gallimard, 1984).

2. Platon, *Phédon*, 118a (P. Vicaire translation) pp. 109-110; Plato, *Phaedo*, p. 98.

3. G. Dumézil, *"Le Moyne noir en gris dedans Varennes"* (Paris: Gallimard, 1984) p. 143; English translation by Betsy Wing as *The Riddle of Nostradamus. A Critical Dialogue* (Baltimore and London: The Johns Hopkins University Press 1999) p. 104.

4. Ibid., Fr. p. 145; Eng. p. 105. Sakyamuni is one of the Buddha's names.

5. Ibid., Fr. p. 136; Eng. p. 99.

6. Platon, *Phédon*, trans. L. Robin (Paris: Les Belles Lettres, 1926) p. 102 n.3.

7. J. Burnet, *Plato's Phaedo* (Oxford: Clarendon Press, 1911) p. 118: "Socrates hopes to awake cured like those who are healed by *egkomēsis (incubatio)* in the Asklepeion at Epidaurus."

8. Friedrich Nietzsche, *The Gay Science*, trans. Walter Kaufmann (New York: Random House, Vintage, 1974) p. 272.

9. L.G. Westerink, ed., *The Greek Commentaries on Plato's Phaedo*, vol. 1: *Olympiodorus* (Amsterdam, Oxford, and New York: North Holland Publishers, 1976).

10. Nietzsche, *The Gay Science*, p. 272.

11. Platon, *Phédon*, 62b, p. 9: "The formula one utters in the Mysteries when one says: 'We are in the place where an eye is kept on us (*en tini phroura*)'"; Plato, *Phaedo*, p. 45: "The allegory which the mystics tell us—that we men are put in a sort of guard post."

12. L. Robin translates it as "day center (*garderie*)," E. Chambry by "post," P. Vicaire by "place where an eye is kept on us," but evokes "prison" and "guard post" (note p. 113). *Phroura* comes from the verb *oraō* (to see) and evokes a place under close supervision.

13. *Phēdon*, p. 9; *Phaedo*, p. 45.

14. Ibid., Fr.: "It is the gods who watch over us (*to tous theous einai epimeloumenous*), and we men are a part that belongs to the gods (*tōn sautou ktēmatōn*)." On *ktēmata* in the sense of "flock," see the translator's, Vicaire's, note p. 113; English, p. 45: "I believe that this much is true, that the gods are our keepers, and we men are one of their possessions."

15. Ibid., Fr. 69d-e, p. 23; Eng. p. 52: "I believe that I shall find there, no less than here, good rulers and good friends."

16. Ibid., 67a, Fr. p. 18; Eng. p. 49: "...we shall continue closest to knowledge if we avoid as much as we can all contact and association with the body, except when they are absolutely necessary, and instead of allowing ourselves to become infected with its nature, purify ourselves from it until God himself gives us deliverance."

17. Platon, *Apologie de Socrate*, 41d, p. 172; Plato, *Socrates' Defense (Apology)*, p. 25: "fix your minds on this one belief, which is certain—that nothing can harm a good man either in life or after death, and his fortunes are not a matter of indifference to the gods."

18. Professor of classical philology, Ulrich von Wiliamowitz-Moellendorff had unleashed a violent polemic against the theses defended by Nietzsche in *The Birth of Tragedy*.

19. U. von Wiliamowitz-Moellendorff, *Platon* (Berlin: Weidmann, 1920) vol. 1: *Leben und Werke*, p. 178; vol. 2: *Beilagen und Textkritik*, p. 58.

20. F. Cumont, "À propos des dernières paroles de Socrate," *Compte rendu de l'Académie des Inscriptions et Belles Lettres*, 1943, pp. 112-126.

21. G. Dumézil, *Le Moyne noir en gris*, p. 143; *The Riddle of Nostradamus*, p. 104.

22. Ibid., Fr. p. 146 et seq.; Eng. p. 106 et seq.

23. Ibid., Fr. p. 140; Eng. p. 102.

24. Platon, *Criton*, 45c, p. 219; Plato, *Crito*, p. 30.

25. Ibid., 45b, Fr. p. 219; Eng. p. 30.

26. Ibid., 44b-c, Fr. p. 218 and 45e-46a, p. 220; Eng. p. 29 and pp. 30-31.

27. Ibid., 47d-e, p. 223: "That which is improved by a healthy regimen (*hupo tou hugieinou*) and is spoiled (*diaphteiromenon*) by an unhealthy regimen... Now is life possible with a wretched and ruined (*diephtarmenou*) body?"; Eng. p. 32: "There is a part of us which is improved by healthy actions and ruined by unhealthy ones... will life be worth living when this part is once ruined?"

28. Ibid., 48a-d, Fr. p. 223; Eng. p. 33: "this part of ourselves, whatever it may be, in which right and wrong operate."

29. Ibid., 47e, Fr. p. 223; Eng. p. 33.

30. Ibid., 48a, Fr. p. 223: "Consequently, my dear friend, it is not so much the views of the many that we should be concerned about (*phrontisteon*) as the judgment of those who alone are knowledgeable about justice and injustice"; Eng. p. 33: "In that case, my dear fellow, what we ought to consider is not so much what people in general will say about us but how we stand with the expert in right and wrong."
31. Dumézil, *Le Moyne noir en gris*, pp. 155-157; *The Riddle of Nostradamus*, pp. 113-115.
32. *Phédon*, 85b-86e, pp. 53-55; *Phaedo*, pp. 68-69.
33. Ibid., 86e-88b, Fr. pp. 55-58; Eng. pp. 69-70.
34. Ibid., 89a, Fr. p. 59: "I marveled at the friendly, benevolent, admiring way in which he received the words of these young people, then his sharpness in grasping the effect on us of their arguments, and finally his skill in curing our ills (*eu hēmas iasato*)"; Eng. p. 71: "what impressed me was, first, the pleasant, kindly, appreciative way in which he received the two boys' objections, then his quick recognition of how the turn of the discussion had affected us, and lastly the skill with which he healed our wounds."
35. Ibid., 90e, Fr. p. 62: "Our soul must not accept the idea that there may be nothing healthy in reasoning. Rather it must accept that it is we who lack health (*oupō hugiōs ekhomen*), and that we must employ our courage and enthusiasm to conduct ourselves healthily, you and the others with a view to your future life, myself with a view to my death itself"; Eng. p. 73: "We must not let it enter our minds that there may be no validity in argument. On the contrary we should recognize that we ourselves are still intellectual invalids, but that we must brace ourselves and do our best to become healthy—you and the others partly with a view to the rest of your lives, but I directly in view of my death."
36. *Le Moyne noir en gris*, p. 159 et seq; *The Riddle of Nostradamus*, p. 116 et seq.
37. On this concept see the last lecture of 1983 on the *Gorgias* in *Le Gouvernement de soi et des autres*, pp. 341-343; *The Government of Self and Others*, pp. 371-373.
38. *Criton*, 45c-d, pp. 219-220; *Crito*, p. 30.
39. Ibid., 50a-53d, Fr. pp. 227-232; Eng. pp. 35-38.
40. *Phédon*, 62b, p. 9; *Phaedo*, p. 45.
41. He will take it later, in 117c.
42. *Phédon*, 115b, p. 105; *Phaedo*, p. 95: "Nothing new, Crito, said Socrates, just what I am always telling you."
43. Ibid.; Eng.: "look after yourselves."
44. *Apologie de Socrate*, 41e, p. 173; *Socrates' Defense (Apology)*, p. 26: "When my sons grow up, gentlemen, if you think they are putting money or anything else before goodness, take your revenge by plaguing them as I plagued you."
45. In the text things actually happen the other way round: Socrates begins by going to take a bath. *Phédon*, 115a, p. 105: "so that I do not give the women the trouble of washing a dead person"; *Phaedo*, p. 95: "rather than give the women the trouble of washing me when I am dead."

seven

22 FEBRUARY 1984

First hour

[
Etymological questions around epimeleia. ∽ *Dumézil's method
and its extension.* ∽ *Plato's* Laches: *reasons for choosing this text.*
∽ *The pact of frankness.* ∽ *The problem of the education of
children.* ∽ *The contradictory judgments of Laches and Nicias on
the demonstration of armed combat.* ∽ *The question of technical
competence according to Socrates.* ∽ *Socrates' reversal of the
dialectical game.*
]

FOR CERTAIN REASONS (BECAUSE, it is true, some people have
asked me) I am not going to talk about the Cynics today, but next week.
I would like instead to make a link between what I was telling you last
week with regard to Socrates and the *Apology* and what I will tell you
next week with regard to the Cynics. That is to say, I will speak to
you about the *Laches*. Before this, a short comment [concerning, first,]
what I was telling you about Dumézil's book and, second, the mission of *epimeleia* and the root of this word. The two things are directly
linked moreover, since it concerns Dumézil. I have had this question
[in mind]: what is the root of the series of terms I have spoken about
on several occasions? There is the word *melō*, which you find above all
in the impersonal form of *melei moi* (I care about; or more precisely: it
concerns me, since it is impersonal), and then a whole series of other
words: the noun *epimeleia*, the verb *epimelein* or *epimeleisthai*, the adjective
amelēs (careless), the adverb *amelōs* (carelessly), and the noun *epimeletēs*

(the person who cares for, who looks after, and which often has a fairly precise meaning in Greek institutions: it is a quasi-official responsibility of being the supervisor of something; at any rate [the term] may refer to a precise responsibility). Where does this series of words come from? The root itself is clear, but what does it refer to? I am completely incompetent in this domain, so I turned to Dumézil. I asked him what this probably Indo-European root (*mel*) was? His first answer was: We don't know; we have no information which allows us to give a signification, a value to this root. And he said straightaway, obviously, we might think of *melos*, that is to say the word found in *melōdia* which signifies: song, rhythmic singing, music. But it is clear that there can be no relation between this *melos* and the small root *mel* found in *epimeleia, melei moi*, etcetera. This was the point I had reached when, yesterday, he sent me a short note to tell me: I have checked in the Chantraine (the dictionary of Greek roots), and there is no plausible etymology for *epimeleia, melei moi*, etcetera.[1] Then, he says, I had an idea, wild at first, and which took hold in my mind: should we really rule out the relation to *melos* as I did the other day? It would be something like: "it appeals to me (*ça me chante*)" with a different orientation towards care and duty; the call of duty instead of freedom and pleasure. That is to say, our expression "it appeals to me (*ça me chante*)" refers in fact to something which is not in the realm of duty, but in the realm of pleasure, of freedom: "I do it because 'it appeals to me.'" But nevertheless, we may very well conceive of an "it appeals to me" which would refer instead to something in your head, which gets into your head, stays in your mind, obsesses you up to a point, and which appeals to you, but in the form of an order, an injunction, a duty to be performed. And he adds that we could find a parallel case from Latin. In Latin there is the verb *camere*, which means "being hot (*être chaud*)." Now, he says, we find this verb again in the old French "*chaloir*," which Hatzfeld and Darmesteter[2] say is a somewhat old-fashioned term which signifies "having an interest in something" and is used only impersonally, in negative and interrogative sentences. For example, it is found in "*il ne m'en chaut*" (it doesn't matter to me). So here, just as "being hot" ended up with the value of "caring about," so "singing (*chanter*)," having a piece of music in one's mind, may well have evolved in the same way to give the value of care.

After receiving this letter, I spoke about it to Paul Veyne last night, and he said to me: But certainly, it is quite conceivable. Without it being wholly incompatible, at any rate as a possibility based on the same idea, maybe we could even point out that *melos* is the call (*chant d'appel*). For example, it is the shepherd's song (*chant*) calling back his flock or calling out to other shepherds, it is the song-signal. Consequently, *melei moi* would mean something like, not exactly "it appeals to me in my head," but: it appeals to me in the sense that it calls out to me or summons me. In our dreadful modern terminology we would say: it says something to me (*ça m'interpelle*)!* This would be more or less what we would have in *melei moi*. Anyway, I am telling you this as information, if you are interested in this problem of *epimeleia*. There would be something like a musical secret, a secret of the musical appeal in this notion of care.

The second thing also refers to what I was telling you last week with regard to Dumézil's book. I imprudently told you [that] among all the interesting things in this book, the central thing is, of course, the coexistence of Dumézil's two commentaries: on the one hand, the commentary on Nostradamus, and on the other, that on Plato. I have tried to read carefully the analyses, commentaries, and reactions which can be found in the press concerning this book, and I have been struck by the fact that some do not mention it at all. Others talk about it, but [only] about the text on Nostradamus. No one talks about the text on Plato and, *a fortiori*, about the fact that there are two texts, one on Nostradamus and the other on Plato. So, what I am going to tell you here does not represent what Dumézil says himself. It is an interpretation which I am suggesting, which is no doubt not entirely foreign to his thought, but is not his explicit intention present as such in the juxtaposition of the two texts. The first, on Nostradamus, is called a satirical allegorical drama: *Sotie nostradamique*. The other is called a *Divertissement*.[3] So these are two texts of diversion, but which do not at all have the same status.

We should also note that these two [studies] put to work a particular form of textual analysis, a certain form of analysis of words, a method of cross-checking different kinds of information found in the text, a sort of crossword method which is entirely in line with

---

* Laughter in the audience.

that employed by Dumézil in his different works of analysis of Indo-European mythologies. And, in a sense, there is a sort of testing of his own methods, an obviously ironic testing, through the asymmetrical symmetry between these two texts and two analyses: one is a satirical allegory (*Sotie*), the other a *Divertissement*. By taking these two texts (of Nostradamus and Plato), Dumézil tested his method, its validity, its rationality, and the demonstrative character of his analyses. He made the test on the basis of two texts which we might say could not be more heterogeneous. [That] of Nostradamus represents of course what we might say is [a piece of writing] which could not be more suspect to any possible rationalism. It is a prophetic, obscure text, weighed down with a series of interpretations which, since the sixteenth century have constantly concealed its meaning and value. Dumézil has thus taken the text most alien to the system of modern and European rationality, the system to which he himself belongs. He takes this text and analyzes it with the methods of his rationality. He produces some results. And then he proceeds to take a text by Plato, and from among Plato's texts, the *Phaedo*, and in the *Phaedo*, the passage which is both terminal and, of course, central: Socrates' death. And, in a sense, we may well say that the meaning and value of Socrates' death is at the heart of Western rationality. After all, Socrates' death, the meaning of this death, is indeed foundational for philosophical discourse, practice, and rationality. For two thousand years no commentator has managed to account for what is said in this text concerning the major event which founded Western rationality (Socrates and his death), for what were very precisely Socrates' last words. Socrates' discourse, which founded our rationality, ended with a phrase which no one, until now, has been able to explain. Dumézil takes up his method again, the method he has employed all his life in the analysis of Indo-European mythology, which he applied to Nostradamus, an example of all that irrationalism may produce in Western discourse, and he employs it in an attempt to resolve this problem of a discourse, a text, a founding event [...*]. He shows that all the commentators and historians of philosophy have been absolutely unable to resolve this little enigma of the sacrifice of a cock: I, Socrates, dying, ask for the sacrifice of a cock.

---

* Some words here are barely audible ["of this pre-rational world" can be heard].

So if we juxtapose these two analyses I think we can see how Dumézil has taken, as it were, the greatest possible distance, has marked out the greatest possible surface for the practice of a certain method, the both philosophical and structural method of analysis that he has employed. And this is what I believe is interesting and almost disconcerting in this text: he employs his method on two registers. He puts to work perfectly the ironic register [with] the analysis of Nostradamus. He shows how far we can go and the limit we may arrive at with such a method. He even says at the end that Nostradamus—like Dumézil—also saw Indo-European tri-functionality. And consequently he reinscribes his own method in that kind of crucible of the irrationalism of Nostradamus. And then, [second register], taking up again and intensifying the same method, he applies it to the crucible of Western rationality: the death of Socrates. He makes an entirely convincing analysis of it which fills a gap that philosophical reflection never managed to resolve concerning Socrates, the death of Socrates [...*]. What is interesting in this book, or one of the interesting things about it, is this interplay between these two texts. These are two short comments I wanted to make as an appendix to last week's lecture.

And now, if you like, let's move on to the text I wanted to analyze, the *Laches*. With regard to the *Apology*, and then, following on from this, with regard to the *Crito* and the *Phaedo*, I have tried to show you how Socrates introduced a certain mode of veridiction which was distinct from, and even explicitly opposed to other modes (those of prophecy, wisdom, and then of teaching, of *tekhnē* and its transmission). I would like to give you an example of the practice of this Socratic veridiction—the principles, rules, and distinctive characteristics of which appear clearly, I believe, in the trilogy of Socratic *parrhēsia*—from the dialogue called the *Laches*. You will, of course, find examples of this *parrhēsia*, of this veridiction peculiar to Socrates—so different from the veridiction of prophecy, of wisdom, and of teaching—being brought into play in many other of Plato's dialogues, and in all the Socratic dialogues in particular. Nevertheless, I have fixed on the *Laches* for a number of reasons.

First, the three fundamental options we encountered in the *Apology*, and which characterize Socratic truth-telling as opposed to the other

---

* The end of the sentence is inaudible.

modes of veridiction, are clearly formulated and explicitly connected to each other in the *Laches*. First, the notion of *parrhēsia* appears quite explicitly and fairly frequently. I think that of all Plato's dialogues, this is the one in which the noun *parrhēsia* or the verb *parrhēsiazesthai* are used most frequently. At any rate, the noun or the verb appear at the start of the dialogue. They describe the different interlocutors. They also mark the commitment of the different interlocutors with regard to each other. A sort of parrhesiastic pact is formulated explicitly at the start of the dialogue. And then, at the very heart of the dialogue, at its center, Socrates appears as the person who possesses *parrhēsia*, who has the right to employ it, and to whom the interlocutors accord the essential right to employ it as he understands it. So the theme of *parrhēsia* is emphatically present. Second, you also encounter this second notion of *exetasis*, as way of testing and examining, which I tried to show you was present and important in the *Apology* and characteristic of Socratic veridiction, [entailing, as well as *parrhēsia*,] a certain procedure of verification, test, investigation, and examination. This notion is present at the very heart of the dialogue of the *Laches*. And before the real and major discussion gets underway, when Socrates' interlocutors accept the game that he proposes, you will see that they are the ones who lay down *exetasis* (the principle of examination) as the basic rule of the game that Socrates will play and that they agree to play with him. [Third,] the notion of *epimeleia* (of care) is constant in the dialogue. At any rate, it appears explicitly near the start of the dialogue. For it is the care of young people, their education, training, and apprenticeship in the qualities and virtues needed in politics, which gives rise to the dialogue. And when this dialogue closes a bit later, Socrates appears as the only person who can lay claim to this care. He is the one who will have to care for the young, and it is to him that parents will turn so that he cares for their children in the same way that their children must in turn have care for themselves. So, throughout the dialogue, we find again the connection, the link, the entwining, as it were, of these three notions: *parrhēsia* as courageous frankness of truth-telling; *exetasis* as practice of the examination and test of the soul; and finally, care as the objective and end of this *parrhēsia*, of this interrogatory frankness. This is the first reason for analyzing the dialogue of the *Laches*.

Second, this dialogue is important, and typical, for the relation it has and maintains with the political scene. Actually, from one point of view, there is nothing exceptional about it. We see Socrates discussing the training of young people, all of them members of the aristocracy from prominent Athenian families and destined, sooner or later, to play their part in the city and to occupy positions with civil or military responsibilities. There is nothing exceptional in this. On the other hand, what is rather odd is that the people with whom Socrates discusses the training of the young are not themselves young. They are adults. And these adults are precisely men who exercise political functions in the period in which the dialogue is supposed to take place. Certainly, we see adults in discussion in other Socratic dialogues. And for the most part they are people who were or are able to exercise political functions, or who belong to families which play an important part in the city. But here, in the *Laches*, they are political men who exercise definite functions at the time they are speaking; they are highly placed historical figures. There is Nicias, who was the main political figure in Athens after Pericles, so at the end of the fifth century. He commanded the Sicilian expedition, and he will die in Sicily. Laches is an important military leader, someone who above all exercised military functions, who was killed at the battle of Potidaea, but who played an important role. So we see something here which is not found in practically any other dialogue: Socrates questioning eminent statesmen precisely at the time they are exercising their office. You recall that this was the situation evoked in the *Apology* when Socrates said that on the instruction of the god, who had entrusted him with different missions, he was to go round Athens seeing the different citizens, from the most eminent and important statesmen down to the craftsmen.[4] Here we have precisely this situation: Socrates establishes direct contact with the political scene and, while speaking directly to politicians and thus connecting up directly with political activity, the whole game of the dialogue will be to show how he proposes a game with a different form from that of the political game. He will propose a type of discourse and veridiction which are not political discourse and political veridiction, and he will get the politicians to enter into this other thing. This is the second reason why the *Laches* seems to me to be interesting and important.

The third reason is, of course, that the theme of courage runs through the whole of this dialogue, since the dialogue's theme is the attempt to define the nature of courage, in order, as it were, to tell the truth of courage. But the theme of courage is not just the object of the dialogue; it is also the hallmark of its different characters. Laches, a military leader, especially, and Nicias, both a political and a military leader, are courageous men. And Socrates moreover—this will be repeated, recalled on at least two occasions—had also been a soldier and had demonstrated his physical courage in battle, in war. But even more, each of these men, who have been courageous on the battlefield, and in civil and military life in defense of the city, also display courage in the dialogue. There is courage, we will see, in admitting some awkward things, the courage of the two generals, the two politicians, Laches and Nicias, in answering Socrates' questions, and there is also Socrates' courage in confronting such important men in the city. So that courage is present as the theme of the dialogue; it is present as civic token, as it were, of the worth of the different characters; and it is also the rule of the moral game within the dialogue in which everything revolves around this question of courage: what is the truth of courage for these men who are truly courageous? But in order to pose this question, in order to confront it properly, one must have the courage of the dialectic. So the intertwining of the themes of courage and truth—the problem of the courage of truth, posed by truly courageous men, who have the courage to confront the question of truth, and of the truth of courage—is at the heart of the dialogue. And it is evident that once I had chosen this theme of the courage of truth as my topic for this year, it was rather difficult not to refer to this text, one of the very few in the whole of Western philosophy to pose the question of courage, and especially of the courage of truth. What is the ethical relationship between courage and truth? Or, to what extent do the ethics of truth entail courage?

The theme of the ethics of truth [...*], the question of the moral conditions which enable a subject to have access to the truth and to speak the truth is, of course, frequently found elsewhere, but we can say that it is central in the construction of this dialogue. We usually

---

* The beginning of the sentence is inaudible.

find the question of the ethics of truth in the form of the question of the subject's purity or purification, and Western reflection devotes most space to the question in this form. From the Pythagoreans to modern philosophy, there is a whole cathartics of truth.[5] This is the idea that to have access to the truth the subject must constitute himself in some kind of break with the sensory world, the world of error, interest, and pleasure, with the whole world which, in relation to the eternity of truth and its purity, constitutes the universe of the impure. The transition for the impure to the pure,* from the obscure to the transparent, and from the transitory and fleeting to the eternal constitutes, or at any rate marks the moral trajectory through which the subject can be formed as a subject capable of truth (of seeing and speaking the truth). All this cathartics is found in the Pythagoreans and still in modern philosophy. Because the Cartesian approach is, after all, a cathartic approach: on what conditions will the subject be able to constitute itself as pure gaze, independent of any private interest, and capable of universality in the possession of the cathartic truth?[6] But the cathartic (the subject's purification as condition of being able to be subject of truth) is only one aspect [of the ethics of truth]. There is another aspect which is that of the courage of truth: what type of resolution, what type of will, what type of not only sacrifice but battle is one able to face in order to arrive at the truth? This struggle for the truth is different from the purification by which one can arrive at the truth. It is no longer the analysis of purification for the truth, but the analysis of the will to truth in its different forms, which may be those of curiosity, battle, courage, resolution, and endurance. Anyway, I think we could find in Plato's text, the *Laches*, one of the elements, one of the starting points for the analysis of this aspect of the ethics of truth.

Finally, my last reason for wanting to dwell a little on the *Laches* is that we see marked out in it the starting point for one of the lines of development of Western philosophy. You remember that last year, or two years ago, we looked at the *Alcibiades* together.[7] The *Alcibiades* is in many respects, at least in some of its themes, quite close to what can be found in the *Laches*. The *Alcibiades* also deals with the training of a young man. As will be the case in the *Laches*, it concerns a

---

* [The French has "from the pure to the impure (*du pur à l'impur*)" which must be a slip; G.B.]

training which has become all the more necessary by the fact that the young man's parents or tutors were unable to provide him with it. In both the *Alcibiades* and the *Laches* it is the relation between education and neglect that founds the principle of care. One must care about the education of young people: all of this is found in the *Alcibiades* and the *Laches*. Only, in the *Alcibiades* this theme of education/neglect/care leads fairly quickly to a classic problem, which is: what is it we must take care of? And you remember that the answer given in the *Alcibiades* is: we must take care of the soul.[8] And then the question arises: what is the soul? What is its nature? In what does taking care of the soul consist? We found here the principle that taking care of the soul is, for the soul, to contemplate itself and, in doing so, to recognize the divine element which is precisely what enables it to see the truth. Hence, in a way, the theme of *epimeleia* quickly and directly led on to the principle of the soul's existence and the possibility and necessity for the soul to contemplate itself, and finally it led to the theme of the divine nature of the soul, or at any rate of the divine element in the soul. And in this sense the *Alcibiades*—you remember the historical problem of the dialogue was raised[9]—brings together fairly quickly the themes of Plato's early dialogues (like the training [...*]), those of the later dialogues, and even Neo-Platonist themes.

In the *Laches*, on the other hand, from a fairly similar starting point, from a [similar]† question about the training of young people, the neglect of their education, and the need to be concerned about them, the dialogue follows a completely different line of development. And in one sense, it never ends up at the point to which the *Alcibiades* leads so quickly. That is to say, the question of what exactly it is that one must take care of is never raised in the *Laches*. The theme is: we must take care of young people, teaching them to take care of themselves. But it is not said what this themselves that they must take care of is exactly. Or rather, it is not said, and yet it is. But precisely it is not said by designating the soul as the immortal reality to which one must turn one's attention and which must be the first and last objective of the care of self. As the dialogue progresses, what is designated as the object one

---

* Some words are inaudible here.
† M.F.: closely related form

must take care of is not the soul, it is life (*bios*), that is to say the way of living. What constitutes the fundamental object of *epimeleia* is this modality, this practice of existence.

When we compare the *Laches* and the *Alcibiades*, we have the starting point for two great lines of development of philosophical reflection and practice: on the one hand, philosophy as that which, by prompting and encouraging men to take care of themselves, leads them to the metaphysical reality of the soul, and, on the other, philosophy as a test of life, a test of existence, and the elaboration of a particular kind of form and modality of life. Of course, there is no incompatibility between these two themes of philosophy as test of life and philosophy as knowledge of the soul. However, although there is no incompatibility, and although in Plato, in particular, the two things are profoundly linked, I think nevertheless that we have here the starting point of two aspects, two profiles, as it were, of philosophical activity, of philosophical practice in the West. On the one hand, a philosophy whose dominant theme is knowledge of the soul and which from this knowledge produces an ontology of the self. And then, on the other hand, a philosophy as test of life, of *bios*, which is the ethical material and object of an art of oneself. These two major profiles of Platonic philosophy, of Greek philosophy, of Western philosophy, are fairly easily decipherable when we compare the dialogues of the *Laches* and the *Alcibiades* with each other.

Here again, a brief comment before getting into this dialogue. Last year[10] I spoke to you about Patočka's book, which has just been translated into French. Patočka was a Czech philosopher who died five years ago,[11] and whose seminar has been published in France with the title *Plato and Europe*.[12] It is a very interesting text because it is, I believe, the only one, among modern books of the history of philosophy at any rate, to give a very important place to the notion of *epimeleia*, of care, in Plato. He sees Western metaphysics, and consequently the destiny of European rationality, as being rooted in this notion of care [...*]. I recommend this book to you. The only point on which I part from him, while recognizing how interesting his book is as an analysis of *epimeleia* and care, is that basically he does not envisage *epimeleia* as care of self,

---

* The end of the sentence is barely audible. Only "generally Husserlian" can be heard.

but as care of the soul. That is to say, it seems to me that he envisages this theme only in the form, in the direction, and from the point of view of the knowledge and ontology of the soul. Everything, on the other hand, belonging to the notion and theme of the care of self as test, questioning, examination, and checking of life (*bios*) disappears in his analysis. And it is precisely this side that I would like to [highlight] starting from the *Laches*, a text in which *bios*, much more than the soul, appears very clearly as the object of care. And this theme of *bios* as object of care [seems] to me to be the starting point for a whole philosophical practice and activity, of which Cynicism is, of course, the first example.

So, the *Laches* as starting point for this question of the care of self, as test of life, and not as knowledge of the soul. I will take three moments in this dialogue, three particular texts which will enable us to pick out precisely what the relationship between frankness (*parrhēsia*, free-spokenness), examination, and care may be. The first passage is right at the start, the setting up of the dialogue. This is what could be called the pact of frankness. The second passage I will try to analyze is towards the end of the first third of the text: this is the definition and acceptance of Socratic examination (*exetasis*). And finally the third moment is right at the end of the text, at the conclusion, when we see the interplay between the problem of the need for, the search for the teacher and the imperative of the care of self.

First, then, at the start of the text, the first line of the page: the pact of frankness. Right at the start, and even before Socrates has been invited to take part, we see four characters. The first is called Lysimachus and the second Melesias. Melesias hardly says anything and keeps a low profile. These first two, Lysimachus and Melesias, are the characters who spark off the dialogue, as it were, who prompt it, give rise to it, and organize it, precisely because they have a question to put and they would like an answer: they try to organize a dialogue in order to get an answer to their question. And in the dialogue they are the ones who from time to time get the discussion going again. And finally, when the discussion has ended and despite the fact that, apparently at least, it has been inconclusive, it is they who resolve to do what is called for. We can say, if you like, that these two, Lysimachus and Melesias, are the dialogue's sponsors.

The real partners of the dialogue will be two other characters, Nicias and Laches. Nicias is a political leader who was very important in Athenian life at the end of the fifth century, and Laches [is a] general. They are the ones who are asked to give their opinion, and Lysimachus and Melesias give them the task of discussing such a serious question. In this presentation of the first four characters we see straightaway and very clearly how the notion of *parrhēsia*, of free-spokenness, and the notion of care are joined together. I will read you all the beginning: "LYSIMACHUS: You have seen this armed athlete fighting, Nicias and Laches. Melesias and I have not told you why we asked you to observe this exhibition: we will now give you our reason, for we think we should be frank with you (*ge humas parrhēsiazesthai*). There are people who ridicule these displays but who, if you ask them what they think, hide their thoughts and, out of consideration for the person they are talking to, do not say what they think. But we reckon you are good judges in the matter, your opinion fully developed, and you will be frank enough to let us know what it is [*haplōs eipein*: you will be able to speak, directly, frankly, simply enough in order to make it known to us; M.F.]. That is why we appeal to you to give your views on the question we are going to put to you. This," he says, "is what this preamble is leading to."[13]

So, Lysimachus and Melesias have taken their two friends, Laches and Nicias, to an exhibition. What is this exhibition? It is a display by a teacher of armed combat—whose name, we learn later is Stesilaus—who shows those present, the spectators, what he can do. First of all, the fact that this is an exhibition is not at all a matter of indifference in all this business. The master of armed combat here (Stesilaus) does not confine himself in fact to explaining verbally what he can do. We find this bragging in some Sophists who appear in other dialogues. Hippias, for example, explains verbally what he can do, although he is no doubt unable to carry out everything he boasts of.[14] Anyway, here we have someone who presents himself as a teacher, as a sort of Sophist more specialized in arms drill, and he demonstrates what in fact he can do. He puts himself to the test. And it is this test that Lysimachus and Melesias, Laches and Nicias watch; they witness it. In this way they are not in danger of being taken in by the flattery of persuasive rhetoric; they will be able to appraise and judge with their own eyes. And the dialogue will recall what Stesilaus can do several times. We have witnesses, eye-witnesses of this. You can see that already we are in a dimension which is not one of verbal presentation, of the ability to present verbally what one is supposed to be able to do; we are in the domain of the test, but of the direct, visual test.

Second, [there is] also what took place, which Lysimachus recalls. Not only did they [go to] see this exhibition with their own eyes in order to test it, and in which the master of armed combat tested himself, but Lysimachus and Melesias were careful not to tell Laches and Nicias why they had taken them, so that the test would be pure and clear cut. They brought Nicias and Laches before the exhibition itself, before the thing itself. And they did not tell them why they had invited them, so that, in actual fact, Nicias and Laches can, without prejudice as it were, accurately evaluate what Stesilaus was doing.

Third, the text shows that yet another precaution was taken. Lysimachus and Melesias chose to take these two men to this exhibition without saying why because Laches and Nicias are, on the one hand, conversant with this topic (they are in fact military leaders, people who have exercised military responsibilities), and, on the other, they are not the kind of people to hide what they think.[15] And while it is true that some people are the kind who laugh at what they see but then lack the courage to say all the bad things they are thinking, Nicias and Laches, after seeing the demonstration, without prejudice, and without even knowing why they have been taken to see it, will have enough character to say what they think without any disguise.

You see therefore the series of precautions taken to set up the conditions, the zone of truth-telling. A well-protected, guaranteed site for the emergence of truth was needed. And whatever might be deceitful in discourse had to be kept away from this site of truth, of the emergence of truth. So, we will see the thing itself. The spectators are silent and Lysimachus puts the question frankly to Nicias and Laches, from whom a frank answer is expected. *Parrhēsia* is in fact the keynote of the dialogue, which will take place thanks to these precautions. What is the object, the raison d'être of all these precautions? Why is it so important that *parrhēsia* operates here, in the [new] question which will be put? [It is because] this question, which is so weighty that one must carefully set out this zone of *parrhēsia*, is that of the care to be given to children and of how one is to take care of them. In fact, Lysimachus explains to Laches and Nicias, you have sons and have no doubt taken care of them. Either you have taken care of them [and] have therefore thought about what is best for them, or you have not been concerned about your sons, in which case it is high time that you were.[16] At any rate, you certainly have something to say about how to take care of children. In any case, [it is a matter] of answering this question: Should we, Lysimachus and Melesias—and possibly you, Nicias and Laches— really entrust our sons to this master of armed combat whose trials and exercises we have just seen directly? Is the teaching they can get from him and that he can give them worthwhile?

Lysimachus and Melesias put this question. But as soon as they have asked it they add a particular reason for having done so. They give the reason why, on the one hand, they are so greatly concerned about their children's education, and why, being concerned about it, they turn to Nicias and Laches as undoubtedly more competent than themselves. Why? Well, Lysimachus says, on behalf of himself and Melesias, the rea- son we are worried about our children and ask your advice about their education is this: when we, Melesias and I, look at our own lives, we realize that we have not done anything good or outstanding. Certainly, we belong to important families, our ancestors had great fame, and our fathers were destined for great things in the city.[17] But it has to be acknowledged that ultimately we have led insignificant and rather mediocre lives without any of those glorious feats which are precisely what might authorize us to advise our children on how they should conduct themselves. In any case, we are not that type of example that children may and should have before their eyes so as to develop their own character and establish their own existence. Our ancestors, they say, may indeed have been important and played a major role in the city, but we have not done so. And Lysimachus immediately adds: But in fact, if we really have led such insignificant lives, is this not precisely because our ancestors, our fathers, attended to the affairs of others? They were so absorbed in the city's affairs, so concerned to deal with *ta tōn allōn pragmata* (the affairs of others)[18] that they could not but neglect us. And it is because we were neglected in our childhood, because no one took care of us, that we have led unremarkable lives.

This neglect of Melesias and Lysimachus when they were children, which was due to the political success of their parents, explains both why Lysimachus and Melesias are so anxious for their own children not to be neglected, and also why they, who are such insignificant and dull examples for their children, turn to the outstanding men, Nicias and Laches, who certainly have things to say about the education of children.*

Now when they have given this explanation concerning *epimeleia* (the word occurs in these passages at least half a dozen times), after having explained why they are so concerned about the care to give their children, they point out that they do not say this without some feeling of shame.[19] For it is not pleasant to confess to Nicias and Laches that their lives' lack of brilliance embarrasses them and makes them particularly concerned about the care to be given to their children. They are thus obliged to give this explanation of their own concern. They are obliged to give them this explanation overcoming their own shame and embarrassment. And to what do they have to resort in order to do this? Well, to *parrhēsia* (to frankness, free-spokenness). This is what Lysimachus says: "It is worth recounting how this idea came to us [of turning to you for advice on the education of our children; M.F.], though it's a bit of a long story... As I was just saying to you, I will be frank. So, each of us finds some fine actions in his father's life that he can recount to young people, actions performed in war and peace, actions concerning the city's affairs; but we two personally have nothing to tell. We are somewhat ashamed before our sons and we reproach our fathers, who gave us a free rein in our youth."[20] You see that the themes of *epimeleia*, of the care one must have for children, and *parrhēsia* are directly linked. They are obliged to call on *parrhēsia*, on their courage to tell the truth, in order to pose the question of the

---

* In the manuscript, finding in ancient morality, on the one hand, a tension "between the care of others in the political form, which seems to make the ethical care of self and others so difficult, and the ethical care of self and others which is so often called upon to lead to the political care as to its raison d'être and accomplishment or as to one of its essential duties," and, on the other hand, a relation of exclusion between "doing what one wants" and "taking care of oneself," Foucault writes:

"An important point in the history of ancient morality is this interplay between the need for direction by which the master or father governs the soul and conduct of others, and the principle of an autonomy and sovereignty of self over self which is the crowning achievement of this effort and work, of this *askēsis* through which one takes care of oneself by oneself."

care of children, since they themselves were neglected and are unable to provide any examples [...*].

That is what I wanted to say about these first lines of the dialogue. I would like now to move on to the more important part of the dialogue, that is to say, the definition of Socratic examination. After Melesias' and Lysimachus' invitation, Nicias and Laches reply favorably to the request. They will give their views on the display they have witnessed; the kind of show or exhibition Stesilaus has given of his abilities as teacher of the art of armed combat. First Nicias, and then Laches give their views. And what needs to be stressed is that this confrontation of the opinions of Nicias and Laches on the teacher of armed combat takes exactly the same form as a political discussion. We are dealing with a sort of *analogon* of the political arena, of an assembly in which the two partners develop their own opinions in turn in a continuous discourse. On the one hand, Nicias finds the teacher's lessons useful. They are useful because they provide good practice for fighting. They are good exercises also inasmuch as they can initiate young people into the art of fighting and ultimately into the whole system of strategy. This is good practice also because it can develop the moral qualities of courage and boldness in the young people who will have to defend their homeland. These exercises are even able to develop physical qualities, not only of strength and endurance, but also a kind of beauty of posture and action, which Nicias says is also important.[21] Laches' discourse, on the other hand, criticizes the exercises [...†]. They only demonstrate the teacher's abilities in precisely those cities where there are scarcely any well trained soldiers.[22] And then, the second reason—and this is very important in contrast with Socrates, as we will see shortly—as a general, Laches has seen how this teacher of the art of fighting conducted himself in battle. He had shown himself to be both not very courageous and above all very clumsy, so that the fighters were doubled up with laughter when they saw how he was unable to put his own lessons into practice.[23] Nicias' discourse and Laches' discourse continue and oppose each other, just as in political sparring or a physical confrontation.

---

* The end of the sentence is inaudible.
† A completely inaudible passage. At the end of the sentence "... their qualities" can be heard.

It is then, after the confrontation of these two speeches and the resulting impasse, that Socrates, already present but silent, is appealed to. As always in dialogues of this kind, Socrates' intervention signals not only a recapitulation of the theme in a different form, but in fact a completely different way of proceeding in the discussion. What transformations does Socrates' intervention bring about? There are three. The simplest is carried out first of all with the least difficulty. It is, as it were, the transition from the political to what could be called the technical model of discussion. We have seen that the political model of discussion is two characters coming forward, one after the other, as if they were taking the floor, to support their theses. That it is this political-judicial model which has been at work until now is very clearly indicated by Lysimachus when we arrive at the impasse. After hearing both Nicias and Laches, Lysimachus says: It is quite clear that there is a divergence, a disagreement in your *boulē* (in your Council: referring to the city's institutions).[24] Nicias and Laches, he says, have given opposite opinions. We must therefore ask Socrates—who is present but has kept quiet until now—who he will vote for (*sumpsēphos*; *psēphos* is the stone, the ballot). So, Lysimachus asks Socrates: Who will you vote for? You can see that all of this refers to the political model. Now—replying to Lysimachus' question: Who gets your vote?—Socrates straightaway explicitly rejects this model, saying: Can the law of the majority, of the greatest number really be applied here? What is actually involved? It is a question—and he employs the word—of *tekhnē*?[25] It is a question of *tekhnē*, and consequently what should prevail is not the greatest number, [but] technique. What kind of technique? Well, precisely what we are looking for is, he says—and we should absolutely hold on to the word—a *teknikos peri psukhēs therapeian* (a technician of the care, of the "therapy," of the soul*).[26]

Now how can we know if someone is competent in the field of *tekhnē* in general, and actually in the field of *this* "*tekhnē*"? It is clear that if we speak as a simple voter [it's enough] for someone to cast their vote for or against an opinion. When what is involved is a problem of *tekhnē*,

---

* The French editor has inserted "[plutôt que]" so that the phrase in brackets reads "(a technician of the care, [rather than] of the 'therapy,' of the soul)," but there do not appear to be any grounds for the addition of these words.

rather than the political arena or political themes, then two criteria must be met for a useful and effective approach to someone. First, we will acknowledge someone as competent in the field of *tekhnē* if we know who taught him, and if these teachers were good and able to train good students. The question of the teacher is the first criterion. And the second could be called the criterion of works. Has the person who claims to be competent and wants to give his views, or the person to whom we turn as someone competent, had only good teachers, and above all, has he been able to do something, and something worthwhile? (We may even accept that he has been able to do something worthwhile without a teacher.)[27] In any case, these are the two necessary criteria. These two criteria, either together or one without the other, are indispensable when we are considering someone's opinion in the field of *tekhnē*.

So, we can bid farewell to the political arena and its procedures, in which two opinions are opposed on every point and voting decides between them according to the law of the greatest number. We can appeal to something else, which is the criterion of competence resting on the two poles of the teacher's quality, on the one hand, and the quality of works, on the other. This becomes apparent when Socrates says: "Likewise, Laches and Nicias, since Lysimachus and Melesias ask for your advice on how to make the souls of their sons as perfect as possible, if we claim to have learned this art we must tell them what teachers we have had, and prove that these teachers, praiseworthy men, have skillfully treated young people before passing on their teaching to us. If any of us claim not to have had a teacher [a perfectly legitimate possibility; M.F.], but can at least show us his works, he must tell us what individuals, Athenians or foreigners, slaves or free men, have become men who are recognized as being praiseworthy thanks to him. If we cannot do this, let us ask our friends to address themselves to others and not expose us to the risk of incurring the gravest responsibility of having corrupted their sons."[28] You can see that we have passed from a political type of veridiction (the scene of an Assembly, a Council, a *boulē*, with conflicting opinions and a vote) to something else. This other scene is that of technical veridiction, which I have spoken to you about and which you can see is well defined here as we saw it was last week: it basically rests on the traditional character of a knowledge handed down from teacher to disciple and manifesting itself [in works]. The veridiction of technique, of teaching, is authorized by this double relation to expertise and works.

But—and here we will see a second transformation—Socrates avoids the issue. Just when he has established the technical, as opposed to the political scene, just when we think that, since it is a question of the technique of the soul, we are now coming to the question of Socrates' teachers and Socrates' works, he avoids the question and says: But as for myself, I have never had a teacher because I could not afford to pay for one [...*]. I was too poor.[29] And I don't have the ability to teach others. So, you should not turn to me if you are really looking for someone skilled who can tell you how to raise your children.

And straightaway he suggests turning the question of competence back to Nicias and Laches. In fact, he says, these are people who are wealthy enough to get teachers. And anyway, they have lived long enough and experienced enough to know what they could teach young people.[30] So we are now in a completely different scene. It is no longer the political, but the technical scene, with the same characters reappearing, thanks to Socrates' ploy which has shifted the scene, but from which he has exempted himself as interlocutor. Again we find Nicias and Laches, we turn to them, and we ask them to speak. Only Socrates has put a hitch in the new scene he has just established. He has introduced a hitch in this [technical] question in which Nicias and Laches are, as it were, put back on the stage. The hitch is this. He says: Since it is now a question of competence, and since Nicias and Laches are to speak as experts, they still have to demonstrate and give evidence of their competence before we ask them for their views. What qualifies them to speak on the question we put to them? We will therefore have to question them on who their teachers were, how they learned what they know, and what their works have been in this domain.[31] Consequently Socrates proposes not only a change of scene from the political to the technical, but a shift, a transformation of the procedure. Laches and Nicias are not simply invited to give their opinion because they are qualified. They are invited and pressured into playing a game in which they will have to reply to questions. They will be questioned on what qualifies them to speak on this technical question of the art

---

* The end of the sentence is inaudible.

of *psukhēs therapeia* (the care of the soul). Lysimachus, as sponsor of the dialogue, accepts this form of questioning proposed by Socrates. He accepts, in fact, Socrates' proposal to change the procedure. And he makes the following proposal to Nicias and Laches: "It seems to me, Nicias and Laches, that Socrates is right. It is up to you to decide if you are agreeable to being questioned and answering. Obviously Melesias and I will be delighted to hear you give your views in answer to Socrates' questions. Because, just as I said at the start, if we have asked you to give us your views it is because we think that you must have thought about this problem, especially because, like us, you have sons who are of an age when they are completing their education. So, if you have no objection, say you will engage in this search with Socrates, asking and answering each other's questions; for as Socrates says, for us this is the most serious question. See then if this project is agreeable to you."[32] So you see: there is a shift from the political to the technical scene, and within the latter a return to Nicias and Laches, but now in the position of people who are going to be questioned.

And it is here that the third change is situated, a change which introduces and marks the emergence of the specifically Socratic game and Socratic *parrhēsia* in the form which I will try to show you shortly. He has therefore transformed the political model into a reference to technique and competence. Second, with regard to this question of competence, he has proposed and got agreement to the rule that these two partners in the discussion will not make direct use of their competence but will first of all be invited to give an account of it by answering the questions Socrates will put to them. Only here we now come to a third transformation, which is the most important. Actually, in proposing this reference to technique and this procedure of questioning, Socrates looks like he is merely drawing his two partners into the domain of technique and so of inviting them to point out their place, as it were, their role, or their game in the passing on of knowledge by the teacher. And when he seems simply to be asking for their qualifications for passing on expertise and knowledge, he is basically devising something completely different. And under the pretext of questioning them about the teachers who can authenticate their competence and their views, he will impose a completely different game on them, one which is neither that of politics, of course, nor even that of technique, [but] which will be the game of *parrhēsia* and ethics, the game of *parrhēsia* oriented towards the problem of *ēthos*. First: how does this Socratic game emerge in the dialogue, that is to say, how is it discovered and accepted by the partners? Second: how is this game described and defined, and in what does it consist? And third: what authorizes Socrates to perform this role of ethical *parrhēsia*?

1. P. Chantraine, *Dictionnaire étymologique de la langue grecque* (Paris: Klincksieck, 1983) p. 683. With regard to this hypothesis of a link, Chantraine says "very doubtful."
2. A. Hatzfeld and A. Darmesteter, *Dictionnaire général de la langue française du commencement du XVIIe siècle jusqu' à nos jours* (Paris: Delagrave, 1964).
3. The full title is: *"The black monk in gray within Varennes." A Nostradamic satirical allegory followed by a Divertissement on Socrates' last words.* The English translation gives a simpler title: *The Riddle of Nostradamus. A Critical Dialogue.*
4. Platon, *Apologie*, 21c-21e and 30a-b, pp. 145-146 and p. 157; Plato, *Socrates' Defense (Apology)*, pp. 7-8 and p. 16.
5. On this point, see the lectures of 6 January 1982, *L'Herméneutique du sujet*, pp. 15-20 and 29-31; *The Hermeneutics of the Subject*, pp. 14-19 and 27-29.
6. In 1982 Foucault spoke of the "Cartesian moment" (distinct from Descartes himself) as escaping the cathartic logic of spirituality (access to truth requires a transformation of the subject). See ibid., Fr. p. 19; Eng. p. 18.
7. See the lectures of 6 and 13 January 1982 in *L'Herméneutique du sujet*; *The Hermeneutics of the Subject*.
8. See, ibid., Fr. pp. 50-57; Eng. pp. 51-58.
9. See, ibid., Fr. pp. 71-72; Eng. pp. 72-74.
10. Foucault did not refer to this book in his 1983 lectures. His first mention of the book is in the lecture of 8 February, 1984, second hour, above p. 65.
11. He died in fact in 1977.
12. J. Patočka, *Platon et l'Europe*, trans. A. Abrams (Paris: Verdier, 1983); Jan Patočka, *Plato and Europe*, trans. Petr Lom (Stanford: Stanford University Press, 2002).
13. Platon, *Lachès*, 178b, p. 90; Plato, *Laches*, p. 124: "LYSIMACHUS: You have seen the exhibition of the man fighting in armor, Nicias and Laches, but we did not tell you at the time the reason why my friend Melesias and I asked you to go with us and see him. I think that we may as well confess what this was, for we certainly ought not to have any reserve with you. Some laugh at the very notion of consulting others, and when they are asked will not say what they think. They guess at the wishes of the person who asks them, and answer according to his, and not according to their own, opinion. But as we know that you are good judges, and will say exactly what you think, we have taken you into our counsels. The matter about which I am making all this preface is as follows."
14. See the beginning of the dialogue, *Greater Hippias*.
15. *Lachès*, 178b, p. 90; *Laches*, p. 124.
16. Ibid., 179b, Fr. p. 91; Eng. p. 124.
17. Lysimachus was the son of the "great Aristides" and Melesias was the son of Thucydides, "not the historian, but one of the main leaders of the aristocratic party in the middle of the fifth century" (note to the *Lachès*, French edition, p. 85).
18. *Lachès*, 179d, p. 91: "We reproach our fathers, who gave us a free rein in our youth, concerned as they were with the affairs of others *(ta de tōn allōn pragmata)*"; *Laches*, p. 124: "we blame our fathers for letting us be spoiled in the days of our youth, while they were occupied with the concerns of others."
19. Ibid., 179c, Fr. p. 92; Eng. p. 124.
20. Ibid.; Eng.: "I will tell you, Nicias and Laches, even at the risk of being tedious, how we came to think of this... And now, as I was saying at first, we are going to be open with you. Both of us often talk to the noble deeds which our own fathers did in war and peace—in managing the affairs of the allies, and those of the city—but neither of us has any deeds of his own which he can show. The truth is we are ashamed of this contrast being seen by them, and we blame our fathers for letting us be spoiled in the days of our youth."
21. Ibid., 181e-182d, Fr. pp. 94-95; Eng. pp. 126-127.
22. Ibid., 183b, Fr. p. 96; Eng. p. 127.
23. Ibid., 184a, Fr. p. 96; Eng. p. 128.
24. Ibid., 184c-d, Fr. p. 98: "It seems to me that our Council *(boulē)* still needs an arbitrator to decide between them... It would be good if you were to tell us to which of the two you give your vote *(sumpsēphos)*"; Eng. p. 128: "because the two counselors disagree, and someone is

in a manner still needed who will decide between them... I should like to hear with which of our two friends you agree."

25. Ibid., 185a, Fr. p. 98; Eng. p. 129.
26. Ibid., 185e, Fr. p. 100; Eng. p. 130.
27. Ibid., 185a-186a, Fr. p. 100; Eng. pp. 129-130.
28. Ibid., 186a-b, Fr. pp. 100-101; Eng. p. 130: "And therefore, Laches and Nicias, as Lysimachus and Melesias, in their anxiety to improve the minds of their sons, have asked our advice about them, we likewise should tell them, if we can, what teachers we know who were in the first place men of merit and experienced trainers of the minds of youth, and then taught also ourselves. Or if any of us says that he has had no teacher but that he has works of his own to show, then he should point out to them what Athenians or strangers, bond or free, he is generally acknowledged to have improved. But if we can show neither teachers nor works, then we should tell them to look for other advisers; we should not run the risk of spoiling the children of friends, and thereby incurring the most formidable accusation which can be brought against anyone by those nearest to him."
29. Ibid., 186c, Fr. p. 101; Eng. p. 130.
30. Ibid., 196c, Fr. p. 101; Eng. p. 130.
31. Ibid., 186e-187d, Fr. p. 101; Eng. pp. 130-131.
32. Ibid., 187c-d, Fr. p. 102; Eng. p. 131: "I very much approve of the words of Socrates, my friends, but you, Nicias and Laches, must determine whether you will be questioned, and give an explanation about matters of this sort. Assuredly, Melesias and I would be greatly pleased to hear you answer the questions which Socrates asks, if you will, for I began by saying that we took you into our counsels because we thought that no doubt you had attended to the subject, especially as you have children who, like our own, are nearly of an age to be educated. Well then, if you have no objection, suppose that you take Socrates into partnership, and do you and he ask and answer one another's questions, for, as he has well said, we are deliberating about the most important of our concerns. I hope that you will see fit to comply with our request."

eight

22 FEBRUARY 1984

Second hour*

[
Socrates and the complete and continuous examination of oneself. ⌒ Bios *as object of Socratic* parrhēsia. ⌒ *The symphony of discourse and action.* ⌒ *Conclusions of the dialogue: final submission to the* logos.
]

FIRST QUESTION: HOW IS this game revealed and accepted? You know that in some of Plato's dialogues it is almost a general rule that at a certain point Socrates' method is presented, outlined, and defined in some of its characteristics, so that the game is never invisible to the reader or unknown to the participants or those who are induced to play it. They are always told something about this game, but, [on the one hand], this description of the Socratic game is very often given by Socrates himself, and not by those who will be, as it were, partners and victims in this game; and on the other hand, the interlocutors frequently, if not always, resist when they become aware of the game into which they have been drawn. At any rate, as you well know, this is what happens with characters like Protagoras, Gorgias, Callicles, and Thrasymachus.[1]

Here, however, we have something very interesting. First of all, at least one of the partners in the discussion is fully aware of who Socrates

---

* We have introduced an artificial break here. It seems that exceptionally there was no break between the first and second hours on this occasion.

is, what he does, and what is special about him. Secondly, not only does he know about Socrates, and agree to his game, [but] the other, Laches, who does not know him, also agrees and enters readily and willingly into the parrhesiastic game which is about to take place. This acceptance of the parrhesiastic game by those who will be its partners, its targets, and to a certain extent its happy and consenting victims is very clearly indicated at the point at which Socrates intervenes. Socrates actually says, and gets it agreed, that he will ask questions to which the others will have to reply. We still think that we are in the domain of competence [and] that Socrates will say: Who are your teachers, or anyway, how were you trained in courage and what works of military ability can authenticate your contribution and the views you give? But just after Socrates has proposed this [...*], Nicias intervenes and says: Don't think that this is how things will proceed. I know Socrates and I know perfectly well what he will do. I am well aware of what happens when "one belongs to the intimate group and usual company of those who discourse with Socrates."[2] He immediately says that he agrees to the game, that he is used to it, and that he enjoys being in Socrates' group.[3] In the event, today, he says: "I am not opposed to Socrates discussing with us in the way he likes."[4] To this prior undertaking by Nicias, based on his knowledge of Socrates and the benevolence and friendship he feels for him, his familiarity with him, Laches adds his own agreement. He does not know Socrates well and he is not at all accustomed to his mode of discoursing, but in the end he agrees, for reasons which we shall see shortly, to all the questions Socrates would like to put to him [and] any possible changes he may impose on the dialogue. And if, unlike Nicias, he does not know exactly how things will proceed, he agrees resolutely to the experiment: "he has my good will," "yes, I consent (*touto gar moi sugkhōreito*),"[5] [and] a bit later: "I invite you [Socrates] to teach me."[6] He ends this intervention, prior to the discussion, by saying: "So speak freely [*leg'oun ho ti soi philon*: speak, say what you like; M.F.] without consideration for my age."[7] We have here the parrhesiastic pact *par excellence*. One will speak frankly, freely, saying all that he has to say in the form that he likes. As for the others, they will not [react], as is so often the case in the political domain or

---

* Inaudible passage.

before someone speaking frankly, by getting annoyed, taking offense, becoming angry, and possibly even punishing the person thought to be abusing the use of *parrhēsia*. There is none of this. Here there is a good, wholly positive game of *parrhēsia* in which Socrates' courage will be repaid with the courage of those who accept his *parrhēsia*. The pact is sealed, full, and I would say it is never revoked. We are dealing with the propitious form of *parrhēsia*.

Second question: now that we know that the two main interlocutors are agreed, what will happen? And what game—to which Nicias agrees because he is familiar with it, and to which Laches, with his courage, also agrees—will Socrates play? It is, of course, Nicias, as someone who knows Socrates, who will set out this parrhesiastic game. This is what he says to Lysimachus: "Because it seems to me that you do not know that if you belong to the intimate group and usual company of those who discourse with Socrates, whatever the subject you start with, you are forced to let yourself be drawn by the discussion into giving an account of yourself, of the kind of life you lead now and have led in the past. And when you have reached this point, Socrates will not let you go before he has well and truly sifted everything. I am used to this character and know that one cannot avoid being treated in this way, and I know that I will not escape now. Because I enjoy, Lysimachus, being in his company, and I find no harm in being reminded of the good or bad things I may have done or still do. I consider that by undergoing this test one becomes more prudent regarding the future, if one is willing, according to Solon's precept, to learn throughout one's life, and not think that old age of itself will bring wisdom. To be examined (*basanizesthai*) by Socrates is not new for me or unpleasant. I have known for a long time that with Socrates not only young people would be questioned, but also ourselves. So I repeat: for my part, I am not opposed to Socrates discussing with us in the way he likes."[8]

So you have the parrhesiastic pact, to which Nicias returns a number of times, and at the same time a description of what will happen. What will happen? Well—this is the hallmark of all Socratic *parrhēsia* and its veridiction—whatever subject you start with, with Socrates it is necessary (*anagkē*)[9] that things take place in the following way: Socrates won't let go until his interlocutor has been led (*periagesthai*:[10] led as by the hand, taken around) to the point where he can give an account of himself (*didonai peri hautou logon*: explain himself).[11] This quotation is obviously very important [...*]. Basically, we are still very close—apparently, if we do not look at it closely—to what was asked shortly before when, having moved from the political to the technical scene, Socrates said: It's all very well to say we are competent and to be consulted as such, but we must still be able to give an account of our competence and say who our teachers were and what works we have actually performed. It seems then that we are in court: it is still a question of giving an account of oneself. But in fact something quite different is involved and this is clearly demonstrated by the dialogue's development. In actual fact, giving an account of oneself does not involve saying who one's teacher is and what works one [has performed]. This Socratic *parrhēsia* does not consist in questioning someone on his antecedents, as it were, in the lineage of tradition which enables knowledge to be handed down, nor does it consist in questioning him, downstream as it were, on the works he has performed thanks to his expertise. He will be asked to give an account of himself, that is to say, to show the relationship between himself and *logos* (reason). How do things stand with you and *logos*, can you justify yourself, can you give the *logos* of yourself? It is not a question of competence, it is not a question of technique, it is not a question of teachers, or of works. Of what is it a question? It is a question—and the text says this a bit further on—of the way in which one lives (*hontina tropon te zē*).

Now compare this, if you like, with, on the one hand, what happened previously, and also with the *Alcibiades*. In the *Alcibiades* you had the problem: who is this "oneself" [to which one] must attend? Here one has to give an account of oneself, but who is this oneself, what domain must be covered by this "giving an account of oneself"? It is not the soul but the way in which one lives (*hontina tropon nun te zē*: how you live now and also how you have lived in the past). It is this domain of existence, of the mode of existence, of the *tropos* of life, on which Socrates' discourse and *parrhēsia* will focus. So it is neither the chain of rationality, as in technical teaching, nor the soul's ontological mode of being, but the style of life, the way of living, the very form that one gives to life.

---

* The end of the sentence is inaudible.

Second, you can see also that what is involved in this "giving an account of oneself" is not, as when just before it was a question of technique, justifying a competence which gives one authority, but of submitting one's life to what he calls a touchstone, a test, which enables one to distinguish between the good and bad one has done in life. There is the verb *basanizesthai* which derives from the word *basanos* (touchstone). This notion of sifting—of the operation by which the touchstone divides things and [enables one to] distinguish between what is and is not gold, between what is and is not good—is a very important notion in all of Socratic practice as Plato defines it. In the Gorgias, at a crucial point in the long dialogue between Socrates and Callicles, Socrates offers a sort of possible parrhesiastic pact to Callicles.[12] In this pact Socrates puts things in a way to make it seem that Callicles will be a touchstone for him, whereas, of course, the opposite will be the case. Here it is indeed the opposite, since Socrates is the *basanos* (touchstone), and by rubbing against him, through confrontation with him, one will be able to distinguish between what is and is not good in one's life. This notion of *basanos* is also employed in a political sense in Book VII of the *Republic* (537b)[13] and in the *Statesman* (308d),[14] where he says that it is important for the constitution of the city to test the people who will belong to it, to submit them to the touchstone so as to be able to distinguish those who are good from those who are bad, those who can be integrated into the city's fabric from those who must be rejected.

So we have here—this was the important element that I especially wanted to hold on to today—the emergence of life, of the mode of life as the object of Socratic *parrhēsia* and discourse, of life in relation to which it is necessary to carry out an operation which will be a test, a testing, sifting. Life must be submitted to a touchstone in order to make an exact division between what is and is not good in what one does, what one is, and how one lives. I forgot something, which is that it is not just a question of testing or forming this mode of life once and for all in one's youth, but—Nicias emphasizes this and it is very important—this principle of the test of life should be followed throughout life. This recalls, you remember, Solon's statement that one should learn throughout one's life: one should undergo this Socratic test even when old. Nicias, who is of a certain age at the time of the dialogue, agrees to undergo the Socratic test. Now, unlike technical competence, which is acquired once and for all in one's life, and can subsequently be employed, the Socratic test is something which one has to repeat and profit from throughout one's life as the organizing and formative principle of one's mode of life. You can see that what is involved here therefore is the constitution, the definition of a particular kind of parrhesiastic practice, of a particular kind of veridiction which is far removed from that of a teacher passing on technical knowledge to those he teaches. This veridiction involves establishing a particular kind of relationship to Socrates which supports the testing and examination of life throughout life.

The first question was: how was this *parrhēsia* accepted? The second: in what does it consist, to what is it related, what is its domain of application? [Answer]: the mode of life. And now the third question: what authorizes Socrates to employ a method with regard to everyone and anyone, what authorized him already to have employed it so often with Nicias, and to employ it now with Nicias and Laches? It is Laches who replies to this question. Nicias described what is involved in Socrates' *parrhēsia*, but it is Laches, who does not know Socrates however, either as a dialectician or as a man of discourse, who explains why Socrates must be given the possibility of employing his discourse in this way.

"As for discoursing," Laches says, "my case is simple, or rather double. I give the impression of sometimes loving and sometimes hating discourses. When I hear a man, who is truly a man and worthy of his words, discoursing on virtue or some knowledge, I experience profound joy contemplating the affinity and harmony in the display I am offered. In my view, such a man is the ideal musician, who is not content with the harmony of his lyre or other frivolous musical instrument, but someone who, in the reality of his life, harmonizes his words and deeds in the Dorian mode, the only truly Greek mode, and not in the Ionian, and even less the Phrygian or Lydian modes. This voice delights me, and I receive his words with such passion that I appear to everyone to be a lover of discourse. But the speechifier who does the opposite annoys me, and the more so the better he seems to speak, and this makes me appear to be an enemy of discourse. As for Socrates, I am not yet familiar with his discourse, but I think I know his actions, and from this point of view I have found him worthy of the finest language and the greatest freedom of speech (*pasēs parrhēsias*). So, if he possesses this quality, he has my good will, I will be happy to be examined by him (*exetazesthai*), and I ask for nothing better than to learn according to Solon's precept, to which I wish to add just one word: yes, I consent to learn in my old age on condition that the teacher is an honorable man[15] [again, the quotation from Solon that Nicias gave earlier; M.F.]. I ask to be allowed this, the honesty of the teacher, so that I will not be accused of being refractory if I do not like what I hear. The fact that the teacher is young, is still not well known, or that he has any other disadvantage of that kind, does not matter to me. So I invite you, Socrates, to teach me and examine me [*elegkhein*] as you like, and I, in return, will teach you what I know. My feelings for you date from the day on which you shared my danger and gave full proof of your courage. So speak freely (*leg'oun ho ti soi philon*) without consideration for my age."[16]

We should read this reply with some care. The passage tends to be interpreted somewhat hastily, ascribing to Laches more or less the following intention. Laches would have said: I agree to Socrates questioning me, he is entitled to put his questions to me concerning courage. Why? Because I have been able to establish that Socrates himself was courageous at the battle of Delium. He was alluding to this famous battle when he said: "My feelings for you date from the day on which you shared my danger":[17] this was the battle in which the Athenians were defeated and Socrates displayed particular courage. The passage is usually interpreted by saying that Laches agrees to this discussion of courage, and to reply to Socrates' questions concerning courage, because he knows that Socrates was courageous at the battle of Delium. Now this interpretation does not keep to the text. First, as you will have been able to see, the question of courage has not yet arisen at this stage of the discussion. We are still dealing with the first question, which was: Lysimachus and Melesias have children and are wondering whether they should entrust them to Stesilaus to learn armed fighting. Who could help them with this? We are still dealing with this question of the care to be given to children. The question of the nature of courage has not yet arisen; it comes in later. Second, if we look at the text we see that not only is it not yet a question of courage in general, but Laches does not even refer exactly to Socrates' courage. He does refer to what took place at the battle of Delium, but he does not employ the word that strictly signifies courage (*andreia*), which will come in later at 190d.[18] He speaks much more generally of Socrates' virtue, worth, or *arretē*. Courage is, of course, a part of virtue, but it is to this virtue, this worth in general that Laches refers.

What actually does he say in all this? I do not think he says: I agree to being questioned by Socrates about courage because Socrates was courageous. [In] the first part of the passage, replying to a question (am I someone who does or does not love discourse?), he says: I both do and do not love discourse; I don't really know much about the matter. Basically, I do not seek to divide discourses into good and bad ones in order to determine those I will welcome and those I will reject, I do not address myself so much to what discourses say as to whether or not there is harmony between what is said (the discourse itself) and the person who is saying it. When the life (*bios*) of the person speaking is in harmony with his discourse, when there is a symphony between someone's discourse and what he is, then I accept the discourse. When the relation between the way of living and the way of speaking is harmonious I accept the discourse and am *philologos* (a friend of discourse). This is precisely the case with Socrates. Laches does not say: Socrates is qualified to talk about courage because he is courageous. Much more generally, he will accept everything that Socrates says freely. He, an old general back at home, will even agree to being tested and examined by Socrates who is still a relatively young man. Why does he agree to all this? Precisely because there is this symphony, this harmony between what Socrates says, his way of saying things, and the way in which he lives. Socratic *parrhēsia* as freedom to say what he likes is marked, authenticated by the sound of Socrates' life. So we do not go from Socrates' courage (at the battle of Delium) to his qualification, his competence to talk about military courage. The line of argument goes from the harmony between Socrates' life and discourse to the practice of a true, free, and frank discourse. Free-spokenness hangs on the style of life. It is not courage in battle that authenticates the possibility of talking about courage.

This passage is rather important and significant precisely for two things in which I am interested this year. First, the link between *epimeleia* (care) and a certain modality of Socratic discourse. Socratic discourse is a discourse which can deal with men's care for themselves inasmuch as Socratic *parrhēsia* is precisely a discourse joined to and ordered by the principle "attend to yourself." When men are taking care of themselves and their children, Socrates is basically the true expert. Neither the political nor the technical form can answer to this fundamental need and care. Only Socratic concern, application, zeal, *epimeleia* is able to answer to the care of men.

[Second], what will Socratic *parrhēsia* speak about? It will not speak of competence; it will not speak of *tekhnē*. It will speak of something else: of the mode of existence, the mode of life. The mode of life appears as the essential, fundamental correlative of the practice of truth-telling. Telling the truth in the realm of the care of men is to question their mode of life, to put this mode of life to the test and define what there is in it that may be ratified and recognized as good and what on the other hand must be rejected and condemned. In this you can see the organization of the fundamental series linking care, *parrhēsia* (free-spokenness), and the ethical division between good and evil in the realm of *bios* (existence). I think we have here the sketch, the already firm outline anyway of Socratic *parrhēsia*, which is not the political *parrhēsia* I talked about last week. It is well and truly an ethical *parrhēsia*. Its privileged, essential object [is] life and the mode of life.

A word more on the end of the text. This is the third passage on which I would like to focus for a moment. I will be briefer here. Questioning Laches and Nicias, who have agreed to play this parrhesiastic game, to find out whether they can give an account (*didonai logon*) of the way in which they live, Socrates asks the question: What is courage? You are in actual fact courageous, can you give an account (give the *logos*) of your behavior, of your way of living? And Laches first of all, and then Nicias apply themselves to this. Both of them fail. Laches, who is courageous, cannot account for (give the *logos* of) his own behavior. His definition of courage fails because it is first of all too narrow, and then too broad.[19] Nicias is also put to the test. He is asked to give an account of his courage, and he cannot do it either, because he tries to account for it simply in terms of knowledge, ability, competence, and *epistemē*.[20] So there is failure. These people, who are courageous in reality and have had the courage to agree to the game of truth proposed by Socrates, have been unable to tell the truth about courage. In this sense there really is failure and the dialogue is broken off with an acknowledgement: "We have not discovered the true nature of courage," Socrates says.[21] No indeed, his partners in the discussion reply.

But at the very point at which they acknowledge their inability to solve the question asked (namely: what is courage in its truth, what is the truth of courage?), the dialogue is nevertheless not limited to this failure and its acknowledgement. Something has taken place in the dialogue which appears, I think, at the very end of the text, and prevents us from seeing a definitive impasse in all the obstacles encountered in the discussion and the effort to define the nature of courage. What has really happened and that to which the dialogue leads is not to be sought in the conclusion, but in the three conclusions, in the superimposition of these three conclusions in the dialogue.

The first is the ironical conclusion by which Socrates' two discussion partners (Nicias and Laches, eminent and courageous politicians) rule themselves out, as it were, and exempt themselves. Nicias, who is more knowledgeable than Laches, has just failed. Laches makes fun of him and sends him back to the person who was and still is Nicias' usual teacher, Damon, a music teacher who was an important figure, both a music teacher and a political adviser, even in Pericles' time. Laches laughs and says to Nicias: You should take some more lessons from Damon.[22] So there is reference to the world of *tekhnē*, of traditional mastery, in which a form of knowledge is passed on from master to disciple. Nicias, thus referred back to his teacher because he has not even been able to define courage, accepts Laches' challenge and states that he will in fact go to Damon to make good his inadequacies, since he has just discovered that he is unable to give a definition of courage.[23] The first conclusion is that he rules himself out.

The second conclusion is that when Laches and Nicias are about to leave the scene, they nevertheless give Lysimachus advice. It is in fact Laches who gives the advice. He says to him: Since neither Nicias nor I have been able to define courage, with regard to your desire to know what to do for your children, Lysimachus, the only advice I can give you is entrust them to Socrates. Why? So that he takes care of them (*tōn meirakiōn epimeleisthai*),[24] and by doing so improves them. We have here precisely the formula, you remember, which we found in the *Apology* when Socrates recalled that the mission assigned to him by the gods was to take care of the citizens of the state, and even of any man in the street, and to improve them.[25] And because this really is the divine mission he has been given, and to which he refers in the *Apology*, it would indeed be ungracious to refuse it here. He accepts it in fact, or at any rate he refuses to shirk the task which Lysimachus asks him to undertake. He says: It would be wrong to "refuse one's aid to anyone who wants to improve himself."[26]

So Socrates is about to become responsible for the education of Lysimachus' children. He is the person to whom this *epimeleia* is entrusted, this care that Lysimachus and Nicias were so concerned about at the start of the dialogue. But Socrates has no sooner said that he cannot refuse than he makes the objection, both to himself and to the others, that, basically, since he was no more able to define courage than were Nicias and Laches, then he is not really capable of taking care of others. And since it has been a general failure (no one has been able to arrive at a definition), we must now look for a teacher and, he adds, regardless of expense and without shame at returning to school.[27] We have the impression that at this point Socrates is doing the same as Nicias when the latter said: As for me, it's very simple; I have not managed to find a definition of courage so I am returning to my schoolteacher. Old as I may be, I am going to start learning again; I will go back to that scene of technical teaching and tradition. I shall speak to my teacher so that he may teach me what I need. Socrates seems to be doing this, but one phrase at least should alert us. This is when he says: Regardless of the expense, let's seek out new teachers. Given, as you know, what Socrates is always saying with regard to those teachers who charge for their lessons, it is clear that this can only be an ironic conclusion. In fact it is quite evident that the schoolteacher to whom one should turn, since one has not arrived at the definition of courage, is not one who charges, like Damon or Stesilaus. This teacher (*maître*), to whom everyone should listen since no one has arrived at the definition of courage, is of course *logos* itself, the discourse which will give access to the truth. And everyone should submit to it, young people of course, but also their parents, and Socrates as well. This is why Socrates ends one of his last interventions, just after having referred to the need to disregard the expense and to return to school, saying: You will no doubt laugh seeing me at school, but let's ignore "those mockers and take care both of ourselves and of these young people (*koinē hēmōn autōn kai tōn meikariōn epimeleian poiēsōmetha*)."[28]

Let us take care, both of ourselves and [the young people]. Taking care of self and of the children is what is in fact at the heart of the Socratic project, the aim of his parrhesiastic practice. It is clear that Socrates is thus in the same situation as the others. Since the true teacher is not the schoolteacher, but *logos*, Socrates must listen to it like the others, and he must take care of himself and of others at the same time. You see however that he inevitably occupies a privileged position. In listening to the teacher that he needs, who is the person who guides, who constantly recalls that one must take care of oneself, and that in order to do this one must listen to the *logos*, if not Socrates himself? So that Socrates rejects the role of teacher (*maître*) in the sense of a teacher of *tekhnē* who can pass on a teaching to his students. He does not want to put himself in this position and is, from this point of view, in exactly the same situation as the others. He will have to take care of himself by listening to the language of mastery (*maîtrise*) that comes from the *logos* itself. However, in this sort of equality—which is not just apparent, [but] real equality—which means that everyone in the Socratic community will have to take care of self and, if they are capable of doing so, take care of others, Socrates nevertheless occupies a position unlike [that] of the others. He is the person who guides the others towards the care of themselves, and maybe towards the possibility of taking care of others. Certainly, Socrates will put himself in the hands of the missing teacher. But at the same time, while putting himself in the hands of the missing teacher (the *logos*), he is the one who guides others on the way of the *logos*. Everyone understands this so well, it is so clearly the lesson of the dialogue, that when Socrates has just said ironically: So let's go to school and let those who will mock us laugh, Lysimachus, who organized the whole dialogue, who raised the question, and who was always in search of someone to take care of his children, says: "I like your discourse, Socrates, and, as the oldest, I want to be the most willing to study with these children. But I ask you this: come to my house tomorrow morning, without fail, to talk again about this project. For the moment, let us part."[29]

So, just after Socrates has said that, like them, he is completely ignorant, and that they all need a teacher, Lysimachus, hearing this, hears something else: he hears that Socrates, and only Socrates, is the teacher of this way leading to the true teacher. And that is why, instead of seeking out the expensive teacher Socrates had referred to ironically, Lysimachus simply says to Socrates: Come to my house then. It is the pact of *epimeleia* that now appears: You will take care of my children, and you will take care not only of them, but of me too—according to the principle evoked at the start of the dialogue when he said that one must question the way in which one lives, even when one is old, and throughout one's life.[30] One's existence, the form of one's style of existence must be constantly subject to the *basanos* (touchstone). It is as *basanos*, as the person who makes each person justify his life, all his life, and throughout his life, that Socrates is called upon for the children of Lysimachus, and for Lysimachus himself. Furthermore, Socrates accepts this mission. His last word is: I will not fail, Lysimachus, "I will come to your house tomorrow" to guide you and your children on the way of the care of self and of listening to the *logos*. I will be at your house tomorrow "if it pleases the gods."[31] This is an entirely banal and ritual expression, but nevertheless it should be understood at two levels, as is often the case with ritual expressions in Plato. We should recall that in actual fact this is, explicitly, what the god wanted. More than a formula, it is the reminder of what the god wanted when, you recall in the *Apology*, he showed Socrates that he had to go among the people and ask them to account for the way in which they live and in this way teach them to take care of themselves.

There you are. So, as promised, this week I have finished with Socrates. As a philosophy professor one really must have lectured on Socrates and the death of Socrates at least once in one's life. It's done. *Salvate animam meam.* Next week, as promised, we will talk about the Cynics.

1. Protagoras and Gorgias appear in the Platonic dialogues named after them. Callicles appears in the *Gorgias*. Thrasymachus is Socrates' interlocutor in Book I of the *Republic*. See what Foucault says about this in the lecture of 9 March, second hour, in *Le Gouvernement de soi et des autres*, p. 338; *The Government of Self and Others*, pp. 367-368.
2. *Lachès*, 187e, p. 103; *Laches*, p. 131: "anyone who is close to Socrates and enters into conversation with him."
3. Ibid., 188a, Fr. p. 103: "I enjoy, Lysimachus, being in his company"; Eng. p. 131: "for I am fond of his conversation, Lysimachus."
4. Ibid., 188c, Fr. p. 103; Eng. p. 132: "I am quite willing to discourse with Socrates in his own manner."
5. Ibid., 189a, Fr. p. 104; Eng. p. 132: "I am of one mind with him, and shall be delighted to be interrogated by a man such as he is."
6. Ibid., 189b, Fr. p. 104; Eng. p. 132: "I invite you to teach and confute me as much as ever you like."
7. Ibid.; Eng.: "Therefore, say whatever you like, and do not mind about the difference of our ages."
8. Ibid., 187e-188c, Fr. p. 103; Eng. pp. 131-132: "Because you seem not to be aware that anyone who is close to Socrates and enters into conversation with him is liable to be drawn into an argument, and whatever subject he may start, he will be continually carried round and round by him, until at last he finds that he has to give an account both of his present and past life, and when he is once entangled, Socrates will not let him go until he has completely and thoroughly sifted him. Now I am used to his ways, and I know that he will certainly do as I say, and also that I myself shall be the sufferer, for I am fond of his conversation, Lysimachus. And I think that there is no harm in being reminded of any wrong thing which we are, or have been doing; he who does not fly from reproof will be sure to take more heed of his afterlife. As Solon says, he will wish and desire to be learning so long as he lives, and will not think that old age of itself brings wisdom. To me, to be cross-examined by Socrates is neither unusual nor unpleasant. Indeed, I was fairly certain all along that where Socrates was, the subject of discussion would soon be ourselves, not our sons, and therefore I say for my part, I am quite willing to discourse with Socrates in his own manner."
9. Ibid., 188a, Fr. p. 103; Eng. p. 131.
10. Ibid., 187a, Fr. p. 103; Eng. p. 131.
11. Ibid.
12. See the earlier analysis of the *basanos* and the Socrates/Callicles confrontation (*Gorgias*, 486d-e) in the lecture of 9 March 1983, second hour, in *Le Gouvernement de soi et des autres*, pp. 335-343; *The Government of Self and Others*, pp. 364-373.
13. Platon, *La République*, Book VII, 537b, p. 180: "This course [of gymnastics] is furthermore a most important test (*tōn basanōn*) for finding out the worth of each of them"; Plato, *Republic*, p. 768: "and moreover one of our tests of them, and not the least, will be their behavior in their physical exercises."
14. Platon, *Le Politique*, 308d, trans. A. Diès (Paris: Les Belles Lettres, 1960) p. 83: "[Our polity] begins by submitting its subjects to the test (*basanon*) of the games"; Plato, *Statesman*, trans. J.B. Skemp, in *The Collected Dialogues of Plato*, p. 1081: "Obviously it will first put the young children to the test in games."
15. *Lachès*, 188c-189a, pp. 103-104; *Laches*, p. 132.
16. Ibid., 189a-b, Fr. p. 104; Eng. p. 132: "I have but one feeling, Nicias, or shall I say two feelings, about discussions? Some would think that I am a lover, and to others I may seem a hater, of discourse. For when I hear a man discoursing on virtue, or of any sort of wisdom, who is a true man and worthy of his theme, I am delighted beyond measure, and I compare the man and his words, and note the harmony and correspondence of them. And such a one I deem to be the true musician, attuned to a fairer harmony than that of the lyre, or any pleasant instrument of music, for he truly has in his own life a harmony of words and deeds arranged—not in the Ionian, or in the Phrygian mode, nor yet in the Lydian, but in the true Hellenic mode, which is the Dorian, and no other. Such a one makes me merry with the sound of his voice, and when I hear him I am thought to be a lover of discourse; so eager am I in drinking in his words. But a man whose actions do not agree with his words is an

annoyance to me, and the better he speaks the more I hate him, and then I seem to be a hater of discourse.

As to Socrates, I have no knowledge of his words, but of old, as appears, I have had experience of his deeds, and his deeds show that he is entitled to noble sentiments and complete freedom of speech. And if his words accord, then I am of one mind with him, and shall be delighted to be interrogated by a man such as he is, and shall not be annoyed at having to learn of him, for I too agree with Solon, 'that I would fain grow old, learning many things.' Socrates must be willing to allow that the teacher himself is a good man, or I shall be a dull and reluctant pupil, but that the teacher is rather young, or not as yet in repute—anything of that sort is of no account with me. And therefore, Socrates, I invite you to teach me and confute me as much as ever you like, and also learn of me anything which I know. So high is the opinion which I have entertained of you ever since the day on which you were my companion in danger, and gave a proof of your valor such as only the man of merit can give. Therefore, say whatever you like, and not mind about the difference of our ages."

17. Ibid., 189b, Fr. p. 104; Eng. p. 132.
18. Ibid., 190d, Fr. p. 106; Eng. p. 134.
19. Ibid., 190e-194c, Fr. pp. 106-112; Eng. pp. 134-137.
20. Ibid., 196d-199e, Fr. pp. 115-120; Eng. pp. 140-143.
21. Ibid., 199e, Fr. p. 120; Eng. p. 143: "Then, Nicias, we have not discovered what courage is."
22. Ibid., 200a, Fr. p. 120; Eng. p. 143.
23. Ibid., 200b, Fr. p. 121; Eng. p. 143.
24. Ibid., 200c, Fr. p. 121; Eng. pp. 143-144. The expression "*tōn meirakiōn epimeleisthai*" appears only in Nicias' summary of Laches' proposal, which speaks rather of "*paideia tōn neaniskōn*" (education of the sons).
25. Platon, *Apologie de Socrate*, 29b-30d, pp. 156-157; Plato, *Socrates' Defense (Apology)*, pp. 15-16.
26. *Lachès*, 200e, p. 121; *Laches*, p. 144: "I should be very wrong in refusing to aid in the improvement of anybody."
27. Ibid., 201a, Fr. p. 121; Eng. p. 144.
28. Ibid., 201b, Fr. p. 122; Eng. p. 144: "Let us then, regardless of what may be said of us, concern ourselves both with our own education and that of the youths, together."
29. Ibid.; Eng.: "I like your proposal, Socrates, and as I am the oldest, I am also the most eager to go to school with the boys. Let me beg a favor of you. Come to my house tomorrow at dawn, and we will advise about these matters. For the present, let us make an end of the conversation."
30. Ibid., 188b, Fr. p. 103; Eng. pp. 131-132.
31. Ibid., 200c, Fr. p. 122. This is the last line of the dialogue: "I will be at your house tomorrow, if it pleases the gods (*ean theos ethelē*)"; Eng. p. 144: "I will come to you tomorrow, Lysimachus, as you propose, God willing."

nine

29 FEBRUARY 1984

First hour

> *The circle of truth and courage.* ⌒ *Comparison of the* Alcibiades *and the* Laches. ⌒ *Metaphysics of the soul and aesthetics of existence.* ⌒ *The true life and the beautiful life.* ⌒ *The articulation of truth-telling on mode of life in Cynicism.* ⌒ Parrhēsia *as the major characteristic of the Cynic: texts from Epictetus, Diogenes Laertius, and Lucian.* ⌒ *Definition of the relationship between truth-telling and mode of life: instrumental, reductive, and test functions.* ⌒ *Life as theater of truth.*

[...*] I HAVE TRIED TO show you the extent to which this practice of veridiction, of [ethical] *parrhēsia* differed from political *parrhēsia* in its form, objectives, domain of application, and also in its procedures, even though, of course, this moral *parrhēsia*, this ethical veridiction puts itself forward and justifies itself, in part at least, by its usefulness for the city and by the fact that it is necessary for the good government and safety of the city. The *Apology* recounted and justified the foundation of this ethical *parrhēsia* in and by Socratic practice. What I tried to show you last week is that the *Laches* gave an example of ethical *parrhēsia* which is noteworthy for two reasons.

---

* The lecture begins with a sentence, only the last words of which can be heard:
"...brought about what could be called, in a rather solemn and barbaric way, the foundation of ethical *parrhēsia*, veridiction, or truth-telling."

The first is that the theme of free-spokenness, of truth-telling (*parrhēsia*), of the courage of speaking the truth was linked to the theme of the truth of courage, at any rate to the question of finding out what courage is in its truth. The truth of courage and the courage of speaking the truth were bound up with each other and connected in the *Laches*. Second, you recall that in the *Laches* we had another, equally strong and essential bond, another relationship, between the employment of free-spokenness (*parrhēsia*) and the principle of having to apply oneself to oneself, to be concerned about self (*epimeleia heautou*). So, on the one hand, there is the bond, the circle of truth of courage/ courage of truth and, on the other, the bond, the affiliation of the practice of *parrhēsia* to the great theme of the care of oneself.

The last point raised very rapidly last week was that it seemed we could make a kind of connection between the dialogue of the *Laches* and that of the *Alcibiades*, which we referred to last year I think.[1] Certainly, there is a great, visible and manifest difference between the *Laches* and the *Alcibiades* with regard to two essential aspects of the dramatic presentation of these dialogues. [The social aspect first of all]: in the *Laches*, Socrates made use of his free-spokenness and of the courage needed to practice it with adults, with respectable, honorable, and important men in the city who had almost reached old age and had themselves actually given evidence of their valor, bravery, and courage but were unable to account for it; in the *Alcibiades*, on the other hand, Socrates addresses his *parrhēsia*, his free-spokenness, to a young man who has not yet displayed all the qualities which are, however, required if he wishes to honor his ambition to govern Athens. The dramatic art of the two dialogues is again different in its conclusion, its end, its philosophical outcome, and not just in its starting point and social framework. In the *Laches* we arrive at the acknowledgement that we do not know what courage is, and no one can say what it is. The *Alcibiades*, on the other hand, ends with the discovery and standpoint of the soul as the reality on which our attention should be focused.

Despite these differences there are some common points, and bringing these dialogues together enables us to discover something which is rather important not only for the Socratic theme, but also, I think, for all Western philosophy. The two dialogues have at least this in common, that both with regard to Laches and Nicias, respectable and honorable men, and with regard to Alcibiades, the desirable adolescent, Socrates' *parrhēsia* serves to ask his interlocutors (Nicias and Laches on the one hand, and Alcibiades on the other) if they are able to give an account of themselves, to explain themselves (*didonai logon*). [Second], this *parrhēsia*, which serves to ask the partners in the discussion to account for themselves, must lead in fact to the discovery that they are forced to acknowledge that they themselves have to take care of themselves. Finally, the third common point in these two dialogues, in this conduction towards the care of oneself, or in this discovery of having to take care of oneself, and in the consequences which [follow on] from this, Socrates appears as the person who, in taking care of others, is capable of teaching them to take care of themselves. This closeness of the two dialogues, despite the differences in their dramatic forms, enables us to grasp the shared underlying root of two different developments in the history of Western philosophy. Very schematically, we can say the following.

On the one hand, you recall that, as a result of Socratic *parrhēsia*, the *Alcibiades*, starting from the principle of the need to give an account of oneself, proceeds to the discovery and establishment of oneself as a reality ontologically distinct from the body. And this reality ontologically distinct from the body is explicitly designated as the soul (*psukhē*). In the *Alcibiades*, Socrates questioned his interlocutors in this way: You have just agreed that you must take care of yourself, but what does "taking care of oneself" mean, and what is this thing we must take care of? And here, proceeding by way of a number of distinctions, Socrates showed Alcibiades that he had to attend to this *psukhē*. And this establishment of the *psukhē*, as reality ontologically distinct from the body that had to be looked after, was correlative with a mode of knowledge of self which had the form of the soul's contemplation of itself and its recognition of its mode of being. You recall all those passages in which Socrates explained that the soul must look at itself, that it is like an eye which, seeking to see itself, is forced to look in the pupil of another eye in order to see itself. In the same way, he says, by contemplating the divine reality, we can grasp what is divine in our own soul.[2] Thus, the establishment of oneself as a reality ontologically distinct from the body, in the form of a *psukhē* which possesses the possibility and ethical duty of contemplating itself, gives rise to a mode of truth-telling, of veridiction, the role and end of which is to lead the soul back to its mode of being and its world. The development of the Socratic veridiction we see in the *Alcibiades*, starting from this fundamental, recurrent, and common theme of the care of self, designates, and up to a point marks out the future site of metaphysical discourse, which will have to speak to man of his being and what in the way of ethics and rules of conduct follows from this ontological foundation of his being.

In the *Laches*, on the other hand, starting from the same common point (giving an account of oneself and taking care of self), the establishment of oneself no longer takes place in the mode of discovery of the *psukhē* as a reality ontologically distinct from the body, [but] as a way of being and doing—this is explicitly stated in the *Laches*—of which one has to give an account throughout one's life. What has to be accounted for, and the very objective of this activity of accounting, is how one lives and has lived. That is to say, giving an account of oneself, which in the *Alcibiades* led us to the ontologically distinct reality of the *psukhē*, leads us to something quite different in the *Laches*. It leads us to *bios*, to life, to existence and the way in which one conducts this existence. This establishment of oneself, no longer as *psukhē* but as *bios*, no longer as soul but as life and mode of life, is correlative to a mode of knowledge of self which, of course, in a way and fundamentally falls under the principle of "know yourself," which is evoked so frequently in the *Alcibiades*. But this *gnōthi seauton*, this self-knowledge, which applies in the *Laches* as well as in the *Alcibiades*, which is valid both for the discovery of the soul and for bringing the problem of the *bios* to light, obviously has a very different form when giving an account of oneself is indexed to the problem of the *bios* (life) rather than to the discovery of the soul as an ontologically distinct reality. This self-knowledge, which in the *Laches* is evoked more than it is employed, does not take the form of the soul's contemplation of itself in the mirror of its divinity. This mode of self-knowledge takes [the form]—the words are in the *Laches*; we noted them—of the test, of examination, and also of exercise concerning the way in which one conducts oneself. And it gives rise to a mode of truth-telling which does not mark out the site of a possible metaphysical discourse, but a mode of truth-telling whose role and end is to give some kind of form to this *bios* (this life, this existence).

So, in one case we have a mode of giving an account of oneself which leads to the *psukhē* and which, in doing this, marks out the site of a possible metaphysical discourse. In the other case, we have a giving an account of oneself, an "accounting for oneself," which is directed towards *bios* as existence, towards [a] mode of existence which is to be examined and tested throughout its life. Why? So as to be able to give it a certain form, thanks to a certain kind of true discourse. This discourse which gives an account of oneself must define the visible figure that humans must give to their life. This truth-telling does not face the metaphysical risk of putting that other reality of the soul above or outside the body; this truth-telling now faces the risk and danger of telling men what courage they need and what it will cost them to give a certain style to their life. Courage of truth-telling when it is a question of discovering the soul; courage of truth-telling also when it is a question of giving form and style to life. In this comparison of the *Alcibiades* and the *Laches* we have the point of departure of the two great lines of development of Socratic veridiction in Western philosophy. From this first, fundamental, and common theme of *didonai logon* (giving an account of oneself), a [first] line will go to the being of the soul (the *Alcibiades*), and the other to forms of existence (the *Laches*). One goes towards the metaphysics of the soul (*Alcibiades*), the other towards a stylistics of existence (*Laches*). And this famous "accounting for self" which constitutes the objective stubbornly pursued by Socratic *parrhēsia*—and here is its fundamental ambiguity, which will leave its mark in the entire history of our thought—may be and has been understood as the task of having to discover and tell of the soul's being, or as the task and work which consists in giving some kind of style to existence. I think this duality of "being of the soul" and "style of existence" signals something important for Western philosophy.

I have emphasized the closeness and fundamental divergence that can be seen in the dialogues of the *Laches* and the *Alcibiades* for the following reason. I have tried in this way to uncover, at least in some of its most ancient and archaic features, the history of what could be called, in a word, the aesthetics of existence. That is to say, not only, not so much for the moment, the different forms the arts of existence may have taken, which would obviously require a whole series of particular studies. But I wanted to grasp, I wanted to try to show you, and myself, how, through the emergence and foundation of Socratic *parrhēsia*, existence (*bios*) was constituted in Greek thought as an aesthetic object, as an object of aesthetic elaboration and perception: *bios* as a beautiful work. This opens up an extremely rich historical field. There is, of course, a history of the metaphysics of the soul. There is also—which is, up to a point, the other side and also alternative—a history of the stylistics of existence, a history of life as possible beauty. For a long time, this aspect of the history of subjectivity, inasmuch as it constitutes life as the object for an aesthetic form, has, of course, been hidden and overshadowed by what could be called the history of metaphysics, the history of the *psukhē*, the history of the way in which the ontology of the soul has been founded and established. This possible study of existence as beautiful form has also been hidden by the privileged study of those aesthetic forms devised to give form to things, substances, colors, light, sounds, and words. But even so, we should recall that man's way of being and conducting himself, the aspect his existence reveals to others and to himself, the trace also that this existence may leave and will leave in the memories of others after his death, this way of being, this appearance, this trace have been the object of his aesthetic concern. They have given rise to a concern for beauty, splendor, and perfection, a continual and constantly renewed work of giving form [to his existence], at least as much as the form that the same men have tried to give to the gods, temples, or the song of words. This aesthetics of existence is an historical object which should not be neglected in favor of a metaphysics of the soul or an aesthetics of things and words.

By structuring the rudiments of this history around the Socratic dialogues, by trying to find in these dialogues the point of departure for what I call the aesthetics of existence—and we should be clear about this—I am not in any way claiming that concern for the beautiful existence is a Socratic invention or an invention of Greek thought or philosophy at the turn of the fifth and fourth centuries. It would be utterly ridiculous to fix so late the point at which concern for a beautiful existence emerges. It would be utterly ridiculous to put it so late when we think that this concern for a beautiful existence was already a completely dominant theme in Homer or Pindar. But, by placing myself at this Socratic moment of the end of the fifth century, I wanted to recover the point at which a certain relationship is established between this no doubt archaic, ancient, and traditional concern in Greek culture for a beautiful, striking, and memorable existence, and the concern with truth-telling. More precisely, what I would like to recover is how truth-telling, in this ethical modality which appeared with Socrates right at the start of Western philosophy, interacted with the principle of existence as an œuvre to be fashioned in all its possible perfection, how the care of self, which, in the Greek tradition long before Socrates, was governed by the principle of a brilliant and memorable existence, [...] was not replaced but taken up, inflected, modified, and re-elaborated by the principle of truth-telling that has to be confronted courageously, how the objective of a beautiful existence and the task of giving an account of oneself in the game of truth were combined. What I wanted to try to recover was something of the relation between the art of existence and true discourse, between the beautiful existence and the true life, life in the truth, life for the truth. The emergence of the true life in the principle and form of truth-telling (telling the truth to others and to oneself, about oneself and about others), of the true life and the game of truth-telling, is the theme, the problem that I would have liked to study. This problem, this theme of the relations between truth-telling and beautiful existence, or again, in a word, the problem of "the true life," would obviously require a whole series of studies. But—once more, forgive me for complaining yet again—it is clear that these are things which I have not yet analyzed myself and which it would be interesting to study and discuss in a group, a seminar. No, I am not able at present to lecture to you properly on this theme of the true life; maybe it will happen one day, maybe never. I would like merely to give you just some sketches and outlines. Anyone interested in this problem can study it more closely.

The second remark I would like to make with regard to this emergence of the question of the true life/aesthetics of existence, is that I have tried therefore to find, with Socrates, the moment when the requirement of truth-telling and the principle of the beauty of existence came together in the care of self. I have also tried to show how two possible developments could emerge from this: that of a metaphysics of the soul and that of an aesthetics of life. In no way am I claiming—and this is the second remark I would like to make—that there was something like an incompatibility or insurmountable contradiction between the

themes of ontology of the soul and aesthetics of existence. On the contrary, we can even say that these two themes were really and constantly
linked. In practice, there is hardly any ontology of the soul which has
not in fact been linked to the definition or requirement of some kind of
style of life, of some kind of form of existence. Just as hardly any style
of existence, any form of life was worked out and developed without
more or less explicitly referring to something like a metaphysics of
the soul. But I would like to emphasize that this relationship between
metaphysics of the soul and stylistics of existence is never a necessary
or unique relationship.

In other words, the stylistics of [existence* could never be] the pro-
jection, application, consequence, or putting into practice of something
like a metaphysics of the soul. The relations between the two are flexible and variable. The relationship exists, but it is sufficiently flexible
for it to be possible to find a whole series of completely different styles
of existence linked to one and the same metaphysics of the soul. While
accepting, on the basis of a schematic and entirely summary view, that
there is a certain degree of constancy in the metaphysics of the soul specific to Christianity, you know very well that Christianity developed
very different styles of existence, both simultaneously and successively,
within the framework of this metaphysics. Several simultaneous modes
of existence have been defined within Christianity. The ascetic's life is
not everyone's life; the lay person's life is not the same as that of the
cleric; the life of the monk or the regular clergy is not the same as that
of the secular clergy, and so on. A whole series of differences, of modulations in the stylistics of existence, or even different styles of existence, have been possible simultaneously within what is, all in all, the
same metaphysical framework. And still with reference to this more or
less constant metaphysics, we can find in Christianity successive styles
of existence which have been very different. For example, the style of
Christian asceticism of the fourth or fifth centuries is very different
from [that of] the asceticism of the seventeenth century. So: a relatively
constant metaphysics and yet a variable stylistics of existence.

But you can also encounter the opposite, that is to say, very different
metaphysics of the soul which serve as the support, reference, or let's

---

* M.F. says: the soul

say theoretical framework for styles of existence which remain relatively stable. For example, we could consider the history of Stoicism
in this way and see how, from the Hellenistic period, or anyway from
the Roman period until late in the European seventeenth century,
Stoicism defined a certain style of existence which, notwithstanding
some modifications in its details, was ultimately fairly constant. Now
you find this Stoicism developing within a rationalist monotheism in
the manner of the Stoicism of the imperial epoch. You could find it
connected to forms of pantheism, or to what might be called the both
humanist and universalist Christianity of the seventeenth century. So
there is a relationship between the metaphysics or philosophies of the
soul and the stylistics of existence which can always be analyzed, but
which is never constant and in actual fact involves possible variations
on both sides.

In this general framework, around this theme of the true life, of the
stylistics of existence, of the search for a beautiful existence in the form
of the truth and the practice of truth-telling, I would like—without
knowing yet how far I will take it, if it will last until the end of the
year, or if I will stop—to take the example of Cynicism for the following basic reason. It seems to me that in Cynicism, in Cynic practice, the
requirement of an extremely distinctive form of life—with very characteristic, well defined rules, conditions, or modes—is strongly connected to the principle of truth-telling, of truth-telling without shame
or fear, of unrestricted and courageous truth-telling, of truth-telling
which pushes its courage and boldness to the point that it becomes
intolerable insolence. This connecting up of truth-telling and mode of
life, this fundamental, essential connection in Cynicism between living
in a certain way and dedicating oneself to telling the truth is all the
more noteworthy for taking place immediately as it were, without doctrinal mediation, or at any rate within a fairly rudimentary theoretical
framework. Here again we must be clear. I am presently giving you a
simple overview, a simple indication of problems. There is, in fact, a
theoretical framework, but it is clear that this framework is infinitely
less important, less developed, and less essential in Cynic practice than
it may be in Platonism, of course, or even in Stoicism or Epicureanism.
We will come back to all this. For the moment, to justify my interest
in Cynicism, I would just like to emphasize some features which mark

it out and distinguish it radically from both Socratic practice, which it frequently invokes however, and again from other philosophical movements in which the mode of life was also very important.

Cynicism appears to me, therefore, to be a form of philosophy in which mode of life and truth-telling are directly and immediately linked to each other. How does this manifest itself? For the moment I am only talking about Cynicism in its ancient form, as we have evidence for it in the texts of the Hellenistic and Roman period, that is to say, [in] Diogenes Laertius, [in] Dio Chrysostom, to a certain extent [in] Epictetus, and also in those satirical or critical texts written by Lucian at the end of the second century, or by the Emperor Julian in his polemic against the Cynics. In these texts we can see that the Cynic is constantly characterized as the man of *parrhēsia*, the man of truth-telling. Of course, the term *parrhēsia* is not reserved for the Cynics and does not refer always and exclusively to them. It is often employed with reference to many other forms of philosophical free-spokenness, of free and truthful speech. You recall, for example, the way in which Arrian, prefacing the *Discourses* of Epictetus, says that by reading these discourses one will be able to understand Epictetus' thought and *parrhēsia*, that is to say, what he thought and the way in which he freely expressed it.[3] So clearly, the word *parrhēsia* is not reserved for the Cynics. But it is nonetheless the case that the word *parrhēsia*, with its polyvalent meaning and ambiguous value (free-spokenness, but also insolence), is very often applied to the Cynics. It is almost always mentioned in the portrait of the Cynic. *Parrhēsia*, free-spokenness, occupies the foreground in depictions of the Cynic and Cynicism.

In Diogenes Laertius, for example, among the many other anecdotes attributed to Diogenes [the Cynic], there is this one. One day he was asked what is most beautiful in men (*to kalliston en tois anthropois*). The answer: *parrhēsia* (free-spokenness).[4] You see how the theme of the beauty of existence, of the most beautiful form it is possible to give to one's existence, and the theme of the exercise of *parrhēsia*, of free-spokenness are directly linked here.

In another example of this presence of *parrhēsia* in the description of Cynicism, in Book III of the *Discourses*, the famous discourse 22 (the portrait of the Cynic), Epictetus, who is not a Cynic himself, gives a portrait of Cynicism which is highly favorable and, to a certain extent, similar to himself. In a way it takes his own philosophy to its extreme consequence (to radical asceticism). Of course, Epictetus' portrait should not be taken as a portrait of what the Cynic really was in his time, but as a sort of ideal definition of what he could be, and of what might be the Cynical essence, as it were, of a certain form of philo-sophical asceticism of which Epictetus gave examples in his life and philosophy. In this chapter, Epictetus explains that the Cynic's role is to exercise the office of spy, of scout. He employs the word *kataskopos*, which has a precise meaning in military vocabulary: they are people sent ahead of the army to observe as unobtrusively as possible what the enemy is doing. This is the metaphor Epictetus employs here, since he says that the Cynic is sent ahead as a scout, in advance of humanity, to determine what may be favorable or hostile to man in the things of the world. The Cynic's function [will be to locate] the enemy armies and where we might find, where we might meet with points of support or aid which will benefit us in our struggle. For this reason, the Cynic, sent ahead as a scout, will not be able to have shelter, a home, or even a country. He is the man who roams, who runs ahead of humanity. And after this roaming, this running ahead of humanity, after having carefully observed and accomplished his task as *kataskopos*, the Cynic must return. He will return to announce the truth (*appaggeilein talēthē*), to announce true things without, Epictetus adds, letting himself be paralyzed by fear.[5] We have here the very definition of *parrhēsia* as the exercise of telling men the truth, announcing it without ever being overcome by fear.

I will take another set of statements, in Lucian, which clearly show the extent to which Cynicism and the practice of *parrhēsia* were linked, to the point that it was impossible to describe a Cynic without refer-ring to his practice of *parrhēsia*. Lucian argued violently against the Cynics and on several occasions portrayed them extremely severely, as in his portrait of Peregrinus for example (we will come back to this later). He also satirized them in a number of texts which he devoted to the criticism of philosophy. And one of these is the famous market for lives (*Bion prasis*) in which Lucian gives an amusing account of how different philosophers come to the market to sell life formulae.[6] The first to appear is Diogenes, who is selling the Cynical life and offers it at a good price (two obols). He presents himself by saying that he is *alētheias kai parrhēsias prophetēs* (the prophet of truth and *parrhēsia*, of truth and frankness).[7]

As I was saying, Lucian multiplied his attacks against the Cynics. But at least one of his texts is favorable to the Cynics, or at least to one particular character who represented Cynicism in Athens in the second century: Demonax. You find praise for Demonax in Lucian, and here, quite clearly this Cynic (the good Cynic, the one who presents a valid and acceptable form of Cynicism) also appears as the man who speaks the truth, the man of *parrhēsia*. This is said explicitly at the beginning of the portrait of Demonax, when Lucian recounts that, from childhood, Demonax felt driven towards philosophy by a natural impulse[8]—we will come back to this; it concerns the problem of the naturalness of the philosophical life [...*]. Starting from this Lucian recalls that this *parrhēsia* (this free-spokenness) and freedom attracted hatred to Demonax as great as the hatred Socrates encountered when he practiced his *parrhēsia* in fifth century Athens. Demonax too had his Meletus and Anytus, was denounced, and accused of impiety.[9] Lucian likens Socrates' trial for impiety to the recent trial of Demonax for impiety. What exactly was the point at issue in the trial for impiety? It is interesting, because *parrhēsia* plays a very precise role here: if Lucian is to be believed, Demonax was first reproached for not having sacrificed to Athena and for having refused initiation into the Eleusinian Mysteries. Dragged before the courts under this double indictment, Demonax answers (he had more luck than Socrates; he got off). But the answer Lucian reports him as giving, concerning his refusal of initiation into the Eleusinian Mysteries, is very interesting. According to Lucian, Demonax said: Certainly I refused to be initiated into the Eleusinian Mysteries. Because, it's either one or the other: either the Mysteries are bad, what takes place in them is bad, and then one has to say so, and it has to be said publicly in order to turn away all those who are not yet initiated and might have the regrettable idea and harmful desire to be initiated in turn; or the Mysteries are good, what takes place in them is good, and then one must attract as many people as possible to them, everyone one can convince. In both cases, telling the whole truth about the Eleusinian Mysteries—that they are good or that

---

* Inaudible passage.

they are bad—is absolutely part of the philosopher's office and role. He had to tell the truth, he had to proclaim it, he had to turn people away from or attract them to the Eleusinian Mysteries. He had to do this, the text says, *hupo philanthropias* ("for love of humanity").[10] His bond with humanity, his function as benefactor of humanity [presupposed] a *parrhēsia* (a freedom of speech) which involves revealing all possible truth concerning the Eleusinian Mysteries. He did not want to become initiated, therefore, because that would entail him having to promise to remain silent. And he, a Cynic, that is to say, the man of *parrhēsia*, cannot promise not to say anything. So, through this series of texts— and dozens of others could be cited—the Cynic does appear in fact as the *prophetēs parrhēsias* (the prophet of free-spokenness).

Only—and this is another important and constant feature concerning the Cynics and their *parrhēsia*—this *parrhēsia* is directly linked to a certain mode of life, in a very particular way which I think is worth closer examination. In the *Laches*, Socrates' *parrhēsia*, his boldness in speaking the truth, the courage which [allows him] to speak quite freely, even to people as honorable, old, respectable, courageous, and esteemed as Nicias and Laches, was basically authorized solely by the fact that he had given certain proofs and guarantees in his life. You recall that when Laches was invited to agree to being examined by Socrates, he said: I like some *logoi* and not others, it all depends. It all depends on what? It all depends on a certain harmony, a certain homophony between what the speaker says and his way of life. We see in this the emergence of the problem of truth-telling and its relation to the life of the person speaking. And yet, while the relationship between truth-telling and mode of life in the Cynics falls, in a way, within the general framework of this homophony between speaking and living which is referred to in the *Laches*, the relation between truth-telling and way of life in the Cynics is, I think, far more complicated and precise. In the first place, this is because the Cynic mode of life is not just a life which demonstrates and manifests virtues like temperance, courage, and wisdom, which Socrates had given evidence that he possessed. The mode of life which is entailed and presupposed, which serves as framework, support, and also justification of *parrhēsia*, is characterized by extremely precise and codified forms of behavior, by highly recognizable forms of behavior. When, late on, the Emperor Julian attacks the Cynics in general, and in particular a certain Cynic called Heracleios who had abused his role and vocation, he questions the latter saying: But to what do you owe Diogenes' staff and his *parrhēsia*?[11] *Parrhēsia* and staff are thus linked together; the Cynic uses *parrhēsia* and carries the staff.

In the discourse *To the Cynic Heracleios*, this staff is actually only one of a well known set of elements for which there is testimony in Antiquity. The Cynic is the man with the staff, the beggar's pouch, the cloak, the man in sandals or bare feet, the man with the long beard, the dirty man. He is also the man who roams, who is not integrated into society, has no household, family, hearth, or country—you remember the text I quoted[12]—and he is also a beggar. We have many accounts which testify that this kind of life is absolutely at one with Cynic philosophy and not merely an embellishment. For example, in Diogenes Laertius, the marriage, the paradoxical and insulting wedding between Crates and Hipparchia is an example of this. Hipparchia really wants to marry Crates, a Cynic philosopher who, as such, has absolutely no desire to marry. So Crates, exasperated by the attentions of Hipparchia, who said she would kill herself if he did not marry her, stood before her, stripped naked, and said: This is your husband, this is what he possesses, decide then, because you will not be my wife unless you share my way of life.[13] The mode of life, defined and formed with the elements I have just mentioned, is an integral part of the Cynic's philosophical practice. Now the role of this mode of life is not just to correspond harmoniously, as it were, to the Cynics' discourse and veridiction. It does not possess just a homophonic function, like that between Socrates' life and his use of *parrhēsia*, which we saw in the *Laches*. The mode of life (staff, beggar's pouch, poverty, roaming, begging) has very precise functions in relation to this *parrhēsia*, this truth-telling.

First, it has instrumental functions. It plays the role of condition of possibility of truth-telling. A moment ago I quoted the text from Epictetus in which we saw the Cynic in the role of *kataskopos* (scout, spy). Actually, if one wishes to be humanity's spy and to return to tell humanity the truth, to tell humanity frankly and courageously all the dangers it might face and where its true enemies are to be found, then one must have no attachments. To be able to play the role of truth teller and scout, one must be free of all attachments. In the discourse xxii of Book III Epictetus says that the Cynic cannot have a family because, ultimately, humankind is his family: "Man, he has fathered all humanity, all men are his sons, all women his daughters."[14] And in paragraphs 69-70 he says: "Ought not the Cynic remain free of all that could distract him, entirely in the service of God, able to mix with men without being tied down by private duties?"[15] How could he observe all these duties "without destroying in him the gods' messenger, scout, and hero"?[16] To be *aggelos*, to be the angel, to exercise this angelic office,[17] this catascopic office of spy and scout, he really must be free of all attachments. The mode of life is therefore a condition of possibility of the exercise of this *parrhēsia*.

Second, this mode of life has another part to play with regard to *parrhēsia*. It is not only a condition of possibility, it has a reductive function: reducing all the pointless obligations which everyone usually acknowledges and accepts and which have no basis in nature or reason. This mode of life as the reduction of all pointless conventions and all superfluous opinions is clearly a sort of general stripping of existence and opinions in order to reveal the truth. For example, there is Diogenes' famous gesture, recounted so frequently in Antiquity, of masturbating in public and saying: But why are you scandalized, since masturbation satisfies a need, just as eating does.[18] I eat in public, so why should I not satisfy this need also in public? So, the mode of life has this reductive function with regard to conventions and beliefs.

Finally, and especially, with regard to the truth, the mode of life peculiar to the Cynics has what could be called a role of test with regard to the truth. It brings to light, in their irreducible nakedness, those things which alone are indispensable to human life or which constitute its most elementary, rudimentary essence. In this sense, this mode of life simply reveals what life is in its independence, its fundamental freedom, and consequently it reveals what life ought to be. Whereas the Socratic approach in the *Alcibiades*, starting from the care of oneself, consisted entirely in being able to define the soul's being in its radical separation, here we have an opposite operation of the reduction of life itself, of life to itself, to what it is in truth, which is revealed by [the very act of] leading the Cynic life. In the discourse xxii of Book III, the Cynic says: "I have no wife, no children, no governor's palace, but only the earth and sky and an old cloak. And what do I lack? Am I not without grief and fear, am I not free?"[19]

So Cynicism is not satisfied with coupling, or establishing a correspondence, a harmony or homophony between a certain type of discourse and a life conforming to the principles stated in that discourse. Cynicism links mode of life and truth in a much tighter, more precise way. It makes the form of existence an essential condition of truth-telling. It makes the form of existence the reductive practice which will make space for truth-telling. Finally, it makes the form of existence a way of making truth itself visible in one's acts, one's body, the way one dresses, and in the way one conducts oneself and lives. In short, Cynicism makes life, existence, *bios*, what could be called an alethurgy, a manifestation of truth.

On this theme of the Cynic life as manifestation, as act of truth, I would like to quote a late but interesting text. It is interesting because, first of all, it shows the tenacity of Cynicism in and to the very end of Antiquity. It is interesting also because it brings out the links between Cynicism and Christianity, which were so important. And finally it is interesting because it calls upon a particularly important term. The text is found in Gregory of Nazianzus (fourth century C.E.), in oration 25. In this oration, Gregory of Nazianzus, who at the time is in Constantinople, praises a certain Maximus, a Christian of Egyptian origin who, born into a Christian family, withdrew for a time into the desert, and whose great reputation for holiness, for asceticism, brought him to the attention of the bishop of Alexandria who sent him to Constantinople. Gregory, at this time the diocesan of Constantinople, welcomes him—actually things turn out very badly; Maximus becomes a heretic, is condemned, and there are violent struggles between Gregory and Maximus, but no matter... So he welcomes this man who has come from Egypt, from the land of monasticism and asceticism; he welcomes this Maximus, who has personally experienced and practiced the ascetic life, and he praises him publicly. He presents him as a philosophical hero, a true Cynic. Praising Maximus, he says quite specifically the following: He detests the impiety of the Cynics and their contempt for the divinity (we will come back to this later when we look at Cynicism in more detail: there was, in fact, a fairly powerful current of impiety in Cynicism, or at any rate of unbelief and skepticism concerning the gods and some religious practices), but he has taken from them frugality, he is like a dog who barks at other dogs. After having thus defined or characterized this Christian ascetic as a philosophical hero, a true Cynic who, independently of all Cynicism's false beliefs or false disbeliefs, has taken up its most important and valuable core, namely its frugality and mode of life, Gregory of Nazianzus continues, now addressing Maximus directly: I liken you to a dog (the comparison with the dog obviously refers to that part of true Cynicism for which Gregory praises Maximus) not because you are impudent, but because of your frankness (*parrhēsia*); not because you are greedy, but because you live openly; not because you bark, but because you mount guard over souls for their salvation.[20] A bit further on he adds: You are the best and most perfect philosopher, the martyr, the witness of the truth (*marturōn tēs alētheias*).[21] Here, of course, *marturōn* ([from the verb] *marturein*) does not designate martyr in the sense we usually give to the word. Bearing witness to the truth is the sense here. But you can see that in Gregory's mouth, it is not a question of just the verbal testimony of someone who speaks the truth. It involves someone who, in his very life, his dog's life, from the moment of embracing asceticism until the present, in his body, his life, his acts, his frugality, his renunciations, and his ascesis, has never ceased being the living witness of the truth. He has suffered, endured, and deprived himself so that the truth takes shape in his own life, as it were, in his own existence, his own body.

This expression "*marturōn tēs alētheias*" (being witness to the truth) is a late one, but I think we can take it as characterizing basically what Cynicism had been throughout Antiquity, and what no doubt a certain kind of Cynicism will be, in different forms, throughout the history of the West. Martyr of the truth understood as "witness to truth": testimony given, manifested, and authenticated by an existence, a form of life in the most concrete and material sense of the word; bearing witness to the truth by and in one's body, dress, mode of comportment, way of acting, reacting, and conducting oneself. The very body of the truth is made visible, and laughable, in a certain style of life. What is manifested in Cynicism is life as the immediate, striking, and unrestrained presence of the truth. Or again: truth as discipline, ascesis, and bareness of life. The true life as life of truth. From its emergence in the fourth century in the Hellenistic period until at least the end of the Roman Empire, and—I would like to show—long after, Cynicism practiced the scandal of the truth in and through one's life. This is the kernel of Cynicism; practicing the scandal of the truth in and through one's life. And this is why it seems to me that with Cynicism we have a quite remarkable point which deserves some attention if we want to study the history of truth and the history of the relations of truth and the subject. This is the justification for why I would now like to dwell for a while on this question of Cynicism.

According to the logic, pedagogy, and rules of teaching I should now speak to you about Cynicism as we may try to locate it in and extract it from the ancient texts, so as then to try to recount, if not its history, at least some of its episodes. In actual fact I will do the opposite, in order to try to justify constantly enclosing you within ancient philosophy. I will make a detour and try to show you why and how Cynicism is not, as is often thought, just a somewhat particular, odd, and ultimately forgotten figure in ancient philosophy, but an historical category which, in various forms and with diverse objectives, runs through the whole of Western history. There is a Cynicism which is an integral part of the history of Western thought, existence, and subjectivity. In the next hour I would like to evoke something of this trans-historical Cynicism. And then, next week, we will return to what may be thought to be the historical core of Cynicism in Antiquity.

1. Foucault analyzed this dialogue at length in the first two sessions of the 1982 lectures: *L'Herméneutique du sujet*; *The Hermeneutics of the Subject*.

2. See the exposition in the lecture of 13 January 1982, second hour, ibid., Fr. pp. 68-70; Eng. pp. 69-71.

3. "Lettre d'Arrien à Lucius Gellius" in Épictète, *Entretiens*, vol. I, trans. J. Souilhé (Paris: Les Belles Lettres, 1943) p. 4: "Everything that I heard from this man [Epictetus] I endeavored to write down while he was speaking, using his own words as much as possible, in order to preserve carefully for my future use the memory of his thought and free-spokenness (*dianoias kai parrhēsias*)"; English translation by W.A. Oldfather, "Arrian to Lucius Gellius" in Epictetus, *Epictetus I. The Discourses, Books I-II* (Cambridge, Mass.: Harvard University Press, Loeb Classical Library, 2000) pp. 5-7: "But whatever I heard him say I used to write down, word for word, as best I could, endeavouring to preserve it as a memorial, for my future use, of his way of thinking and the frankness of his speech." For an earlier analysis of this text, see the lecture of 3 March 1982, second hour, in *L'Herméneutique du sujet*, pp. 349-350: *The Hermeneutics of the Subject*, p. 367.

4. Diogène Laërce, *Vies et doctrines des philosophes illustres*, trans. M.-O. Goulet-Cazé, Book VI, §69, p. 736; Diogenes Laertius, *Lives of Eminent Philosophers*, vol. II, p. 71: "Being asked what was the most beautiful thing in the world, he replied, 'Freedom of speech.'"

5. Épictète, *Entretiens*, Book III, discourse XXII, 24-25, p. 73: "In reality, for men the Cynic is a scout (*kataskopos*) of what is favorable to them and what hostile. And he must first explore exactly, then return to announce the truth (*apaggeilai talēthē*), without letting himself be paralyzed by fear"; English translation by W.A. Oldfather, Epictetus, *Epictetus II. The Discourses, Books III-IV* (Cambridge, Mass.: Harvard University Press, Loeb Classical Library, 2000) p. 139: "For the Cynic is truly a scout, to find out what things are friendly to men and what hostile; and he must do his scouting accurately, and on returning must tell the truth, not driven by fear..."

6. Lucien, *Les Sectes à l'encan*, in *Œuvres complètes de Lucien de Samosate*, vol. 1, trans. E. Talbot (Paris: Hachette, 1912) pp. 199-214; English translation by A.M. Harmon as, Lucian, *Philosophies for Sale*, in *The Works of Lucian*, vol. II (Cambridge, Mass.: Harvard University Press, Loeb Classical Library, 1913).

7. Ibid., §8, Fr. p. 203: "I wish to be the interpreter of truth and frankness (*alētheias kai parrhēsias prophetēs*)"; Eng. p. 465: "I desire to be an interpreter of truth and free speech."

8. Lucien, *Démonax*, in *Œuvres complètes*, vol. I, §3, p. 525: "I was led to the study of wisdom by a natural inclination to virtue and an innate love of philosophy"; English translation by A.M. Harmon as, Lucian, *Demonax*, in *The Works of Lucian*, vol. I (Cambridge, Mass.: Harvard University Press, Loeb Classical Library, 1913) p. 145: "he felt the stirring of an individual impulse toward the higher life and an inborn love for philosophy."

9. Ibid., §11, Fr. p. 527: "The popular hatred was, for him as for Socrates, the fruit of his frankness and freedom"; Eng. p. 149 "he ran counter to public opinion and won from the masses quite as much hatred as his prototype by his freedom of speech and action."

10. Ibid.; Eng. p. 151.

11. Julien (l'Empereur), *Contre Héracleios*, 225b-c, in *Œuvres complètes*, vol. II-1, trans. G. Rochefort (Paris: Les Belles Lettres, 1963) §19, p. 71; English translation by Wilmer C. Wright as, *Oration VII* (To the Cynic Heracleios) in Julian, *The Works of the Emperor Julian*, vol. II (Cambridge, Mass.: Harvard University Press, Loeb Classical Library, 1913) p. 125.

12. Épictète, *Entretiens*, III, XXII, 47-48, p. 77: "You see me, I have no shelter, no country, no resources, no slaves. I sleep on the ground. I have no wife, no children, no governor's palace, but only the earth and sky and an old cloak"; Epictetus, *Epictetus II*, p. 147: "'Look at me,' he says, 'I am without a home, without a city, without property, without a slave; I sleep on the ground; I have neither wife nor children, no miserable governor's mansion, but only earth, and sky, and one rough cloak.'"

13. Diogène Laërce, *Vies et doctrines*, Book VI, §96, p. 760; Diogenes Laertius, *Lives of Eminent Philosophers*, vol. II, p. 101.

14. Épictète, *Entretiens*, III, XXII, 81, p. 82; Epictetus, *Epictetus II*, p. 159: "Man, the Cynic has made all mankind his children; the men among them he has as sons, the women as daughters."

15. Ibid., 69-70, Fr. p. 80; Eng. p. 155: "... it is a question, perhaps, if the Cynic ought not to be free from distraction, wholly devoted to the service of God, free to go about among men, not tied down by the private duties of men."

16. Ibid.; Eng.: "if he observes them, he will destroy the messenger, the scout, the herald of the gods, that he is."

17. Ibid., 23, Fr. p. 72: "The true Cynic... must know that he has also been sent by Zeus as a messenger (*aggelos*) to men"; Eng. pp. 137-138: "the true Cynic... must know that he has been sent by Zeus to men, partly as a messenger."

18. Diogène Laërce, *Vies et doctrines*, Book VI, §46, p. 722 and §69, p. 736; Diogenes Laertius, *Lives of Eminent Philosophers*, vol. II, p. 47 and p. 71.

19. Épictète, *Entretiens*, III, XXII, 48, p. 77; Epictetus, *Epictetus II*, p. 147: "'I have neither wife nor children, no miserable governor's mansion, but only earth, and sky, and one rough cloak. Yet what do I lack? Am I not free from pain and fear, am I not free?'"

20. Grégoire de Nazianze, *Discours*, 24-26, trans. J. Mossy (Paris: Éd. du Cerf, "Sources chrétiennes" no. 284) 1981; 1200B, 25, I,2, p. 159: "You, philosopher and sage... you, dog, not in impudence, but in frankness (*parrhēsian*), not in greediness, but in improvidence, not in barking, but in the protection of the good, in spiritual vigilance"; English translation by Martha Pollard Vinson as *Oration 25* in Saint Gregory of Nazianzus, *Select Orations* (Catholic University of America Press, 2003) p. 158: "Come, wise man and lover of wisdom... and Dog, not in shamelessness but in your openness, not in ravenous ways but in your hand-to-mouth existence, not in barking but in your defense of the good and your vigilant watch over souls."

21. Ibid., 1200A, 25, I,1, Fr. p. 159: "You, the best and most perfect of philosophers—and I would add: of martyrs of the truth (*marturōn tēs alētheias*)"; Eng. p. 158: "Come then, step forward, best and most consummate of philosophers and, I shall add, witnesses of the truth."

ten

29 FEBRUARY 1984

Second hour

[
Hypotheses concerning the descendants of Cynicism. ∿ *Religious descendants: Christian asceticism.* ∿ *Political descendants: revolution as style of existence.* ∿ *Aesthetic descendants: modern art.* ∿ *Anti-Platonism and anti-Aristotelianism of modern art.*
]

I AM GOING TO ask for your indulgence. What I am now going to offer you is no more than a stroll, an excursus, a wander. Imagine that we were able to work as a group or that we wanted to write a book on cynicism as a moral category in Western culture: how would we go about it? If I had to project a study of this kind in advance, this is more or less what I would say ... Next week we will return to historical Cynicism (that of Antiquity), but now, having been rather stimulated by Cynicism over these last weeks, I felt like putting forward the following.

There is no doubt that Cynicism is apt to appear as a somewhat trivial and not just marginal figure in ancient philosophy. There are a number of reasons for this. In the first place, of course, there is the very strong discredit, which we will come back to, which weighed on Cynicism in Antiquity, or anyway the standpoint which meant that established, institutional, and recognized philosophy always had an ambiguous attitude towards Cynicism, trying to distinguish between a set of practices which were despised, condemned, and severely criticized, and then, on the other hand, something which was like the core of Cynicism, and which was worth saving. This attitude towards Cynicism was frequent in Antiquity and was no doubt a strong influence on its later discredit. The other reason is that some ancient philosophies have handed down to Western thought extremely strong and well specified doctrinal cores, as in the cases of Plato and Aristotle—and to some extent Stoicism, although this is already much less clear. This is clearly not the case with Cynicism for the good reason that we have very few Cynic texts, a fairly large number of which did exist however, [but] also because the theoretical framework of Cynicism, even in Antiquity, seems to have been extremely rudimentary. Cynic doctrine has therefore disappeared, as it were. But doesn't this mean that Cynicism, rather like Stoicism, Epicureanism, and especially Skepticism—we will have to come back to this in more detail—was basically handed down, kept up, and carried on much more as an attitude, a way of being, than as a doctrine? We could therefore conceive of the history of Cynicism, not, once again, as a doctrine, but much more as an attitude and way of being, with, of course, its own justificatory and explanatory discourse. So it seems to me that we could study the history of Cynicism through the centuries, from Antiquity to our own time, from this point of view.

I have to say that we are somewhat lacking in works which deal with this long history of Cynicism. As far as I know, apart from some German texts, I can find hardly any reference to this problem of Cynicism in its long history, and especially any writings devoted to the relationship between, let's say, modern cynicism (cynicism in modern European thought and culture) and ancient Cynicism. We would need more precise research. For the moment, I have found the following. In German there is, first, a text by Tillich from 1935 which is called *Der Mut zum Sein* (the courage to be, or courage with regard to being), in which there is a clear reference both to Nietzsche (will to power, courage to be) and, at the same time, of course, to existentialism.[1] In this text a distinction is made—I do not know if this is the first time this distinction appears, anyway it is explicit here—between *Kynismus* and *Zynismus*. Tillich employs the term *Kynismus* to designate ancient Cynicism, which he defines, which he describes as the Cynics' criticism of contemporary culture from the standpoint of nature and reason. From this Cynicism he derives, but with notable and considerable differences, contemporary *Zynismus*, contemporary cynicism, which, he says, is the courage to be one's own creator. In *Parmenides und Jona*,[2] Heinrich, in 1966, also takes up this distinction between *Kynismus* and *Zynismus* and, right at the beginning of his book if I remember rightly, devotes a very interesting chapter to the long history of Cynicism with, once again, the contrast between ancient *Kynismus* and contemporary *Zynismus*. According to him, in response to the destruction of the city state and of the political community of classical Antiquity, ancient *Kynismus* was a form of assertion of oneself which, no longer able to refer to or get support from the political and communitarian structures of ancient life, was indexed [to], sought its point of reference and foundation [in] animality. According to Heinrich, the core of ancient *Kynismus* would be assertion of oneself as animal. Like ancient *Kynismus*, the contemporary *Zynismus* of modern Europe is also a form of self-assertion—and he notes the filiation or at least continuity of the experience of the cynical form—but this self-assertion does not take place by reference to animality, but is effectuated in the face of and in relation to absurdity and the universal absence of meaning. The third text to which we can refer is Gehlen's book entitled *Moral und Hypermoral*.[3] In the first chapter he defines cynicism as a form of individualism, an assertion of the self (*Ichbetonung*). Finally, [the] fourth book, by someone called Sloterdijk, which someone pointed out to me recently, but which I have not read, appeared last year in Germany, published by Suhrkamp, and bears the solemn title *Kritik der zynischen Vernunft (Critique of Cynical Reason)*.[4] No critique of reason will be spared us, not of pure, or of dialectical, or of political reason, and so now we have: "critique of cynical reason." It is a book in two volumes about which I know nothing. I have been given some, let's say, divergent views on the book's interest. In any case, in contemporary German philosophy since the war you can certainly find a whole problematization of Cynicism in its ancient and modern forms. And it is undoubtedly something to be studied more closely: why and in what terms has contemporary German philosophy posed this problem?

If I restrict myself to the first three texts I have cited, since I do not know the fourth, it seems to me that these interpretations, which at least have the great interest of posing the problem of Cynicism as a trans-historical category, nevertheless call for some comment. First of all, it seems to me that these authors systematically contrast a Cynicism with a rather positive value, ancient Cynicism, and a cynicism with a rather negative value, modern cynicism. Of course, faced with this it needs to be pointed out that there was always considerable ambiguity in the way in which ancient culture regarded and perceived Cynicism. I reminded you of this a moment ago. And then, if we want to give Cynicism its true dimensions as a form of existence in Christian Europe and modern Europe, we cannot just subject it to a uniformly negative judgment. I think that these first three analyses—I am not talking about the fourth—are constructed on the hypothesis of a fairly strong and pronounced discontinuity between ancient Cynicism and modern cynicism, as if there were no intermediate forms, and as if there were just these two, no doubt more or less related, but strongly contrasting forms. If there has been a long, continuous history of Cynicism, implying of course diverse forms, different practices, and styles of existence modeled according to different schemas, it is easy to show the permanent existence across all European culture of something which may appear as Cynicism itself (le *cynisme*).

Finally and especially, in these interpretations, whether of Gehlen, Heinrich, or Tillich, Cynicism is always presented as a sort of individualism, of self-assertion, an intensification of the specific existence, of natural and animal existence, of existence at any rate in its extreme singularity, whether this is in opposition or reaction to the break up of the social structures of Antiquity, or faced with the absurdity of the modern world. By basing the analysis of Cynicism on this theme of individualism, however, we are in danger of missing what from my point of view is one [of its] fundamental dimensions, that is to say, the problem, which is at the core of Cynicism, of establishing a relationship between forms of existence and manifestation of the truth. It seems to me that it is the form of existence as living scandal of the truth that is at the heart of Cynicism, at least as much as the famous individualism we are in the habit of finding so frequently with regard to everything and anything. Well, if we were to agree—these are hypotheses, for possible work—to consider the long history of Cynicism on the basis of this theme of life as scandal of the truth, or of style of life as site of emergence of the truth (*bios* as alethurgy), it seems to me that there are some things we could bring out and tracks we could follow. In the long history of Europe we could see at least three factors, three elements which were able to relay, again in diverse forms, the Cynic schema, the Cynic mode of existence, first in Christian Antiquity, and then in the modern world.

The first support for the transfer and penetration of the Cynic mode of being in Christian Europe was of course [formed] by Christian culture itself: the practices and institutions of asceticism. In Christian asceticism we find what I think was, for a long time, for centuries, the major medium of the Cynic mode of being across Europe. There is a great deal of evidence for the fact that the [ascetic practices] of ancient Christianity were lived and brought into play as bearing witness to the truth itself, that the Christian ascetic wanted to give concrete shape to the truth by these same practices of ascesis in the manner of the Cynic. Furthermore we have a thousand [examples] of the extreme closeness of the practice of Cynic destitution as witness, martyr of the truth, and Christian ascesis as also bearing witness to the truth (although involving a different truth). One of the oldest is found precisely in Lucian with regard to Peregrinus. Peregrinus was a philosopher, a Cynic, whose theatrical death Lucian recounts. He was burnt alive, at the Olympic Games I believe.[5] Lucian writes an extremely violent text about this death in which he recounts Peregrinus' life and how at a certain point he was a Christian and on his own took up and practiced all the renunciations typical of the Christian life. Why? Out of faithfulness and obedience to the person Lucian calls the sophist crucified in Palestine.[6] So Peregrinus is a Cynic who passed through Christianity, or a Christian who has become a Cynic. Anyway, the interaction between the two forms of life is close enough for someone like Lucian, obviously quite distant from these problems, quite hostile to all these forms of practice, to blend them together without too much difficulty. Similarly, in his criticism of the Cynics, Julian later emphasizes the closeness of the Cynic life and the Christian life. And it is notable that Saint Augustine, for example, in a text I would like to quote, refers to this problem of the Cynics. It is in a passage in the *City of God* (Book XIX) where he raises the question: can someone who leads the Cynic mode of life really be admitted to the Christian community and be recognized as Christian (which proves that the Cynic mode of life was still practiced in Christian communities, or at any rate that those who practiced the Cynic mode of life wanted and sought integration in Christian communities)? Saint Augustine answers: "It matters little to this city whether one adopts this or that kind of life in professing the faith which leads to God ... So when the philosophers become Christians it does not require them to change their appearance and their ways of living if these are not contrary to religion, but to give up their false doctrines."[7] Saint Augustine's lesson is clear therefore: when the doctrine is good, one may perfectly accept into the Christian community someone who leads the Cynic life, adopts the Cynic way of dressing, and lives like a Cynic. We will find, in Saint Jerome for example, (*Against Jovinianus*, Book II, paragraph IV, chapter 14), something on the death of Diogenes, capped with a eulogy. He exhorts Christians not to be inferior to a philosopher like Diogenes.

There is obviously nothing very surprising in the fact that at the beginning of Christianity there was a noticeable interaction between Cynic practice and Christian asceticism. But what we should also note is that, through the intermediary of Christian asceticism and monasticism of course, the Cynic mode of life was passed on for a very long time. And even if explicit references to Cynicism, and to Cynic doctrine and lives disappear, along with the term "dog" referring to the Cynicism of Diogenes, many of the themes, attitudes, and forms of behavior which are observable in the Cynics are found again in many spiritual movements of the Middle Ages. After all, the mendicant orders—those people who, stripping themselves of everything, adopting the simplest and coarsest clothing, go bare foot to call men to look to their salvation and questioning them in diatribes whose violence is well known[8]—take up in fact a mode of behavior which is the Cynic mode of behavior. The Franciscans, with their destitution, wandering, poverty, and begging, are, up to a point, the Cynics of medieval Christianity. As for the Dominicans, you know that they called themselves the *Domini canes* (the Lord's dogs). Even if the link established with ancient Cynicism was probably only *a posteriori*, it is in fact this model, passed on through Christianity, which was revived. We could find many other examples [of this revival] in the more or less heretical movements which flourished and developed throughout the Middle Ages. The following is the description of Robert d'Arbrissel, that spiritual inspirer who was very important in the West of France, in Anjou and Touraine at the end of the eleventh century: dressed in rags, he went bare foot from village to village, fighting against the demoralization of the clergy and calling on all Christians to perform acts of penitence. Or again, you find this description in the Waldensian movement: they have no fixed abode, they travel in pairs like the Apostles (*tanquam Apostolicum*), naked, following the nakedness of Christ (*nu nudum Christum sequentes*). And this theme (naked, following Christ's nakedness, following the nakedness of the Cross) was extremely important in all this Christian spirituality and, here too, it refers, at least implicitly, to the famous Cynic nudity, with its double value of being at the same time a mode of life of complete destitution and the manifestation, in complete nakedness, of the truth of the world and of life. The choice of life as scandal of the truth, the bareness of life as a way of constituting the body itself as the visible theater of the truth, seems to have been not only a theme throughout the long history of Christianity, but a particularly lively, intense, and strong practice in all the efforts at reform which were opposed to the Church, its institutions, its increasing wealth, and its moral laxity. There is a Christian Cynicism, an anti-institutional Cynicism, a Cynicism that I would say was anti-ecclesiastical, whose living forms and traces could still be seen on the eve of the Reformation, during the Reformation, even within the Protestant Reformation, or even the Catholic Counter Reformation. All this long history of Christian Cynicism could be followed up.

Second, coming closer to our own time, it would also be interesting to analyze another support of the Cynic mode of being, of Cynicism understood as form of life in the scandal of the truth. This would no longer be found in religious practices and institutions, but in political practices. Here, of course, I am thinking of revolutionary movements, or at least of some of these movements, which you know, moreover, borrowed a lot from the different, orthodox and other forms of Christian spirituality. Cynicism, the idea of a mode of life as the irruptive, violent, scandalous manifestation of the truth is and was part of revolutionary practice and of the forms taken by revolutionary movements throughout the nineteenth century. Revolution in the modern European world—this is a fact which is known and I think we talked about it last year—was not just a political project; it was also a form of life. Or, more precisely, it functioned as a principle defining a certain mode of life. And if, for convenience sake, you want to call "militantism" the way in which life as revolutionary activity, or revolutionary activity as life, was defined, described, organized, and regulated, we can say that militantism, as revolutionary life, as life devoted wholly or partially to the Revolution, took three great forms in nineteenth and twentieth century Europe. Two in particular are known (the oldest and the most recent), but I shall be interested in the third.

[First, we find] the revolutionary life in the form of sociality and the secret, the revolutionary life in the secret society (associations, plots against present and visible society, formation of an invisible sociality ordered according to a millenarian principle and aim). This aspect of revolutionary life was obviously very important at the beginning of the nineteenth century.

Second, at the other extreme, there is the militantism which no longer takes the form of secret sociality but of visible, recognized, established organization, and which seeks to assert its aims and dynamic in the social and political field. This militantism no longer hides itself in secret sociality, but appears and gains recognition in trade union organizations and political parties with a revolutionary function.

And then, the third important way of being militant is militancy as bearing witness by one's life in the form of a style of existence. This style of existence specific to revolutionary militantism, and ensuring that one's life bears witness, breaks, and has to break with the conventions, habits, and values of society. And it must manifest directly, by its visible form, its constant practice, and its immediate existence, the concrete possibility and the evident value of an *other* life, which is the true life. Here again, right at the center of the experience, of the life of revolutionary militantism, you find the theme, so fundamental and at the same time so enigmatic and interesting, of the true life, of that problem of the true life which was already raised by Socrates and which I do not think has ceased to run through all Western [thought].

Revolutionary life, life as revolutionary activity has had these three aspects: secret sociality, established organization, and then bearing witness by one's life (bearing witness to the true life by one's life itself). These three aspects of revolutionary militantism (sociality, organization, and style of existence) were continuously present in the nineteenth century. But clearly they have not all or always had the same importance. Schematically we could say that they have been dominant in turn: the aspect of secret sociality clearly dominated the revolutionary movements of the beginning of the nineteenth century; the organizational aspect became crucial in the last third of the nineteenth century with the institutionalization of the political parties and trade unions; and the aspect of bearing witness by one's life, of the scandal of the revolutionary life as the scandal of the truth was, roughly speaking, dominant much more in the movements of the mid-nineteenth century. Dostoyevsky should of course be studied, and with Dostoyevsky, Russian nihilism; and after Russian nihilism, European and American anarchism; and also the problem of terrorism and the way in which anarchism and terrorism, as practice of life taken to the point of dying for the truth (the bomb which kills the person who places it), appear as a sort of dramatic or frenzied taking the courage for the truth, which the Greeks and Greek philosophy laid down as one of the fundamental principles of the life of the truth, to its extreme consequence. Going after the truth, manifesting the truth, making the truth burst out to the point of losing one's life or causing the blood of others to flow is in fact something whose long filiation is found again across European thought.

But when I say that this aspect of bearing witness by one's life was dominant in the nineteenth century, that we find it especially in those movements which go from nihilism to anarchism or terrorism, I do not mean by that that this aspect has completely disappeared and was only an historical figure in the history of European revolutionism. In fact this problem of life as scandal of the truth constantly resurfaces. You see the problem of the style of revolutionary life reappearing fairly constantly in what may be called leftism. The resurgence of leftism as a permanent tendency within European revolutionary thought and projects has always taken place not by basing itself on the organizational dimension, but on the dimension of militantism comprising secret sociality or style of life, and sometimes the paradox of a secret sociality which manifests itself and makes itself visible in scandalous forms of life. Moreover, it should not be thought that the dimension of the secret and style of life, or of life as scandal of the truth, completely disappears where revolutionism takes the form of organization in political parties. Here obviously we would need a close analysis of the revolutionary parties in France (the Socialist and Communist parties). It would be interesting to see how the problem of the style of life was raised in the Communist Party, how it was posed in the 1920s, and how it was gradually transformed, elaborated, modified, and finally reversed, since we end with that paradoxical result, but which in a sense only confirms the importance of style of life and the manifestation of truth in the militant life. In the present situation, all forms and styles of life which might have the value of a scandalous manifestation of an unacceptable truth have been banished, but the theme of the style of life nevertheless remains absolutely important in the militantism of the French Communist Party, in the form of the, as it were, inverted injunction to adopt and assert persistently and visibly in one's style of life all the accepted values, all the most customary forms of behavior, and all the most traditional schemas of conduct. So that the scandal of the revolutionary life—as form of life which, breaking with all accepted life, reveals the truth and bears witness to it—is now inverted in these institutional structures of the French Communist Party, [with] the implementation of accepted values, customary behavior, and traditional schemas of conduct, as opposed to bourgeois decadence or leftist madness. One can quite well imagine this analysis of the style of life in European revolutionary movements, and, however important it would be to make this analysis, so far as I know, it has never been done: how the idea of a cynicism of the revolutionary life as scandal of an unacceptable truth clashed with the definition of a conformity of existence as the condition of militantism in the so-called revolutionary parties. This would be another object of study.

After religious movements, throughout the Middle Ages and over a long period, [after] political practice since the nineteenth century, I think there was a third great medium of Cynicism in European culture, or of the theme of the mode of life as scandal of the truth. We would find it in art. And here again, it would be a lengthy and complex history. We would no doubt have to go back a long way, because however clearly asserted and violent Cynicism's opposition to the different rules of conduct and cultural and social values was in Antiquity, there was nonetheless a Cynical art and literature in this period. Satire and comedy were often permeated by Cynical themes, and even better, they were, up to a point, a privileged site for their expression. In medieval and Christian Europe we would no doubt have to consider a whole aspect of literature as a sort of Cynical art. The fabliaux would no doubt belong to this domain, as well as the literature studied by Bakhtin,[9] who relates it particularly to the festival and carnival, but which I think also certainly falls under this manifestation of the Cynic life: the problem of the relations between the festival and the Cynic life (naked, violent life, the life which scandalously manifests the truth). We would again come across many of the themes concerning the carnival and carnivalesque practice. But I think it is especially in modern art that the question of Cynicism becomes particularly important. That modern art was, and still is for us the vehicle of the Cynic mode of being, of the principle of connecting style of life and manifestation of the truth, came about in two ways.

First, with the appearance—at the end of the eighteenth century, during the nineteenth, I don't know, again, this would all have to be studied—of something quite remarkable in European culture: the artistic life. [Notwithstanding this], the idea that the artist alone, as artist, must have a singular life, which is not entirely reducible to the usual dimensions and norms, was already fully accepted. We only need to read Vasari's *The Lives of the Artists*,[10] for example, or Benvenuto Cellini's autobiography,[11] in which the idea that the artist, as artist, cannot have a life exactly like the lives of others is clearly and easily accepted. The artist's life and the lives of others are not commensurable. But at the end of the eighteenth and the beginning of the nineteenth century something new appears which is different from what might be found in the Renaissance, in Vasari. This is the, I think, modern idea that the artist's life, in the very form it takes, should constitute some kind of testimony of what art is in its truth. The artist's life must not only be sufficiently singular for him to be able to create his work, but it must in some way be a manifestation of art itself in its truth. This theme of the artistic life, which is so important throughout the nineteenth century, basically rests on two principles. First: art is capable of giving a form to existence which breaks with every other form, a form which is that of the true life. The other principle is that, if the artistic life does in fact have the form of the true life, then this in turn guarantees that every work which takes root in and starts from this life truly does belong to the dynasty and domain of art. So I think that this idea of the artistic life as the condition of the work of art, as authenticating the work of art, as work of art itself, is a way of taking up again, in a different light, from a different angle, and with a different form of course, that Cynic principle of life as manifestation of a scandalous break by which the truth becomes clear, manifests itself, and becomes concrete.

That is not all, and there is another reason why art has been the vehicle of Cynicism in the modern world. This is the idea that art itself, whether it is literature, painting, or music, must establish a relation to reality which is no longer one of ornamentation, or imitation, but one of laying bare, exposure, stripping, excavation, and violent reduction of existence to its basics. This practice of art as laying existence bare and reducing it to its basics stands out in an increasingly noticeable way from the mid-nineteenth century. Art (Baudelaire, Flaubert, Manet) is constituted as the site of the irruption of what is underneath, below, of what in a culture has no right, or at least no possibility of expression. To that extent there is an anti-Platonism of modern art. If you have seen the Manet exhibition this winter,* it stands out: there is an anti-Platonism of modern art which was the great scandal of Manet and which, I think, without characterizing all art possible today, has been a profound tendency which is found from Manet to Francis Bacon, from Baudelaire to Samuel Beckett or Burroughs. Anti-Platonism: art as site of the irruption of the basic, stripping existence bare.

And art thereby establishes a polemical relationship of reduction, refusal, and aggression to culture, social norms, values, and aesthetic canons. This is what makes modern art since the nineteenth century the endless movement by which every rule laid down, deduced, induced, or inferred from preceding actions is rejected and refused by the following action. In every form of art there is a sort of permanent Cynicism towards all established art. We could call this the anti-Aristotelian character of modern art.

Anti-Platonic and anti-Aristotelian modern art: reduction, laying bare the basics of existence; permanent refusal and rejection of every form of established art. In these two aspects, modern art has what

---

* Foucault, who is certainly not referring to the big Manet retrospective at the Grand Palais (22 April to 1 August 1983), has in mind rather the exhibition at the Centre Georges Pompidou ("Bonjour Monsieur Manet") from June to October 1983, and which presented, sometimes very provocatively, some views and visions of Manet's works by contemporary artists.

could be called an essentially anti-cultural function. The consensus of culture has to be opposed by the courage of art in its barbaric truth. Modern art is Cynicism in culture; the cynicism of culture turned against itself. And if this is not just in art, in the modern world, in our world, it is especially in art that the most intense forms of a truth-telling with the courage to take the risk of offending are concentrated. To that extent, I think we could undertake a history of the Cynic mode, of Cynic practice, of Cynicism as mode of life linked to a manifesta-tion of the truth. We could do this with regard to modern art as with regard to revolutionary movements, and as we have been able to do with regard to Christian spirituality. Forgive these superficial surveys; they are notes for possible work. Next week we will return to some more serious things about ancient Cynicism. Thank you.*

---

* Foucault does not deliver here an important development which is found in the manuscript and continues thus:

"...there are obviously many questions which could be developed around all this: the genesis of this function of art as Cynicism in culture. See in *Rameau's Nephew* the first portents of this process which will become striking in the course of the nineteenth century. Scandal around Baudelaire, Manet, (Flaubert?); the relationship between the Cynicism of art and the revolutionary life: proximity, the fascination of one for the other (constant attempt to link the courage of revolutionary truth-telling to the violence of art as unrestrained irruption of the true); but also an essential unsuperimposability, which is no doubt due to the fact that if this Cynic function is at the heart of modern art, it is only marginal in the revolutionary movement as soon as the latter became dominated by organizational forms: when revolutionary movements are organized into parties and parties define the "true life" as flawless uniformity within the norms, as social and cultural uniformity. It is clear that far from being a link, Cynicism becomes a point of incompatibility between the *ēthos* peculiar to modern art and the *ēthos* peculiar to political practice, even revolutionary political practice. We could find this same question again formulated in a different way: how Cynicism, which seems to have been a fairly widespread popular movement in Antiquity, became in the nine-teenth and twentieth centuries both an elitist and marginal attitude, important in our his-tory even though the term cynicism itself is almost only ever referred to negatively. To add one other thing: Cynicism may be grouped with another form of Greek thought: Skepticism. It too is much more style than doctrine, more a way of being, doing, and speaking; it too has an ethical attitude towards the truth; attitude of being, doing, and speaking; attitude of test, examination, and questioning of principles. But with this big difference: Skepticism is an attitude of examination deployed systematically in the domain of knowledge, most of the time leaving the practical implications aside; whereas Cynicism is focused above all on practical attitude and is structured around a lack of curiosity or a theoretical indifference and the acceptance of a few basic principles. Nevertheless, it remains the case that the com-bination of Cynicism and Skepticism in the nineteenth century was a source of "nihilism" understood as a way of living with a certain attitude towards the truth. We should abandon the habit of only ever thinking of nihilism in the aspect in which it is considered today: either in the form of a destiny peculiar to Western metaphysics, a destiny which one can only escape by returning to that which the forgetting of which made this metaphysics pos-sible; or in the form of a vertigo of decadence peculiar to a Western world henceforth unable to believe in its own values. First of all nihilism should be considered as a very precise his-torical figure in the nineteenth and twentieth centuries, which does not mean that it should

1. P. Tillich, *Der Mut zum Sein* (Stuttgart: Steingrüben, 1953, republished Berlin: De Gruyter, 1991); Paul Tillich, *The Courage To Be* (New Haven and London: Yale University Press 2000 [1952]).
2. K. Heinrich, *Parmenides und Jona* (Frankfurt/Main: Suhrkamp, 1966).
3. A. Gehlen, *Moral und Hypermoral. Eine pluralistische Ethik* (Frankfurt/Main: Athanäum Verlag, 1969).
4. P. Sloterdijk, *Kritik der zynischen Vernunft* (Frankfurt/Main: Suhrkamp, 1983); English translation by Michael Eldred as *Critique of Cynical Reason* (London: Verso, 1988).
5. See *Œuvres complètes de Lucien de Samosate*, vol. II, §36-39, trans. E. Talbot, pp. 395-396; English translation by A.M. Harmon, as Lucian, *The Passing of Peregrinus*, in *Lucian V* (Cambridge, Mass.: Harvard University Press, Loeb Classical Library, 1962) pp. 41-45.
6. Ibid., §11, Fr. p. 387; Eng. p. 13: "the man who was crucified in Palestine."
7. Saint Augustin, *La Cité de Dieu*, XIX, 19, t. 37, trans. G. Combès (Paris: Desclée de Brouwer, 1960) p. 135; English translation by Henry Bettenson as Augustine [Saint], *City of God* (Harmondsworth: Penguin, 1972) p. 879: "It is completely irrelevant to the Heavenly City what dress is worn or what manner of life adopted by each person who follows the faith that is the way to God, provided that these do not conflict with the divine instructions. Hence, when even philosophers become Christians, they are not obliged to alter their mode of dress or their dietary habits, which offer no hindrance to religion. The only change required is in their false teachings."
8. Norman Cohn, *The Pursuit of the Millenium. Revolutionary Millenarians and Mystical Anarchists of the Middle Ages* (London: Pimlico, 2004).
9. M. Bakhtin, *Rabelais and His World*, trans. Hélène Iswolsky (Bloomington: Indiana University Press, 1984).
10. Giorgio Vasari, *The Lives of the Artists*, trans. Julia Conaway Bondanella and Peter Bondanella (Oxford: Oxford University Press, 2008). See the 1962 text, "Le 'non' du père," on Hölderlin, which already contains a discussion of the philosophy of these *Lives*. In *Dits et Écrits*, vol. I, pp. 192-193; English translation by D.F. Bouchard and S. Simon as "The Father's 'No'" in Michel Foucault, *Aesthetics, Method, and Epistemology. Essential Works of Foucault 1954-1984*, Vol. 2, ed. James Faubion (New York: The New Press, 1998) pp. 8-9.
11. Benvenuto Cellini, *The Autobiography of Benvenuto Cellini*, trans. Anne Macdonell (London: Everyman's Library, 2010).

---

not be inserted in the long history of what preceded and prepared it: Skepticism, Cynicism. And by the same token, it should be considered as an episode, or rather as an historically well situated form of the problem posed long ago in Western culture: that of the relation between will to truth and style of existence.

Cynicism and Skepticism have been two ways of posing the problem of the ethics of truth. Their intersection in nihilism manifests something essential, something central in Western culture. What this is can be stated briefly: where concern for the truth constantly calls truth into question, what is the form of existence which makes this questioning possible; what life is necessary given that truth is not necessary? The question of nihilism is not: if God does not exist, everything is permitted. Its formula is rather a question: how to live if I must face up to the fact that 'nothing is true'? At the heart of Western culture there is the difficulty of defining the link between the concern for the truth and the aesthetics of existence. This is why Cynicism seems to me to be an important question, although, of course, there are many texts about it and they do not enable us to identify a stable doctrine. The history of the doctrine matters little, what is important is to establish a history of arts of existence. In this West, which has invented many different truths and fashioned so many arts of existence, Cynicism constantly reminds us that very little truth is indispensable for whoever wishes to live truly and that very little life is needed when one truly holds to the truth."

eleven

7 MARCH 1984

First hour

[
Bibliographical information. ◠ *Two contrasting Cynic characters:*
Demetrius and Peregrinus. ◠ *Two contrasting presentations of*
Cynicism: as imposture or universal of philosophy. ◠ *Doctrinal*
narrowness and broad social presence of Cynicism. ◠ *Cynic teach-*
ing as armature of life. ◠ *The theme of the two ways.* ◠
Traditionality of doctrine and traditionality of existence. ◠
Philosophical heroism. ◠ *Goethe's* Faust.
]

THIS WEEK I HAVE received a letter from an auditor concerning
parrhēsia and the different and new meanings of the word in Christian
literature. She has sent me some very interesting references in Cassian,
John Climachus, the *Sayings*, the Church Fathers, etcetera. Then, self-
effacement: she does not put her name or address. So I cannot reply.
Anyway, I say to her that she is in fact quite right. Her references are
interesting, that is precisely the direction I would like to take this
year, if I have time: to show you how, through the evolution of the
term *parrhēsia* in Greco-Roman Antiquity, we arrive with Christianity
at a sort of breaking up of the meanings of the word *parrhēsia* in
Christian literature. Certainly, when Gregory of Nazianzus praises
Maximus, presenting him as a Cynic endowed with *parrhēsia*, the word
is employed with its completely traditional meaning.[1] But a whole set
of other meanings will be brought to the word *parrhēsia*. This is what
I would like to study a bit later. That is the brief answer to this letter,

simply in the form of a promise, which I am not even sure I will be able to keep.

Second, still with regard to Cynicism. I have finally found a book, I don't mean *the* book, but a book on Cynicism, which is certainly much more interesting, much more documented anyway, than those I referred to last week. It is again a German book, since clearly the historical and philosophical problem of cynicism has preoccupied the Germans a great deal, at least since the end of the Second [World] War. It can be found in the Bibliothèque Nationale, was written by someone called Heinrich Niehues-Pröbsting, and is entitled *Der Kynismus des Diogenes und der Begriff des Zynismus*.[2] You see the two spellings of the word cynicism: *Kynismus* (ancient Cynicism) and *Zynismus* (the general notion of cynicism). The book was published in 1979 and I recommend it to you. There is both a very interesting analysis of ancient Cynicism and a history of the concept of cynicism which is very different moreover, in its references, from the very vague sketch I gave you last week when I tried to locate at least some of the vehicles of Cynicism, of the Cynic life, the Cynic attitude in Western culture (within Christian institutions, political life, and artistic practice). In Pröbsting's book you will find instead a whole series of references to theoretical reflection on Cynicism, to the way in which it has been represented in the history of philosophy from the sixteenth century to the present, and to authors who have referred more or less directly to Cynicism, sometimes quite explicitly, like Wieland,[3] Friedrich Schlegel,[4] but also others like Nietzsche[5]—[the author gives some] good indications on how Nietzsche's cynicism was perceived, considered, and criticized in his own time, or immediately afterwards, in particular by someone called Ludwig Stein, who in 1893 wrote a book about Nietzsche's *Weltanschauung* and its dangers, and in which he identifies, picks out, and denounces Nietzsche's cynicism.[6] You will find all this in the book. I have not read it all and I cannot swear to you that [there is nothing] about *Rameau's Nephew*, which is nevertheless a moment, a turning point in the history of reflection on Cynicism in the West, and nor is there anything on Sade.[7] So there you are, for anyone interested in Cynicism. I add—and for this forgive my error, of course—that I have not spoken about Glucksmann's book, *Cynisme et Passion*, which is indeed a reflection on the possible meanings and values of Cynicism in the present.[8]

So let us return, humbly and modestly, to the history of Cynicism in Antiquity, to which I would like to devote this session. If I do not have time to finish we will continue next week, but I would like to try to finish now. I will begin by indicating some problems concerning Cynicism which both single it out from other forms of philosophical reflection and practice in Antiquity and make it difficult to analyze. To say some very basic, very schematic things, the first difficulty and singularity concerning Cynicism is the variety of attitudes and conducts which were picked out and recognized in the same period as falling under Cynicism. Of course, there is always a central core, or at least a sort of stereotype which is regularly stamped as Cynicism in everyone's eyes. The blazon of Cynicism is—we have already spoken about this— the man in the short cloak, with the long beard, bare and dirty feet, begging pouch, and staff, who is found on the street corner, in the public square, and at the temple door questioning people and telling them some home truths. But beyond, or beside this stereotype, on both sides of this familiar character, who is reported already in the fourth century [B.C.E.] and is found again facing Julian in the third century [C.E.], there are many other forms of life which put themselves forward at the time and were perceived, described, vaunted, and deprecated as Cynic forms of life. I will take two extreme examples, or at any rate extremely different examples.

There is the famous character Demetrius, who was very important in the history of Cynicism and in the relations between Cynic thought and life and Stoic thought, and very important for Seneca in particular. Seneca often quotes him, always with enormous praise, calling him "our Demetrius"[9] and saying that he is without doubt one of the most remarkable figures of the philosophy of his time, if not of all time. As we see him in Seneca's texts, Demetrius is clearly someone who certainly leads a simple, poor life, since in one of his letters (62, 3) Seneca says that he prefers the company of Demetrius to that of those who wear purple. And he contrasts the *"seminudus"* (half-naked) Demetrius with those who wear purple.[10] Seneca recounts in *On Benefits* (Book VII) how this same Demetrius flatly and vigorously refused a significant sum of money which the Emperor, Caligula, had offered him. Demetrius is supposed to have accompanied his refusal with a commentary. Sounding just like a Cynic, he said: If he wanted to tempt me, he should have offered me the whole Empire.[11] Of course, he did not mean by this that if he had been offered the whole Empire he would have accepted and succumbed to temptation, but given that temptation is a test of one's resilience, by which one strengthens oneself and assures one's own sovereignty before the world, if he had needed a truly serious test by which he could have perfected himself, strengthened himself, and increased his resilience, then what was needed was obviously not the offer of a sum of money, it was at least the offer of the whole Empire. That was the offer he would have had to resist, and which would have given his victory value and meaning. With this *seminudus* [individual], who refuses any offer one may make him, and who accompanies his refusal with firm, insolent words referring to the stamp he gives to his whole life as a test, we have a character who is in fact completely Cynic, corresponding to at least some of the fundamental features of Cynic existence. But we should not forget that Seneca also portrays Demetrius as a man of culture, certainly far removed from all those street preachers to which the image of the Cynic was often reduced. Again in *On Benefits*, Book VII, Seneca speaks of his eloquence. He describes how Demetrius speaks and portrays him in this way: he is a man of perfect wisdom, whose eloquence is suited to important subjects, and who speaks without affectation, a studied use of words, or ornate language. His eloquence pursues its object with great strength of mind, carried by its impulse (its *impetus*).[12] This is a definition of sober, effective eloquence, of Cynic eloquence up to a point, inasmuch as it is stripped of all embellishment. But it is clear that the form of eloquence Seneca is describing here has nothing to do with the shrieking, insolence, and insults hurled at the crowd by street preachers. Moreover, the life led by Demetrius had nothing to do with the life of the popular agitator. He was linked to the Roman aristocracy and was counselor to a whole group which included Thrasea Paetus and Helvidius Priscus. When Thrasea Paetus was condemned to death, or at any rate, forced by the Emperor to kill himself, Demetrius was exiled at the same time along with several members of this group, like Helvidius Priscus. He was able to return only when Vespasian took power in sixty nine. Once again he became part of an opposition group, which seems to have been organized particularly around those who rejected the principle of a hereditary Empire. He was again in the group of Helvidius Priscus and was expelled once more with other philosophers in the years seventy one to seventy five.[13] We have here the typical model, not of a court philosopher, but of a philosopher counselor, a soul counselor and political counselor of aristocratic groups. Nothing to do with the street orator.

At the other extreme, Cynicism may be symbolized by someone like Peregrinus, who we spoke about last week. He is quite the opposite, an ostentatious vagabond who was no doubt linked to the anti-Roman popular movements of Alexandria, addressing his teaching at Rome to the *idiotai* (those without culture or social and political status). He was expelled from Rome. If we are to believe Lucian, later he probably became a Christian.[14] Before his death—we shall see how he died shortly—Peregrinus sent his testament, advice and laws, to different towns. He played, or wanted to play, Lucian says in his highly critical portrait, the role of prophet, leader of the thiase.[15] The people thought him a pontiff, a legislator, and even a god.[16]

Doubtless nothing symbolizes better the contrast between these two characters—Peregrinus, who wanders over the Mediterranean world and mixes with the different popular and religious movements, and Demetrius, well located in the Roman aristocracy—than their relation to death and suicide. We do not know how Demetrius dies, but we know through the account given by Tacitus that he was counselor to Thrasea Paetus at the latter's suicide.[17] When Thrasea Paetus was forced to kill himself, on the Emperor's orders, Demetrius was the only person who had access to him. Thrasea Paetus shut himself away with him and, in the manner of Socrates, they discussed the immortality of the soul. It was a typically Greco-Roman suicide in the great tradition of ancient culture, quite clearly philosophical and at the same time fully in line with a practice which existed in Rome and in the Roman aristocracy at that time. On the other hand, there is the suicide of Peregrinus. For Peregrinus killed himself, but in a completely different way. He killed himself by having himself burned alive, near Olympia, after having organized this suicide—if we are to believe Lucian who, again, gives a highly critical portrait of Peregrinus—calling the people around him and turning his death into a sort of grand popular festival.[18]

So a family of very different attitudes is brought together in the characterization of Cynicism, which covers an extremely wide spectrum

with regard to social rules as well as to political life or religious traditions. Basically, Cynicism presents quite different models of attitudes
and this makes it rather difficult to define what would be the, or a
Cynic attitude par excellence. This is the first difficulty, the first source
of confusion we encounter when we want to study Cynicism.

The second reason why this analysis is rather difficult—which is,
if you like, more interesting for making headway in the study of what
Cynicism was—is the ambiguity of the attitude towards it, especially in
the period of its greatest development, that is to say, from the first century B.C.E. to the third century C.E., let's say to Julian. During this
long period of four centuries we find that the attitude towards Cynicism
is in fact characterized by two things. First, of course, there are a great
many very vigorous denunciations. Whatever zeal ancient philosophers
had for arguing with each other, whatever the severity with which
certain philosophical schools, like the Epicureans for example, were
opposed, I do not think that any portraits of the philosopher reach the
level of violence that we find in the portraits of Cynicism. The Cynic
is reproached for his coarseness, ignorance, and lack of culture. Here is
an example of this from the end of the second century, [the portrait]
of the Cynic given by Lucian, who was, of course, a great adversary of
philosophy in general and of Cynicism in particular. It is in a dialogue
called *The Runaways*, in which Philosophy is speaking.

It is an interesting text and we will come across it twice (I would
like to cite it now as one of the many portraits of Cynicism which
circulated in Antiquity; we will come back to it again later for a more
precise reason). In this text, Philosophy speaks and gives, as it were,
its own history and the history of the people who have come to frequent it, or who have tried to take up the principles and rules of the
philosophical life. In paragraph twelve of *The Runaways* it says: "He
belongs to that species of contemptible men, for the most part servile
and mercenary, who, given over to rough work since childhood, have
been unable to form any relationship with me; they are in the grip of
slavery, occupied with earning their wages, and practicing the trades
appropriate to their condition, cobblers, joiners, fullers, and wool carders...Trained in these professions from a very young age, they never
heard my name spoken. But when they arrived at manhood, and seeing the multitude showing the deepest respect towards my intimates

[that is to say, the true philosophers; M.F.], tolerating their frankness, seeking their friendship, listening to their advice, and yielding to their slightest reproach, they imagined that philosophy was dominating everyone with its absolute power. To learn what is needed for this profession appeared to them to take too long or rather to be impossible. On the other hand, their lowly and hard occupations were scarcely enough for their existence, and the yoke of servitude became hard, as it is in fact. What do they do? They resolve to drop the final anchor ..., ride at anchor in the port of Madness, call to their aid their usual allies, Insolence, Ignorance, and Impudence, equip themselves with a new provision of insults, which they keep ready at hand; then ... they disguise themselves as best they can and put on an appearance similar to my own."[19] This text is interesting for the social landscape—I will come back to this shortly—in which Cynicism is placed. There is also the idea here that a certain form of Cynicism is only the imitation, caricature, grimace, and imposture of genuine Cynicism. In any case, you have a portrait of the crudeness, ignorance, and lack of culture of those who generally practice Cynicism.

Another extremely harsh and negative portrait of Cynicism is found in the Emperor Julian, author of two texts directed specifically against Cynicism: *To the Cynic Heracleios* and *To the Uneducated Cynics*. In paragraph V of *To the Cynic Heracleios*, Julian writes: "Now, in the name of the Muses, answer me this question about Cynicism: is it a form of insanity, a kind of life unworthy of a man, not to say a brutish tendency of the soul which denies all beauty, honesty, and goodness? ... The disappearance of all reverence for the Gods and the discredit of all human prudence leads not only to the laws we identify with honor and justice being trampled under foot, but even those the Gods have engraved in our souls and which we fully believe without having to be taught that a divine being exists: it is to him that our eyes are turned ... Moreover, let us suppose also the rejection of the second, naturally sacred and divine law which orders total and absolute respect for the rights of others, and which calls on us not to introduce any confusion into this by speech, deeds, or secret impulses of the soul ... Does not this attitude deserve the barathrum?[20] Should not those who preach these doctrines be banished, without blows of the thyrsi[21] like expiatory victims ..., but put to death by stoning? For how do they differ ... from desert pillagers and coastal bandits who rob those who disembark? They despise death, it is said, as if these bandits were not affected by the same insanity!"[22] Here we have an equally violent portrait of the Cynics, which this time does not attack the hypocritical imitation of philosophy so much as the fact that the Cynics are opposed to divine and human laws, and to all the forms of tradition or social organization. These are the two major points to which criticism of the Cynics are usually attached, but there are many others.

Nevertheless, at the same time, and in contrast with this ostentatious, noisy, and aggressive Cynicism which denies the laws, traditions, and rules, even its fiercest adversaries always point out the value and merits of another, measured, thoughtful, well-bred, discreet, honest, and really austere Cynicism. There is practically no criticism of the Cynics which is not accompanied by an explicitly favorable judgment on true Cynicism, whether this be an original Cynicism, which one thinks one can discern, or which one honors in Diogenes or Crates, or an essential Cynicism which is practiced by good Cynics, or a principled Cynicism which one practices oneself.

For example, Lucian, whose violent opposition to the Cynics we have seen, both when directly attacking Peregrinus personally (in the text on his death), and when attacking them generally, as in *The Runaways*, nonetheless gives an extremely positive portrait of a certain Demonax, about whom we know little except through this long and beautiful portrait of what, according to Lucian, the authentically Cynic life would be. On a number of points this portrait is actually true to some of the general principles of Cynicism. Demonax is presented in Lucian's text as a man who was first brought to philosophy naturally, by an innate impulse.[23] In fact, one of the important themes of Cynicism was that the impulse towards philosophy basically did not require culture, training, or an apprenticeship. One is essentially a philosopher by nature, and is born a philosopher. In the obviously mythical dialogue Dio Chrysostom reports between Diogenes and Alexander, Diogenes explains that "king," in the philosophical sense of the word, is not something one becomes. One is king by nature, because one is born a son of Zeus.[24] In this sense, Demonax is also a sort of son of Zeus. He is brought to philosophy naturally, by an innate impulse, but, Lucian immediately adds, this does not mean that he is not educated. Being led to philosophy by this natural impulse does not entitle him to remain uneducated. On the contrary, he has read a great deal and learned much from the poets. He has familiarized himself with the principles of philosophy and has taken care, furthermore, not to enclose himself in a particular philosophy, but has striven to combine the best elements of different philosophies. [Lucian] adds that Demonax has completed this literary and philosophical culture with exercises in physical endurance, enabling him to resist deprivation and suffering: physical exercises for the cold and for hunger. In his portrait Lucian emphasizes another trait which shows that there is indeed a true and good Cynicism which even he can recognize. He portrays Demonax in fact as a sort of practitioner of the truth who has been devoted to liberty (*eleuthēria*) and *parrhēsia* all his life and who provides an example of self-knowledge for everyone. But according to Lucian, in Demonax this concern for the truth does not take the form of violence, aggression, and insult, as it does in so many Cynics.[25] As a good physician of human beings who is concerned about the cure of their souls, Demonax practiced mildness and, despising all wealth and honor, he strove to take part in the life of the city.[26] The portrait ends by evoking the ageing Demonax: close to death, he is welcomed, taken in, supported, and looked after by different Athenian citizens, he is received in different households and gives to each the advice needed or useful for assuring peace and harmony in the family or even in the whole city.[27] A man of truth to be sure, a man who never feared speaking it—this is evident—Demonax is at the same time someone for whom the practice of truth is a mild, curative, therapeutic practice, a practice of peace and not of insults and assaults.[28] You see that even Lucian can give a positive portrait and image of Cynicism.

In a mind much closer to philosophical care, the Emperor Julian, in his discourse *To the Cynic Heracleios*, praises the true Cynic philosophy, which he claims to find [in] Diogenes and Crates, who he sees as the authentic founders of this true Cynicism and whose example is now neglected. Among the principal qualities of Diogenes and Crates, which distinguishes both of them from present day Cynicism, Julian stresses the absence of any distinction, gap, or contradiction between their words and deeds. Here is an example of what Julian writes: "So what form did the dealings of our philosophers [Diogenes and Crates;

M.F.] take? Their deeds preceded their words. Those who honored poverty [Diogenes and Crates; M.F.] demonstrated that they were the first to despise their patrimony [a reference to the fact that Crates gave away all the goods he had inherited from his family; M.F.]; those who prized modesty [still Diogenes and Crates; M.F.] were the first to practice simplicity in everything; those who removed the theatrical pomp and arrogance from others' lives were the first to live on the public squares and in the precincts consecrated to the gods. Before waging a war of words against libertinage, they fought it with their actions and proved by deeds, not by vociferations, that it is possible to reign with Zeus when one has hardly any needs and is not bothered about the body."[29] So there is a true Cynicism, the Cynicism demonstrated by Crates and Diogenes in words, but above all by their actions.

Not only is there this original Cynicism, to which Julian refers and pays homage, but, and this is interesting, Julian also makes Cynicism a sort of universal philosophy which is valid for and accessible to everyone. This is found in the second discourse, *To the Uneducated Cynics*. This is what he says: "As for myself, who would speak with deference of the gods and those who have made their way towards the divine life, I am convinced that even before him [he is referring to Heracles who, in line with Cynic tradition, he has just made the founder of philosophy, especially ascetic philosophy; M.F.], there were men—not only among Hellenes, but even among Barbarians—who professed this philosophy [the Cynic philosophy whose core, according to Julian, is found in Crates and Diogenes, in Heracles and before him: there were men everywhere, among Hellenes or Barbarians, who professed this philosophy; M.F.], which is, as it seems to me, universal, entirely natural, and demands no special study. It is sufficient to choose what is decent out of desire for virtue and aversion to vice; there is no need to work on thousands of volumes, for, it is said, 'erudition does not give one sense.' One does not have to submit oneself to any other discipline than that which the followers of the other various philosophical schools endure."[30]

So there is this very interesting representation of Cynicism, which is late but very revealing. Cynicism appears here as an ancient philosophy, since it goes back to Heracles, beyond even historically, or pseudo-historically identified philosophers like Diogenes and Crates. It goes back to men before Heracles, to all men, Hellenes or Barbarians. There is, if you like, cultural universality as well as antiquity. Second, one does not have to undertake any particular or special study to acquire such an ancient and universal philosophy. Very little is required in the way of knowledge: the practice of some ultimately basic virtues, which everyone can know and practice, is enough to form the core of Cynicism. The third idea is that this antiquity, universality, and ease of access is at the same time a sort of philosophical syncretism, since to arrive at the Cynic modality of existence it is enough to extract from each of the existing philosophies a basic core related to the practice of the virtues. At this point Cynicism appears as what is universal in philosophy, what is universal and no doubt also what is banal. But you can see that there is a very strange paradox here, since, on the one hand, we have seen Cynicism described as a very particular form of life, on the fringe of institutions, laws, and recognized social groups: the Cynic is someone truly on the fringes of society who moves around society itself without being acceptable or taken in. The Cynic is driven out; he wanders. And at the same time Cynicism appears as the universal core of philosophy. Cynicism is at the heart of philosophy and the Cynic moves around society without being admitted to it. An interesting paradox. We get the impression that people of the Imperial, and even late Imperial period, who were interested in philosophy, had a double attitude towards Cynicism. On the one hand, there is an attempt to distinguish and eliminate a certain form of Cynic practice. And on the other hand, there is an effort to extract from this Cynic practice, or from other philosophical practices, some kind of core which was recognized as the essence, the specific, pure essence of Cynicism itself.

This constantly resumed effort to discriminate between a sham and a true Cynicism, between a perverted Cynicism and an essential core of Cynicism seems to me quite unusual. Still, there are a number of question marks. For we could find a similar attitude with regard to other philosophies. For example, with regard to the Epicureans it has become usual to distinguish carefully between the lesson of the first master, Epicurus, and the way in which disciples, and corrupt disciples, practiced Epicureanism. But with regard to Cynicism it seems to me we are dealing with something a bit different which appears to be quite unusual in the history of ancient philosophy. It is not just a matter in fact of distinguishing between the first lesson (the master's) and then the way in which it is later corrupted and forgotten by the disciples. In the case of Cynicism, on the one hand one seeks to expel the Cynic and his mode of existence from the honorable and recognized philosophical field, but, on the other hand, this expulsion cannot be carried out without referring at the same time to a universally valid Cynicism, and without claiming to be a Cynic oneself or to represent true Cynicism. The criticism of Cynicism is always made in the name of an essential Cynicism. You are well aware, of course, that if this kind of procedure is fairly unusual in Antiquity, it has often been employed since. After all, you are quite familiar with, or at least have seen the same phenomenon in recent years with the criticism of socialism, which could only be made in the name of socialism, of an essential socialism. Anyway, there is this form of the development of a quite unusual thought.

The third reason why the study of ancient Cynicism is difficult and singular is that the Cynic tradition contains no, or very few, theoretical texts. At any rate, we can say that the doctrinal framework of Cynicism seems to have been entirely rudimentary. This rudimentary character obviously has to be associated with the popular form of this philosophy. With regard to this link between the rudimentary character of the theory and the popular form of the philosophy, we do not need to speculate about whether this philosophy had to be doctrinally simple because it was popular, or conversely whether Cynicism's theoretical crudity made it a popular philosophy and facilitated its fairly widespread presence in society. In any case, the fact is attested: Cynicism was a philosophy which, on the one hand, had a broad presence in society and, on the other, had a limited, meager, and elementary theoretical framework.

A few words on these two aspects of Cynicism. With regard to the first aspect, many accounts attest to the popular character of this philosophy. We know that its discourses and interventions were addressed to a wide and consequently not very cultured public, and its recruits came from outside the educated elites who usually practiced philosophy. You have seen Lucian's account, taken from *The Runaways*, in which Philosophy recounts the birth of Cynicism: the people who are said to dedicate themselves to Cynicism are described as given over to rough work since childhood, forced to earn their living and practice trades suited to their condition. They were—and Lucian is extremely precise on this point—cobblers, joiners, fullers, and wool carders. And he attributes the interest of these people in philosophy to a sort of political and social ambition: seeing the respect accorded to the true disciples of true philosophy, seeing how philosophers were welcomed, how their frankness was tolerated, their friendship sought after, and their advice listened to, these people, in reality simple cobblers, joiners, fullers, and wool carders, decided to become philosophers, or rather to imitate the philosophical kind, the philosophical style of life. This is fairly clear evidence for how the popular character of Cynicism was critically perceived.

We have another interesting text concerning this popular recruitment and character of Cynicism. In Dio Chrysostom, Discourse 32,[31] you find a no doubt much more historically reliable description than the one given in Lucian's satire. It is a discourse which Dio Chrysostom addressed to the inhabitants of Alexandria, reproaching them for not [listening to the truth]—referring to the misfortune of Athens when the Athenians demonstrated their inability to listen to the truths they were told. Dio Chrysostom (second century C.E.) addresses the inhabitants of Alexandria saying: You too do not listen to the truth. But no doubt a primary reason for you not listening to the truth is that no one tells you this truth. No one tells you the truth because those who could or should tell you the truth do not exercise their profession properly. And he distinguishes three categories of philosophers—we would say now, more or less, three categories of intellectuals. There are intellectuals or philosophers who remain silent, and they remain silent because they think the crowd cannot be convinced, and however much one employs forceful arguments with them and for them, they are never able to understand. Consequently these philosophers withdraw into themselves and keep quiet. The second category of philosophers are those who keep their remarks for the classroom and lectures for a select public and who refuse to confront the general public and address themselves to the city as such. There is a third category of philosophers which, this time, he names (he does not say who the first two categories are): they are the Cynics. He describes these Cynics, posted on street corners, in the lanes, at the doors of the temple, holding out the begging bowl, playing on the credulity of lads, sailors, and people like that, stringing together their crude farcical remarks, and, Dio Chrysostom continues, doing the greatest harm to genuine philosophy by turning the philosopher into a laughing stock (just as one may ruin teaching by getting children to laugh at their teacher). Here again we have a portrait of Cynicism and Cynic practice as a popular practice which uses very precise and particular places as its stage: the streets, the doors of the temple. The Cynic begs. And who does he address? Who does he convince? What is his public? From whom does he get support? They are kids, sailors, people like that.

Cynicism thus seems to have been, at least to a large degree, a popular philosophy. And to that extent we can understand its theoretical poverty. But outside of or correlated with this, there was in Cynic doctrine itself a justification of this theoretical poverty, of the thinness and banality of its doctrinal teaching: the two aspects, doctrinal thinness and popular recruitment, refer back to each other [through] a sort of circular induction.

That philosophy not only can, but must have a limited, poor, schematic doctrinal framework was asserted by the Cynics for a number of reasons which affect the very conception they had of the philosophical life and of the relationship between philosophical teaching and philosophical life. In fact, for the Cynics, the function of philosophical teaching was not essentially to pass on knowledge but, especially and before all else, to give both an intellectual and moral training to the individuals one formed. It was a matter of arming them for life so that they were thus able to confront events. Diogenes Laertius gives an example of this conception of teaching as passing on an armature for life, and not a body of knowledge, when he shows how Diogenes the Cynic conceived of the teaching he had to give to the children of Xeniades. Diogenes had been bought as a slave by Xeniades. To the latter, who asked him: I do want to buy you, but what can you do? Diogenes replied: I can command.[32] Xeniades reacted to this parrhesiastic answer, saying: Fine, you will educate my children. Diogenes Laertius recounts the legend of Diogenes' education of Xeniades' children. What did this teaching consist of? The text begins by saying that Diogenes the Cynic had taught Xeniades' children all the sciences. This would seem to indicate an encyclopedic type of education such as could be found in other philosophical schools, in the Platonists or Peripatetics in particular. But Diogenes Laertius immediately adds: Diogenes had taught Xeniades' children all these sciences in the form of summaries and synopses, in such a way that they would remember them more easily.[33] That is to say, the sciences are not taught in all their ramifications, but in the essential principles which are necessary and sufficient for living properly. This teaching was completed by an apprenticeship in endurance. Xeniades' children had to be able to wait on themselves, that is to say, without calling on servants and slaves. This is the apprenticeship in independence. He taught them always to wear only very simple clothes, without tunic and without shoes. He also taught them to hunt—no doubt a reference to Spartan teaching—which enables people to manage by themselves, to be independent, to practice autarky: one eats what one catches and kills on the hunt. He also taught them physical posture, a rigorous physical stance. They were not allowed to walk in the street without keeping their eyes lowered and speaking to no one. It is this type of apprenticeship, an apprenticeship in endurance, of battle, an apprenticeship in the form of an armature for existence, which characterizes Cynic teaching. Furthermore, if we are to believe Diogenes Laertius, the Cynics expelled logic and physics from the philosophical domain. They considered morality to be the only genuinely philosophical discipline.[34] They also rejected Geometry and Music from their teaching. Diogenes Laertius quotes a comment of Diogenes the Cynic replying with these two verses to someone who wanted to teach him music: "Men rule their lives and households with wise thought, not with tunes on the lyre and warbling."[35]

You can find the theory, or at any rate the development of this conception of Cynic teaching as training and armature for life in an important text by Seneca. At the beginning of Book VII of *On Benefits*, Seneca recounts how Demetrius conceived of learning the sciences. I am sorry, but as the library was closed, I am reading this in a poor translation, but it is not too serious: "Demetrius the Cynic, a great man in my view, even when compared with the greatest, was right when he used to say that it is better to know a small number of wise precepts which one has ready to hand for one's use than to learn many which one does not have at hand. In the same way a clever wrestler is not one who has learned all the postures and complicated movements which one rarely has to use in fights, but one who, after having carefully practiced one or two of these moves for a long time, watches out attentively for the opportunity to apply them. For it is not important for him to know a great deal provided that he know enough to win; similarly in this study there are many things which give pleasure, but very few assure victory."[36] The teaching is therefore essentially a teaching of struggle, which must teach what is needed for the struggle and indispensable for gaining victory. On that basis, Demetrius, quoted by Seneca, shows that what is difficult to know in Nature is really only hidden because knowledge of it is of no use for life. For example, there is no point in knowing the origin of storms or why there are twins. We do not know these things and it would be very difficult to know them. They are hidden, since they serve no purpose. On the other hand, all that is necessary to existence, to the struggle which the Cynic life must be, is available to everyone. These are the most familiar and obvious things that Nature has set out around us so that we learn them and make use of them. Cynic teaching is simple and practical. It is a teaching which the Cynics themselves said was a short cut, a short way. It is frequently stated that Cynic doctrine is a short cut to virtue, a short way (*suntomos odos*). It was so characteristic of Cynicism that, in the definition of Cynicism given in the *Souda*, it is [presented] as the quick way to virtue.[37]

This notion of the quick way to virtue, short-circuiting the lengthy and theoretical teaching, is interesting. In the first place it is interesting because it is inserted in the long history, which should no doubt be studied, of that figure which appears so frequently in Western philosophical thought and spirituality: that of the two ways. This figure is found very frequently; we might say that it is a constant. There is the distinction between the two ways in Parmenides' Poem. The first way says what Being is and this is the way of certainty, for it accompanies truth. The other way says what Being is not. This way, says Parmenides, is the narrow path on which one can learn nothing.[38] You also find an image of the two ways, with a different meaning, in the mythical story told by Prodicus in Book II of Xenophon's *Memorabilia*. Prodicus recounted that at a certain point Heracles found himself at the parting of two ways: the hard and difficult road of austerity, but which finally leads to true and stable happiness; and the easy road of debauchery and constant pleasures on which one can never arrive at a stable and definitive happiness because incessant pleasures disappear, are mixed with suffering, and have to be renewed.[39] This theme of the two ways is frequently found in Antiquity, but also in early Christianity. The text called the *Didache*, which is so characteristic of ancient Christianity, also opens on the distinction between two ways, but these are not the two ways of Parmenides, or those of Heracles, or Prodicus. They are the way of life and the way of death. The text begins in this way: "There are two ways: one of life and the other of death; but the difference between the two ways is great."[40]

The Cynics also had a conception of the two ways, but it is not like that of Parmenides, or that of Prodicus, or, of course, the future distinction found in early Christianity. There are two ways, one of which is lengthy, relatively easy, and does not call for great effort, which is the way by which one achieves virtue through the *logos*, that is to say, through discourses and learning them (through school and doctrinal apprenticeship). Then there is the other, short way, which is the difficult, arduous way which rises straight to the summit over many obstacles and which is, as it were, the silent way. Anyway, it is the way of exercise, of *askesis*, of practices of destitution and endurance. Many Cynic texts refer to this distinction of the two ways. Diogenes Laertius alludes to it in paragraph 104 of his life of Diogenes the Cynic. There is also a reference in Plutarch's *Dialogue on Love*.[41] And you find a fairly lengthy description of it in an obviously apocryphal pseudo-letter by Crates. Crates was the first disciple of Diogenes, and in the first century C.E. a number of apocryphal letters by Diogenes or Crates were circulated. These texts are characteristic, not, of course, of what Crates and Diogenes might have said or thought, but of Cynicism as it was recognized, valued, accepted, and circulated at the beginning of the Empire. In this pseudo-letter by Crates (letter 21), there is this description of the two ways: long is the way which leads to happiness through discourse (so: the way of discourse is the long way). The one which goes by daily exercises is a short cut (*suntomos*). But many of those who follow the same aim as the dogs (the Cynic philosophers) flee those who put forward this way when they note how difficult it is. They cannot become dogs by this way, for exercise is naturally much more effective than discourse.[42] Short way: the way of exercise. Long way: the way of discourse. So you can understand how and why Cynic doctrine is so difficult to pinpoint to the extent that the passing on of the Cynic life essentially took place through this short way, without discourse, which was the way of exercise and apprenticeship.

Finally, and related to this moreover, the final reason why the case of Cynicism is unusual and its study difficult, is that Cynicism had a quite particular mode of traditionality. What I mean is this: since, as we have just seen, they are less concerned with teaching a doctrine than with passing on schemas, then to pass on these schemas of life the Cynics make use not so much of a theoretical, dogmatic teaching as of above all models, stories, anecdotes, and examples. These examples, anecdotes, and stories may be attributed to precise historical figures, or founding fathers—like Crates and Diogenes, who assuredly existed, but whose historical reality was later overlaid with elements of entirely fictional accounts, so that it is very difficult to find the core of their doctrine—or even to entirely legendary and mythical figures like Heracles. So, with this passing on of schemas of life through examples and anecdotes, it is understandable that it is very difficult to know both what Cynic doctrine might have been and also the history of Cynicism and the sequence of historical figures who punctuated it. But through these uncertainties about the history of Cynicism and the reality of its doctrine, it seems to me that Cynic teaching, in the way in which it passed itself on through examples and anecdotes, found and gave rise to an interesting and important mode of traditionality. The traditionality of Cynic teaching, which was conveyed through models of behavior, frameworks of attitudes, took the form of brief anecdotes called *khreiai*, which reported in a few words a gesture, a retort, or an attitude of a Cynic in a given situation; or of longer stories, *apomnēmoneumata* (memories),[43] in which a whole episode of the Cynic life was recounted; and also jokes and anecdotes, which were called *paigna*, and which provoked laughter (*paizei*) and were sorts of comical, ironical *khreiai*.[44]

This form of passing on schemas of conduct through exemplary anecdotes founded a traditionality which was very different from what could be called doctrinal traditionality. What does doctrinal traditionality actually consist of? In Antiquity it consisted in reactualizing a forgotten and misunderstood core of thought in order to make it the point of departure and source of authority of a thought which is given in a variable and complex relationship of identity and otherness with the original thought. This traditionality of teaching, this doctrinal traditionality was obviously very important for passing on philosophical doctrines like Platonism and Aristotelianism—and for Stoicism to a certain extent, already much less so for Epicureanism, and almost not at all for Cynicism.

Alongside this, Cynicism—and, it should be said, Epicureanism to a certain extent—practiced what could be called, not a traditionality of doctrine, but a traditionality of existence. And the traditionality of existence set itself the objective, not of reactualizing a core of original thought in the present, but of recalling elements and episodes of lives—of the life of someone who really existed or of someone who existed mythically, without it really mattering which—, elements and episodes which are now to be imitated, to which life must be given again, not because they have been forgotten, as in doctrinal traditionality, but because now, today, we are no longer equal to these examples, because a decline, an enfeeblement, a decadence have removed the possibility of our doing as much. Let's say, schematically, that doctrinal traditionality enables a meaning to be maintained or retained beyond forgetfulness. Traditionality of existence, on the other hand, enables the strength of a conduct to be restored beyond a moral enfeeblement.

This traditionality of existence, as distinct from the traditionality of doctrine, was undoubtedly important in several philosophical sects, and even in all the philosophical sects to some extent, but the way in which it comes to terms and combines with the traditionality of doctrine is not the same. It is clear that the traditionality of doctrine was the essential part in Platonism or Aristotelianism, and the traditionality of existence, through the passing on of examples of lives, had only a very limited role. In Stoicism and Epicureanism, the combination between traditionality of doctrine and traditionality of existence was more balanced, either one or the other being a little more important. But in the case of Cynic traditionality, the form of traditionality of existence very largely prevailed, obliterating the traditionality of doctrine almost entirely, or rendering it pointless. And through this traditionality of existence we see emerging—and this is very clear in the Cynics, much more than in any other form of philosophy, much more even than in Epicureanism or Stoicism—that figure, which is so important, of the philosophical hero.

The philosophical hero is different from the sage, from the traditional sage, from the sage of high Antiquity, from the sage like Solon
or Heraclitus. The philosophical hero is no longer the sage, but he
is not yet the Christian holy man or ascetic. Between the sage—the
divine man—of the archaic tradition and the ascetic of the last centuries of Antiquity, the philosophical hero represents [a certain] mode
of life which will be extremely important in the period in which it
was formed and the model passed on, inasmuch as this figure of the
philosophical hero modeled a number of existences and represented
a sort of practical matrix for the philosophical attitude. You see then
why Cynicism performed this role, which is seen so clearly in Julian, as
a sort of essence or commonplace of any possible philosophy. Cynicism
was precisely the form of philosophical heroism in its most general,
rudimentary, and also demanding aspect. Cynicism as the essence of
philosophical heroism ran through the whole of Antiquity and made
it, whatever its theoretical poverty, an important event not only in the
history of forms of life, but in the history of thought. Philosophical heroism, the philosophical life as heroic life, was something put in place
and handed down by this Cynic tradition.

So, by informing this image and affirming the values of the philosophical hero, Cynicism had a considerable influence on the development of a Christian asceticism rooted, to a not inconsiderable extent,
in [this model] of heroism. This philosophical heroism formed what
could be called a legendary dimension, a philosophical legend which
modeled in a particular way how the philosophical life itself has been
conceived of and practiced in the West up until now. On the basis of
this we can conceive of the idea of a history of philosophy which would
be somewhat different from the history traditionally taught today, a
history of philosophy which would not be a history of philosophical
doctrines, but a history of forms, modes, and styles of life, a history of
the philosophical life as a philosophical problem, but also as a mode of
being and as a form both of ethics and heroism.

Obviously, this history of philosophy as ethics and heroism would
come to a halt when, as you know, philosophy became a teaching profession, that is to say, at the beginning of the nineteenth century. But
even so, we should note that when philosophy becomes a teaching
profession, with the result that the philosophical life, philosophical

ethics, philosophical heroism, and the philosophical legend no longer have a raison d'être, the moment when philosophy can no longer be entertained except as an historical set of doctrines, is also the moment when the legend of the philosophical life receives its highest and last literary expression. This is, of course, Goethe's *Faust*.[45] Goethe's *Faust* appears to me to be—it can, at any rate, be interpreted in this way—the last great image, but also the last great expression of the philosophical legendary as it was formed, developed, and left its deposits over the centuries in our West. Goethe's *Faust* is that final expression of the philosophical legend. When philosophy becomes a teaching profession, the philosophical life disappears. Unless one were to want to recommence this history of the philosophical life, of philosophical heroism, in exactly the same period, but in a completely different, displaced form. Philosophical heroism, philosophical ethics will no longer find a place in the practice of philosophy as a teaching profession, but in that other, displaced and transformed form of philosophical life in the political field: the revolutionary life. *Exit* Faust, and enter the revolutionary.

That's it. I have taken a long time. In a moment we will return to the problem of historical Cynicism and the question of the true life in the Cynics.

1. Grégoire de Nazianze, homélie 25; Gregory of Nazianzus, Oration 25. See above, lecture of 29 February, first hour, pp. 172-173.

2. H. Niehues-Pröbsting, *Der Kynismus des Diogenes und der Begriff des Zynismus* (Munich: W. Fink, 1979).

3. Ibid., pp. 228-231.

4. Ibid., pp. 245-250.

5. Ibid., pp. 250-278.

6. L. Stein, *Friedrich Nietzsche's Weltanschauung und ihre Gefahren* (Berlin: Deutsche Rundschau, 1893).

7. The book contains nothing on Sade, but it does refer to *Rameau's Nephew*, ibid., pp. 36-41.

8. A. Glucksmann, *Cynisme et Passion* (Paris: Grasset, 1981); English translation as *Cynicism and Passion* (Stanford French and Italian Studies, vol. 76, September 1995).

9. Sénèque, *Lettres à Lucilius*, vol. II, Books V-VII, ed. F. Préchac, trans. H. Noblot (Paris: Les Belles Lettres, 1969) Letter 62, 3, p. 95: "Our Demetrius (*Demetrius autem nostem*) lives not like a man who despises all goods, but like a man who has given possession of them to others"; English translation by Richard M. Gummere as Seneca, *The Epistles*, Vol I (Cambridge, Mass.: Harvard University Press, Loeb Classical Library, 1989) p. 429: "Our friend Demetrius, however, lives not merely as if he has learned to despise all things, but as if he has handed them over to others to possess."

10. Ibid. Fr.: "Demetrius is virtue itself: I take him everywhere with me, and, leaving those in purple in the lurch, I converse with this man in rags (*illo seminudo*), I admire him"; Eng.: "Demetrius, for instance, the best of men, I take about with me, and, leaving the wearers of purple and fine linen, I talk with him, half-naked as he is, and hold him in high esteem."

11. Sénèque, *Des bienfaits*, VII, XI, 1, trans. F. Préchac (Paris: Les Belles Lettres, 1961) p. 88: "When C. Caesar wanted to make him a gift of two hundred thousand sesterces, he laughingly refused it, this refusal doing him no credit in his eyes... 'If he meant to test me,' he said, 'the whole Empire was not enough for this'"; English translation by John W. Basore, as Seneca, *On Benefits*, in *Moral Essays*, vol. III (Cambridge, Mass.: Harvard University Press, Loeb Classical Library, 1989) p. 483: "And so, when Gaius Caesar wanted to give Demetrius two hundred thousand, he laughingly refused it, not even deeming it a sum the refusal of which was worth boasting about!... 'If he meant to tempt me,' said he, 'he ought to have tested me by offering me his whole kingdom.'"

12. Ibid., VII, VIII, 2, Fr. p. 85: "A man perfect in wisdom, although he denies this; of rigorous logic in his conduct; with an eloquence appropriate to the most manly thoughts, without ornament or studied form of expression, but which pursues (*impetus tulit*) the exposition of personal ideas with magnificent pride together with fiery inspiration"; Eng. p. 477: "a man of consummate wisdom, though he himself disclaimed it, of steadfast firmness in all his purposes, of an eloquence fitted to deal with the mightiest subjects, not given to graces, nor finical about words, but proceeding to its theme with great spirit, as impulse inspired it."

13. On this history, see Dio Cassius, *Roman History, Volume VIII, Books 61-70*, trans., Earnest Cary (Cambridge, Mass.: Harvard University Press, Loeb Classical Library, 1925), Book 66, §12-13, and Tacitus, *Annals, Books XIII-XVI*, trans. J. Jackson (Cambridge, Mass.: Harvard University Press, Loeb Classical Library, 1937) Book XIV. See also Foucault's earlier reference to this history in the lecture of 27 January, first hour, in *L'Herméneutique du sujet*, pp. 137-138; *The Hermeneutics of the Subject*, pp. 142-143.

14. Lucien, *Sur la mort de Pérégrinos*, §11, pp. 386-387; Lucian, *The Passing of Peregrinus*, p. 13.

15. The thiase is a group of faithful loudly honoring their divinity (the term is used above all with reference to Dionysian circles). Lucian refers to Peregrinus as a "thiasarch" [the English translation has "cult leader"].

16. Ibid.

17. Tacitus, *The Annals, vol. I*, trans. John Jackson (London and Cambridge, Mass.: William Heinemann, and Harvard University Press, "Loeb Classical Library," 1937), Book XVI, 34-35, pp. 386-389.

18. Lucien, *Sur la mort de Pérégrinos*, §20-39, pp. 390-396; Lucian, *The Passing of Peregrinus*, pp. 23-45.

19. Lucien, *Les Fugitifs*, §12-13, in *Œuvres complètes de Lucien de Samosate*, vol. II, p. 402; English translation by A.M. Harmon as Lucian, *The Runaways* in *Lucian, vol. V* (Cambridge, Mass.: Harvard University Press, Loeb Classical Library, 1936) pp. 69-71: "There is an abominable class of men, for the most part slaves and hirelings, who had nothing to do with me in childhood for lack of leisure, since they were performing the work of slaves or hirelings or learning such trades you would expect their like to learn—cobbling, building, busying themselves with fuller's tubs, or carding wool... Well, while they were following such occupations in their youth, they did not even know my name. But when they began to be reckoned as adults and noticed how much respect my companions have from the multitude and how men tolerate their plain-speaking, delight in their ministrations, hearken to their advice, and cower under their censure, they considered all this to be a suzerainty of no mean order. Now to learn all that was requisite for such a calling would have been a long task, say rather an impossible one. Their trades however, were petty, laborious, and barely able to supply them with just enough. To some, moreover, servitude seemed grievous and (as indeed it is) intolerable. It seemed best to them, therefore, as they reflected upon the matter, to let go their last anchor, when men that sail the seas call the 'sacred' one; so, resorting to good old Desperation, inviting the support too of Hardihood, Stupidity, and Shamelessness, who are their principal partisans, and committing to memory novel terms of abuse, in order to have them at hand... they very plausibly transform themselves in looks and apparel to counterfeit my very self."

20. A deep pit in Athens into which condemned criminals were thrown.

21. The thyrsus, a staff wound round with vine branches and ivy and topped with a pine cone, is the traditional attribute of Dionysius and the Maenads.

22. Julien (l'Empereur), *Contre Héracleios*, 209b-210a, §5, pp. 50-51; Julian, *Oration VII* (To the Cynic Heracleios), pp. 85-87: "But now in the Muses' name answer me this question about the Cynic philosophy. Are we to think it a sort of madness, a method of life not suitable for a human being, but rather a brutish attitude of mind which seeks naught of the beautiful, the honourable, or the good? ... This then is his aim, to do away with all reverence for the gods, to bring dishonour on all human wisdom, to trample on all law that can be identified with honour and justice, and more than this, to trample on those laws which have been as it were engraved on our souls by the gods, and have impelled us all to believe without teaching that the divine exists, and to direct our eyes to it... Furthermore, suppose that one should discard also that second law which is sanctified both by nature and by God, I mean that law that bids us keep our hands altogether and utterly from the property of others, and permits neither by word or deed, or in the inmost and secret activities of our souls to confound such distinctions... is not this conduct worthy of the pit? And ought not those who applauded such views to have been driven forth, not with blows by wands, like scapegoats... but put to death by stoning? For tell me, in Heaven's name, how are such men less criminal than bandits who infest lonely places and haunt the coasts in order to despoil navigators? Because, as people say, they despise death; as though bandits were not inspired by the same frenzied courage!"

23. *Démonax*, §3, p. 525; *Demonax*, p. 145.

24. Dion Chrysostome, Discours IV: *Sur la royauté*, in L. Paquet, ed., and trans., *Les Cyniques grecs. Fragments et témoignages* (Paris: Le Livre de poche, 1992) §21-23, pp. 205-206; English translation by J.W. Cohoon as Dio Chrysostom, *The Fourth Discourse, On Kingship*, in *Dio Chrysostom, I: Discourses 1-11* (Cambridge, Mass.: Harvard University Press, Loeb Classical Library, 1932) pp. 177-179.

25. Lucien, *Démonax*, §7, p. 526; Lucian, *Demonax*, p. 147.

26. Ibid., §3, Fr. pp. 525-526: "despising all the goods of this world"; Eng. p. 145: "he despised all that men count good."

27. Ibid., §63, Fr. p. 534: "He lived almost one hundred years, without illness or pain, disturbing no one, demanding nothing, useful to his friends, and making no enemies. The Athenians, and all Greece, held him in such great affection that the magistrates stood up when he passed by and everyone fell silent. At the end, in his extreme old age, he entered without invitation into the first household, and dined and passed the night there. The occupants regarded this event as the appearance of a god, and believing that a good spirit had come to visit their dwelling. When he passed by, the bakers fought among themselves to get

him and begged him to accept a loaf of bread: the one who gave it to him considered himself entirely happy. Even children brought him fruit and called him their father"; Eng. p. 171: "He lived almost a hundred years, without illness or pain, bothering nobody and asking nothing of anyone, helping his friends and never making an enemy. Not only the Athenians but all Greece conceived such an affection for him that when he passed the magistrats rose up in his honour and there was silence everywhere. Toward the end, when he was very old, he used to eat and sleep uninvited in any house which he chanced to be passing, and the inmates thought that it was almost a divine visitation, and that good fortune had entered their doors. As he went by, the bread-women would pull him toward them, each wanting him to take some bread from her, and she who succeeded in giving it thought that she was in luck. The children, too, brought him fruit and called him father."

28. Ibid., §7, Fr. p. 526: "He was never heard to shout, argue violently, or give way to anger when he had to go over things again. He pursued vices, but he forgave the guilty: he wanted to model himself on physicians who cure diseases but who do not get angry with their patients"; Eng. p. 147: "He was never known to make an uproar or excite himself or get angry, even if he had to rebuke someone; though he assailed sins, he forgave sinners, thinking that one should pattern after doctors, who heal sickness but feel no anger at the sick."

29. Julien (l'Empereur), *Contre Héracleios*, 214b-c, §9, pp. 56-57; Julian, *Oration VII. To the Cynic Heracleios*, pp. 97-99: "Now what was the manner of their intercourse with men? Deeds with them came before words, and if they honoured poverty they themselves seem first to have scorned inherited wealth; if they cultivated modesty, they themselves first practised plain living in every respect; if they tried to expel from the lives of other men the element of theatrical display and arrogance, they themselves first set the example of living in the open market places and the temple precincts, and they opposed luxury by their own practice before they did so in words; nor did they shout aloud but proved by their actions that a man may rule as the equal of Zeus if he needs nothing or very little and so is not hampered by the body."

30. Julien (l'Empereur), *Contre les cyniques ignorants*, 187c-d in *Œuvres complètes*, vol. I, II-1, §8, p. 153; English translation by W.C. Wright as *Oration VI. To the Uneducated Cynics* in Julian, *The Works of the Emperor Julian, vol. II*, p. 23: "But for my part, while I desire to speak with due reverence of the gods and of those who have attained to their functions, I still believe that even before Heracles, not only among the Greeks but among the barbarians also, there were men who practised this philosophy. For it seems to be in some ways a universal philosophy, and the most natural, and to demand no special study whatsoever. But it is enough simply to choose the honourable by desiring virtue and avoiding evil; and so there is no need to turn over countless books. For as the saying goes, 'Much learning does not teach men to have understanding.' Nor is it necessary to subject oneself to any part of such a discipline as they must undergo who enter other philosophical sects."

31. Dio Chrysostom, *Discourse, 32. To the People of Alexandria*, in *Dio Chrysostom, Discourses 31-36*, trans. J.W. Cohoon (Cambridge, Mass.: Harvard University Press, Loeb Classical Library, 1939-1951), §8-12, pp. 178-183.

32. Diogène Laërce, *Vies et doctrines des philosophes illustres*, trans. M.-O. Goulet-Cazé, Book VI, §29, pp. 710-711: "In his *Sale of Diogenes*, Menippus says that the philosopher, a prisoner and put on sale, was asked what he could do. He replied: 'I can command men.' and he told the crier: 'Make this announcement: does anybody want to buy a master?'"; Diogenes Laertius, *Lives and Opinions of Eminent Philosophers*, vol. II, p. 31: "Menippus, in his *Sale of Diogenes* tells how, when he was captured and put up for sale, he was asked what he could do. He replied, 'Govern men.' And he told the crier to give notice in case anybody wanted to purchase a master for himself."

33. Foucault follows the old translation of R. Genaille, *Vie, doctrines et sentences des philosophes illustres*, p. 17: "These children also learned many passages from the poets and prose writers and even some writings of Diogenes, who presented them with summaries and synopses of each science so that they would remember them more easily." The new translation by M.-O. Goulet-Cazé, *Vies et doctrines des philosophes illustres*, Book VI, §31, p. 712, has: "These children learned by heart many passages from the poets, prose writers, and work by Diogenes himself; and he got them to practice every method enabling them to remember quickly and well"; *Lives and Opinions of Eminent Philosophers*, vol. II, p. 33: "The boys used to get by heart

many passages from poets, historians, and the writings of Diogenes himself; and he would practice them in every short cut to a good memory."

34. Ibid., Fr., Goulet-Cazé, §103, p. 766: "They [the Cynics] maintain, like Ariston of Chios, that the subjects of Logic and Physics must be rejected, and that one should apply oneself solely to Ethics"; Eng., p. 107: "They are content then, like Ariston of Chios, to do away with the subjects of Logic and Physics and to devote their whole attention to Ethics."

35. Ibid., Fr., Genaille, p. 48, Goulet-Cazé, §104, p. 767; Eng., p. 107: "By men's minds states are ordered well, and households,/Not by the lyre's twanged strings or flute's trilled notes."

36. The French editors do not give a reference for this quotation. English translation by John W. Basore as Seneca, *On Benefits*, in *Moral Essays*, vol. III (Cambridge, Mass.: Harvard University Press, Loeb Classical Library, 1935) Book VII, §3-4, pp. 455-457: "For Demetrius the Cynic, a great man, even if compared with the greatest, is fond of stating, very admirably that it is far better for us to possess only a few maxims of philosophy that are nevertheless always at our command and in use, than to acquire vast knowledge that notwithstanding serves no practical purpose. 'Just as,' he says, 'the best wrestler is not one who is thoroughly acquainted with all the postures and grips of the art, which he will seldom use against an adversary, but he who has well and carefully trained himself in one or two of them and waits eagerly for the opportunity to use them—for it makes no difference how much he knows if he knows enough to give victory—, so in this effort of ours there are many points that are interesting, few that are decisive.'"

37. The *Souda* is a tenth century encyclopedia attributed to an author who is supposed to have been a very erudite Greek lexicographer named Suidas.

38. Parmenides, *Parménide. Le Poème*, II, trans. Jean Beaufret (Paris: PUF, 1955): "I will tell you what are the only two roads of research to be thought of: the first—how it is and is not possible that it not be—is the path in which to trust—for it follows the Truth—. The second, that it is not and that not-being is necessary, I tell you is only a track on which one finds absolutely nothing in which to trust"; English translation by Jonathan Barnes in Jonathan Barnes, *Early Greek Philosophy* (Harmondsworth: Penguin, 1987) p. 132:
    "But come, I will tell you—preserve the account when you hear it—
    the only roads of enquiry there are to be thought of:
    one, that it is and cannot not be,
    is the path of persuasion (for truth accompanies it);
    another, that it is not and must not be—
    this I say to you is a trail devoid of all knowledge."

39. Xénophon, *Mémorables*, II, 1, 21-34, trans. P. Chambry (Paris: Garnier-Flammarion, 1966) pp. 320-323; English translation by E.C. Marchant as Xenophon, *Memorabilia* in *Xenophon IV* (Cambridge, Mass.: Harvard University Press, Loeb Classical Library, 1979), pp. 94-103.

40. W. Rordorf and A. Tuilier, trans., *La Doctrine des Douze Apôtres: Didachè* (Paris: Éd. du Cerf, 1978) p. 141; English translation by Aaron Milavec in Aaron Milavec, *The Didache: Text, Translation, Analysis, and Commentary* (Liturgical Press, 2004) p. 3: "There are two ways: one of life and one of death! (And) [there is] a great difference between the two ways."

41. Plutarque, *Dialogue sur l'amour*, Traité 47, 759c, trans. M. Cuvigny, in *Œuvres morales*, vol. X (Paris: Les Belles Lettres, 1980) p. 75: "Thus attracted, the lover crossed a great distance in an instant, as by that 'straight and short path' that the Cynic philosophers say they have found and which leads to virtue"; English translation by W.C. Helmbold, *The Dialogue on Love* in Plutarch, *Moralia, IX* (Cambridge, Mass.: Harvard University Press, Loeb Classical Library, 1961) p. 369: "By these he is led to make a long journey with great swiftness; he has found, as the Cynics say, the passage to virtue 'strenuous and short at the same time.'"

42. Letter 21 in G. Rombi and D. Deleule, *Lettres de Diogène et Cratès* (Paris: Babel, 1998) p. 22: "You will learn to conduct yourself in this way for other things too, by becoming accustomed to not fearing, instead of only reasoning: long in fact is the way of happiness when one goes by reasoning, whereas exercise, which passes through the actions of everyday life, offers a short cut. But most, while pursuing the same ends as the dogs, flee those who call out to them when they see how difficult it is. But by this way, one has to become the dog, one must be it from birth: for by nature exercise is much more effective than that way"; English translation by Ronald F. Hock, "The Epistles of Crates," 21, To Metrocles the

Cynic" in Abraham J. Malherbe, ed., *The Cynic Epistles. A Study Edition* (Atlanta, GA: Society of Biblical Literature, 2006 [1977]) p. 71: "And you will learn how to do other things in this manner if you make it a habit not to be afraid of words nor merely to use them. For the way that leads to happiness through words is long, but that which leads through daily deeds is a shortened regimen. But the masses, although they desire the same end as the Cynics, flee those who preach the regimen, when they see how difficult it is. One must not become a Cynic because of this way, but must be born one. For the regimen is naturally more effective than the way itself." At the time Foucault would have been able to refer to the Greek text in R. Hercher, *Epistolographi Graeci* (Paris: Firmin Didot, 1873) pp. 208-217.

43. The *apomnēmoneumata* also evoke a memorable action. See the title of Xenophon's book on Socrates: Memorabilia *(les Memorables)—Ta Apomnēmoneuta.*

44. On all these genres, and particularly the *khreaia*, see M. Alexandre, "The Chreia in Greco-Roman education," *Ktèma*, 1989, 14, pp. 161-168; R.F. Hock, *The Chreia in Ancient Rhetoric*, vol. 1: *The Progymnasmata* (Atlanta: Scholars Press, 1986); and R.F. Hock and E.N. O'Neil, *The Chreia and Ancient Rhetoric* (Leiden-Boston, Mass.: Brill Academic Publishers, 2002).

45. On this character, see what Foucault said in 1982, *L'Herméneutique du sujet*, pp. 296-297; *The Hermeneutics of the Subject*, pp. 309-311.

twelve

7 MARCH 1984

Second hour

[
The problem of the true life. ∽ *The four meanings of truth: unconcealed; unalloyed; straight (droit)*; unchanging.* ∽ *The four
meanings of true love in Plato.* ∽ *The four meanings of the true
life in Plato.* ∽ *The motto of Diogenes: "Change the value of
the currency."*
]

FORGIVE ME, I HAVE taken too long with this general presentation of Cynicism. I would like now to return to the problem which
concerns and interests me, and for and in which Cynicism plays at least
an important, if not exclusive role. The problem is the following. As I
was saying last week, Cynicism presents itself essentially as a certain
form of *parrhēsia*, of truth-telling, but which finds its instrument, its
site, its point of emergence in the very life of the person who must thus
manifest or speak the truth in the form of a manifestation of existence.
Everything I have just been saying to you was a way of finding in the
general characteristics of Cynicism the elements which enable us to
understand how [and] why the Cynic's truth-telling takes the privileged form of life as testimony of the truth. From one end to the other,

---

* [Both senses of the French *"droit"* and the English "straight" should be borne in mind here:
that of the property of a line, object, or route being without curve, deviation, or twists, being
direct, vertical, or upright, and that of the moral quality of a person or conduct as honest,
upright, not crooked, and hence law-abiding or, in this context, not deviating from a line of
conduct; G.B.]

from Diogenes, to whom Lucian attributes the assertion that he is the prophet of the truth (very precisely of *parrhēsia: prophetēs parrhēsias*),[1] to Gregory of Nazianzus saying of Maximus, both Christian ascetic and true philosopher, that he is *marturōn alētheias* (bears witness, testifies to the truth),[2] Cynicism appears as this way of manifesting the truth, of practicing alethurgy, the production of truth in the form of life. It seems to me that I have found a theme here—which obviously should be developed much more than I have been able to do in this framework—, which was really very important in ancient philosophy, in Christian spirituality, much less in contemporary philosophy no doubt, but certainly in what could be called political ethics since the nineteenth century: this is the theme of the true life. What is the true life? Given that our mental framework, our way of thinking leads us, not without problems, to think of how a statement can be true or false, how a statement can have a truth value, then what meaning can we give to this expression "true life"? When talking about life—and the same could be said with regard to a form of behavior, a feeling, or an attitude—how can we qualify it as true? What is a true feeling? What is true love? What is the true life? This problem of the true life has been absolutely crucial in the history of our philosophical or spiritual thought. I would like to refer to this theme of the true life in a general way, but taking Cynicism as the point of application.

First of all—this is what I would like to analyze for you now—even before Cynicism, or alongside it, what did Greek philosophy understand by the "true life"? This expression is sometimes found, and a not insignificant number of times, in Plato. Before addressing the question of the true life (*alēthēs bios, alēthinos bios*), I will give some extremely elementary reminders about the notion of truth itself. *Alētheia*: the truth. *Alēthēs*: true. In classical Greek thought, what is generally understood by *alētheia*, what is *alēthēs* (true)? I think we can—once again, forgive me, very schematically—distinguish four meanings or see four forms in which, according to which, and because of which something may be said to be true.

First, of course, forgive me for reminding you of this: that which is not hidden, not concealed is true. The negative structure of the term— *a-lētheia, a-lēthēs*–is frequently found in Greek. The word *a-trekēs*, for example, which means straight, etymologically means quite precisely "not curved." *Ne-mertēs*, which means sincere, etymologically [signi-fies]: which does not deceive, does not dupe. The *a-lēthēs* is that which, not being hidden, not concealed, is given to view in its entirety, is com-pletely visible, no part of it being concealed or secret. First value of the word *alēthēs*. But not only is that which is not concealed called *alēthēs* (true), but also that which is not added to or supplemented, which is not mixed with something other than itself. That whose being is not only not hidden or concealed, but also whose being is not altered by any foreign element which would thus distort it and end up concealing what it is in reality, [is *alēthēs*].*

Third meaning: that which is straight (*euthus*: direct) is *alēthēs*. This rectitude is the opposite of twists and turns which precisely conceal it. For that which is true, being *euthus* is also opposed to the multiplic-ity and mixture which distorts. From this point of view, that *alēthēs* is straight, that *alētheia* (the truth) is also a rectitude, derives directly from the fact that the truth is not concealed and is without multiplicity and unalloyed. So it will be quite natural to say that conduct and a way of doing things are *alēthai* inasmuch as they are straight, in accordance with rectitude, with what is right.

Finally, the fourth meaning, the fourth value of the term *alēthēs* is that which exists and remains beyond any change, which remains in its identity, immutability, and incorruptibility. By virtue of the fact that it is without deviation, concealment, mixture, curvature, or disturbance (it is really straight), this unconcealed, unalloyed, and straight truth can thereby remain what it is in its unchangeable and incorruptible identity.

These are, very schematically, the four essential values that can be found [in] these terms, *alēthēs* and *alētheia*. You see then that this notion of truth, with its different values and field of meanings, divided up according to these four axes, can be applied to many things other than propositions and statements. This notion of truth—as the unconcealed, the unalloyed, the straight, and the unchanging and incorruptible—is applicable, either in all four of its meanings, or in one or some of them,

---

* In the manuscript Foucault constructs another meaning of truth, which he abandons (passage crossed out): "*alēthēs* is also contrasted with what is only reflection, image, shadow, imitation, appearance; that which is adequate to its essence, which is identical, is *alēthēs*."

to ways of being, ways of doing things, ways of conducting oneself, or forms of action. Moreover, this notion of truth, with its four meanings, is applied to *logos* itself, not to *logos* understood as proposition, as statement, but *logos* as way of speaking. *Logos alēthēs* is not just a set of propositions which turn out to be exact and can take the value of truth. *Logos alēthēs* is a way of speaking in which, first, nothing is concealed; in which, second, neither the false, nor opinion, nor appearance is mixed with the true; [third], it is a straight discourse, in line with the rules and the law; and finally, *alēthēs logos* is a discourse which remains the same, does not change, or become debased, or distorted, and which can never be vanquished, overturned, or refuted.

But you understand also how and why these same words, *alēthēs* and *alētheia*, can be applied to something other than *logos*. There is at least one domain in which the application of this qualifying term *alēthēs* was of major importance. We should no doubt focus on this for a moment, at least by way of an invitation to think about it, for this description in terms of truth will certainly have considerable importance in Western culture. This is quite simply the notion of *alēthēs erōs* (true love).[3] What is this strange, remarkable notion, true love, which is crucial in Platonic philosophy, of course, but generally in Greek ethics? Well, in true love we find precisely the values I have just been talking about. True love is first, love which does not conceal, and it does not conceal in two senses. First, it does not conceal because it has nothing to hide. It has nothing shameful which has to be hidden. It does not shun the light. It is willing, and is such that it is always willing to show itself in front of witnesses. It is also a love which does not conceal its aims. True love does not hide the true objective that it seeks to obtain from the one it loves. It is without subterfuge and does not employ roundabout means with its partner. It does not keep itself out of sight of witnesses, or of its partner. True love is love without disguise. Second, true love is an unalloyed love, that is to say, without mixture of pleasure and displeasure. It is also a love in which sensual pleasure and the friendship of souls do not intermingle. To that extent it is therefore a pure love because unalloyed. Third, true love (*alēthēs erōs*) is love which is in line with what is right, with what is correct. It is a direct (*euthus*) love. It has nothing contrary to the rule or custom. And finally, true love is love which is never subject to change or becoming. It is an incorruptible love which remains always the same.

If you look at the definition, description, and portrait of true love in the Socratic and Platonic texts, it is easy to find these four values of *alētheia*. And I think that this definition of true love may enable us to make some headway in the investigation of the nature of the true life (*alēthēs bios*), which is our problem now. Moreover, it is not entirely without significance that true love was, in Platonic philosophy—but also, as you know, in a whole sector, a whole domain of Christian spirituality and mysticism—the form par excellence of the true life. Since Platonism, true love and the true life have traditionally belonged together, and to a large extent Christian Platonism will take up this theme. Let's leave this, but it would be a very interesting and vast domain to study.

Now we come to the *alēthēs bios*, which I would like to locate first of all outside of its Cynic sense and the very paradoxical and curious form it takes in Cynicism. [Take the true life] as it appears in the philosophical texts of the classical epoch, essentially in Plato, but you could find at least some rudiments of it, less interesting, less developed for sure, in Xenophon. Let's take this definition. I am not going to try to take the notion of *alēthēs bios* in its final philosophical elaboration in Plato, but in its obvious, everyday meanings which we find in the Platonic texts, apart from any particular philosophical elaboration.

The *alēthēs bios* is first, of course, an unconcealed life, that is to say, a life which does not harbor any shadowy part. It is a life which can face the full light of day and appear without reticence to the sight of all. A way of being and of conducting oneself therefore is true and falls within the domain of the true life if it hides nothing of its intentions and aims. There is a reference to this conception of the true life, as life which does not conceal anything, in the *Lesser Hippias*, paragraphs 364e-365a, which concerns the famous parallel, the frequently invoked contrast between Ulysses and Achilles. The text Socrates quotes at this point is from *The Illiad*, Book Nine, in which Achilles, speaking to Ulysses and calling him "ingenious Ulysses" (*polumēkhan'Odusseu*), says to him: "I must tell you my intentions straightforwardly, as I will carry them out, and as I know they will be accomplished. I detest as much as the doors of Hades the person who hides one thing in his mind and says something else."[4] Commenting on Achilles' challenge to Ulysses,

Socrates says: Ulysses, is the man *polutropōtatos*,[5] the man of a thousand roundabout means, that is to say, the man who hides from his partners what he has in mind and wants to do. On the other hand, as opposed to Ulysses, Achilles—who precisely has just said to the ingenious Ulysses: I will tell you my intentions straightforwardly, as I will carry them out, not only as I want to carry them out, but as I will in actual fact carry them out, as I know [I will carry them out]—appears as the man of truth, without circumlocution. Between what he thinks and what he says, between what he says and what he wants to do, between what he wants to do and what he will in actual fact do, there is no concealment, no deviation, nothing which hides the reality of what he thinks and what will be the reality of what he does. We are in broad daylight, and Socrates says of Achilles: Here is a man *haploustatos kai alēthestatos* (the simplest, most direct, and truest; *haplous*, someone straightforward).[6] The conjunction *haplous/alēthēs* is fairly frequent when referring to a man, a character, an existence, a form of life. The coupling of *haplous* and *alēthēs* is found in Book II of the *Republic*, where in this case what is characterized as truth, true life, true mode of being, is the god's existence, which the *Republic* says, is simple and true (*haploun kai alēthēs*: straightforward and true): "Simple and true in deeds and words, God does not change himself, and nor does he deceive others by phantoms, or discourse, or by signs sent in waking or in dreams."[7] So you can see how this simplicity which is truth of existence, true life, is characterized here: no change, but no possibility of deceptions being produced by the disconnection, the discrepancy between what happens and discourse, phantoms, and signs.

The second value [of the expression] *alēthēs bios* corresponds to what I was just telling you, [namely] that *alēthēs* designated what is without mixture. In Plato, the *alēthēs bios* appears as the unalloyed life, without mixture of good and evil, pleasure and suffering, vice and virtue. A true life is one which cannot be variegated. All that well known variegation (of the part of the soul which is susceptible to lust or irascible, of democratic or tyrannical cities in which all desires have a place, in their violence or singularity) is precisely what gets in the way of leading the true life. That the variegated man, the man prey to the multiplicity of his desires, appetites, and impulses of his soul, is not capable of the truth is precisely what is said in the description of the democratic man in Book VIII of the *Republic*. This is how Plato describes him: "He establishes then a sort of equality between the pleasures and he lives by giving up the command of his soul to the first-comer..., until he has his fill of it, then he abandons himself to another, treating them on an equal footing... Today he is intoxicated by the sound of the flute; tomorrow he diets; sometimes he exercises in the gymnasium, sometimes he is idle and cares about nothing, and at other times one might think him buried deep in philosophy; he is often a politician, leaping onto the platform and saying and doing whatever comes into his head."[8] This life of the democratic man, sometimes idle and at others busy, sometimes given over to pleasure and at others to politics, and when given over to politics saying anything and everything that comes into his head, this life without unity, this mixed life dedicated to multiplicity is a life without truth. It is unable, Plato says, to give way to *logos alēthēs* (true discourse).[9] We can quote another text in which the true life is contrasted in this way with the life of mixture. At the end of the *Critias*, Plato quickly evokes the decadence of Atlantis—this is just before the text breaks off, the end of which is lost—and he explains: After the happy life that men were able to lead in Atlantis, a time came when the share, the part given by the gods to the men of Atlantis became mixed with many mortal elements.[10] This mixture of the divine share, which characterized the true life of the men of Atlantis, with mortal elements, is what caused their fall from the true life, from its happiness and accompanying beauty. When life is mixed, it is no longer the true life.*

Third, in Plato, the true life is a straight (*euthos*) life. According to the characterization of truth as rectitude, of the true as that which is straight, the true life is a straight life, that is to say, a life in line with the principles, the rules, the *nomos*. In his famous *Letter VII*, Plato recounts how he was led to go to Sicily at Dion's request and how he hesitated to accept this invitation. But he let himself be persuaded when he realized how easily Dion had accepted his [Plato's] principles

---

* The manuscript contains at this point a passage corresponding to the fifth meaning of truth, which Foucault leaves out (conformity to the essence):

"The *alēthēs bios* is a life which does not don the appearance of that which it is not. It does not imitate a form which is not its own. A true life is the life which allows its *ēthos* to be easily recognized" (his reference here is to Book V of Plato's *Laws*, 738d-e).

and modeled his life according to the rules [he] gave him.[11] Dion's conversion to philosophy, the training he received anyway, allowed Plato to hope that, through Dion, the city of Syracuse, and maybe the whole of Sicily, would agree to settle down under this form of law. And, he says, there was the hope of everyone having an *alēthinos bios* (a true life).[12] The true life, which is Plato's promise to the Sicilians, or rather his hope when he went to Sicily, is life according to the rules that Plato, that philosophy, can propose not just to men in their individual life, as in the case of Dion, but also in their social life, their public and political life. These are the laws, the political order that Plato wants to propose to the Sicilians and Syracusans.*

This passage may be brought together with one from the *Gorgias* in which we also find this notion of the true life. It is right at the end when Plato is referring to the Judgment of souls. In the myth of the *Gorgias*, we see the souls presenting themselves after death to those who will be their judges, and in particular to Rhadamanthus. Socrates says: Rhadamanthus, the judge of souls and the underworld, will no doubt have his work cut out. The souls of great kings will come before him. He will not let himself be impressed by these souls, for he will see straightaway that there is nothing in them that is healthy, "everything is deformed by lies, vanity, [and imposture; M.F.], nothing is straight (*euthus*)."[13] Why is nothing straight? Because this soul has lived without truth (*aneu alētheias*):[14] "the license, laxity, pride, and intemperance of its conduct have filled it with disorder and ugliness."[15] Plural, variegated souls traversed by desire, license, and laxity; souls without truth. Consequently Rhadamanthus will send these souls to suffer the punishment they deserve.[16] But, Socrates continues, Rhadamanthus also discovers a completely different type of soul, the souls maybe of philosophers, or even possibly of citizens like any other ordinary citizen. But whether these souls are the souls of philosophers or of someone like everyone else, they are souls which have lived in a holy way (*hosiōs*)[17] and with truth (*met'alētheias*), without dedicating themselves to sterile restlessness. Rhadamanthus "admires the beauty" of these souls which have lived with truth (*met'alētheias*), and sends them to the Isles of the

---

* The manuscript gives here a quotation from Book X of Plato's *Republic*, 604b-c, concerning the reproach that the poets only propose imitations. But the passage is crossed out.

Blessed.[18] Hence, after this reference to the contrasting destinies of souls (some punished because they have been without truth; the others rewarded and sent to eternal happiness because they have lived with the truth), Socrates resolves: I will strive, through the pursuit of the truth, to make myself as perfect as possible "in life and in death."[19] The life with truth is then the straight life.

Finally, the fourth meaning, the fourth value of the expression *bios alēthēs, alēthinos bios* in Plato: the true life is one which shuns disturbance, change, corruption, and the fall, and which remains without change in the identity of its being. And it is this identity of life with regard to itself which ensures that it escapes every element of alteration and, on the one hand, assures it a freedom understood as independence, as non-dependence and non-slavery with regard to everything which could subject it to domination and control, and, on the other, assures it happiness (*eudaimonia*), understood as self-mastery and self-enjoyment. We have just seen that this true life as a life of perfect mastery and complete happiness was evoked in the *Critias*: this was the existence of the inhabitants of Atlantis who led a true and blissful life before their mortal elements mixed with their divine element. The truth of the life is its happiness, its perfect happiness. In the same way, according to fairly analogous values, there is a well known passage in the *Theaetetus*, 174c-176a, in which Plato describes the busy, tumultuous life without leisure of those who are familiar with all the problems of practical life and perfectly able to deal with them, but who spend all their time doing so. Plato contrasts this with the life of those who, because they are contemplating the real truth, are clumsy and ridiculous in everyday activities and provoke the laughter of Thracian maidservants. But these people who are so clumsy in everyday life can "adapt to the harmony of discourse in order to sing fittingly of the true life (*bion alēthē*) lived by the gods and blessed men."[20] The true life is therefore the divine and blessed life. These are, if you like—very schematically, and again, without seeking more precise philosophical elaboration as *background** for the analysis I would now like to make—the recognized meanings of the notion of true life (*alēthēs bios*).

---

* In English in the original; G.B.

What we now have to grasp—I will just begin and will develop things next week—is [how] Cynicism played on this notion of *alēthēs bios*. Right at the start of Diogenes' life, recounted by Diogenes Laertius, there is a series of important episodes or allusions. In the first place there is reference to the fact that Diogenes was the son of a money changer, a banker, someone who had to handle coins and exchange them against each other. There is also reference to the fact that it was following an embezzlement—to tell the truth, an activity of counterfeiting—that Diogenes or his father were exiled from Sinope, where they were from and where they lived. The third reference, finally, to this problem of money is Diogenes, exiled from Sinope, going to Delphi and asking the god, Apollo, for advice. And Apollo's advice was supposed to have been to falsify the currency, or to change its value.[21]

This principle, "Change the value of the currency," was regularly utilized in the Cynic tradition to two ends. First: to balance, bring together, and establish symmetry between Socrates and Diogenes. Just as Socrates had received from the god of Delphi the prophecy, the indication, the role assignment that he was the wisest man, so, in the same way, Diogenes, going to Delphi and asking the god how things stood with himself, gets this answer: "change, alter (*altérer*)* the value of currency." So both Socrates and Diogenes find themselves charged with a mission. This symmetry, this proximity of Socrates and Diogenes will be maintained throughout the Cynic tradition. In the texts he writes in the fourth century against the Cynics and in favor of true Cynicism, Julian, who speaks about Diogenes with great respect, never fails to speak of Socrates and Diogenes at the same time: one heard the god's words at Delphi, knew himself to be the wisest man, and sought to know himself; the other received another, very different mission from

---

* [The French *altérer* can mean to change, modify, etc. in a neutral sense, and also to degrade, distort, adulterate, disfigure, etc. When referring to *monnaie* (currency or coinage), as here, it is usually rendered as to falsify. However, Foucault clearly wants to distinguish the meaning of *altérer* here from that of falsifying (*falsifier*). The editors and contributors to R. Bracht Branham and Marie-Odile Goulet-Cazé, eds., *The Cynics. The Cynic Movement in Antiquity and Its Legacy* (Berkeley: University of California Press, 1996) translate the Cynic motto *parakharattein to nomisma* as "deface the currency," which is closer to Foucault's intention than "falsify." I have generally opted for leaving the verb in its neutral sense, since Foucault's commentary makes clear the meaning he gives to the Greek. It also seems possible that in choosing the verb *altérer* Foucault wanted to suggest a connection with the theme of "otherness" (*altérité*) he develops in later lectures; G.B.]

the god at Delphi, which was to change the value of the currency. So there is symmetry between these two characters.

The second meaning of this imperative is obviously much more difficult to pinpoint. What in fact does "alter the value of the currency" (*parakharattein to nomisma*) mean? It is around this theme that I will try to develop the problem of the Cynic true life next week. For now I would just like to point out that what should be stressed first of all with this theme of "change, alter the value of the currency" is the connection—indicated by the word itself—between currency and custom, rule, law. *Nomisma* is currency; *nomos* is the law. To change the value of the currency is also to adopt a certain standpoint towards convention, rule, or law. Second, still with regard to this notion of *parakharaxis; parakharattein* (change, alter) does not mean devalue the money. We can sometimes find the important sense of "defacing (*altérer*)" a coin so that it loses its value, but here the verb essentially and especially signifies: starting from a certain coin which carries a certain effigy, erase that effigy and replace it with another which will enable this coin to circulate with its true value. That the coin is not misleading about its true value, that its own value is restored to it by stamping it with another, better, and more adequate effigy, is what is defined by this important Cynic principle of altering and changing the value of the currency.

It seems to me—and I will end with this and continue with it next week—that what is involved in Cynicism regarding the true life is, first of all, actually taking up the coin of the *alēthēs bios*, and taking it back as close as possible to its traditional meaning. From this perspective, the Cynics do not, as it were, change the metal itself of this coin. But they want to modify its effigy and, on the basis of these same principles of the true life—which must be unconcealed, unalloyed, straight, stable, incorruptible, and happy—, by going to the extreme consequence, without a break, simply by pushing these themes to their extreme consequence, they reveal a life which is precisely the very opposite of what was traditionally recognized as the true life. Taking up the coin again, changing its effigy, and, as it were, making the theme of the true life grimace. Cynicism as the grimace of the true life. The Cynics tried to make the traditional philosophical theme of the true life grimace. Instead of seeing Cynicism as a philosophy which broke with the themes of the true life because it was popular, or because it was never accepted by the educated philosophical consensus and community, it should rather be seen as taking these themes to their extreme consequence, as an extrapolation of the themes of the true life rather than as external to them. With regard to the question of the true life, what is involved is much more a sort of carnivalesque continuity of the theme, than of a break with the received values of classical philosophy.

Forgive me, I am far from having fulfilled my contract and from having told you what I should have told you this week. I will try to finish with Cynicism next week.

1. Lucien, *Les Sectes à l'encan*, §8, p. 203: "I [Diogenes] wish to be the interpreter of the truth and frankness (*alētheias kai parrhēsias prophetēs*)"; Lucian, *Philosophies for Sale*, p. 465: "I desire to be an interpreter of truth and free speech."

2. Grégoire de Nazianze, *Discours*, 24-26, 1200A, 25, I,2, p. 159; Saint Gregory of Nazianzus, *Select Orations*, "Oration 25," p. 158. See above, lecture of 29 February, first hour.

3. See *L'Usage des plaisirs*, ch. 5, "Le véritable amour"; *The Use of Pleasure*, Part Five, "True Love."

4. Platon, *Hippias Mineur*, 365a, in *Œuvres complètes*, vol. 1, trans. M. Croiset (Paris: Les Belles Lettres, 1970) p. 28; English translation by Benjamin Jowett, Plato, *Lesser Hippias*, in Plato, *The Collected Dialogues*, p. 202: "crafty Odysseus, I will speak out plainly the word which I intend to carry out in act, and which will, I believe, be accomplished. For I hate him like the gates of death who thinks one thing and says another."

5. Ibid., 364c: Fr. p. 27; Eng. p. 202: "wiliest."

6. Ibid., 364e. In fact it is Hippias who describes Achilles in this way. Fr: "[Homer] made [Achilles] the simplest and most sincere (*haploustatos kai alēthestatos*) of men"; Eng: "[Achilles] is the most straightforward of mankind."

7. Platon, *La République*, Book II, 382e, trans. E. Chambry (Paris: Les Belles Lettres, 1943) p. 89; Plato, *Republic*, in Plato, *Collected Dialogues*, p. 630: "Then God is altogether simple and true in deed and word, and neither changes himself nor deceives others by visions or words or the sending of signs in waking or in dreams."

8. Ibid., Platon, *La République*, Book VIII, 561b-561d, trans. E. Chambry (Paris: Les Belles Lettres, 1934) pp. 32-33; Plato, *Republic*, pp. 789-790: "then he establishes and maintains all his pleasures on a footing of equality... and so lives turning over the guardhouse of his soul to each as it happens to come along until it is sated, as if it had drawn a lot for that office, and then in turn to another, disdaining none but fostering them all equally.... And does he not... live out his life in this fashion... indulging the appetite of the day, now... abandoning himself to the lascivious pleasing of the flute and again drinking only water and dieting, and at one time exercising his body, and sometimes idling and neglecting all things, and at another time seeming to occupy himself with philosophy. And frequently he goes in for politics and bounces up and says and does whatever enters his head."

9. Ibid., 561b: Fr. p. 32: "As for reason and truth (*logon alēthē*), I said, he rejects them and does not allow them entry to the garrison"; Eng., p. 789: "And he does not accept or admit into the guardhouse the words of truth."

10. Platon, *Critias*, 121a-b, trans. A. Rivaud (Pasis: Les Belles Lettres, 1949) p. 274: "But, when the divine element diminished in them, through the effect of repeated crossing with many mortal elements, when the human character dominated, then they fell into indecency, no longer able to bear their present prosperity. To clear-sighted men they seemed ugly, for they had allowed themselves to lose the most beautiful and precious goods. On the other hand, in the eyes of those who could not discern what kind of life truly contributes to happiness (*tois adunatousin alēthinon pros eudaimonian bion horan*), it was then that they seemed perfectly beautiful and happy"; English translation by A.E. Taylor, *Critias*, in Plato, *Collected Dialogues*, p. 1224: "But when the god's part in them began to wax faint by constant crossing with much mortality, and the human temper to predominate, then they could no longer carry their fortunes, but began to behave themselves unseemly. To the seeing eye they now began to seem foul, for they were losing the fairest bloom from their most precious treasure, but to such as could not see the true happy life, to appear at last fair and blessed indeed..."

11. Plato, *Letter VII*, 327a-b, Fr. p. 31; Eng. p. 1576. See above, pp. 70-71, note 9.

12. Ibid., 327d, Fr. p. 32: "That if now he inspired the same desire in Dionysius, as he attempted, he had the greatest hope of establishing, without massacres, murders, and all the evils that actually took place, a happy and true life (*bion eudaimona kai alēthinon*) throughout the land"; Eng. p. 1577: "If, accordingly, he were now to succeed in his attempt to bring about the same result once again in the case of Dionysius, he had great hopes of creating, without bloodshed or slaughter or such misfortunes as have actually occurred, a happy and genuine way of living throughout the land."

13. Platon, *Gorgias*, 525a, trans. A. Croiset (Paris: Les Belles Lettres, 1968) p. 221; English translation by W.D. Woodhead, *Gorgias*, in Plato, *The Collected Dialogues*, p. 305: "there is

no sign of health in his soul...everything is crooked through falsehood and imposture, and nothing is straight..."

14. Ibid., Eng.: "because it has been reared a stranger to truth."

15. Ibid., Eng.: "owing to the license and luxury and presumption and incontinence of its actions the soul is surcharged with disproportion and ugliness."

16. Ibid.

17. Ibid., 526c, Fr. p. 222; Eng. p. 306: "in piety and truth."

18. Ibid., Fr. p. 223; Eng. p. 306: "is filled with admiration."

19. Ibid., 527e, Fr. p. 224; Eng. p. 307: "let us follow the guidance of the argument...that this is the best way of life—to live and die in the pursuit of righteousness and all other virtues."

20. Platon, *Théétète*, 176a, trans. A. Diès (Paris: Les Belles Lettres, 1967) p. 207. The French translation gives "the reality of life" for "*bion alēthē*," which Foucault rightly re-translates as "true life." English translation by F.M. Cornford, *Theaetetus*, in Plato, *The Collected Dialogues*, p. 880: "caught the accent of discourse that will rightly celebrate the true life of happiness for gods and men."

21. Diogène Laërce, *Vies et doctrines*, Book VI, §20-21, trans. M.-O. Goulet-Cazé, pp. 703-705; Diogenes Laertius, *Lives of Eminent Philosophers*, II, p. 23.

thirteen

14 MARCH 1984

First hour

[
*The Cynic paradox, or Cynicism as scandalous banality of phi-
losophy.* ∽ *Eclecticism with reverse effect.* ∽ *The three forms of
courage of truth.* ∽ *The problem of the philosophical life.* ∽
*Traditional components of the philosophical life: armature for life;
care of self; useful knowledge; conformable life.* ∽ *Interpretations
of the Cynic precept: transform the values.* ∽ *The label "dog."* ∽
The two lines of development of the true life: Alcibiades *or*
Laches.
]

TODAY I WILL SPEAK about the Cynic life, about the *bios kunikos*
as true life. As I tried to show you last week, what seems to me to be
both difficult and important to understand in Cynicism is the following
paradox, which is nonetheless fairly simple in itself. On the one hand,
Cynicism appears in the form of a set of features which it shares with
many philosophies of the time; there is something commonplace and
ordinary in the theses it advances and the principles it recommends. On
the other hand, it is stamped by a scandal which has constantly accompanied it, a disapproval which surrounds it, a mixture of mockery, repulsion, and apprehension in reaction to its presence and manifestations.
Throughout its existence, from the Hellenistic epoch to the beginning of
Christianity, Cynicism was both very familiar and nevertheless strange
in the landscape of Greco-Roman philosophy, thought, and society.
It was ordinary, commonplace, and it was unacceptable. All in all we

could say that a sizable number of eminent philosophers found it fairly easy to recognize themselves in Cynicism and gave a positive image of it. There is some evidence of this in important texts. You remember that Seneca gave a portrait of Demetrius the Cynic, backed up by quotations and references, as one of the most important philosophers of his time.[1] You remember Epictetus, Discourse 69 in Book III of *The Discourses*, presenting his famous portrait of the ideal Cynic. Even amongst [its] declared opponents there is a positive characterization of a certain form of Cynicism. The Emperor Julian, precisely when he is criticizing it, lays claim to Cynicism as a universal philosophical standpoint, as old as philosophy itself. Lucian too, despite his harsh criticisms of not only a Cynic like Peregrinus, but of practically all philosophers, gives a positive portrait of Demonax.

So, at the same time as philosophers find it so easy to recognize themselves in Cynicism, they vehemently distinguish themselves from it by a repulsive caricature. They present it as a sort of unacceptable adulteration of philosophy. Cynicism would be the broken mirror, as it were, for ancient philosophy. It is the broken mirror in which every philosopher can and must recognize himself, in which he can and must recognize the very image of philosophy, the reflection of what it is and should be, and of what he is and would like to be. And at the same time, the philosopher sees in this mirror something like a grimace, a violent, ugly, unsightly deformation in which there is no way in which he could recognize either himself or philosophy. All of this amounts to saying, quite simply, that Cynicism was seen, I think, as the banality of philosophy, but its scandalous banality. Cynicism made a scandal of philosophy grasped, practiced, and clad in its banality.

In conclusion, I would say that, in Antiquity, Cynicism appears to me to be basically like a sort of eclecticism with reverse effect. By this I mean that if eclecticism is the form of thought, discourse, and philosophical choice which combines the commonest and most traditional features of the different philosophies of an epoch, this is generally so that they can be made acceptable to everyone and the organizing principles of an intellectual and moral consensus. Generally speaking, this is the definition of eclecticism. I would say that Cynicism is an eclecticism with reverse effect: it is eclecticism because it does take up some of the most fundamental features found in the philosophies contemporary with it; but it has a reverse effect, because it turns this re-use of these features into a shocking practice which far from establishing a philosophical consensus, establishes rather a strangeness in philosophical practice, an exteriority, and even hostility and a war.

The paradox of Cynicism is that it formed the commonest elements of philosophy into so many breaking-points for philosophy. This is what we must try to understand: how can Cynicism be basically what everyone says and yet make the very fact of saying it unacceptable? This paradox of Cynicism, if we can characterize it in this way, is worth some attention for two reasons. The first is that it enables Cynicism to be situated in the history, or prehistory, of what I wanted to outline this year, that of the courage of truth. It seems to me that Cynicism sheds a new light on, gives a new form to that grand old political and philosophical problem of the courage of truth, which was so important in all of ancient philosophy. We could draw up the following very schematic outline.

We first came across the problem of the courage of truth—this is what I tried to study last year—in the form of what could be called political boldness, that is to say: the courage of the democrat or the bravery of the courtier when they tell the Assembly or the Prince something other than what this Assembly or Prince thinks. The political boldness of both the democrat and courtier thus consists in saying something other than and contrary to what the Assembly or Prince thinks. The politician, if he is courageous, risks his life for the truth against the opinion of the Prince or Assembly. This is, very schematically, the structure of what could be called the political bravery of truth-telling.

We came across a second form of courage of truth, which I sketched out a bit last year and took up again this year. This is no longer political bravery but what could be called Socratic irony, which consists in telling people, and getting them gradually to recognize, that they do not really know what they say and think they know. In this case, Socratic irony consists in risking the anger, irritation, and vengeance of the people, and even being put on trial by them, in order to lead them, despite themselves, to take care of themselves, of their souls, and of the truth. The simplest case, political bravery, involved opposing the courage of truth-telling to an opinion, an error. In the case of Socratic irony, it involves introducing a certain form of truth into a knowledge that men do not know they know, a form of truth which will lead them to take care of themselves.

With Cynicism, we have a third form of courage of truth, which is distinct from both political bravery and Socratic irony. Cynic courage of truth consists in getting people to condemn, reject, despise, and insult the very manifestation of what they accept, or claim to accept at the level of principles. It involves facing up to their anger when presenting them with the image of what they accept and value in thought, and at the same time reject and despise in their life. This is the Cynic scandal. After political bravery and Socratic irony we have, if you like, Cynic scandal.

In the first two cases the courage of truth consists in risking one's life by telling the truth, risking one's life in order to tell the truth, and risking one's life because one has told the truth. In the case of Cynic scandal—and this is what seems to me to be important and worth holding on to, isolating—one risks one's life, not just by telling the truth, and in order to tell it, but by the very way in which one lives. In all the meanings of the word, one "exposes" one's life. That is to say, one displays it and risks it. One risks it by displaying it; and it is because one displays it that one risks it. One exposes one's life, not through one's discourses, but through one's life itself. This is the first reason for keeping hold of this Cynic scandal, in its very structure, which always operates within the framework of the grand theme of having the courage of truth, but which makes it work in a different way from political courage or Socratic irony.

The second reason for focusing for a moment on this problem of the Cynic life is that in Cynic practice, in Cynic scandal, the question Cynicism constantly puts to philosophy in Antiquity, and also in Christianity or the modern world, the permanent, difficult, and perpetually embarrassing question, is basically that of the philosophical life, of the *bios philosophikos*. If we take up the problem and theme of Cynicism on the basis of this great history of *parrhēsia* and truth-telling, we can say that whereas all philosophy increasingly tends to pose the question of truth-telling in terms of the conditions under which a statement can be recognized as true, Cynicism is the form of philosophy which constantly raises the question: what can the form of life be such that it practices truth-telling?

From the origin of philosophy, and maybe in fact until now, still and despite everything, the West has always accepted that philosophy cannot be separated from a philosophical existence, that the practice of philosophy must always be more or less a sort of life exercise. This is what distinguishes philosophy from science. But while loudly proclaiming that philosophy is fundamentally not just a form of discourse, but also a mode of life, Western philosophy—and such was its history and perhaps its destiny—progressively eliminated, or at least neglected and marginalized the problem of this philosophical life, which to start with, however, it posited as inseparable from philosophical practice. It has increasingly neglected and marginalized the problem of life in its essential connection with the practice of truth-telling. We can take it that the forgetting, neglect, elimination, and exteriorization of the problem of the true life, of the philosophical life in relation to philosophical practice and discourse, are the effects of, or manifest certain phenomena.

The absorption and, to a certain extent, confiscation by religion of the theme and practice of the true life has certainly been one of the reasons for this disappearance. It is as if philosophy was able to disburden itself of the problem of the true life to the same extent as religion, religious institutions, asceticism, and spirituality took over this problem in an increasingly evident manner from the end of Antiquity down to the modern world. We can take it also that the institutionalization of truth-telling practices in the form of a science (a normed, regulated, established science embodied in institutions) has no doubt been the other major reason for the disappearance of the theme of the true life as a philosophical question, as a problem of the conditions of access to the truth. If scientific practice, scientific institutions, and integration within the scientific consensus are by themselves sufficient to assure access to the truth, then it is clear that the problem of the true life as the necessary basis for the practice of truth-telling disappears. So, there has been confiscation of the problem of the true life in the religious institution, and invalidation of the problem of the true life in the scientific institution. You understand why the question of the true life has continually become worn out, faded, eliminated, and threadbare in Western thought.

The question of the true life is always gradually removed from philosophical reflection and practice, except of course at some remarkable points and moments. The problem of the philosophical life could perhaps be taken up again, from Montaigne[2] to the *Aufklärung*. For if the traditional history of philosophy, and particularly of classical philosophy, is almost exclusively interested in the problem of the systematic character of philosophical thought and the formal and systematic structure of its truth-telling, there is no doubt that the problem of the philosophical life nevertheless arises with a certain intensity and force from the sixteenth to the eighteenth century. After all, Spinoza—read *On the Improvement of the Understanding*—in fact puts the question of the philosophical life and the true life at the very source of the philosophical project.[3] And, subject to much more precise analyses, we might say that with Spinoza we have, as it were, the last great figure for whom philosophical practice was inspired by the fundamental and essential project of leading a philosophical life. And we could contrast Spinoza, and the way in which he lived, with Leibniz, who might be the first modern philosopher inasmuch as for him, far from implying the choice of a philosophical life, as in Spinoza, philosophy always manifested itself and was practiced through a number of what could be called modern activities: he was a librarian, a diplomat, a politician, an administrator, etcetera. We have there a modern form of philosophical life which could be contrasted with Spinoza's philosophical practice, which implied a true life of a completely other type than that of everyday life. But to tell the truth, we could even argue about Leibniz. Anyway, it would be interesting to study the history of classical philosophy starting from the problem of the philosophical life, considered as a problem of a choice which may be identified through biographical events and decisions, but also through the place [it is] given in the system itself.

In any case, I would simply like to suggest that if it is true that the question of Being has indeed been what Western philosophy has forgotten, and that this forgetting is what made metaphysics possible, it may be also that the question of the philosophical life has continued to be, I won't say forgotten, but neglected; it has constantly appeared as surplus in relation to philosophy, to a philosophical practice indexed to the scientific model. The question of the philosophical life has constantly appeared like a shadow of philosophical practice, and increasingly pointless. This neglect of the philosophical life has meant that it is now possible for the relation to truth to be validated and manifested in no other form than that of scientific knowledge.

In this perspective, Cynicism, as a particular figure of ancient philosophy as well as a recurring attitude throughout Western history, raises the question of the philosophical life in a peremptory fashion, [in] the form of scandal. The fact that Cynicism is always both inside and outside philosophy (the familiarity and strangeness of Cynicism in relation to the philosophy which serves as its context, milieu, vis-à-vis, opponent, and enemy), the Cynic constitution of the philosophical life as scandal, is the historical stamp, the first manifestation, the point of departure for what has been, I think, the great exteriorization of the problem of the philosophical life in relation to philosophy, to philosophical practice, to the practice of philosophical discourse. This is why Cynicism interests me and what I would like to pinpoint with it. You can see how, for me, its study can be connected to the question of the practices and arts of existence: it is because it was both the most rudimentary and most radical form in which the question of this particular form of life, the philosophical life—which is obviously only one particular form, but extremely important and central through the problems it poses—was raised.

I would now like to study how Cynicism posed the question of the philosophical life and how it practiced it. Let us take Cynicism in those aspects which are the most common, usual, familiar, well known, and close to all the philosophies contemporary with it. Once again, going back over some of what I was saying last week, we do not know a great deal about Cynicism, the essentials coming from late sources dating from the first centuries C.E. Consequently it is very difficult to know whether there was an evolution of Cynicism. It is even difficult to know what the historical reality of the tradition was, and what continuity there was with those semi-legendary figures of Antisthenes, Diogenes, and Crates. I am taking Cynicism as it manifested itself, as it was expressed in the texts of the first two or three centuries C.E., independently of any historical question of chronology, succession, influence, or anything else. At the point of departure of Cynic practice, as described in the texts I am talking about, we find a number of very common, standard elements as general, basic principles, which manifestly link Cynic practice to the old Socratic tradition on the one hand, and themes common to other philosophies on the other.

First, for Cynicism, philosophy is a preparation for life; certainly a very common and easily recognized theme. For example, the aphorism that to prepare for life one needs either *logos* or the *brokhos* is attributed to Diogenes. That is to say: either reason (*logos*) which organizes life, or the cord (*brokhos*) with which one hangs oneself.[4] Either you will hang yourself, or you will prepare your life according to *logos*. Philosophy is preparation for life.

Second, this preparation for life—which again, is a very familiar, easily recognizable principle—entails above all else that one takes care of oneself. There are many statements in the Cynics on the importance of this care of self, of the rule: "take care of yourself." There is the following anecdote (*khreia*) about Diogenes. One day he was on a public square, or on the street corner, speaking seriously of solemn, weighty things, and no one was listening to him. So he breaks off his discourse and begins to whistle like a bird. Straightaway a crowd of curious people gather around him. Then he insults the gaping onlookers who form a circle around him, telling them that they hurried to "listen to foolish things, but that they hardly rushed to hear serious things."[5] There are lots of accounts on the same theme that one must take care of oneself, which is the only serious thing. Demonax, for example—this is cited in Stobaeus—reprimanded people who went to great pains for their body while neglecting themselves. It is, he said, as if you wanted to look after your house without taking care of those living in it.[6] And Julian, in his discourses where he tries to give the pure, essential, and valid image of Cynicism, says: Whoever desires to be a serious (*spoudaios*) Cynic must begin by imitating Diogenes and Crates, by taking care of himself, and he employs the famous expression I have quoted so many times: *hautou proteron epimelētheis*.[7] Diogenes and Crates are therefore teachers of care of self, as we have seen Socrates was. This is again an entirely common-place and standard theme in philosophy.

The third principle we find constantly taken up and repeated by the Cynics, and which is also a completely familiar theme, is that in order to take care of oneself one must only study what is really useful in and for existence. Diogenes Laertius quotes these remarks of Diogenes the Cynic. The latter "was surprised to see the grammarians devote so much study to the morals of Ulysses, and to neglect their own, to see musicians tune their lyre so well, and forget to tune their soul, to see mathematicians study the sun and moon, and forget what is beneath their feet, to see orators full of zeal for speaking well, but never pressed to act well."[8] Entirely in the same spirit, again in a text quoted by Stobaeus, when someone asked Demonax whether the world was or was not spherical, he replied: "You go to great pains over the subject of the cosmic order, but you are completely unconcerned about your own internal disorder."[9] So, if you want to take care of yourself, it is not the cosmic order, not things of the world, not grammar, mathematics, or music you should study, but things immediately useful for life, that is to say, for the care of yourself.

Finally, fourth, one must make one's life conform to the precepts one formulates. According to Diogenes Laertius, Diogenes the Cynic rebuked those who despised wealth but envied the wealthy, he rebuked those who sacrificed to the gods in order to obtain health but feasted during these same sacrifices.[10] There can only be true care of self if the principles one formulates as true principles are at the same time guaranteed and authenticated by the way one lives.

In all this you can recognize quite common and traditional principles. But to these four general and common principles, which you find in Socrates, as in the Stoics and even the Epicureans, the Cynics add a fifth, which is very different and completely specific to them, singling them out. I referred to this principle at the end of last week.* This is the principle that one must *"parakharattein to nomisma"* (alter, change the value of the currency). This is a difficult, obscure principle which has been interpreted in many different ways. We can accept that the expression *parakharattein to nomisma* means "change the currency," but in two senses, a pejorative sense and a positive, or at any rate neutral sense. It may actually be a dishonest alteration (*altération*) of the currency. It may also be a change of the effigy stamped on the coin, a change which enables the true value of the coin to be reestablished. Anyway, in all the doxography and most of the references to Cynicism, this principle, with its ambiguous meaning (positive or negative value), is constantly associated with Diogenes and Cynic principles. Thus,

---

* [See above p. 226, and footnote; G.B.]

Diogenes Laertius gives several versions of the beginnings of Diogenes' life, his vocation, and his philosophical choice.

First version: the father of Diogenes was a money changer at Sinope, but he falsified (*falsifié*) it—in the pejorative, negative sense of the term. As a result, his son, Diogenes, was forced to leave the town, to emigrate, and go into exile in Athens.[11] Diogenes Laertius relates other versions around the same theme. According [to some]—he cites Eubulides—it was Diogenes himself, not his father, who falsified the money.[12] According to still other sources, in reality Diogenes went to Delphi spontaneously to consult the oracle—in this version neither he nor his father would seem to have falsified the money—and the oracle is supposed to have told him: "Falsify the currency," or "alter," "change the value of the currency."[13] Finally, in a more complicated version, Diogenes Laertius combines the previous versions he has just referred to and says: According to some, in his childhood and youth, Diogenes falsified some coins his father had given him—here we find again the father and his relation to money—as a result of which the father, as the person responsible for this falsification, was imprisoned and died. Diogenes either exiled himself or was sent into exile as punishment. He went to Delphi and asked the god: How can I become famous? To this the oracle replied: Alter the currency.[14] You see everything brought together in this account: the father, the falsification of the currency by Diogenes, and then the Delphic precept "alter the currency" (*parakharaxon to nomisma*).

The principle of altering the currency is regularly associated with Cynicism and, in the lives of philosophers recounted by Diogenes Laertius, there is a whole series of anecdotes which regularly associate the Cynics with money, to its practice and correct or corrupt use. Thus, again according to Diogenes Laertius, Monimus, the first disciple of Diogenes the Cynic, was the servant of a banker and, feigning madness, stole some money from him.[15] Crates was supposed to have been an extremely rich man who abandoned the wealth he inherited from his father, distributing the money to the poor, or else, as another version has it, throwing all his inherited cash into the sea.[16] In his *Life* of Menippus, Diogenes Laertius says that, according to Hermippus, Menippus was a money lender who accumulated a great fortune but was ultimately ruined by his enemies and, in despair, hanged himself.[17]

As for Bion of Borysthenes—who is on the borders of a particular form of Platonism and Cynicism—he recounted, again according to Diogenes Laertius, how his father, having evaded taxation, was sold into slavery with all his family. This was how Bion of Borysthenes became a slave.[18] As you can see, there is very often a story of money, banking, and exchange whenever the Cynics are involved.

What is important, or what at any rate I would like to stress, is that the principle that you must "alter your currency" or "change the value of your currency," is regarded as a principle of life, and even as the most fundamental and typical Cynic principle. When Julian, for example, writes his two great discourses against the Cynics, he refers at several points to the principle: alter the currency, change the value of the currency. In *To the Uneducated Cynics*—you remember, I spoke about this last week—Julian presents Cynicism as a kind of universal philosophy, the essential features of which are found in all the other philosophies, its basic principles going back not only to Hercules, but even before, to the beginning of humanity. In this same passage, Julian states what, according to him, are the two principles of Cynicism; he comments that these two principles go back as far as the Pythian Apollo. These two principles are, in fact, first: "know yourself"; second: "*parakharaxon to nomisma*" (revalue your currency, alter your currency, change its value). And he adds that if the [first; G.B.] principle, with which the Cynics are linked and by which they are inspired, was not addressed solely to Diogenes, since it was also addressed to Socrates in particular and, even more generally, to everyone (it was inscribed, engraved on the very door of the temple), the principle "*parakharaxon to nomisma*," on the other hand, was addressed to Diogenes alone. So that, according to Julian, of these two great fundamental principles, of these two most universal principles of philosophy, one was addressed to everyone and to Socrates ("know yourself"), and the other was reserved for Diogenes alone ("revalue your currency").[19]

In the other discourse (*To the Cynic Heracleios*), recalling once again the two Delphic principles ("know yourself" and "alter the value of your currency"), Julian raises the important, interesting question of the relation between these two principles.[20] Must one revalue one's currency in order to know oneself or is it that by knowing oneself one can revalue one's currency? Julian opts for the second solution when he says that the person who knows himself will know exactly what he is, and not merely what he passes for being. So the meaning Julian gives to the juxtaposition and coordination of these two precepts would be the following: the fundamental precept is "revalue your currency"; but this revaluation can only take place through and by means of "know yourself," which replaces the counterfeit currency of one's own and others' opinion of oneself, with the true currency of self-knowledge. One can handle one's own existence, take care of oneself as something real, and have the true currency of one's true existence in one's hands, on condition that one knows oneself. And Julian comments that when Diogenes obeyed the Pythian Apollo, when he began to get to know himself, the coin he was took on its true value. To get to know himself, Diogenes had to be able to recognize himself, and be recognized by others, as superior to Alexander himself. This refers to the famous confrontation between Diogenes and Alexander. Alexander says: If I had not been Alexander, I would have liked to be Diogenes.[21] Diogenes replies to him: But I am the true king (the true coin). You see that throughout the history and representation of Cynicism, the theme of the *parakharaxis tou nomismatos*, the precept *"parakharaxon to nomisma"* (change the currency) appears at the heart of Cynic experience and practice.

There are, of course, a number of interpretations of this principle, essentially around the theme that *nomisma*, the currency, is also *nomos*, the law, custom. The principle of altering the *nomisma* is also that of changing the custom, breaking with it, breaking up the rules, habits, conventions, and laws. It is very likely that this is how it was received and understood, whatever the original meaning of this expression. So it is this that, in a sense, we should bear in mind. But it seems to me that we can make some headway in the analysis of this principle.

Maybe we could clarify the meaning of this expression by recalling the characterization that the Cynics seem to have given of themselves when they commented on the term "dog" which was applied to them. There are different interpretations of why Diogenes was called "the dog." Some are of a local order: it was because of the place Diogenes chose as his home.[22] According to other interpretations it was because, in actual fact, he led a dog's life. Called dog by others, he took on the epithet himself and declared himself dog. Here again, the origin of the expression is not important. The problem is the value it was given, and how it functioned in the Cynic tradition that we can take up to the first century C.E.

In a commentator of Aristotle,[23] but many other authors refer to it, we find the following interpretation of this *bios kunikos*, which seems to have been canonical. First, the *kunikos* life is a dog's life in that it is without modesty, shame, and human respect. It is a life which does in public, in front of everyone, what only dogs and animals dare to do, and which men usually hide. The Cynic's life is a dog's life in that it is shameless. Second, the Cynic life is a dog's life because, like the latter, it is indifferent. It is indifferent to whatever may occur, is not attached to anything, is content with what it has, and has no needs other than those it can satisfy immediately. Third, the life of the Cynic is the life of a dog, it received the epithet *kunikos* because it is, so to speak, a life which barks, a diacritical (*diakritikos*) life, that is to say, a life which can fight, which barks at enemies, which knows how to distinguish the good from the bad, the true from the false, and masters from enemies. In that sense it is a *diakritikos* life: a life of discernment which knows how to prove, test, and distinguish. Finally, fourth, the Cynic life is *phulaktikos*. It is a guard dog's life, a life which knows how to dedicate itself to saving others and protecting the master's life. Shameless life, *adiaphoros* (indifferent) life, *diakritikos* life (diacritical, distinguishing, discriminating, and, as it were, barking life), and *phulaktikos* (guard's life, guard dog's life).

You can see that it is not difficult to recognize a close kinship between these four, once again, canonical characteristics, picked out and distinguished in these terms in the traditional representation of the Cynics, and those characteristics I tried to identify last week which traditionally defined the true life. Basically, the Cynic life is at once the echo, the continuation, and the extension of the true life (that unconcealed, independent, straight, sovereign life), but also taking it to the point of its extreme consequence and reversal. What is the shameless life if not the continuation, the pursuit, but also the scandalous reversal of the unconcealed life? The *bios alēthēs*, the life in *alētheia*, you recall, was a life without concealment, which holds nothing back, a life which was capable of having nothing to be ashamed of. Well, ultimately, this is the shameless life of the Cynic dog. The indifferent, *adiaphoros* life which needs nothing, which is content with what it has, with what it happens across, with what it is thrown, only continues, extends, takes to the extreme consequence, and scandalous reversal, of the unalloyed, independent life which was one of the fundamental characteristics of the true life. The diacritical, barking life which distinguishes between good and bad, friends and enemies, masters and others, is the continuation, but also the scandalous, violent, polemical reversal of the straight life, of the life which obeys the law (the *nomos*). The life of the guard dog, of combat and service, which characterizes Cynicism, is also the continuation and reversal of that tranquil, self-controlled, sovereign life which characterized the true existence.

I will try to develop all this more precisely shortly. What I would like to emphasize now is you can see that the alteration of the currency, the change of its value, which is constantly associated with Cynicism, no doubt means something like: the forms and habits which usually stamp existence and give it its features must be replaced by the effigy of the principles traditionally accepted by philosophy. But by the very fact of applying these principles to life itself, rather than merely maintaining them in the element of the *logos*, by the fact that they give a form to life, just as the coin's effigy gives a form to the metal on which it is stamped, one thereby reveals other lives, the lives of others, to be no more than counterfeit, coin with no value. By adopting the most traditional, conventionally accepted and general principles of current philosophy, by making the philosopher's very existence their point of application, site of manifestation, and form of truth-telling, the Cynic life puts the true currency with its true value into circulation. The Cynic game shows that this life, which truly applies the principles of the true life, is other than the life led by men in general and by philosophers in particular. With this idea that the true life is an *other* life (*vie autre*), I think we arrive at a particularly important point in the history of Cynicism, in the history of philosophy, certainly in the history of Western ethics.*

---

* [Foucault introduces here the important theme of otherness (*altérité*) with the distinction and interplay between: an *other* life (*une vie autre*), in the sense of the mode of existence of the true life in this world, which is radically other than common or traditional forms of existence; the other world (*l'autre monde*), in the sense of the transcendent Platonic world of pure Forms, or the Christian hereafter; and an *other* world (*un monde autre*), in the sense of this world, but radically

We come to the heart of an important problem if we accept that Cynicism is in fact this movement by which life changes as a result of being really and truly, in actual fact, stamped with the effigy of philosophy. In this respect, Cynicism was not just the insolent, rough, and rudimentary reminder of the question of the philosophical life. It raised a very grave problem, or rather, it seems to me that it gave the theme of the philosophical life its cutting edge by raising the following question: for life truly to be the life of truth, must it not be an *other* life, a life which is radically and paradoxically other? It is radically other because it breaks totally and on every point with the traditional forms of existence, with the philosophical existence that philosophers were accustomed to accepting, with their habits and conventions. Will not the true life be a radically and paradoxically other life, since all it will do is implement the principles most commonly accepted in current philosophical practice? Is not and must not the true life be an *other* life is an important philosophical question with long-term significance. Maybe—and again forgive the schematism, these are hypotheses, dotted lines, outlines of possible directions for work—it could be said that with Platonism, and through Platonism, Greek philosophy since Socrates basically posed the question of the other world (*l'autre monde*). But, starting with Socrates, or from the Socratic model to which Cynicism referred, it also posed another question. Not the question of the other world, but that of an *other* life (*vie autre*). It seems to me that the other world and other life have basically been the two great themes, the two great forms, the great limits within which Western philosophy has constantly developed.

Maybe we could put forward the following schema. You remember that Heraclitus, refusing to lead the solemn, stately, isolated, and withdrawn life of the sage, went among the artisans and sat and warmed himself at the baker's oven, saying to those who were astonished and indignant: *kai enthauta theous* (but the gods are also here).[24]

---

transformed and made other than its present form. It is often difficult to render the distinctions between these forms clearly in English while retaining the French play on the word *autre* and the possible implicit reference to the theme of otherness and, perhaps, to the idea of *penser autrement*, "thinking otherwise," expressed by Foucault in *L'Usage des plaisirs* (Paris: Gallimard, 1984) p. 15. Where it seems necessary or helpful to make the distinction clear I have included the French in brackets. See too, "Course Context," below, pp. 354-356; G.B.]

Heraclitus [conceived of] a philosophy, a philosophical practice, a philosophizing which is fulfilled with the principle of *kai enthauta theous* (here too there are gods, even in the baker's oven). Philosophy is fulfilled in the thought of the world itself, and in the form of the common life.

But with the Socratic care of self, with the *epimeleia heautou* I have been talking to you about for so long, we see two great lines of development emerging along which Western philosophy stretches out. On the one hand, on the line which, as all the Neo-Platonists recognized, starts from the *Alcibiades*, the care of self leads to the question of the truth and specific being of that which one must be concerned about. What is this "me," this "self," we must care about? These are the questions we encountered in the *Alcibiades*, and they led the dialogue to the discovery of the soul as what we must attend to, the soul we must contemplate.[25] What do we discover in the mirror of the soul contemplating itself? The pure world of truth, that other world, which is the world of truth and the world to which we must aspire. And to that extent, on the basis of the care of self, through the soul and the contemplation of the soul for itself, the *Alcibiades* founded the principle of the other world (*l'autre monde*) and marked the origin of Western metaphysics.

On the other hand, still on the basis of the care of self, but starting now from the *Laches* rather than the *Alcibiades*, taking the *Laches* as the point of departure, the care of self does not lead to the question of what this being I must care for is in its reality and truth, but to the question of what this care must be and what a life must be which claims to care about self. And what this sets off is not the movement towards the other world, but the questioning of what, in relation to all other forms of life, precisely that form of life which takes care of self must and can be in truth.

This other line of development gives to the question of the art of living and of the way of living, if not its origin, at least its philosophical foundation. We do not encounter Platonism and the metaphysics of the other world (*l'autre monde*) on this line. We encounter Cynicism and the theme of an *other* life (*vie autre*). These two lines of development—one leading to the other world, and the other to an *other* life, both starting from the care of self—are clearly divergent, since one give rises to Platonic and Neo-Platonic speculation and Western metaphysics, while the other gives rise to nothing more, in a sense, than Cynic crudeness. But it will revive, as a question which is both central and marginal in relation to philosophical practice, the question of the philosophical and true life as an *other* life. May not, must not the philosophical life, the true life necessarily be a life which is radically other?

Clearly, it should not be thought that these two major lines of divergence, which are, I think, foundational for all Western philosophical practice, were completely and definitively foreign to each other. After all, Platonism also raised the question of the true life in the form of an *other* existence. And we have seen that Cynicism, precisely, could perfectly well connect up, combine, and occupy itself with philosophical speculations quite foreign to the primitive, rudimentary, and crude tradition of Cynicism itself. So there was constant interaction. And it is important to bear in mind the fact which has been crucial in the history of Western philosophy, morality, and spirituality, that Christianity, but also all the Gnostic currents[26] around Christianity, were precisely movements in which one tried to think systematically and coherently the relationship between the other world and the life which is other.

In the Gnostic movements, in Christianity, there was the attempt to think an *other* life (*vie autre*), the life of severance and ascesis, without common measure with [usual] existence, as the condition for access to the other world (*l'autre monde*). And it is this relation between an *other* life and the other world—so profoundly marked within Christian asceticism by the principle that it is an *other* life which leads to the other world—which is radically challenged in Protestant ethics, and by Luther, when access to the other world will be defined by a form of life absolutely conformable to existence in this world here. The formula of Protestantism is, to lead the same life in order to arrive at the other world. It was at that point that Christianity became modern.

We will stop for three minutes, and we will take up again afterwards the problem of the other life.

---

1. The portraits of Demetrius are found in Seneca, *On Benefits*, VII, i-ii and xi, and *The Epistles of Seneca*, 69.

2. In 1982 Foucault gave Montaigne as the perfect illustration of the Renaissance attempt to "reconstitute an aesthetics and an ethics of the self": *L'Herméneutique du sujet*, p. 240; *The Hermeneutics of the Subject*, p. 251.

3. Foucault had already called on Spinoza and his *On the Improvement of the Understanding* in 1982 to show the persistence and requirements of spirituality within classical philosophy: *L'Herméneutique du sujet*, p. 29; *The Hermeneutics of the Subject*, p. 27.

4. Diogenes Laertius, Book VI, §24, Fr. (Goulet-Cazé) p. 708: "He always repeated that, if one wishes to be equipped for living, one needs reason or a rope"; Eng. p. 27: "He would continually say that for the conduct of life we need right reason or a halter."

5. Ibid., §27, Fr. (Genaille) p. 16; (Goulet-Cazé, p. 709); Eng. p. 29: "he reproached them with coming in all seriousness to hear nonsense, but slowly and contemptuously when the theme was serious."

6. Stobée, W.H. II, I, 11, in L. Paquet, trans. and ed., *Les Cyniques grecs*, p. 281: "Demonax reprimanded those people who take great care over their body while neglecting themselves, as if one were to look after one's house without being concerned about those who live in it."

7. Julien (l'Empereur), *Contre les cyniques ignorants*, 201d, §18, p. 171: "Whoever desires to be a Cynic and a serious man (*kunikos einai kai spoudaios anēr*) must begin by attending to himself, imitating Diogenes and Crates"; Eng., Julian, *Oration VI. To the Uneducated Cynics*, p. 59: "Then let him who wishes to be a Cynic, earnest and sincere, first take himself in hand like Diogenes and Crates."

8. Diogenes Laertius, Book VI, §27-28, Fr. (Genaille) pp. 16-17, (Goulet-Cazé, p. 710); Eng. pp. 29-31: "And he would wonder that the grammarians should investigate the ills of Odysseus, while they were ignorant of their own. Or that the musicians should tune the strings of the lyre, while leaving the dispositions of their own souls discordant; that the mathematicians should gaze at the sun and the moon, but overlook matters close at hand; that the orators should make a fuss about justice in their speeches, but never practise it."

9. Stobée, W.H. II, I, 1, in *Les Cyniques grecs*, Demonax, no. 61, p. 282.

10. Diogenes Laertius, VI, §28, Fr. (Genaille) pp. 16-17, (Goulet-Cazé, p. 710); Eng. p. 31.

11. Ibid., §20, Fr. (Goulet-Cazé) p. 703: "According to Diocles, Diogenes was exiled because his father, who kept the public bank, falsified the money"; Eng. p. 23: "Diocles relates that he went into exile because his father was entrusted with the money of the state and adulterated the money."

12. Ibid., Fr. pp. 703-704: "Eubulides, in his book *On Diogenes*, says that it is Diogenes himself who commits the misdeed and that he went in exile accompanied by his father"; Eng. p. 23: "But Eubiulides in his book on Diogenes says that Diogenes himself did this and was forced to leave home along with his father."

13. Foucault refers here to the third version offered by Diogenes Laertius, which is actually much more complex. According to this version, Diogenes, as public superintendant, was persuaded by some functionaries of finance to falsify the money. He went to Delphi to get advice on this point and the oracle replied "falsify," but referring to established customs. Diogenes misunderstood and falsified the money.

14. Diogenes Laertius, VI, §21, Fr. (Goulet-Cazé) p. 705: "It is said that he received the money from his father and that it was he who adulterated it: the father was imprisoned and died, while he went into exile; he went to Delphi where he did not ask if he should falsify the money, but what he should do to become famous; this was how he received that answer from the oracle"; Eng. p. 23: "One version is that his father entrusted him with the money and that he debased it, in consequence of which the father was imprisoned and died, while the son fled, came to Delphi, and inquired, not whether he should falsify the money, but what he should do to gain the greatest reputation; and that then it was that he received the oracle."

15. Foucault is misled here by Genaille's old translation. In fact, Monimus does not steal the money but scatters it far and wide. Ibid., §82, Fr. (Goulet-Cazé) p. 749: "Monimus pretended to be mad and scattered the small change everywhere, as well as the money on the banker's counter, until his master dismissed him"; Eng. p. 85: "For he forthwith pretended

to be mad and proceeded to fling away the small change and all the money on the banker's table, until at length his master dismissed him."

16. Ibid., VI, 87, Fr. (Goulet-Cazé) p. 754: "When he had converted his goods into money—he was in fact one of the prominent people—and had got for them two hundred talents, he distributed that sum to his fellow citizens.... According to Diocles, Diogenes persuaded him to abandon his land to sheep pasture and to throw any money he might have into the sea"; Eng. p. 91: "So he turned his property into money, —for he belonged to a distinguished family, —and having thus collected about 200 talents, distributed that sum among his fellow-citizens.... Diocles relates how Diogenes persuaded Crates to give up his fields to sheep pasture, and throw into the sea any money he had."

17. Ibid., VI, 99-100, Fr. pp. 762-763; Eng. p. 103.

18. Ibid., IV, 46, Fr. p. 525; Eng. p. 425.

19. Julien (l'Empereur), *Contre les cyniques ignorants*, 188a-b, §8, pp. 153-154; Eng., Julian, *Oration VI. To the Uneducated Cynics*, p. 25: "Falsify the common currency."

20. Julien (l'Empereur), *Contre Héracleios*, 211b-d, §8, pp. 23-24; Julian, *Oration VIII. To the Cynic Heracleios*, pp. 89-91: "give a new stamp to the common currency."

21. Diogenes Laertius, VI, §32, Fr. (Goulet-Cazé) p. 713; Eng. p. 35.

22. It is actually a matter of Antisthenes, the first Cynic. See ibid., VI, §13, Fr. p. 691; Eng. p. 13: "He [Antisthenes] used to converse in the gymnasium of Cynosarges (White hound) at no great distance from the gates, and some think that the Cynic school derived its name from Cynosarges."

23. It is Élias. See A. Busse, ed., *Commentaire sur les* Catégories, *proemium*, 1-32 (Berlin) IV, 2, 1888, p. 111. See also, C.A. Brandis, *Commentaria in Aristotelem graeca* (Berlin: Akadamie der Wissenschaften, [1836] 1882-1909) p. 23; J. Humbert, *Socrate et les petits socratiques* (Paris: P.U.F., 1967).

24. "Héraclite," A 9, in J.-P. Dumont, ed., *Les Écoles pré-Socratiques* (Paris: Gallimard, coll. "Folio Essais") p. 57: "As Heraclitus is reported to have said to the strangers who wanted to meet him, but who, on entering his house, saw him warming himself in the kitchen and remained rooted to the spot, he invited them not to be afraid to enter, since, 'there are gods even in such a place *(einai gar kai enthauta theous)*'." This passage is taken from Aristotle, *Parts of Animals*, I, 5, 645a,17-23, English translation by W. Ogle, in Aristotle, *The Complete Works*, Vol. One, ed. Jonathan Barnes (Princeton: Princeton University Press, 1984) p. 1004: "as Heraclitus, when the strangers who came to visit him found him warming himself at the furnace in the kitchen and hesitated to go in, is reported to have bidden them not to be afraid to enter, as even in that kitchen divinities were present." Foucault moves Heraclitus from the "kitchen" to the "baker's oven." It seems in fact that in Aristotle's text it was the "toilets," but tradition has preferred to think of "kitchens." See the translation by J.-F. Pradeau in *Héraclite. Fragments* (Paris: Garnier-Flammarion, 2002) p. 193 and the note on p. 234.

25. On this point, see the lecture of 13 January 1982, second hour, in *L'Herméneutique du sujet*, pp. 68-71; *The Hermeneutics of the Subject*, pp. 69-72.

26. On this movement, see Foucault's pointers in the 1982 lectures, ibid., Fr. p. 246, and pp. 402-403; Eng. pp. 256-257 and pp. 420-422.

fourteen

14 MARCH 1984

Second hour

[The unconcealed life: Stoic version and Cynic transvaluation. ∽
The traditional interpretation of the unalloyed life: independence
and purity. ∽ Cynic poverty: real, active, and indefinite. ∽ The
pursuit of dishonor. ∽ Cynic humiliation and Christian humility.
∽ Cynic reversal of the straight life. ∽ The scandal of animality.]

IN THE ANALYSIS OF the Cynic life I have pointed out four aspects:
the unconcealed life, the independent life, the straight life, and the
sovereign life, master of itself. I have tried to show how by basing
themselves on these themes and putting them to work, Cynic practice
and the Cynic life consisted precisely in turning them round, to the
point of making them scandalous.

First, the unconcealed life. Last week I tried to show you that the
notion of true life (*alēthēs bios*) was first and foremost constructed in
terms of the general principle that the *alēthēs* is the unhidden, the
unconcealed. The true life was therefore the unconcealed life, the life
which hides no part of itself, and which does so because it does not
commit any shameful, dishonest, or reprehensible action which could
incur the censure of others and cause the person committing it to
blush. The unconcealed life is therefore the life which does not make
one blush because one has nothing to be ashamed of. And there are
many examples of this conception of the true life as unconcealed life
which does not make one blush. Thus, you remember what was said in

Plato's *Phaedrus* and *Symposium*: true love is love which does not have to hide any shameful action and which never seeks out the dark to fulfill its desires.[1] It is a love which may be lived out, engaged in always under the warranty and guarantee of others. You could also find a whole series of very interesting arguments on this unconcealed life in Seneca. For Seneca, the true life is the life one should live as if always under the eyes of others in general, but especially and preferably under the watchful eye, the gaze, the supervision of the friend who is at once a demanding guide and a witness. For Seneca, the practice of correspondence, of the exchange of letters, had precisely this role of, as it were, putting the existence of each correspondent under the watchful eye of the other by making author and addressee of the missive present to each other.[2] On the one hand, the author of the letter is a sort of eye, a sort of source of supervision for the person to whom he addresses his advice and opinion. Seneca tells Lucilius: When I send you a letter giving you advice, in a way it is as if I myself were coming to see you and check what you are doing. But on the other hand, inasmuch as he recounts his own life, what he is doing, his choices, hesitations, and decisions, the person who writes the letter puts his own life under the watchful eye of his addressee. The two correspondents, author and addressee of the missive, are thus subject to each other's watchful eye. Correspondence is a practice of the true life as unconcealed life, that is to say, as life under the both real and virtual eye of the other.

You find yet another formulation, other variations of this theme of the unconcealed life, in Epictetus. The unconcealed life in Epictetus is not the life which exposes itself to the other's gaze in letters; it is a life which knows that it is taking place entirely under a certain internal gaze of the divinity which dwells within us. The absence of concealment becomes then a consequence of the ontological structure of the human being, since the *logos* in the soul is a divine principle (*daimōn*). This is how Epictetus, in some passages with which you are familiar, evokes the principle of the unconcealed life, but unconcealed to this internal gaze, very different from that control over love evoked by Plato, as well as from that practice of spiritual correspondence in Seneca. In Epictetus, the absence of concealment is living, and knowing oneself to be living, under this internal gaze. In Book I, Discourse 14, he says: "Zeus... has placed next to each man a particular spirit as guardian,... and it is a guardian who is never deceived... Also, when you close your doors and make it dark within, remember and never say that you are alone: you are not alone in fact, but God is within, and your spirit is there also. And what need do they have of light to see what you are doing?"[3] And in Book II, Discourse 8, you read: "You are a fragment of God. You have in you a part of that God... Will you not remember, when you are eating, who you are that is eating, and who it is you are nourishing? In your sexual relationships, who you are when you engage in them?... You carry God within yourself and do not realize that you sully him with your impure thoughts and dirty actions."[4]

This theme of the unconcealed life was extremely important and took on a series of very different forms, but it is central in the philosophical tradition as a characterization of the true life. It seems to have been continually taken up in Cynicism. But it is only taken up through a sort of alteration, a sort of transvaluation which made its application a scandal.

How does this alteration, this transvaluation take place? First of all in the, as it were, simplest, most immediate, most direct way: by a dramatization of this principle of non-concealment in and by life itself. For the Cynics, the rule of non-concealment is no longer an ideal principle of conduct, as it was for Epictetus or Seneca. It is the shaping, the staging of life in its material and everyday reality under the real gaze of others, of everyone else, or at any rate of the greatest possible number of others. The life of the Cynic is unconcealed in the sense that it is really, materially, physically public. These elements of the Cynic life as public life appear in the well-known more or less legendary accounts concerning Diogenes. Diogenes Laertius recounts: "He resolved to eat, sleep, and speak in any place."[5] Absence of home—the home being understood, as with us, but even more so in Greece, as the place of the secret, of isolation, and of protection from others. Absence even of clothes: the Cynic Diogenes is naked, or almost naked. It is also the choice of the places where he stops: Corinth. Dio Chrysostom says that Diogenes chose to go to Corinth so often because it was a big, public town where one could live in public and meet sailors, travelers, and people from all over the world on the street corners and in the temples. It was under this gaze that Diogenes chose to live. And finally he dies in a gymnasium of Corinth, wrapped in his cloak like a sleeping beggar. His cloak was drawn aside and he was seen to be dead.[6] There is no privacy, secret, or non-publicity in the Cynic life. We constantly come across this theme afterwards: the Cynic lives in the street, in front of the temples. He eats and satisfies his needs and desires in public.[7] He heads for all the big public gatherings. He is seen at the games and the theaters. He gives his own life as testimony to everyone. You remember also the famous Peregrinus whom Lucian detested so much and who decided to kill himself by fire—no doubt the meeting point of an old Herculean theme and maybe also of a practice coming from India. Peregrinus decided to burn himself, but in public, during the Games, so that there was the greatest possible number of spectators at his death. Absolute visibility of the Cynic life.

But this dramatization, this theatrical staging of the principle of non-concealment is immediately accompanied by a reversal of its effects, so that this Cynic life, which is the most truly faithful to the principle of non-concealment, by the very fact of this radicalization, appears radically other and irreducible to all other lives. The game, which makes this dramatization turn round into scandal and inversion of the unconcealed life of the other philosophers, is the following. An unconcealed life would neither hide anything bad nor do anything bad since it would not conceal anything. Now, the Cynics say, can there be anything bad in what nature wills and in what she has placed in us? And conversely, if there is something bad in us or if we do something bad, is this not because men have added to nature with their habits, opinions, and conventions? So that if non-concealment must guarantee and stand security for an entirely good life, of a life which is good because entirely visible, then this non-concealment must not take up and accept the usual, traditional limits of propriety, those limits on which men are agreed and which they imagine to be indispensable. Rather, it must bring to light what is natural in the human being, and therefore what is good. That is to say, non-concealment, far from being the resumption and acceptance of those traditional rules of propriety which mean that one would blush to commit evil before others, must be the blaze of the human being's naturalness in full view of all. This blaze of the naturalness which scandalizes, which transforms into scandal the non-concealment of existence limited by traditional propriety, manifests itself in the famous Cynic behavior. Diogenes ate in public, which was not easily accepted in traditional Greece.[8] In particular, Diogenes masturbated in public.[9] Crates too, having agreed to get married because his wife promised to lead exactly the same style, the same mode of life as him, made love with her in public.[10] All of this constitutes the form of this non-concealed life, in terms of the principle that Diogenes and Crates often repeat, namely: how can we consider making love, having sexual relations to be an evil, since it has been implanted in our very nature? Since it has been implanted in our very nature, it cannot be an evil. So it does not have to be concealed. The Cynic public life will therefore be a life of blatant and entirely visible naturalness, asserting the principle that nature can never be an evil. The Cynic dramatization of the unconcealed life therefore turns out to be the strict, simple, and, in a sense, crudest possible application of the principle that one should live without having to blush at what one does, living consequently in full view of others and guaranteed by their presence. But as a result, this strict, simple, and crude application of the most general principle overturns all the rules, habits, and conventions of propriety which this principle basically accepted spontaneously, renewed, and strengthened. Under the slogan of the unconcealed life, traditional philosophy basically assumed or renewed the requirement of propriety; it accepted its customs. Applying the principle of non-concealment literally, Cynicism explodes the code of propriety with which this principle remained, implicitly or explicitly, associated. This is the shameless life, the life in *anaideia* (the brazen life). The philosophical life thus dramatized by the Cynics deploys the general theme of non-concealment but frees it from all the conventional principles. As a result, the philosophical life appears as radically other than all other forms of life.

Second, now, the unalloyed life. You remember that the true life was the life without mixture, that is to say, the life without bonds, without dependence on anything which might be foreign to it, in accordance with the principle that what is *alēthēs* is pure, without otherness, perfectly identical to itself. In ancient philosophy this characterization of the true life as unalloyed life led to two quite different but often linked stylistics: an aesthetic of purity, found especially in Platonism, which involves freeing the soul from anything that may introduce an element of disorder, of involuntary discord (so freeing it from everything material and physical); and then a stylistic of independence, self-sufficiency, and autarchy, which involves freeing life from anything that may make it dependent on external elements, on uncertain events. In any case, it is a question of defining an attitude which is entirely detached from those events over which one has no control. The indifference of the Cynic life, their indifferent life (*adiaphoros bios*) follows the tradition common to these different themes of the independent life. But here again, it takes off from this consensus, but in a form such that it alters its principle. It revalues the currency; it changes the value of this coin and makes the philosophical life appear as being or having to be a life which is radically other. In what way? First of all, here again it is by what could be called a material, physical, bodily dramatization of the principle of life without mixture or dependence. And this dramatization of the principle of independence in the form of life itself, of physical, material life, obviously takes the form of poverty.

We touch here on a theme which is both important and difficult. In fact, the theme that the true life must be a life of poverty is obviously culturally very widespread and can be found in many other civilizations, philosophies, and, of course, in a great many religions. Also the idea that the true life, the philosophical life cannot be a life of wealth, a life attached to wealth, is certainly found early on in Greece; Socrates is an example of this. Nonetheless, it remains the case that the problem of poverty raised a number of difficulties in Greco-Roman ethics, philosophy, and philosophical practice for the reason that Greco-Roman culture constantly played on a certain socially recognized, validated, and structuring contrast: that between the foremost, the best, the most powerful, those with education and power, and the rest, the crowd, those without any kind of power, education, or wealth. This contrast between the foremost and the others, the best and the crowd, continued to organize ancient Greek and Roman societies, and to a quite noticeable extent it continued to shape the moral and philosophical thought of Antiquity. Even here, and even in those like Seneca, for example, who say that there is no difference between the soul of a slave and that of a knight or a senator, the contrast between the best and the rest, the foremost and the crowd, continued to hold sway. And by his own attitude, Seneca unfailingly and constantly makes it clear that he absolutely wants to be among the foremost, the best, as opposed to the crowd, in which, however, rich and powerful people can be found. But the opposition, the foremost and best/the others and the crowd, structures these societies and that form of thought.

Consequently, the problem of poverty as a component of the true life was not a simple one in ancient society, culture, and thought, no doubt much less so than in medieval Christianity. And no doubt because of this uncertainty, because of the difficulty of reconciling the principle that the true life cannot be a life of wealth with the idea that the true life is, at the same time, the life of the best, we find a somewhat mixed stance with regard to poverty; at any rate, we see the idea being privileged that what is important is not so much having or not having money, but adopting a stance and an attitude towards money, towards wealth, so that one does not let oneself be absorbed by the concerns of wealth, be worried by the idea that one might lose it, or be upset in the event that one really does lose it. What this true life spoken of by the philosophers involves is rather a certain attitude towards fortune and misfortune, and towards the change of fortune into misfortune. This, above all else, is what is at issue in this true life. And once again, Seneca, an extremely rich swindler, expounds at length on the idea that the true life is a life of virtual detachment with regard to wealth.

On the other hand, and in contrast with this, Cynic poverty is, of course, a real, material, and physical poverty. Cynic poverty is real, active, and indefinite.

First, Cynic poverty is real, that is to say, it is not at all a simple detachment of the soul. It is a stripping of existence which is deprived of the material elements to which it is traditionally linked and on which it is usually thought to depend. For example, Cynic poverty will focus on clothes, habitat reduced to the minimum, and possessions—Crates actually gives away his goods.[11] It concerns food, which one tries to reduce to the minimum. We may compare this Cynic life with several passages in Seneca's correspondence with Lucilius where he evokes those kinds of periods of poverty training which it is good to undertake from time to time.[12] Seneca says: For a few, three or four days, you should wear homespun clothes, sleep on a pallet, and eat as little as possible; I promise it will do you good, not just because it will restore your capacity for pleasure—which is what some dissolute people do—but also because it will teach you to have an attitude towards all this such that you would not suffer if, by chance, you were to lose everything. It is protection against the possible event, and not a real practice. It is, if you like, a virtual exercise. Cynic poverty is a real poverty which carries out a real stripping of possessions.

Second, it is an active poverty in the sense that it is not the kind of poverty that would be satisfied with giving up all concern with wealth, acquisitive conduct, and economy. Cynic poverty is not satisfied with maintaining the mediocre state with which one started. Thus, although the Cynics' attitude towards Socrates was always one of veneration and respect, continually referring to him at any rate, they nevertheless attributed to Diogenes a criticism of Socrates in which they said: even so, Socrates had a house, a wife, children, and even slippers.[13] That is to say, the Socratic attitude, which consisted in being content with the petty mediocrity of his life, is not the Cynic attitude. Cynic poverty cannot be indifference to wealth and acceptance of a given situation. Cynic poverty must be an operation one carries out on oneself in order to obtain positive results of courage, resistance, and endurance. The dramaturgy of Cynic poverty is far from that indifference which is unconcerned about wealth, whether this be the wealth of others or one's own; it is an elaboration of oneself in the form of visible poverty. It is not an acceptance of poverty; it is a real conduct of poverty.

Finally, third, Cynic poverty is unlimited. It is real, it is active, and it is unlimited, or indefinite, in the sense that it does not halt at a stage which is thought to be satisfying because one thinks one is, all in all, free from everything superfluous. It continues and is always looking for possible further destitution. It is a restless, dissatisfied poverty which strives to get back to the ground of the absolutely indispensable. There is a whole series of anecdotes on this theme. The most famous, of course, is that of the small bowl. Diogenes, whose only dish was a small bowl from which he drank water, saw a small boy at a fountain who drank from his hands cupped like a bowl. Then Diogenes threw away his bowl, saying that it was pointless wealth.[14]

You can see that the typical poverty of the Cynic life is not the virtual poverty of an attitude, as in Seneca. Nor is it a middling poverty of the kind Socrates accepted. It is a real poverty of dispossession, an indefinite poverty endlessly at work on oneself.

Only this dramaturgy of real, unlimited poverty leads to some paradoxical effects. Out of faithfulness to the principles of this active poverty, as visible form of the unalloyed life, of the pure and self-sufficient life, the Cynic actually ends up leading a life of ugliness, dependence, and humiliation. And thus the radical application of this principle leads to its reversal: the Cynic's life of scandalous, unbearable, ugly, dependent, and humiliated poverty. Here again there is plenty of evidence for this. Although it is important, we will quickly pass over the paradoxical valorization of dirtiness and ugliness, of hairy and unsightly destitution. In societies so attached to the values of beauty, to plastic values in the human body and actions, in the bearing and posture of individuals, it is easy to imagine that it was not very easy to accept this valorization of dirtiness, ugliness, and lack of grace which is a part of Cynicism. This inversion of physical values undoubtedly played a role which was not slight. In any case, this inversion understandably gave rise to a scandal. Certainly, we could find in Socrates also a number of things concerning the interplay between the valuation and devaluation of the beautiful and the ugly. But precisely, Socrates of course stresses that we should not be attached to the beauty of the body, and that we should prefer exercises of the soul to those which embellish and strengthen the body. We find too in Socrates the idea that we should recognize the beauty of the soul beneath the inelegance of a body lacking beauty. But the source of this relative, and always merely relative disqualification of beauty and physical values is precisely the preference of one beauty to another, the privilege of one beauty in relation to another.

Cynic poverty, on the other hand, is the assertion of the specific and intrinsic value of physical ugliness, dirtiness, and destitution. This is important and has introduced values of ugliness into ethics, the art of conduct, and unfortunately philosophy as well, which have still not been abandoned.

Only, there is more than this valorization of ugliness in itself. There is the fact that in this absolute poverty the individual ends up in a situation of dependence. The principle of the unalloyed life, of life without subordination, independent of everything, ends up being reversed. For what do we encounter when we obtain this base of absolute poverty? We encounter slavery, which, as you know, was unacceptable to a Greek or Roman, and generally it becomes acceptable only when it is a fate one suffers and to which one must submit with indifference.

In the Cynics, on the other hand, there is something like a direct, positive acceptance of the situation of slavery. There is the story of Diogenes who, when put on sale in the market, wants to sit down, because it is more comfortable, and when the slave merchant who is selling him refuses him the right to sit down, Diogenes replies: "No matter, fish are purchased lying on their belly."[15] And he lay down like a fish, thus agreeing to play the role of merchandise for sale. So poverty leads to the acceptance of slavery. It leads to something which was even more serious than slavery for a Greek or Roman (for after all, slavery could always be one of life's misfortunes): begging. Begging is poverty pushed to the point of dependence on others, on their good will, on the chance encounter. For the Ancients, holding out one's hand was the gesture of ignominious poverty, of dependence in its most unbearable form. Begging was Cynic poverty pushed to the point of voluntary scandal.

And finally, beyond even begging, beyond material dependence, Cynic poverty confronted something which was even more serious than slavery and begging: *adoxia*. *Adoxia* is the bad reputation, one's image after being insulted, despised, and humiliated by others, none of which, obviously, ever had any positive value for the Greeks and Romans. *Adoxia* could not be given any positive value in a society in which relations of honor were so important, where glory, a good reputation and the record one leaves in men's memory, was one of the desired forms of afterlife. Precisely *adoxia* now forms part of the Cynic's bare life. Here again, someone like Socrates was, of course, not afraid to accept even an unjust condemnation to death. But when he accepts this sort of dishonor, Socrates is not at all practicing the *adoxia* of the Cynics. He knows perfectly well that if majority opinion sees him as no more than someone who has committed a crime and been condemned to death, nonetheless, from a certain point of view, and in the eyes of those who really know, he, Socrates, is just and no dishonor is attached to his life.

For the Cynics, the systematic practice of dishonor is on the contrary a positive conduct with meaning and value. And no doubt there is something in this that is extremely strange in all of ancient morality and which really makes the Cynics an exception. I have found an article [about] *adoxia* in the Cynics which, in the way the author poses the problem, deals with it in an interesting way, [but] I do not know if it is historically well founded. The article is in the *Harvard Studies in Classical Philology* from 1962, written by someone called Ingalls, and is entitled "The Seeking of Dishonor." The author shows that he is aware of the fact that Cynicism was fully part of the Greek milieu. And he emphasizes that, basically, the Cynics were nothing other than a sort of particularly concentrated and vigorous expression of some themes peculiar to Greek morality. But there is a point on which the Cynics cannot at all be thought to represent Greek morality, and this is precisely the problem of *adoxia* (of dishonor). And he introduces here the influence of India, of—how to put it?—a certain practice found in some Hindu religious groups in which dishonor and the pursuit of dishonor take on a positive value. So he makes the insertion of *adoxia* into Greek morality the effect of an external influence.

In fact, I don't know whether or not this is historically true. In any case, what interests me is that this idea of *adoxia* seems justifiable and comprehensible on the basis of the reversal of that principle of the independent life which cannot fail to encounter dependence and dishonor when it is dramatized to the point of absolute poverty. [Now] this dishonor is actually sought after by the Cynics who actively look for humiliating situations which are valuable because they train the Cynic in resistance to everything to do with opinions, beliefs, and conventions. There is an example of this in the anecdote of Diogenes refusing to respond after being struck on his head with a fist, or a stick, I don't recall. This is not a question of honor. He says: next time I will wear a helmet.[16] For the blow is no more than the blow, and the dishonor which is supposed to accompany such a situation—receiving a blow—has no importance and literally does not exist. So: indifference towards all those humiliating situations, and even an active seeking out of humiliating situations, because first of all there is the side of exercise, of the reduction of opinions, and then also there is the fact that, within the accepted humiliation, one is able to turn the situation around, as it were, and take back control of it. There is the story of Diogenes who, eating on the public square, is treated by the passers-by as a dog: You eat like a dog, they tell him. And Diogenes immediately turns the situation around, accepting the humiliation. He accepts the humiliation and turns it around by saying: But you too are dogs, since only dogs form a circle around a dog which is eating. I am a dog, but so too are you, no less than I am.[17] One day he was at a dinner where he was thrown a bone, since he is a dog. At that point he left with his bone, returned, and pissed on the guests, like a dog.[18]

You see that this Cynic game of humiliation is interesting and [may] be compared with something which, up to a point, derives from it but changes its values, meaning, and forms: Christian humility. From Cynic humiliation to Christian humility there is an entire history of the humble, of disgrace, shame, and scandal through shame, which is very important historically and, once again, quite foreign to the standard morality of the Greeks and Romans. And I think we should distinguish the future Christian humility, which is a state, a mental attitude manifesting itself and testing itself in the humiliations one suffers, from this Cynic dishonor, which is a game with conventions of honor and dishonor in which the Cynic, at the very point when he plays the most disgraceful role, brings out his pride and supremacy. Cynic pride relies on these tests. The Cynic asserts his sovereignty, his mastery through these tests of humiliation, whereas Christian humiliation, or rather, humility, is a renunciation of oneself. All of this—Cynic humiliation and Christian humility—should no doubt be developed much more than I am doing now. I am just pointing out a few things. On the basis of this theme of the independent life, and through its dramatization in the form of poverty, slavery, begging, *adoxia*, dishonor, there is a reversal of the classical philosophical theme and the emergence of the true life as other, scandalously other.

We could say the same thing about the straight life, which is one of the characteristics of the true life in the traditional sense of the term. The straight life as characteristic of true life was a life in accordance with a certain *logos*, which is itself indexed to nature. The straight life was a life according to nature, but it was also a life in conformity with the laws, or at least with some laws, rules, and customs agreed between men. There was a sort of fundamental ambiguity in this traditional notion of the true life as straight life. Actually, this straight life was in rather ambiguous conformity with a core of naturalness and a never wholly defined, somewhat fuzzy ensemble which, depending on the schools and philosophers, varied in relation to the human, social, and civic laws which were recognized as having to serve as the framework, grid, and organizing principle of the true life.

The Cynic will take up this theme of the true life as straight, conformable life. It's just that he will take it up in such a way that this conformable life will become a life which is wholly other. Actually, the conformity to which the Cynics index the principle of the true life, the straight life, is based upon and concerns solely the domain of the natural law. Only that which belongs to the domain of nature can be a principle of conformity for defining the straight life according to the Cynics. No convention, no human prescription may be accepted in the Cynic life if it does not conform exactly to what is found in nature, and in nature alone. Thus the Cynics, of course, reject marriage and the family, and they practice, or claim to practice free union.[19] Thus they reject all taboos and conventions concerning food. Diogenes was supposed to have tried to eat raw meat.[20] He even seems to have died from trying to eat a live octopus, on which he choked—we will come back to this.[21] According to Diogenes Laertius, Diogenes would not have considered eating human flesh so heinous and intolerable.[22] The Cynic might not reject even cannibalism.

It is again for the same reason that the Cynics reject any ban on incest. On this I refer you to a very interesting passage in Dio Chrysostom. The Tenth Discourse of Dio Chrysostom, devoted largely to the Cynic life and to Diogenes, ends with a criticism of Laius, which amounts to saying: Basically, Laius wasn't very smart, since he badly misunderstood the oracle. The oracle at Delphi said to him: Do not have a child, or expose it. And, according to Dio Chrysostom, painting the ideal portrait of Diogenes, the latter is supposed to have said that what the oracle really said was: You should neither have a child nor expose it. That is to say: Do not have a child; but in the event of you having one, do not expose it. And Laius, foolishly, had a child, which was one way of not listening to the oracle, and he exposed it, which was a second way of not understanding and transgressing the oracle's order.[23] Anyway, Laius has committed this foolishness of which Oedipus is both the result and heir. He is the heir to this foolishness because it is quite clear that Oedipus was not really that clever when he solved the Sphinx's riddle.[24] Anyone could have found the answer to that famous riddle. But it is above all with regard to his incest that Oedipus showed his foolishness and naivety. What in fact should Oedipus have done? He should have truly practiced the Delphic principle of "know yourself." In that case he would not have consulted Teiresias to find out what was involved. He would not have sent Creon to consult the oracle at Delphi; he would have gone himself. Receiving the oracle, he would have understood that he had married his mother, killed his father, and produced children with his mother. Knowing all this, what would he have said, if he had been smart? He would have said: But this is what I see every day in my hen house, it is what happens with all animals, where in fact one kills one's father, marries one's mother, and ends up both father and brother to one's children, to one's brothers and sisters.[25] So there is a natural model which Oedipus failed to recognize because he was incapable of knowing himself and finding within himself one of the cores of his naturalness.

There are still a great many things that could be said about this naturalness in the Cynics.* This principle of a straight life which must be indexed to nature, and solely to nature, ends up giving a positive value to animality. And, here again, this is something odd and scandalous in ancient thought. In general terms, and summarizing considerably, we may say that in ancient thought animality played the role of absolute point of differentiation for the human being. It is by distinguishing itself from animality that the human being asserted and manifested its humanity. Animality was always, more or less, a point of repulsion for the constitution of man as a rational and human being.

---

* The manuscript includes the following development which Foucault does not take up in the lecture:
"But it is not just by turning to the most immediate naturalness that the Cynic life carries out the reversal of the straight life. Here again, what is involved is an active, aggressive, polemical, militant turn. The Cynic's natural life has a maieutic function. It involves trying and testing all the truths which may be accepted and revered by men. The militancy of the Cynic life is opposed here also to philosophical existence in the most general form. Seneca and Epictetus assert that they give no more credit to a powerful man than to any other. The Cynic cites Diogenes who tells Alexander that he is only an opaque body between himself and the Sun. All the philosophers are severe against those who enjoy elaborate dishes. They always recommend simple, natural food which satisfies the appetite. Diogenes is known for having tried raw meat. All the philosophers recommend not practicing the secret pleasures except in cases of need and when necessary and in accordance with the laws of the city. The Cynics refer to a natural model which does not rule out incest."

In the Cynics, in accordance with the rigorous and systematic application of the principle of the straight life indexed to nature, animality will play a completely different role. It will be charged with positive value, it will be a model of behavior, a material model in accordance with the idea that the human being must not have as a need what the animal can do without. There is a whole series of anecdotes on this: Diogenes observing how mice live,[26] and Diogenes seeing a snail carrying its house on its back and deciding to live in the same way.[27] When need is a weakness, a dependence, a lack of liberty, man must have no other needs than those of the animal, those satisfied by nature itself.

In order not to be inferior to the animal, one must be capable of taking on that animality as reduced but prescriptive form of life. Animality is not a given; it is a duty. Or rather, it is a given, offered to us directly by nature, but at the same time it is a challenge to be continually taken up. This animality, which is the material model of existence, which is also its moral model, constitutes a sort of permanent challenge in the Cynic life. Animality is a way of being with regard to oneself, a way of being which must take the form of a constant test. Animality is an exercise. It is a task for oneself and at the same time a scandal for others. Assuming, in front of others, the scandal of an animality as a task for oneself is what the principle of the straight life indexed to nature leads to when this principle becomes the real, material, concrete form of existence itself. The *bios philosophikos* as straight life is the human being's animality taken up as a challenge, practiced as an exercise, and thrown in the face of others as a scandal.

There remains the fourth element, that of the unchangeable life, of life without corruption or fall, the life of sovereignty. I should show you how this life is reversed by the Cynics. I will try to do this next week because it will lead us precisely to another moment, another figure: the true life in the spirituality of Christian asceticism.

1. See L'Usage des plaisirs, ch. V, "Le véritable amour," pp. 251-269; The Use of Pleasure, Part Five, "True Love," pp. 229-246.

2. See L'Herméneutique du sujet, pp. 343-344; The Hermeneutics of the Subject, pp. 360-361.

3. Epictetus, Discourses, I, 14, Fr. pp. 57-58; Eng. p. 103: "Zeus ... has stationed by each man's side as guardian his particular genius ... a guardian who ... is not to be beguiled. ... Wherefore, when you close your doors and make darkness within, remember never to say that you are alone; nay, God is within, and your own genius is within. And what need have they of light in order to see what you are doing?"

4. Ibid., II, 8, 11-14, Fr. p. 30; Eng. pp. 255-257: "you are a fragment of God; you have within you a part of Him ... Will you not bear in mind, whenever you eat, who you are that eat, and whom you are nourishing? Whenever you indulge in intercourse with women, who you are that do this? ... It is within yourself that you bear Him, and do not perceive that you are defiling him with impure thoughts and filthy actions."

5. Diogenes Laertius, VI, §22, Fr. (Genaille) p. 15; (Goulet-Cazé, p. 706); Eng. p. 25: "he used any place for any purpose, for breakfasting, sleeping, or conversing."

6. Ibid., VI, §77, Fr. (Goulet-Cazé) p. 743; Eng. pp. 79-81.

7. Ibid., VI, §69, Fr. p. 736; Eng. p. 71.

8. Ibid., VI, §58 and 69, Fr. p. 730 and p. 736; Eng., p. 59 and p. 71.

9. Ibid., VI, §46 and 69, Fr. p. 722 and p. 736; Eng., p. 47 and p. 71.

10. Ibid., VI, §96-97, Fr. p. 760; Eng. pp. 99-101.

11. Ibid., VI, §87, Fr. p. 754; Eng. p. 91.

12. On poverty exercises in Seneca, see L'Herméneutique du sujet, pp. 410-411; The Hermeneutics of the Subject, pp. 428-430.

13. Diogène no. 186, Elien, Histoire variée, IV, 11, in Les Cyniques grecs, p. 110: "Diogenes asserted that Socrates himself led a soft life: he shut himself away in a nice little house, with a little bed, and some slippers that he wore from time to time."

14. Diogenes Laertius, VI, §37, Fr. p. 715; Eng. p. 39.

15. Ibid., VI, §29, Fr. (Genaille) p. 17; (Goulet-Cazé, p. 711); Eng. p. 31: " 'It makes no difference,' said he, 'for in whatever position fishes lie, they still find purchasers.' "

16. Ibid., VI, §41, Fr. (Goulet-Cazé) p. 719; Eng. p. 43: "When some one hit him a blow with his fist, 'Heracles,' said he, 'how came I forgot to put a helmet on when I walked out?' "

17. Ibid., VI, §61, Fr. p. 732; Eng. p. 63.

18. Ibid., VI, §46, Fr. p. 722; Eng. p. 49.

19. Ibid., VI, §72, Fr. p. 738: "[Diogenes] demanded community of wives, not even speaking of marriage, but of the coupling of a man with the woman he has seduced"; Eng. p. 75: "He advocated community of wives, recognizing no other marriage than a union of the man who persuades with the woman who consents." See also the horrified comments of Philodemus, Sur les Stoiciens = Papyrus d'Herculanum 155 and 339, XV-XX, in Les Cyniques grecs, p. 117.

20. Diogenes Laertius, VI, §34, Fr. p. 713; Eng. p. 37.

21. Actually, the two versions concerning a death of Diogenes due to an "octopus" do not speak of choking: either Diogenes was struck down by cholera after eating raw octopus (ibid., VI, §76, Fr. p. 742; Eng. p. 79), or it is said that "while wanting to share an octopus with some dogs he was bitten on the tendon of his foot, as a result of which he died" (ibid., VI, §77, Fr. p. 743; Eng. p. 79: "while trying to divide an octopus amongst the dogs, he was so severely bitten on the sinew of the foot that it caused his death").

22. Ibid., §73, Fr. p. 739; Eng. p. 75.

23. Dion Chrysostome, Discours X: Diogène, ou Des domestiques, §24-25, in Les Cyniques grecs, p. 253; English translation by J.W. Cohoon, Dio Chrysostom, "The Tenth Discourse, On Servants" in Dio Chrysostom I. Discourses I-XI (Cambridge, Mass.: Harvard University Press, Loeb Classical Library, 1932) p. 437.

24. Ibid., §31, Fr. p. 255; Eng. p. 441.

25. Ibid., §30, Fr. p. 254: "Well! cockerels don't make so much fuss about such experiences, nor do dogs or asses"; Eng. p. 441: "But domestic fowls do not object to such relationships, nor dogs, nor any ass."

26. Diogenes Laertius, VI, §22, Fr. p. 706: "According to Theophrastus in his Megarian dialogue, it was because he saw a mouse running about, without seeking a resting place,

without fear of the dark, and with no desire for sources of enjoyment, that Diogenes found a remedy for the difficulties in which he found himself"; Eng. p. 25: "Through watching a mouse running about, says Theophrastus in the Megarian dialogue, not looking for a place to lie down in, not afraid of the dark, not seeking any of things which are considered to be dainties, he discovered the means of adapting himself to circumstances."

27. Diogenes, Letter 16, "À Apoplexis" in *Lettres de Diogène et Crates*, p. 45: "I addressed myself to you to have somewhere to live; thank you for promising me accommodation; but the sight of a snail gave me the idea of somewhere to live sheltered from the wind, my Metroon jar"; English translation by Benjamin Fiore, Diogenes, Epistle 16, "To Apoplexis, greetings," in Abraham J. Malherbe, ed., *The Cynic Epistles. A Study Edition*, p. 109: "I asked you about a dwelling. Thank you for undertaking to arrange one. But when I saw a snail, I found a house to keep off the wind. I mean the earthenware jug in the Metroon."

fifteen

21 MARCH 1984

First hour

[
The Cynic reversal of the true life into an other *life* (vie autre).
⌢ *The traditional sense of the sovereign life: the helpful and exem-
plary sage.* ⌢ *The theme of the philosopher king.* ⌢ *The Cynic
transformation: the confrontation between Diogenes and Alexander.*
⌢ *Praise of Heracles.* ⌢ *The idea of philosophical militancy.* ⌢
The king of derision. ⌢ *The hidden king.*
]

[...*] I WOULD HAVE LIKED to finish today what I began last week,
that is to say the Cynic reversal of the themes of the true life. We have
tried to see how the practice of the true life, when it is pushed to its
extreme consequence in the Cynics, and dramatized in a number of
forms, becomes the scandalous manifestation of the other life. And this
change, this turning round, this transformation of the true life into
other life seems to me to have been the source and heart of the Cynic
scandal.

We saw first of all that the theme of the unconcealed life was pushed
to its extreme consequence and dramatized by the Cynics in the form
of the shameless life. We saw too how the theme of the unalloyed life,
without dependence, self-sufficient, was also dramatized in the form

---

* M.F. begins with the following remarks: "I will try to lecture for two hours today, but I am
not absolutely sure of getting to the end because I have a bit of the flu, and even the whole thing.
So I will do what I can. You will forgive me if we stop after a time."

of poverty and was turned into a practice of voluntary destitution, of begging, and ultimately even of dishonor. Finally, third, with regard to the theme of the straight life, of the life according to nature, reason, and the *nomos*, we saw how the Cynics dramatized this in the form of the natural life, of the life outside convention, and how on that basis it was turned round and appeared in the form of a life manifesting itself as challenge and exercise in the practice of animality.

With the Cynics, a naked, begging, and bestial life, or a life of shamelessness, destitution, and animality looms up on the borders of ancient philosophy—on the borders of what, in a sense and in a way, ancient philosophy was more or less accustomed to thinking, since all these themes are basically only the continuation, the extrapolation of some fairly common principles of that philosophy. In short, Cynicism appears as the point of convergence of some entirely standard themes and, at the same time, this figure of the other life, the shameless life of dishonor and animality, is what is most difficult for ancient philosophy, thought, ethics, and all ancient culture to accept. Cynicism is thus this kind of grimace that philosophy makes to itself, this broken mirror in which philosophy is at once called upon to see itself and fails to recognize itself. Such is the paradox of the Cynic life as I have tried to define it; it is the fulfillment of the true life, but as demand for a life which is radically other.

We still have a fourth aspect of this reversal to study. You remember that if we take [this notion] of the true life in its most common form, it concerned first the theme of the unconcealed life, then that of the independent, unalloyed life, and finally that of the straight life. The fourth aspect I referred to was, you recall, the theme of the sovereign life. It seems to me that here too we can see this theme taken to its extreme consequence and reversed, and this is the most fundamental, characteristic, and also paradoxical component of this Cynic life. So, the fourth reversal: the reversal of the theme of the sovereign life.

Again, this is a traditional, standard theme. It seems to me that the traditional form of the theme of the sovereign life, that is to say, of the life master of itself, superior to any other, is generally characterized by two main features. First, in ancient philosophy the sovereign life is generally one which tends to establish a relationship to self of enjoyment, in both senses of the word: possession and pleasure. The sovereign life is a life in possession of itself, a life of which no fragment, no element escapes the exercise of its power and sovereignty over itself. Being sovereign is first and foremost being one's own, belonging to oneself. There are a series of formulations of this. The most explicit is in Seneca, where there are a whole set of expressions, like, for example: *in se potestatem habere* (having possession of oneself: letters 20,[1] 62,[2] 75[3]), or just simply again *sui juris esse* (being one's own law, not falling under any foreign law: *On the Shortness of Life*[4]), there is also the expression *se habere* (self-possession, owning oneself, as it were: letter 42[5]), and quite simply *suum esse* or *suum fieri* (being, becoming one's own: *On the Shortness of Life*).[6]

This relationship of enjoyment-possession is also a relationship of enjoyment-pleasure. One takes pleasure in oneself in the sovereign life, one delights in oneself, one finds in oneself all the sources and foundations of the true delight, which is not that of the body, or that which depends on external objects, but the delight one can have indefinitely without ever being deprived of it. Here again, there are many expressions in Seneca which revolve around this theme. For example, in letter 23 we find the principle *suo gaudere* (delighting in oneself, taking one's pleasure in oneself),[7] or again you see the principle of having to seek all of one's joy in oneself (*intra se omne gaudium petere*: ask within oneself, seek within oneself for all of one's joy: *To Helvia On Consolation*, V).[8] So in these general formulations the sovereign life is a life of enjoyment: enjoyment-possession, enjoyment-pleasure.

But—and this is another equally very important aspect in the general theme of the sovereign life in Antiquity—when the sovereign life is a relationship to self and enjoyment of itself, and by virtue of this, it also founds, or opens out onto a relationship to the other and others. The sovereign life is a life beneficial to others and, underpinned by the relationship of possession, enjoyment, and pleasure in oneself, this relationship to others may take two forms. It may be a personal relationship of direction, spiritual help, and assistance: this is the direction, help, assistance, or support that may be given to a student who comes to listen to the lesson. I refer you to Epictetus where you will find many important formulations in which the teacher must not merely give the student lessons in skill, pass on knowledge to him, teach him logic or how to refute a sophism, and nor is this what the student demands from his teacher. A different relationship must be established between them, a relationship of care, assistance, and help. You have come here, [Epictetus] says to his student, as to an *iatreion* (a clinic), you are here to be taken care of, treated. And when you return home, it is not just as an individual who is able to resolve sophisms or get himself admired for his abilities in discussion. You must return home as someone who has been treated, and whose ills have been alleviated.

This personal relationship is the relationship between teacher and student. It is also, and very often, the relationship of friend to friend, as was the case with Seneca, for example. Seneca offers assistance to Lucilius, a friend roughly his own age, a bit younger. There are dozens of texts and I will merely cite one from the Preface to *Natural Questions*, in which Seneca writes to Lucilius, who has just been made procurator in Sicily: The sea will now separate us, however I want to continue to be of service to you. You are still unsure of your way, your path; I will take you by the hand to guide you.[9]

The sovereign life is therefore a life of assistance and help to others (student or friend). But it is useful and beneficial to others in yet another form: this is inasmuch as it is in itself a sort of lesson of universal significance which is given to humankind by the very way in which one lives and by the conspicuous way in which one leads this life in full view of everyone. The sage, leading the sovereign life, can and will be useful to humankind through the example he offers, and through the texts he writes. One of Seneca's texts explains that his decision to retire is not so that he can cut himself off from humankind and lead a selfish life. On the contrary, he will now devote his time to writing, and his texts will be able to circulate as lessons for life and existence for humanity in general. Again, quite simply, the sovereign life is a lesson of universal significance through its splendor, through the brilliance with which it adorns humankind. This is an idea which you find expressed very clearly in Epictetus when he says that the sage is like that small red thread on the senator's toga, (the laticlave). The ornament of the senator's toga is the red thread, the red stripe, which indicates the person's rank and status. In the same way, the sage must be like the red thread in the fabric of humanity which assures the brilliance and splendor of humankind.

What is interesting in these themes concerning the sovereignty of the sage's life and its beneficial character is that this relationship of advice, assistance, encouragement, and example is obviously something obligatory which cannot be shirked. As we have just seen, even in the case of Seneca, where the sage retires and consequently leads a withdrawn and hidden life, far from human eyes, even when he gives up all ambition and active political life, when he distances himself from the city in general or the town in order to live in the country, he must nevertheless still be useful to others. He is bound to this obligation to be useful to others, and it is that obligation which Seneca fulfills through his letters, his discussions, conversations with his friends, and the texts he writes. So it is true that being beneficial to others, in the very exercise of a sovereign life which enjoys itself, is, in a sense, an obligation.

But it is important to understand that this activity, by which one is useful to others in the exercise of a sovereign life on itself, is a surplus, as it were, an excess, or rather it is nothing more or less than the other side of the relation to self. Exercising perfect mastery over oneself, bearing witness to this mastery in the eyes of others and, through this testimony, helping them, guiding them, serving as an example and model, are only different aspects of one and the same sovereignty. Being sovereign over self and being useful to others, enjoying oneself and solely oneself and at the same time giving others the assistance they need in their predicaments, their difficulties, or possibly their misfortunes, basically comprises one and the same thing. The same founding act of taking possession of self by self gives me enjoyment of myself, on the one hand, and enables me to be useful to others in their trouble or misfortune, [on the other].

This is, if you like, very schematically, what might be said about this theme of the true life, taken in its most common and standard dimensions. Well, this theme—the true life as exercise of sovereignty over self which is at the same time beneficial to others—is taken up by the Cynics. It is taken up, but once again the theme is pushed to its extreme consequence, accentuated, intensified, and dramatized in the form of the assertion, the arrogant assertion, that the Cynic is king. Of course, the Cynics were not the first, and certainly not alone in linking the theme of monarchy as political sovereignty to that of the philosophical life as sovereignty of self over self. We could find many examples of this; I will cite just two.

First of all, in Plato the relation between monarchy and philosophy is of course very important, intense, and highly valorized. However, subject obviously to closer examination, it seems to me that in Plato the relation between philosophy and monarchy, between being philosopher and being king, appears in two ways. It appears first in the form of a structural analogy, since, basically, the philosopher is someone who is able to establish a type of hierarchy and a type of power in his soul and in relation to himself which is of the same order, has the same form, the same structure as the power exercised in a monarchy by a monarch, if at least the latter is worthy of this name and his government really corresponds to the essence of monarchy. So, there is in fact an essence, form, or structure which is common to political monarchy and sovereignty of self over self. But this theme of the link between monarchy and philosophy is also found in Plato in another form, which is that of the "ought to be." That is to say, one has to or should try to get to that ideal point where the philosopher will really be able to exercise a monarchy over others and where the identification of the monarch and the philosopher will assure, on the one hand, sovereignty of self over self to each soul and, on the other, the form that will enable the city as a whole to be happy and stable. We also encounter the theme, the principle of a bond between monarchy and philosophy, in the Stoics. In the Stoics, the philosopher is, in a sense, close to being a king; or rather he is more than a king. He is more than a king in the sense that he is someone who is not only capable of governing himself (he guides his own soul), but also of governing the souls of others, and not merely of others such as they are defined and live within a city, but the souls of men in general, of humankind. In that sense the philosopher is more than a king. This is in fact Seneca's objection to Attalus, a Cynic to whom, when he said he was king, Seneca replied: In actual fact the philosopher is something other than a king, in a sense he is even better than a king, for he is capable of managing, directing, and guiding a king's soul, and through the king's soul, he is capable of directing also the souls of men and the whole of humankind.

The king and the philosopher, monarchy and philosophy, monarchy and sovereignty over self are frequent themes. But in the Cynics I think they take a completely different form, simply because the Cynics make the very simple, bald, utterly insolent assertion that the Cynic himself is king. This is not just the ideal of a city in which philosophers would be kings. This is not that kind of game between the otherness and superiority of the philosopher in relation to the king. The Cynic himself is a king; he is even the only king. Crowned sovereigns, visible sovereigns, as it were, are only the shadow of the true monarchy. The Cynic is the only true king. And at the same time, vis-à-vis kings of the world, crowned kings sitting on their thrones, he is the anti-king who shows how hollow, illusory, and precarious the monarchy of kings is.

This stance of the Cynic as anti-king king, as the true king who, by the very truth of his monarchy, denounces and reveals the illusion of political kingship, is very important in Cynicism. This explains the role of the famous historical meeting (probably mythical, of course) between Alexander and Diogenes as one of those, as it were, matrix scenes to which the Cynics constantly refer. An historic encounter: nothing actually excludes it having taken place. A mythical encounter, in view of all the commentaries, analyses, and accounts which the Cynic tradition has produced and added to, quite simply because in this idea of the philosopher as anti-king king we have something which is at the very center of the Cynic experience and Cynic life as true life and other life and of the Cynic as true king and other king.

There are many examples of this contrast between the Cynic king and the political king of men. I would just like to consider one important text, which is the longest we have on this meeting between Alexander and Diogenes, whose episodes are, once again mythical. It is in Dio Chrysostom (or Dio of Prusa), in roughly the first third of his Fourth Discourse.[10] His first four discourses are devoted to the problem of monarchy, and at the start of the fourth discourse there is a long account of the famous meeting between Diogenes and Alexander. I would like simply to focus on some elements which will enable me to make some headway in the analysis of this figure of the anti-royal king.

First, in this account we find the idea of Diogenes and Alexander facing each other in a sort of wholly dissymmetrical and unequal equality. Alexander is the all powerful king. He already has all the splendor of his glory. He has not yet conquered Persia, but he is already the master of Greece. He is surrounded by an army and courtiers. And he decides to visit Diogenes, because in his eyes Diogenes is the only one who could vie with him. This is Alexander's well known and frequently quoted phrase: Had I not been Alexander, I should have liked to be Diogenes.[11] So Diogenes and Alexander are face to face and, from that point of view, completely symmetrical.

But at the same time, there is total dissymmetry, since facing Alexander in all his glory, Diogenes is the wretch in his barrel. But Alexander displays his true greatness and shows that he could be close to what truly makes a king in the fact that when he visits Diogenes he does not rely on the splendor of his glory and his armed strength for his authority. He meets Diogenes face to face. He leaves his court and entourage, Dio Chrysostom explains, and goes to confront Diogenes.[12] You can see the game of symmetry and dissymmetry, of equality and inequality, marked in the very staging of this relationship between Diogenes and Alexander. And the dialogue stage manages this confrontation in order to show that the person who thinks he is king is not the true king. The true king is, of course, Diogenes.

I will not go over all this rather lengthy discussion again; I would just like to pick out some elements. First, Alexander is a king, a king of the world, of men, a political king. But to assure this monarchy and be able to exercise it, he is forced to depend and actually does depend on certain things. To exercise his monarchy he needs an army, guards, allies, he needs armor (he appears with his sword). Diogenes needs absolutely nothing to exercise his sovereignty. He stands before Alexander naked in his barrel with no army, court, allies, or anything else. Alexander's monarchy is therefore quite fragile and precarious, since it depends on something else. That of Diogenes, on the other hand, is unshakeable and cannot be overturned, since he needs nothing to exercise it.[13] This is the first argument.

Second, is the true king someone who has to become a king, either through education or by inheriting the office from his parents or people who may have adopted him? This is the case with Alexander: he received the monarchy from his parents, and he also received a training (a *paideia*) which supposedly makes him capable of exercising the office of monarch. Against this, Diogenes sets the nature of a true king, like him. In the first place, a true king like Diogenes comes directly from Zeus. He is a son of Zeus, and not of a monarchical [lineage]. He is a son of Zeus in the sense that he has been formed directly on the model of Zeus himself. The sage's soul has been formed in full and perfect sovereignty. It is princely by nature and consequently needs no *paideia*. The sage's soul is not a cultivated soul; it did not have to acquire the monarchy and the ability to be a monarch through education. The princely soul is such by nature, without any *paideai*. It is endowed with what Dio Chrysostom calls *andreia* (both courage and, more generally, virility). He is quite simply a man. And his monarchy manifests itself in this virility, in the fact that he is a man. It is also *megalophrosunē* (greatness of soul). Virility and greatness of soul are what distinguish the son of Zeus, as opposed to the *paideia*, the education which the hereditary son of a king needs in order to become king in turn.[14] This is the second contrast.

The third is the following: what distinguishes the kingship of a sovereign like Alexander, the condition for him to be able to exercise this sovereignty, is his ability to triumph over his enemies. It is by triumphing over his enemies that he assures his sovereignty over men. This is what Alexander says to Diogenes: When I am not only king of the Greeks, since I am that already, but also king of the Medians and the Persians whom I will have really vanquished, will I not then be fully and completely king? To which Diogenes replies: What! You will have defeated the Greeks, you will have defeated the Medians, and you will have defeated the Persians. But will you have defeated your true enemies? And these are the internal enemies, your faults and vices.[15] The sage has no faults or vices. The king of the world, of men, may well battle against all his enemies. He may well defeat them one by one. There will still always be this first and last, fundamental battle to be waged.

And finally, the last characteristic, the last contrast between the king of men and the philosopher-king, the Cynic-king, is that the king of men is obviously exposed to every misfortune and reversal of fortune. He may lose his monarchy. The philosopher-king, the Cynic-king, on the other hand, will never cease being king. He is king forever, since he is king by nature. It is at this point that Dio Chrysostom refers, or makes Diogenes refer, to the famous Persian ritual in which, in certain ceremonies, a prisoner of war was taken and for a time was treated like a king, given courtesans, and all his needs, desires, and fancies satisfied. And after thus having him lead a truly royal life, he is stripped of everything, flogged and finally hung.[16] That, says Diogenes, according to Dio Chrysostom, is the fate of all kings of men. The sage has no need of all those satisfactions, pleasures, and ornaments which characterize the life of a king. But, doing without all that, he will remain king indefinitely. You see, the Cynic is the true king. And this idea of the Cynic as true king is, I think, quite different from the Platonic idea of the relations between monarchy and philosophy, as also from the Stoic conception.

But that is not all. The Cynic is a true king; only he is an unrecognized, unknown king who, by the way he lives, by the existence he has chosen, and by the destitution and renunciation to which he exposes himself, deliberately hides himself as king. And in this sense he is the king, but the king of derision. He is a king of poverty, a king who hides his sovereignty in destitution. Not only in the form of destitution but, we saw this last week, also in the form of deliberate endurance, of endless work on self by which he is always pushing back the limits of what he can bear. At the heart of this monarchy of the Cynic, which is a monarchy in fact and not just ideal, you find again the relentless work of self on self. The king Diogenes rolls in the burning sand in summer and in the snow in winter, solely in order to be able to practice on himself an ever more complete, harsh, and accomplished endurance. So it is a real, but also unrecognized monarchy, hidden beneath destitution and derision. The third characteristic is that it is a monarchy of dedication. It is a kingship of dedication, but of a dedication which is quite different from that kind of overflowing or conversion of sovereignty over self into benefits for others that we saw in Seneca, for example, where sovereignty of self over self was of benefit to others.

The dedication of the Cynic king, of that real and derisory king, is marked by three features. First, the singular dedication of this king of poverty is a mission he has been given, a task imposed on him. The nature which has made him king has charged him at the same time to care for others. Caring for others is not just giving them lessons, through discourse or example, which will enable them to conduct themselves; it is really taking care of them, seeking them out wherever they may be, sacrificing oneself, one's own life, so as to be able to take care of others. And it is not the enjoyment of self, but much more a certain form of self renunciation that enables one to take care of others. It is a hard mission, and one which one might be inclined to call sacrificial, if the Cynics did not say at the same time that the philosopher really finds his joy and the fulfillment of his existence in this sacrifice of oneself.

Second, the mission received in this way is not a legislator's or even a governor's mission. It is a care relationship, a medical relationship. The Cynic treats people. He brings them medication thanks to which they will really be able to assure their own cure and their own happiness. He is the instrument of the happiness of others. For example, Crates, a historical-mythical figure, one of the first disciples of Diogenes, is described by Apuleius as someone who goes from house to house, knocking on doors and bringing advice to those who need it, so that they can be cured.[17] There is a medical interventionism, as it were, in the Cynic's mission, which is in complete contrast with that sort of overabundance through which the happy life of the wise philosopher, like Seneca, simply gave itself as an example to others, whom it assisted merely with advice, examples, and writings. There is a physical interventionism, a social interventionism of the Cynics.

Finally, third, this Cynic mission takes the form of a battle. It has a polemical, bellicose character. The medications offered by the Cynics are harsh. We can say that the Cynic is a sort of benefactor, but he is essentially, fundamentally, and constantly an aggressive benefactor whose main instrument is, of course, the famous diatribe. We have a number of texts, examples, and descriptions of this: the Cynic gets up in the assembly—whether this is a theater, a political assembly, in the middle of a festival, or just simply on the street corner, or in the market—and he speaks out and attacks. He attacks his enemies, that is to say, he attacks the vices afflicting men, affecting those he is speaking to in particular, but also humankind in general.

So you see that the Cynic is of service in a very different way than through leading an exemplary life or giving advice. He is useful because he battles, because he bites, because he attacks. And the Cynics frequently apply these qualities to themselves, this description of their own mission as a battle, comparing themselves to those competitors who, in the games and contests, try to prevail over others—and then the Cynic defines himself as an athlete—or comparing themselves to soldiers of an army who have to mount guard or confront enemies and engage in physical combat.

Of course, here again, the Cynics are not the only ones to employ this athletic or military comparison to indicate the true philosophy. You know that it is very easy to find a whole series of comparisons, of metaphors of the same kind in ancient philosophy, from the Socratic tradition at least. You remember Socrates as a soldier, more able to endure the pain, toil, and harshness of a soldier's life than anyone else, to the extent of arousing the admiration of Laches. Socrates says of himself that he is like an athlete (*athlētēs*).

These fairly traditional themes of military or athletic combat do seem to be found again in the Cynics. Only, with a certain inflection. In Socrates and the Stoics, the enemies this athletic or military combat was directed against, a combat which required life-long training in order to be able to confront the possible misfortunes of existence, were essentially their own desires, appetites, and passions. For each individual, or at least for all those who agreed to take up the battle, it involved ensuring the victory of reason over his own appetites or of his soul over his body. The Cynic's military or athletic battle is also the individual's struggle against his desires, appetites, and passions. But it is also a battle against customs, conventions, institutions, laws, and a whole condition of humanity. It is a battle against vices, but these are not just the individual's vices. They are vices which afflict humankind as a whole, the vices of men which take shape, rely upon, or are at the root of their customs, ways of doing things, laws, political organizations, or social conventions. The Cynic battle is therefore not simply that military or athletic battle by which the individual ensures self-mastery and thereby benefits others. The Cynic battle is an explicit, intentional, and constant aggression directed at humanity in general, at humanity in its real life, and whose horizon or objective is to change its moral attitude (its *ēthos*) but, at the same time and thereby, its customs, conventions, and ways of living.

The Cynic is a combatant whose struggle for others and against enemies takes the form of endurance, destitution, and the constant test of self on self, but also of struggle in humanity, in relation to humanity, and for the whole of humanity. The Cynic is a king of poverty, endurance, and dedication. But this is a king who battles both for himself and for others.

It is in this representation of the Cynic battle that we encounter the figure of Heracles. The great model for the Cynic king, this king of poverty and battle, is Heracles, son of Zeus—we found the theme that the sage stems directly from Zeus, fashioned by his own hands. In the famous anecdote, the famous account given by Prodicus in Xenophon, Heracles chooses the life of exercise and endurance rather than the easy life of license and sensual pleasure.[18] At the crossroads of two ways, it is the hard, arduous road that Heracles chooses at the start of his life. Heracles has been given a mission; he serves Eurystheus and in that sense does what he is told to do. And in carrying out this service, in this mission he has been given by Eurystheus, he does not wage a battle against his vices (he has none) or his evils (he has no evils either). He wages a battle against the vices of the world and the evils of men. He has to clean up the world and take on, as it were, the ugliness and infamy of humanity.

This reference to Heracles is a constant of Cynic practice and discourse. A particularly developed example is found again in Dio Chrysostom, at the end of the Eighth Discourse devoted to virtue.[19] Dio Chrysostom develops the Heracles theme in this discourse and presents him as the Cynic hero. Here again we can pick out some features from this text, because they are rather interesting for grasping this reversal of the sovereign life in the Cynics. Dio Chrysostom first of all contrasts Heracles with other heroes, with other athletes who were famous in mythology for their beauty, wealth, or power. Heracles is not like Zetes, one of the Argonauts.[20] He is not like Peleus, father of Achilles. He is not like Jason[21] and Cinyras.[22] He is not like Pelops with his ivory shoulder.[23] Far from being one of these brilliant heroes, recognized by all and happy in their exploits, Heracles, says Dio Chrysostom, is always represented by everyone as suffering (*ponounta*) and struggling (*agōnizomenon*).[24] Consequently, he is someone for whom one cannot but feel pity. He is the most pitiable of men (*anthrōpōn athliotaton*). *Athlios* is a word—but I do not know if this is well founded etymologically—which refers to *athlētes*.[25] *Athlētes* is athlete. *Athlios* is someone who is wretched. The theme of the wretched athlete (*athlētes, athlios*) runs through the whole of this passage from Dio Chrysostom. In contrast with all the great and, as it were, positive, visible, and striking legendary heroes, Heracles is characterized as a wretched athlete, a battler who arouses pity for his harsh destiny. Heracles appears as what he is, he is finally recognized, and his wretched kingship becomes brilliant kingship only after his death. He is recognized, hailed, honored, and deified after his death, and he is given Hebe as wife.[26]

Dio Chrysostom develops this contrast between Heracles and the other heroes, the other athletes, by portraying him physically as a true hero of endurance. Physically, Heracles is a man who is as alert as a lion. He has a piercing eye and keen hearing. He is utterly indifferent to extreme heat and biting cold. He never sleeps in a bed, always on the ground. He needs no cover, only a dirty hide.[27] This is exactly the beggar whose portrait we saw last week. And this hidden, wretched, beggar king accomplishes the various exploits known as the Labors of Hercules. Dio Chrysostom lists these different exploits, giving each a symbolic meaning according to an interpretation which was very common in Antiquity. Diomedes the Thracian, whom he defeats in battle and smashes with his club like an old jar, was the unjust, tyrannical sovereign who sat on a gold throne and killed all the strangers who passed through his territory. So he was the unjust sovereign, unable to recognize the universality of humankind. Heracles sets himself against this political aberration and kills Diomedes.[28] Geryones is wealth, and Heracles steals his cattle.[29] The Amazons, of course, are immodesty and physical pleasure. In an interesting interpretation, Dio Chrysostom represents Prometheus, whom Heracles frees, as a Sophist. This is a fairly typical theme of the Cynics. Prometheus was actually a negative figure for the Cynics because he had removed men from their original animality, the nature they started with, by giving them the invention of fire and initiating them into techniques and know-how. Prometheus separated man from his original naturalness and consequently doomed him to all his later ills. So Prometheus is precisely the Sophist. By setting Prometheus free Heracles does not liberate this Sophist so that he can continue with his bad actions and exercise his bad influence on humanity. If Heracles freed Prometheus, it means that he freed him from his opinions (from his flattering opinion of himself and from everything he believed concerning knowledge, technique, and teaching).[30] The deliverance of Prometheus means the return of Prometheus and humanity to original naturalness.

Dio Chrysostom puts this praise of Heracles in the mouth of Diogenes, and he ends his account by saying that Diogenes' discourse aroused the enthusiasm of those listening. But in the midst of this enthusiasm, Diogenes remained silent. He sat on the ground and performed an indecent act. Seeing him perform this indecent act, the crowd, which had been favorable to his discourse in favor of Heracles, became angry and claimed he was mad. The Sophists surrounding Diogenes, listening to him, recommenced their uproar, like frogs which no longer see the water snake.[31] This [episode] is rather interesting for the game, the staging of that anti-royal monarchy of the Cynics. Diogenes, then, has aroused everyone's enthusiasm. Everyone is ready to follow him, and then he commits the indecent act. He squats on the ground (in contrast with the sovereign's royal attitude seated on his throne) and performs an indecent act (return to the first animality which is the true form of monarchy as it should be understood and which is not recognized). And it is at this point that, once again, this king of poverty hides himself. He disappears like the water snake, leaving the frogs to make their din. Diogenes having disappeared, the true monarchy hidden once more, the Sophists resume their discourse. Anti-king king, concealed king, shadowy king, poor and derisory king. This dramatization of sovereignty in this monarchy of derision is typical of the Cynics. The final Cynic reversal is characterized by this dramatization of happy and beneficial sovereign life into a life of wretched kingship of tests of oneself and struggle with others.

Accordingly, we could say the following. Through the various themes we have referred to, we have seen that the Cynics reversed the idea of the unconcealed life by dramatizing it in the practice of nakedness and shamelessness; they reversed the theme of the independent life by dramatizing it in the form of poverty; and they reversed the theme of the straight life by dramatizing it in the form of animality. Well, we can also say that they reverse and invert the theme of the sovereign life (tranquil and beneficial: tranquil for oneself, enjoyment of self, and beneficial for others) by dramatizing it in the form of what could be called the militant life, the life of battle and struggle against and for self, against and for others.

I know that by employing this term "militant life" I am guilty of an obvious anachronism. The very terms militant, militantism, militancy cannot be translated or given any equivalent in Greek and Latin vocabularies. Nevertheless, notwithstanding this, it remains that we have here a certain core which is rather important in the history of ethics. I would like to say this. First, there are a number of notions, images, and terms employed by the Cynics which seem to me to cover quite well what will later become the theme of the militant life in Western ethics. You recall the way in which the Cynics interpreted the term "dog" which others applied to them and they applied to themselves. It seems to me, in fact, that the idea of the guard dog which accosts enemies and bites them, the theme of the combatant-soldier or combatant-athlete who fights against the evils of the world, and the idea of the battler always hard at work, unsparing in his efforts, and enduring his own poverty for the greatest good of all, are all quite close to the much more modern notion of militantism. And this notion of militantism covers, it seems to me, many of the dimensions of that Cynic life which turns the beneficial sovereignty of the *bios philosophikos* into combative endurance.

The idea of a philosophical militancy is, of course, not peculiar to the Cynics; it is frequently found in ancient philosophy and in the Stoics in particular. However—and this is the second thing I would like to say—if Cynic militancy belongs to a whole set of practices of proselytism, it seems to me that it is singular and distinct from all the others in the sense that the militancy of the philosophical schools and sects of Antiquity essentially operated within a closed world. It was a matter of gaining other adherents, of winning the greatest possible number of individuals to the cause through the power of proselytism or propaganda. But philosophical militancy was always practiced in the form of the sect, of the small privileged number.

It seems to me that we have a somewhat different idea in the Cynics. This would be the idea of a militancy in the open, as it were, that is to say, a militancy addressed to absolutely everyone, which precisely does not require an education (a *paideia*), but which resorts to harsh and drastic means, not so much in order to train people and teach them, as to shake them up and convert them, abruptly. It is a militancy in the open in the sense that it claims to attack not just this or that vice or fault or opinion that this or that individual may have, but also the conventions, laws, and institutions which rest on the vices, faults, weaknesses, and opinions shared by humankind in general. It is therefore a militancy which aspires to change the world, much more than a militancy which would seek merely to provide its followers with the means for achieving a happy life. If we are to talk of Cynic militancy, it is important not to forget the system to which it belongs, that it exists alongside many other forms of philosophical proselytism in Antiquity. But we should also recognize a particular form in this militancy: an overt, universal, aggressive militancy; militancy in the world and against the world. This, I think, is the singularity of Cynic sovereignty.

A history of philosophy, morality, and thought which took forms of life, arts of existence, ways of conducting oneself and behaving, and ways of being as its guiding theme would obviously be led to accord considerable importance to Cynicism and the Cynic movement. In particular, it seems to me that we could see in the idea of Cynic sovereignty as derisory and militant monarchy the origin of two things which are important for our culture.

First, an event in what could be called the imaginary or mythological of our political thought: the figure of the king of derision. This theme of the relationship between monarchy and derision should be studied. I think we could find it in a range of forms. For example, there is the couple formed by the king and his fool: the fool alongside the king, the king's vis-à-vis, in a sense the anti-king, who is, at the same time, closest to the king, his confidant, the only one who can speak to him freely, who can use his *parrhēsia* with the king, and who knows the truth even better than the king, and what's more, knows the truth of the king.

We could also study the theme of the hidden king, the unrecognized king who passes through humanity without ever being recognized by anyone, although it is he who possesses the highest form of virtue and true power. Here we find a theme whose importance for Christianity you know. To some extent, the Christlike theme of the hidden king has certainly taken up some elements of this theme of the Cynic king of destitution. This is also the theme in all the frequently found figures of the banished king who has been driven from his land and travels through the world without being recognized by anyone. This is the concealed personage, king, saint, hero, or knight, whose truth, heroism, and highly beneficial value for humanity are not recognized by the whole of humanity. At the point of confluence of all this you could obviously find the figure of King Lear. King Lear is actually a certain episode, no doubt the highest expression of this theme of the king of derision, the mad king, and the hidden king. After all, *King Lear* begins with a story of *parrhēsia*, a test of frankness: who will tell the king the truth? And King Lear is precisely someone who is unable to recognize the truth that was there. And on the basis of this failure to recognize the truth, he in turn is unrecognized. Unrecognized as king, he wanders through the world, accompanied by those who protect him and do what is good for him, without him being aware of this, until the end which covers all at once the death of his daughter, Cordelia, his own death, and the fulfillment of his wretchedness, but a fulfillment which is at the same time the triumph and restoration of the truth itself. I think that Cynicism has played a large role in this, as it were, political imaginary of the unrecognized monarchy.

I think too—and here things would no doubt be easier, but they should also be studied closely—that Cynicism forms the matrix, the point of departure for a long series of historical figures in Christian asceticism, an asceticism which is at once both a spiritual battle in itself, against one's own sins and temptations, and also a battle for the whole world. The Christian ascetic is someone who purges the whole world of its demons. There is the idea of combative dirtiness. And then, of course, in the various movements which have run through and accompanied Christianity throughout its history, there is also that idea of the hidden sovereign, of the sovereign of derision who struggles for humanity and to free it from its evils and vices. There is the development of the mendicant orders in the Middle Ages, and there are the movements which preceded and also followed the Reformation. The principle of militantism constantly [recurs] in these movements, an open militantism which is the critique of real life and of men's behavior, and which, in personal renunciation and destitution, conducts the battle which must lead to the change of the whole world. And after all, the revolutionary militantism of the nineteenth century is still this; it is still that kind of kingship, that kind of monarchy hidden under the rags of poverty, or under the practices of destitution and renunciation at any rate, that monarchy of an aggressive, constant, and endless battle to change the world. And, very briefly, in these conditions we can say that not only has Cynicism pushed the theme of the true life to the extreme point of its reversal into the theme of the life which is scandalously other, but it has laid down this otherness of an *other* life, not simply as the choice of a different, happy, and sovereign life, but as the practice of a combativeness on the horizon of which is an *other* world (*un monde autre*).

Thus you see that the Cynic is someone who, taking up the traditional themes of the true life in ancient philosophy, transposes them and turns them round into the demand and assertion of the need for an *other* life. And then, through the image and figure of the king of poverty, he transposes anew the idea of *an other* life into the theme of a life whose otherness must lead to the change of the world. An *other* life for an *other* world.

You can see that we are, of course, a long way from most of the themes of the ancient true life. But we have here the core of a form of ethics which is wholly characteristic of the Christian and the modern world. And inasmuch as it was through this movement that the theme of the true life became the principle of an *other* life and aspiration for another world (*un autre monde*), Cynicism is the matrix, the embryo anyway of a fundamental ethical experience in the West.

I will stop now. In the second hour, if you like, despite being in bad shape, I will try to comment quickly on a text by Epictetus (the famous discourse 22 of Book III) in which there is a very precise description of the Cynic mission. And in this passage we will find that these themes are again brought into play by Epictetus.

1. Sénèque, *Lettres à Lucilius*, trans. H. Noblot and F. Préchac (Paris: Les Belles Lettres, 1947), letter 20, 1, p. 81: "If you are well and judge yourself worthy of one day being your own master (*fias tuus*), I am delighted"; English translation by Richard M. Gummere, Seneca, *The Epistles of Seneca* (Cambridge, Mass.: Harvard University Press, Loeb Classical Library, 1917) vol. I, 20, 1, p. 133: "If you are in good health and if you think yourself worthy of becoming at last your own master, I am glad."

2. Ibid., 62, 1, Fr. p. 94: "My liberty, Lucilius, is full and complete: wherever I am, I am my own (*ibi meus sum*)"; Eng. p. 427: "As for me, Lucilius, my time is free; it is indeed free, and wherever I am, I am master of myself."

3. Ibid., 75, 18, Fr. p. 55: "'But,' you will ask me, 'what is total independence?' Not fearing men, not fearing the gods; wanting nothing immoral, nothing immoderate; exercising an absolute power over oneself (*in se ipsum habere maximam potestatem*)"; Eng. vol. II (1920), p. 147: "You ask what this freedom is? It means not fearing either men or gods; it means not craving wickedness or excess; it means possessing supreme power over oneself."

4. Sénèque, *De brevitate vitae*, V, 3, trans. A. Bourgery (Paris: Les Belles Lettres, 1923) p. 53: "[The sage] will never be half-free, his freedom will always be intact and all of a piece, he will live free, independent (*sui juris*), above all others"; English translation by John W. Basore, Seneca, *On the Shortness of Life*, V, 3, in *Moral Essays*, vol. II (Cambridge, Mass.: Harvard University Press, Loeb Classical Library, 1932) p. 301: "But, in very truth, never will the wise man... be half a prisoner—he who always possesses an undiminished and stable liberty, being free and his own master and towering over all others." Letter 75, 18, could also be cited: Fr. *Lettres*, p. 55: "inestimable good of succeeding in belonging to oneself (*suum fieri*)"; Eng. *Epistles*, vol. II, p. 147: "And it is a priceless good to be master of oneself."

5. Ibid., 42, 10, Fr. p. 5: "Who possesses himself (*se habet*) has lost nothing; but how many are they who have the happiness of possessing themselves (*habere se*)?"; Eng., vol. I, p. 285: "He that owns himself has lost nothing. But how few men are blessed with ownership of self!"

6. *On the Shortness of Life*, II, 4, Fr. p. 49: "This one is the servant of that one, that one the servant of some other; no one belongs to himself (*suus nemo est*)"; Eng. pp. 291-293: "A cultivates B and B cultivates C; no one is his own master."

7. Letter 23, 6, Fr. *Lettres*, p. 99: "Be happy with your own funds (*de tuo gaude*)"; Eng. *Epistles*, p. 163: "rejoice only in that which comes from your own store."

8. Sénèque, *Consolation à Helvia*, V, 1, trans. R. Waltz (Paris: Les Belles Lettres, 1961) p. 63: "He [the sage] strives ceaselessly to rely only on himself, to seek contentment only in himself (*a se omne gaudium peteret*)"; English translation by John W. Basore, Seneca, *To Helvia On Consolation*, in *Moral Essays*, vol. II, p. 425: "the wise man... has always endeavoured to rely entirely upon himself, to derive all of his joy from himself."

9. Sénèque, *Questions naturelles*, IVa, 20, trans. P. Oltramare (Paris: Les Belles Lettres, 1961) vol. II, p. 178: "Although separated by the sea, I will try often to be of service to you by being harsh with you to conduct you on the best path"; English translation by Thomas H. Corcoran, Seneca, *Natural Questions* (Cambridge, Mass.: Harvard University Press, Loeb Classical Library, 1972) vol. II, p. 17: "Even though we are separated by the sea, I will try to supply this help to you; taking your hand in mine I will at once lead you away to a better life."

10. Dion Chrysostome, Discours IV: *Sur la royauté*, in *Les Cyniques grecs*, pp. 202-225; English translation by J.W. Cohoon, Dio Chrysostom, *Fourth Discourse On Kingship*, in *Dio Chrysostom I, Discourses I-XI* (Cambridge Mass.: Harvard University Press, Loeb Classical Library, 1932).

11. Diogenes Laertius, VI, §32, Fr. p. 713; Eng. p. 35.

12. Dio Chrysostom, *Fourth Discourse On Kingship*, §11, Fr. p. 204; Eng. p. 173.

13. Ibid., §8, Fr. p. 203; Eng. p. 171.

14. Ibid., §30, Fr. p. 207; Eng. pp. 181-183.

15. Ibid., §§55-56, Fr. p. 211; Eng. p. 195.

16. Ibid., §67, Fr. p. 213; Eng. p. 199.

17. Apulée, *Florides*, XXII, 1-4, trans. V. Bétolaud, *Œuvres complètes*, vol. III (Paris: Garner Frères, 1836): "The famous Crates, disciple of Diogenes, was honored by his contemporaries in Athens as the guardian spirit of every home. No house was ever closed to him;

a father had no secret so intimate that Crates did not enter into, always appropriately; he was the conciliator and arbitrator of all disputes and quarrels between relatives"; English translation by H.E. Butler, Apuleius, *Florida* in Lucius Apuleius, *The Apologia and Florida of Apuleius of Madaura* (Dodo Press: 2010 [this is a reprint of Oxford: Clarendon Press, 1909]) pp. 123-124: "Crates, the well-known disciple of Diogenes, was honoured at Athens by the men of his day as though he had been a household god. No house was ever so closed to him, no family had ever so close a secret as to regard Crates as an unseasonable intruder: he was always welcome; there was never a quarrel, never a lawsuit between kinsfolk, but he was accepted as mediator and his word was law." Diogenes Laertius, VI, 86, Fr. p. 753: Diogenes Laertius calls Crates the "'Door-opener,' because he entered every house and dispensed his admonishments"; Eng. p. 89: "He was known as the 'Door-opener'...from his habit of entering every house and admonishing those within." There is a similar portrait in Plutarch, *Moralia*, trans. Paul A. Clement and Herbert B. Hoffleit (Cambridge, Mass.: Harvard University Press, 1969) vol. VIII, 632e, p. 127.

18. Xénophon, *Mémorables*, II, 1, 21-34, pp. 320-33; Xenophon, *Memorabilia*, pp. 95-103.

19. Dion Chrysostome, *Discours VIII: Diogène ou De la vertu*, in *Les Cyniques grecs*, pp. 233-241; Dio Chrysostom, *The Eighth Discourse: Diogenes or On Virtue*, in *Dio Chrysostom I, Discourses I-XI*, pp. 376-399.

20. Ibid., §27, Fr. p. 239; Eng. pp. 391-393. Zetes, with Calaïs, was one of the two sons of Boreas; they both took part in the expedition of the Argonauts.

21. Jason was the leader of the Argonauts, captain of the mythical expedition to fetch the Golden Fleece.

22. Son of Apollo and Paphos, the first king of Cyprus, he came from Asia. Loved by Aphrodite, who bestowed considerable wealth on him, he lived for 160 years and became proverbial for his longevity and wealth.

23. *Diogenes or On Virtue*, §28. The son of Tantalus, Pelops was cut into pieces, cooked, and served up as a dish for the gods by his father, who wanted to test their omniscience. The gods quickly distinguished the human flesh from animal meat, with the exception of Demeter, who ate the young man's shoulder. Tantalus was consigned to the Underworld and his son put back together again, apart from the eaten shoulder, which was replaced by a piece of ivory.

24. Ibid.

25. Ibid., Fr.: "Our toiling and struggling Heracles was greatly pitied: he was called the most unhappy man and for that reason, moreover, one began to call his labor and works 'toils,' as if a life of labor was a life of struggle (and a miserable life)"; Eng: "As for Heracles, they pitied him while he toiled and struggled and called him the most 'trouble-ridden,' or wretched of men; indeed this is why they gave the name 'troubles,' or tasks, to his labors and works, as though a laborious life were a trouble-ridden or wretched life."

26. Ibid.

27. Ibid., §30, Fr. p. 239; Eng. pp. 393-395.

28. Ibid., §31, Fr. p. 239; Eng. p. 395.

29. Ibid.

30. Ibid., §33, Fr. p. 240; Eng. pp. 395-397.

31. Ibid., §36, Fr. pp. 240-241: "So spoke Diogenes, and the crowd around him took a lively pleasure in hearing his words. But dwelling, I suppose, on this final image of Heracles, he cut short his words, squatted on the ground and did something vulgar. The people then began to mock him, to treat him like a madman, and the Sophists resumed their din, like frogs in a pond when they no longer see the water snake"; Eng. pp. 397-399: "While Diogenes thus spoke, many stood about and listened to his words with great pleasure. Then, possibly with this thought of Heracles in his mind, he ceased speaking and, squatting on the ground, performed an indecent act, whereat the crowd straightway scorned him and called him crazy, and again the sophists raised their din, like frogs in a pond when they do not see the water-snake."

sixteen

21 MARCH 1984

Second hour

[
Reading of Epictetus on the Cynic life (Book III, xxii). ∽ *Stoic
elements of the portrait.* ∽ *The philosophical life: from rational
choice to divine vocation.* ∽ *Ascetic practice as verification.* ∽
*Ethical elements of the Cynic mission: endurance, vigilance, inspec-
tion.* ∽ *The responsibility for humanity.* ∽ *Government of the
world.*
]

I WILL TRY QUICKLY to read with you chapter 22 from Book III of
Epictetus' *Discourses*. It is an extremely interesting text inasmuch as it
is well and truly the description of the Cynic mission. Following what I
have just been saying, if we accept that the reversal of the theme of the
sovereign life in the Cynics leads to the assertion that, on the one hand,
the Cynic is a king, and that, on the other, he has a hard mission to
fulfill, we find the second aspect (the mission) developed in Epictetus,
whereas Dio Chrysostom lays more stress on the theme of Cynic kingship (Fourth and Eighth Discourses). So Epictetus is interesting for
this definition of Cynic sovereignty as mission.

All the same, it is a complex text and it cannot be taken as a
Cynic's direct expression of his forms of life: Epictetus was a Stoic.
You know—this is very complicated, difficult, and not very clear—that
there were many close relations and contacts between a certain form of
Stoicism and a certain form of Cynicism. With Epictetus we have then
a Stoic's representation of what would be easiest for a Stoic to accept

and recognize in the Cynic life, what a Stoic would find most essential and pure in this life.

Epictetus excludes the more clamorous, garish, and scandalous features of the Cynic life from this representation. He brushes aside the theme of shamelessness and says that the Cynic does not have to be dirty and disgusting, that on the contrary he should attract people to himself, not by luxury, of course, but by cleanliness and decency. So he eliminates some things from the Cynic life. He adds some specifically Stoic elements to the description of the Cynic life, in particular everything concerning the examination of representations, the theory of propensity and repulsion, of desire and aversion. He takes up all these Stoic categories in his description of the Cynic life, so that he presents a sort of combination, a mixture, a Stoicizing description of Cynicism as the militant practice of the philosophical life, and I would like to focus on this. So: the philosophical life as militancy.

How does Epictetus present this Cynic militancy, this courage of the Cynic to assert the truth of a philosophy in his life and with regard to others? The first thing to stress is that in talking about Cynic practice, Epictetus does not define a choice of life exactly, but a mission one is given. It seems to me that this difference or inflection from a choice of life to a mission one has received is important.

Taking Stoicism as our reference point, we can say that, for the Stoics, every man living in a city had a status, wealth, and possibly responsibilities and obligations. And the Stoics thought it would be dishonorable, or at any rate morally blameworthy to shirk these different tasks. One has to marry, have children, exercise public office if need be, and so on. These were responsibilities one received and which could not be shirked.

On the other hand, what did philosophy [represent] in contrast with these responsibilities? Philosophy was precisely a choice, the choice of a certain form of existence which enabled one to exercise these offices, these responsibilities, and one's status in a certain way. Philosophy was a choice in relation to a sort of social mission which one received. The Cynic life, [as] Epictetus depicts it, transforms this idea of philosophy as pure choice as opposed to missions and responsibilities one has received. Epictetus does not describe the *kunizein* (the fact of being a Cynic, of leading the Cynic life) as a choice one might make on one's own, quite the contrary. Speaking of those people who start to lead the Cynic life (wearing a rough cloak, sleeping on the ground), he says that all these choices of existence, these voluntary, self-imposed practices cannot constitute the true *kunizein* (the true Cynic practice).

Epictetus' interlocutor in this dialogue, a disciple who wants to be a Cynic, says: "I already wear a rough cloak, so shall I wear one then. I already sleep on the ground, so shall I sleep there then. In addition I will take a beggar's pouch and a staff, and I will go on my way, begging and insulting those I meet."[1] So this disciple thinks or believes that being a Cynic means making this choice of clothes, appearance, and mode of life. To which Epictetus replies: "If this is how you see things, keep away from it; don't come near it, it has nothing to do with you."[2] What I think Epictetus means is that all the external aspects of the Cynic life (rough cloak, beggar's pouch, staff) are tawdry rags which do not enter into the real Cynic life. But there is another reason. It is not just because they are tawdry materials which have nothing to do with the relationship of self to self; it is also because that in doing this the individual sets himself up as a Cynic; he proclaims himself Cynic. Now this is precisely what one must not do. For Epictetus, someone who, independently of the gods (*dikha theous*), "undertakes such an important matter, incurs divine anger and wishes nothing else than to cover himself with shame in the eyes of everyone."[3]

Consequently, the adoption of the Cynic life cannot be a choice made spontaneously of one's own accord, for oneself on the basis of one's own decision, it cannot be made *dikha theous* (independently of the gods). At this point Epictetus makes a comparison: Imagine someone entering a well-ordered household. He declares himself steward of this household and sets about exercising the steward's functions, knowing nothing about the household or the order reigning within it. Naturally, immediately there will be the greatest disorder. And seeing this disorder, the master of the household will soon drive out the impostor.[4] Well, the same thing happens in the order of the Cynic life. One has to be designated for the Cynic life by God, just as the true steward, who establishes the proper order of a household, is someone appointed by the master of the household. One does not appoint oneself steward in a household; one does not appoint oneself Cynic.

Epictetus gives a prosopopoeia of God on this subject, lending him the following speech: "You, you are the sun ... Carry out your revolution and thus set everything in motion, from the greatest to the smallest."[5] Then, turning to an animal, he says to it: "You, you are a bull, advance and fight, for this is your business, what suits you and what you can do."[6] Finally, turning to a man, he tells him: "You, you are capable of commanding an army against Ilium, you will be Agamemnon. You, you are capable of defeating Hector in combat: be Achilles."[7] The comparison is clear: just as God has assigned each thing its place in the world and the role it is to perform, so God designates certain individuals among humans in the same way, entrusting them with a certain mission. This mission, moreover, is represented metaphorically by these different elements: the philosopher is like the sun which gives light to the world and sets everything in motion, great and small; the philosopher is like the bull who advances and fights (militancy); the philosopher is also like someone who can command men, just as Agamemnon commanded against Ilium; finally the philosopher is capable of withstanding the hardest battles against faults and vices, just as Achilles was capable of fighting Hector. So, the sun, the bull, Agamemnon, and Achilles are designated by God to exercise their function and their role. In the same way, the Cynic philosopher is designated; he cannot be self-appointed.

So I think we should make the following distinction on this point. Epictetus does not say at all that to practice the philosopher's life we must wait to receive this mission from God. For Epictetus, whatever one's status, magistrate or married, poor or rich, philosophy, the philosophical way of life, really is the result of a choice. But within the philosophical life there is a particular function of being the advanced party, of combat, and also of service to humanity. This function is precisely Cynicism. Within this general domain of philosophy, which rests on choice, there are a few who have a philosophical mission. One can only be entrusted with this philosophical mission by a god, and no one can set himself up as a professional philosopher, as it were, if he has not been given this mission. Choosing between the philosophical and the non-philosophical life is a matter of choice and freedom. Claiming to be a Cynic and undertaking the task of addressing humankind in order to battle with it and for it, and possibly against it for the change of the world, is a mission one is given by God, and only by God. One must wait for it, not bestow it on oneself.

You can see that there is, in a sense, the same Socratic theme of the divine mission. Socrates too was given a mission. You remember that in the *Apology* Socrates was bound to this mission, and what the effect of this was, what consequence it had? In the *Apology* Socrates said that he had a mission and concluded from this that, since he had been given this mission, he could not rid himself of it. Despite the fact that this mission met with hostility, despite him incurring the citizen's anger because of it, and not only his anger, but a trial, and not only a trial, but death, despite all this, since he had been given this mission, he would keep to it and fulfill its tasks until the end. The mission bound him, personally, to a certain task.

In the text by Epictetus the philosophical mission takes on a somewhat different sense. Through the mission, the Cynic is certainly bound to himself, to this obligation, but the effect of this idea of mission is essentially to rule out from the Cynic profession all those who have no right to it and all those who have not been designated for it. The divine mission constrains Socrates to be a philosopher, despite the dangers. The divine mission [according to] Epictetus excludes from this philosophical mission, from this philosophical task, all those who do not have a right to it, all those who are not capable of it, and all false philosophers. So it seems to me that these two notions of mission do not have exactly the same effect, even though the Cynic mission does echo the Socratic theme of the philosophical mission received [from the god].

So one receives the mission to be a Cynic. Again, everyone must be capable of the choice of the philosophical life. On the other hand, some are missionaries of philosophy; they profess philosophy. In the Budé translation, the title given to the chapter—which was added later; it is not by Epictetus or Arrian—is: "On the Cynic profession"[8] (in Greek: *peri kunismou*, on the subject of Cynicism). It is a translation we can take up again, giving, of course, both meanings to the term "profession." This is philosophy as an occupation to which one entirely devotes oneself. It is also a profession in the sense of the attitude by which one manifests before everyone the philosophy in which one believes, the fact that one believes in this philosophy, and that one really identifies oneself with the philosophical role one has been given. So it will in fact be a question of the philosophical profession.

There are many things that could be said about the emergence, more or less in this period (in the second century), of this, as it were, professional conception of activities. In Marcus Aurelius there are some considerations on the exercise of imperial power as a profession and almost as a job.[9] Now how do we recognize this mission of becoming professional philosophers, which only some of those who have made the philosophical choice have received? Are there signs, as there will be signs of divine grace or divine vocation in Christianity? In fact, for Epictetus, there is no prior mark which enables one to recognize oneself as charged with a philosophical mission. One can recognize oneself as charged with this philosophical mission only on condition that one puts oneself to the test. It is here that self-knowledge plays an important role. Whoever wishes to become Cynic should not look for external signs of God having chosen him. He must do something else: "Examine the thing more seriously, know yourself, question the deity, do not attempt the undertaking without God."[10] Shortly before this he said: "Do you see how you must undertake such an important business? Begin by taking a mirror, look at your shoulders, examine your loins and thighs."[11] What is involved in this text, which is a clear reference to the athlete and to the battle? We will recognize that we are made for the job of Cynic and have been given this mission if we train for the Cynic life, and if in the exercise of this life we really can recognize our ability to fulfill it. There is no self-appointment, but test of self by self, recognition of what one is and what one can do in the attempt to live in the Cynic way. How is this series of tests and experiences one has to conduct on oneself in order to recognize oneself as Cynic set out? It is very simple, and you will recognize straightaway some of the elements we know already: "First of all, in all that concerns you personally [Epictetus says to the person who wishes to undertake the Cynic life; M.F.], you must change completely your present way of acting, accusing neither God nor man; you must suppress your desires entirely, seek to avoid only that which depends on you, and feel no anger, envy, or pity; you must find no young girl beautiful, or vainglory, or boy, or any delicacy good. For you must know this: other men have the shelter of their walls, their houses, and the dark to perform actions of that kind, and they have a thousand ways to hide them: one keeps his door closed."[12] As for the Cynic, what must he do? He must not wish to hide anything that concerns him; he has only his modesty (*aidōs*) to hide himself: "There is his house, his door, the guards to his bedroom, his darkness."[13]

It is absolutely clear that this is the ideal of the unconcealed life which we find again here, with, first, that specifically Stoic mutation, inflection: the principle of the unconcealed life is immediately connected, not to *anaideia* (shamelessness), but rather to *aidōs* (modesty). That is to say, Epictetus restores the traditional meaning of the unconcealed life. Life must be unhidden because whoever leads the philosophical life, conducting himself according to the rules of modesty, does not have to hide, and everyone can see what he does. You recognize the principle of the unconcealed life, but with this revocation of *anaideia*. Second, you see that the first test by which an individual will recognize whether he is able to be Cynic and to recognize the mission with which he is charged is this: will he or won't he be able to lead an unconcealed life?

The second test consists precisely in finding out whether he can lead a life which needs nothing, a bare life of poverty, that is to say, the true life without mixture or dependence. Epictetus sets out this second test of the Cynic life a bit further on when he says that the Cynic is someone with material to work on. What is this material? Just as the carpenter has wood as the material on which he works, so the Cynic has to work on his own soul. "The wretched body is nothing to me ... Exile? And to what place can I be expelled? ... Wherever I go there will be the sun, the moon, stars, dreams, omens, and conversation with the gods."[14] We have here the second Cynic test, the test of a life of poverty and wandering that nothing ties down and keeps to a native land. It is a life under the sun, the moon, and the stars, a life which talks with the gods, listens to dreams, and understands omens. But beyond this, it is the life not bound to anything; it is *adiaphoros*, the independent life we talked about last week, the life of poverty and destitution.

The third test of the Cynic life is that of the diacritical (*diakriticos*) life, the life which distinguishes. Can one lead the life of the barking dog which can tell friends from enemies and recognize those who are favorable to [its] master and those who are hostile? The Cynic is someone who can show men that they are entirely in error and looking for the nature of good and evil where it cannot be found. The Cynic must be, and recognizes himself in the fact that he is, Epictetus says, a scout (*kataskopos*), pointing out to men what is favorable and what is hostile to them.[15] This is very precisely that diacritical function [which consists in] distinguishing between what is favorable and what hostile, between friends and enemies.

You see that the three aspects of the Cynic life which I analyzed last week are clearly found again in this text. They are at once the manifestation of the Cynic life, the way of leading it, and at the same time the way of providing oneself with the signs that one is capable of leading it. This is at once the expression and the test, the measure and the affirmation of the Cynic life.

So there is no need to look for external signs of the Cynic mission. The Cynic mission will be recognized only in the practice of *askēsis*. The ascesis, exercise, and practice of all this endurance, which means that one lives unconcealed, non-dependent, and distinguishing between what is good and what is bad, will in itself be the sign of the Cynic mission. One is not called to Cynicism, as Socrates was called by being given a sign by the god of Delphi, or as the Apostles will be, by receiving the gift of tongues. The Cynic recognizes himself, and he is, as it were, alone with himself in order to recognize himself in the test of the Cynic life he undergoes, of the Cynic life in its truth, the unconcealed, non-dependent life which remakes, unravels the division between good and evil.

Now, granted that Cynicism is a mission and that one recognizes one's ability to see this mission through by constantly putting oneself to the test, in what will this mission consist? Here is the third point, the third stage of reflection found in this text. In what will the Cynic mission consist according to Epictetus? Right at the end of the text there is what I think is a crucially important, decisive passage. Ending his discussion with the candidate Cynic, Epictetus reminds him of the difficulty of the task he will have to accomplish, and therefore of the care with which it is advisable he prepare for it. To describe this task, Epictetus resorts to a quotation from Homer. In the *Illiad* (Book VI, 492), just before the battle with Achilles, Hector says to Andromache (I am not absolutely sure if it is the battle with Achilles at this point, but it doesn't matter): Go home to your weaving, *"war will be the respon-sibility of men/of all men, and especially of me."* So the Cynic mission is a mission of combat. There are women, the others who must return home to their weaving; and then there are "some," the soldiers who will have to fight and accomplish their mission of war. The Cynic is a philosopher at war. He is someone who wages philosophical war for others.

What does this mission of philosophical war comprise? First, it com-prises everything we already know: harshness towards oneself, all the hardships that the Cynic imposes on himself. Epictetus reminds him: the Cynic has no clothes, shelter, or hearth, he lives in the dirt, and he has neither slave nor homeland. The Cynic evoked by Epictetus says of himself: "I am without shelter, without homeland, without resources, without slaves. I sleep on the ground. I have no wife, no children, no palace to govern, only the earth, the sky, and one old cloak."[16] Only, for Epictetus, he is not characterized by this simple deprivation. There is more, and we see here something which I referred to last week: the acceptance of the violence, blows, and injustice which others may inflict on him. This is a typical feature of Cynicism. For the Cynics, blows, insults, and humiliations are an exercise, and this exercise is valuable as training both in physical endurance and in indifference towards opinion. And you recall that it was equally a way of carrying out a reversal and of appearing stronger than others, of showing that one can prevail over others. There were those scenes in which Diogenes accepts an insult or a blow, and then turns the situation round and appears stronger than the others.

We find again in Epictetus all these themes of the acceptance of suf-fering and injustice, which, once again, are rather unusual in Antiquity, an acceptance which is also valuable as test and training. In paragraph 53 Epictetus says: If God advises you to take the Cynic path, this is not because he loves seeing you receive blows, it is so "that you become great."[17] Blows, therefore, make one great; they test, train, and perfect. A bit further on he says again: When you receive blows, you must not run to Caesar or the Proconsul. The Cynic is convinced that he must endure the suffering; Zeus is exercising him.[18] So you see the idea that the suffering the Cynic accepts, the humiliation he does not seek to avoid, is valuable exercise.

But what does this exercise lead to? On the one hand, it leads, of course, to distinguishing the body and the soul. "The Cynic's capacity for endurance must be such that common people take him to be insensitive, a stone. Nobody can abuse him, strike him, or offend him. He has himself given his body to whoever wants it to treat as he sees fit."[19] But there is another aspect of Cynic endurance, of the value of the acceptance of these humiliations, insults, and blows as exercise—this is important and no doubt marks a certain proximity to Stoicism, as if Cynic thought is contaminated by Stoic thought in Epictetus—and this is that the exercise of endurance manifests and strengthens the philanthropic bond which may exist between philosophers and the whole of humankind. To the suffering and injustice he suffers at the hands of someone else, the Cynic responds in a completely dissymmetrical way with the assertion that he, the Cynic, is linked by a bond of friendship, or anyway by a bond of philanthropy to the very people who do him harm. He will put up with the violence and injustice, not only so as to become resistant, and to prepare himself for all the misfortunes which may occur—which is the classical form—but as an exercise of friendship, of affection, or at any rate of the intense bond with the whole of humankind. In paragraphs 54-55, Epictetus says: It is a sort of pleasant good which is prepared for the Cynic, "he must be beaten like an ass and, being beaten, must love those who beat him as though he were the father and brother of all."[20]

The relationship of insult, humiliation, and violence established between the Cynic and others, and which we saw served in Diogenes as a sort of recovery of mastery, of ironic domination, appears here therefore, through an interesting inflection in the history of ethics, as the occasion of a reversal, not of domination, or of strength, or making possible a different form of mastery, but a reversal which means that the insult gives the Cynic the opportunity to establish a relationship of affection with the very people who do him harm and, through them, with the whole of humankind.

If Cynicism thus constructs bonds with the whole of humanity in this practice of endurance, what then will the Cynic's activity now be, given this bond of friendship, and what will his missionary task be? He will be—we have just found the word—the *kataskopos* (scout),[21] or the *episkopos* (I was going to say: bishop) of the humankind he addresses.[22] For the analysis of this mission of the Cynic, I think we need to refer to the long passage in which Epictetus explains why the Cynic should not marry. It was actually a Stoic thesis that, except in particular circumstances which may prevent it, every man should marry because marriage was precisely part of humanity's responsibilities. As human being, member of a family, citizen, and above all part of humankind, there is no question of shirking this general obligation. Now, Epictetus says in this passage, if every man should marry (the Stoic thesis), the Cynic, on the other hand, not only may not, but must not marry. Why must he not marry? Because if he had to take care of his household, then he would have to heat the water for his son's bath, he would have to provide wool for his wife when she is pregnant, he would have to provide services for his father-in-law, and provide for all his family.[23] Now it is quite clear that the Cynic must "remain free from anything that might distract him." He must be "entirely in the service of God [reference to the mission I have just been talking about; M.F.], able to go among men without ever being tied down by private duties."[24] And at this point the Cynic appears as a man whose poverty, destitution, lack of home and country are nothing other than the condition for being able to exercise, in a positive way, the positive mission he has been given. At this point, free of everything and all his impulses, he appears as a sort of universal night-watchman who keeps watch over the sleep of humanity. As a universal night-watchman, he must keep watch over all the others, over all those who are married, over all those who have children. He has to observe who treats his wife well and who treats her badly, to see "which people quarrel among themselves, which household enjoys peace, and which does not." He must "make his rounds like a physician and feel everyone's pulse."[25]

Universal missionary of humankind, who watches over men whatever they may be doing and wherever they may be, who knocks on doors, enters, checks what is going on, and says what is good and what is bad. All this, you see, is the Cynic's mission, which is nothing other than the reverse, positive side of his necessary detachment. This image of the missionary, of the physician of everyone, of the overseer who gives advice and counsel to all, this image of the benefactor who pushes everyone to do what they should, is something new in relation to what could be called the usual and traditional proselytism or militantism in the different philosophical sects of Antiquity. The Cynic is a functionary of humanity in general; he is a functionary of ethical universality.

And this man, of whom one demands detachment from every particular tie of family, homeland, and civic and political responsibility, is freed from these ties only so that he can accomplish the great task of ethical universality, which is not the political universality of the group (city, or State, or even the whole of humankind), but the universality of all men. An individual bond with individuals, but with all individuals, is what characterizes, in its freedom as well as in its obligatory form, the Cynic's bond with all the other men who make up humankind.

The Cynic is therefore responsible for humanity. This humble, rough, harsh task, which demands so many renunciations, is at the same time the most beneficial and highest task. In the first place, it is useful to men, and to all men. "Who," Epictetus asks, "provides the greatest service to men, those who bring two or three ugly-snouted brats into the world [that is to say, those who marry and have children; M.F.], or those who, to the best of their ability, exercise supervision (*hoi episkopountes*) over all men, observing what they do, how they spend their life, what they care for, and what they neglect contrary to their duties?"[26] We find here reference, of course, to the theme of *epimeleia*, a double *epimeleia* which means that the philosopher (here, the Cynic) is someone who sees to that which men take care of. Their care, their *epimeleia*, is to look after men's care. To take care of men's care appears here as the Cynic philosopher's actual task. This task is therefore useful to all men; it is every bit as worthwhile as any private activity. It is more worthwhile to watch over the whole world than to produce two or three ugly-snouted brats. But it is also more worthwhile than any public activity. No doubt, Epictetus says, the Cynic will not mount the rostrum to speak about public income, or peace and war in the framework of the city.[27] But, if the Cynic doesn't do this, he will, on the other hand, address everyone, Athenian, Corinthian, or Roman. And he will not discuss taxes, income, or peace and war. What will he discuss with all these men, Athenians, Corinthians, and Romans? "Happiness and unhappiness, good and ill fortune, slavery and freedom." Can he exercise any greater authority than that? Is that (speaking to all men of happiness and unhappiness, good and ill fortune, slavery and freedom) not the true political activity, the true *politeuesthai*?[28]

The Cynic, who was only a king of poverty, and a hidden and unrecognized king, now appears as someone who exercises the true function of *politeuesthai*, the true function of the *politeia*, understood in the true sense of the term, that *politeia* where it is not just a question of war and peace, of duties, taxes, and revenues in a city, but of the happiness and misfortune, the freedom and slavery of the whole of humankind. As a result the Cynic is associated with the government of the universe. The *politeuesthai* is no longer that of the cities and States, it is that of the whole world. Epictetus evokes the Cynic's hard daily round, which, through all his asceticism, deprivations, and suffering has led him to call out to men and to help them wherever they are. And, in the evening of this heavy day's work, which is the Cynic's life, well, Epictetus says, he may sleep with a pure heart, knowing that "all his thoughts are the thoughts of a friend and servant of the gods, of one who takes part in the government of Zeus."[29] This, then, is the Cynic in the evening of his life, restored, beyond his hidden monarchy, in true sovereignty, which is that of the gods over the whole of humankind. This is the reversal of the theme of sovereignty in the Cynics.*

Next week, which will be the last, I will try to take up again this theme of *parrhēsia* and show you how, through the Cynic mode of being, the values of *parrhēsia* are inflected and what shape they begin to take in Christianity.

---

* The manuscript has a development here which is not taken up in the lecture:
"We will stop there for a moment. On the one hand, I know that it is or would be an exaggeration to credit Cynicism with having invented philosophical militancy. In the first place because it does seem to have implanted its own practice in a pre-existing tradition. Then, and especially, because a kind of militancy existed, to different degrees and in different forms, in the most numerous of the philosophical movements of Antiquity: the school, general teaching. Cynic militancy was part of a whole set of practices of proselytism. But what makes it singular and distinguishes it from all the others is that it does not develop in a closed circuit but in the open, that it does not require an education, a *paideia*. It will employ harsh, drastic means to shake up the people. In short, it is that it alone claims to take on conventions, laws, and institutions. It is a militancy that claims to change the world. But when we speak of Cynic militancy, we should not forget the whole of which it is part; we should not forget that we find around it forms of philosophical proselytism. Nor should we forget that the Stoics often practice a very similar form of activity, of propaganda. So: situating Cynicism in all this family; but nonetheless recognizing in it a form of open, aggressive militantism; a militantism in the world and against the world. What gives this Cynic activity its historical importance is also the series in which it is inserted: the activism of Christianity, which is at the same time spiritual battle, but battle for the world; other movements which have accompanied Christianity: the mendicant orders, preaching, movements which preceded and followed the Reformation. In all these movements we find the principle of an open militantism. Revolutionary militantism of the nineteenth [century]. The true life as an other life (*une vie autre*), as a life of combat, for a changed world."
[However, see above, in the first hour of this day's lecture, pp. 283-285, where many of these points are in fact developed; G.B.]

1. Epictète, *Entretiens*, Book III, chapter xxii, 10, trans. J. Souilhé and A. Jagu (Paris: Les Belles Lettres, 1963) p. 71; English translation by W.A. Oldfather, Epictetus, *Epictetus II. The Discourses Books III-IV* (Cambridge, Mass.: Harvard University Press, 1928) pp. 133-135: "I wear a rough cloak even as it is, and I shall have one then; I have a hard bed even now, and so I shall then; I shall take to myself a wallet and a staff, and I shall begin to walk around and beg from those I meet, and revile them."

2. Ibid., III, xxii, 11, Fr. p. 71; Eng. p. 135: "If you fancy the affair to be something like this, give it a wide berth; don't come near it, it is nothing for you."

3. Ibid., III, xxii, 2, Fr. p. 70; Eng. pp. 131-133: "the man who lays his hand to so great a matter as this without God, is hateful to Him, and his wish means nothing else than disgracing himself in public."

4. Ibid., III, xxii, 3-4, Fr. p. 70; Eng. p. 133.

5. Ibid., III, xxii, 5-6, Fr. p. 70; Eng. p. 133: "*You* are the sun... arise, make the circuit of the heavens, and so set in motion all things from the greatest to the least."

6. Ibid., III, xxii, 6, Fr. p. 70; Eng. p. 133: "*You* are a bull; come on and fight, for this is expected of you, it befits you, and you are able to do it."

7. Ibid., III, xxii, 7-8, Fr. p. 70; Eng. p. 133: "*You* are able to lead the host against Ilium; be Agamemnon. *You* are able to fight a duel with Hector; be Achilles."

8. Ibid. [The title given to Oldfather's English translation is: "On the calling of a Cynic"; G.B.]

9. On this point see *L'Herméneutique du sujet*, pp. 192-194; *The Hermeneutics of the Subject*, pp. 200-202. The texts of Marcus Aurelius are the *Meditations*, VI, 30 and VIII, 5.

10. Epictetus, III, xxii, 53, Fr. p. 77; Eng. p. 149: "Think the matter over more carefully, know yourself, ask the Deity, do not attempt the task without God."

11. Ibid., III, xxii, 51, Fr. p. 71; Eng. p. 149: "Do you see the spirit in which you are intending to set your hand to so great an enterprise? First take a mirror, look at your shoulders, find out what kind of loins and thighs you have."

12. Ibid., III, xxii, 13-14, Fr. p. 71; Eng. p. 135: "First, in all that pertains to yourself directly, you must change completely from your present practices, and must cease to blame God or man; you must utterly wipe out desire, and must turn your aversion toward the things that lie within the province of the moral purpose, and these only; you must feel no anger, no rage, no envy, no pity; no wench must look fine to you, no petty reputation, no boy-favourite, no little sweet-cake. For this you ought to know: Other men have the protection of their walls and their houses and darkness, when they do anything of that sort, and they have many things to hide them. A man closes his door ..."

13. Ibid., III, xxii, 15-16, Fr. p. 72; Eng. p. 135: "His self-respect is his house, his door, his guard at the entrance to his bedroom, his darkness."

14. Ibid., III, xxii, 21-22, Fr. p. 72; Eng. p. 137: "My paltry body is nothing to me... Exile? And to what place can anyone thrust me out? ... wherever I go, there are sun, moon, stars, dreams, omens, my converse with gods."

15. Ibid., III, xxii, 24-25, Fr. p. 73: "In reality, the Cynic is for men truly a scout (*kataskopos*) of what is favorable to them and what is hostile. And he must first explore exactly and then return to announce the truth without being paralyzed by fear"; Eng. p. 139: "For the Cynic is truly a scout, to find out what things are friendly to men and what hostile; and he must first do his scouting accurately, and on returning must tell the truth, not driven by fear to designate as enemies those who are not such, nor in any other fashion be distraught or confused by his external impressions."

16. Ibid., III, xxii, 47-48, Fr. p. 77; Eng. p. 147: "I am without a home, without a city, without property, without a slave; I sleep on the ground; I have neither wife nor children, no miserable governor's mansion, but only earth, and sky, and one rough cloak."

17. Ibid., III, xxii, 53, Fr. p. 78; Eng. p. 149.

18. Ibid., III, xxii, 56-57, Fr. p. 78; Eng. p. 151.

19. Ibid., III, xxii, 100, Fr. p. 85; Eng. p. 167: "Now the spirit of patient endurance the Cynic must have to such a degree that common people will think him insensate and a stone; nobody reviles him, nobody beats him, nobody insults him; but his body he has himself given for anyone to use as he sees fit."

20. Ibid., III, xxii, 53, Fr. p. 78; Eng. p. 149: "For this too is a very pleasant strand woven into the Cynic's pattern of life; he must needs by flogged like an ass, and while he is being flogged he must love the men who flog him, as though he were the father or brother of them all."

21. Ibid., III, xxii, 24-25, Fr. p. 73; Eng. p. 139.

22. Ibid., III, xxii, 77 and 98, Fr. p. 81 and p. 84; Eng. pp. 157-159 and p. 165.

23. Ibid., III, xxii, 68-71, Fr. p. 80; Eng. p. 155.

24. Ibid., III, xxii, 69, Fr. p. 80; Eng. p. 155: "wholly devoted to the service of God, free to go about among men, not tied down by the private duties of men."

25. Ibid., III, xxii, 73, Fr. p. 80; Eng. p. 157: "who is treating his wife well, and who ill; who quarrels; what household is stable, and what not; making his rounds like a physician, and feeling pulses."

26. Ibid., III, xxii, 77, Fr. p. 81; Eng. pp. 157-159: "who do mankind the greater service? Those who bring into the world some two or three ugly-snouted children to take their place, or those who exercise oversight, to the best of their ability, over all mankind, observing what they are doing, how they are spending their lives, what they are careful about, and what they undutifully neglect?"

27. Ibid., III, xxii, 84, Fr. p. 82; Eng. p. 161.

28. Ibid., III, xxii, 85, Fr. p. 82; Eng. p. 161.

29. Ibid., III, xxii, 95, Fr. p. 84; Eng. p. 165: "every thought which he thinks is that of a friend and servant to the gods, of one who shares in the government of Zeus."

seventeen

28 MARCH 1984

First hour

[
The two aspects of the Cynic life as sovereign life: bliss and mani-
festation of truth. ⌇ *The Cynic standpoint: conformity to the truth,*
self-knowledge, and supervision of others. ⌇ *The transformation of*
self and the world. ⌇ *Transition to Christian asceticism: continu-*
ities. ⌇ *Differences: the other world and the principle of obedience.*
]

FIRST OF ALL SOME words on the Cynic's *parrhēsia*, followed by
some indications on the evolution of the term *parrhēsia* in Christian
authors of the first centuries. And then possibly, if I have time, I would
like to situate a little all that I have told you, in this and previous
years, within the more general framework I wanted to give to these
analyses.

So first, return to the problem of *parrhēsia* in Cynic life and practice. You remember how the Cynic life defined itself and presented
itself as a royal life, and even as the royal life par excellence, fully
sovereign over itself. I think that this sovereignty, by which the Cynic
life characterized itself, expressed a double derision towards political
sovereignty, the sovereignty of kings of the world. First, because Cynic
sovereignty asserted itself aggressively, in a critical, polemical mode,
as the only real monarchy. What basically was at issue in the meeting
between Diogenes and Alexander was which of them was the true
king. And Diogenes, of course, asserted himself and revealed himself
as the true king, facing Alexander, who held his monarchy, in the true

sense of the term, only inasmuch as he too shared in the sovereignty of
that wisdom.

On the other hand—this was the other side of the Cynic derision
of monarchies—the Cynic's real monarchy inverted all the signs and
distinguishing features of political monarchies. It practiced solitude,
whereas sovereigns were surrounded by their court, soldiers, and allies.
It practiced destitution, whereas kings of the world gave themselves
all the outward signs of wealth and power. It practiced endurance and
ascetic exercises, whereas monarchs of the world practiced the enjoyment of pleasures. So there is a double derision of this real monarchy.
But through this double derision of real, political monarchies, the Cynic
sovereign found the true monarchy, the universal monarchy which was
that of the gods. On the evening of his day's work, you recall, the Cynic
could go to sleep with a pure heart knowing that "all his thoughts
are the thoughts of a friend and servant of the gods, of one who takes
part in the government of Zeus [*metekhōn tēs arkhēs tou Dios*: someone
who takes part, shares in the government, the power of Zeus; M.F.]."[1]
This exercise of Cynic sovereignty, on which I dwelt last week, has, I
think, two consequences. I will pass over the first quickly and spend a
bit more time on the second. First, Cynic sovereignty founds a blessed
mode of life for whoever exercises it. Second, this Cynic sovereignty
founds a practice of the manifested truth, of truth to be manifested.

Cynic sovereignty establishes the possibility of a blessed life in a
relation of self to self in the form of acceptance of destiny. In the passage I have just referred to, in which he goes to sleep with a pure heart,
recognizing that he takes part in the government of the gods, the Cynic,
Epictetus says, can then recite the verse of Cleanthes: "*Lead me, O Zeus,
and thou Destiny.*"[2] The Cynic says yes to his own destiny therefore. He
agrees to be led by Zeus. And to that extent, everything Zeus wishes
for him, everything Zeus sends him in the way of tests, all the harshness of life he may experience, will be accepted. He accepts them while
making them bear the mark of bliss and happiness. No matter that he
be deprived of everything, he will be able to say: "What then do I lack?
Am I not without sorrow and fear, am I not free? ... Has any one of you
seen me with a sad face? ... Who, seeing me, does not think he is seeing
his king and his master?"[3] You see: return to the theme of kingship, of
sovereignty; to that sovereignty which manifests itself in the radiance

of the joy of someone who accepts his destiny and consequently knows no lack, sorrow, or fear. All the harshness of existence, all the deprivation and frustration, is turned into a positive exercise of the sovereignty of self over self. And in comparison with this bliss, all the disorders of a politically royal life, of the kings of the world exercising their political sovereignty, appear in their negativity. Epictetus says that Diogenes habitually compared "his own bliss with that of the great king."[4] Or rather, he thought that no comparison was possible between the great king's bliss and his own, "for where there are disorders, grief, terror, unsatisfied desire, the realization of everything that should be avoided, envies, and jealousies [in short, wherever there reigns all those things that characterize the king's actual existence; M.F.], where could bliss make its way?"[5] No bliss for the kings of the world. Bliss, however, for someone who, like the Cynic, accepts his destiny. This is a first aspect.

The other side of this sovereign life, on which I would like to lay more stress, is that as well as being a blissful life, it is also manifestation of the truth. The Cynic, says Epictetus, is someone with the courage to tell the truth (*tharein parrhēsiazesthai*).[6] And in paragraph 25 he says that the Cynic is charged with announcing the truth. He is, as it were, the angel of the truth, the angel who tells, who announces the truth (*appaggeilein talēthē*: he announces true things).[7]

In this text, which, once again, I am using to define this final, border-figure (you will see why shortly) of the Cynic, in the way Epictetus defines this Cynic life and practice, we see that the practice of the truth takes on different aspects. The function of veridiction, the manifestation of the truth in and through the Cynic life, takes different paths simultaneously. There are several ways of telling the truth in the Cynic life.

The first route, the first way: the relationship to the truth is an immediate relationship of conformity to the truth in conduct, in the body. This conformity is a very common, familiar theme which we have already encountered. It was essential in the *Laches*, you recall, where Socrates was able to gain the confidence of Laches because of the conformity, the harmony, the homophony between what he, Socrates, said and how he lived.[8] The Cynic must have this same homophony, this same conformity. Epictetus explains that the Cynic is not someone, for example, who tells others that they must not steal while he is hiding a cake under his arm or in his cloak.[9] The Cynic who says one should not steal, does not steal. This is all easy and simple, but there is also this idea that there is not only a relationship of conformity of conduct, but also a relationship of physical, corporal conformity, so to speak, between the Cynic and the truth. There is an interesting passage on this in Epictetus, because he uses it at the same time to criticize a certain exaggerated form of Cynic poverty. For a number of reasons, Epictetus rejects the dramatization of Cynic poverty I have spoken to you about. The main reason, and we will come back to it, is that he limits, or regulates as it were his portrait of the Cynic in terms of what are quite simply Stoic principles. In this passage, he says that Cynics should avoid excess poverty, dirt, and ugliness. For the truth must attract; it must serve to convince. The truth must persuade, whereas dirt, ugliness, and hideousness repel. The Cynic must lead an ascetic life, but also one of cleanliness, as the visible figure of a truth which attracts. He is the physical model itself of the truth, with all the positive effects this model may have. Epictetus describes this modeling of the truth in the Cynic's body and comportment in this way: "He must not be content with displaying the qualities of his soul in order to convince the uninitiated that one can be honest and good in all that they admire," but must also, "prove with the qualities of his body that the simple, frugal life in the open air does not harm even the body."[10] This is what Diogenes did: he went about in fact "blooming with health, his body alone attracting the crowd's attention."[11] The Cynic is therefore like the picture of the truth. Stripped of all vain ornament, of everything that would be, as it were, the equivalent of rhetoric for the body, he appeared at the same time in full, blooming health: the very being of the true, rendered visible through the body. This is one of the first ways, the first paths by which the Cynic life must be a manifestation of the truth.

But the Cynic life has other responsibilities, other tasks in relation to the truth. The Cynic life must also include precise self-knowledge. The Cynic life is not just the picture of the truth; it is also the work of the truth of self on self. And this work of self-knowledge on self must take two aspects. First, the Cynic must always be able to make a proper, correct appraisal of what he can do so that he can confront the tests he may face, and so that, in his work on himself, he avoids situations in

which he could be defeated. The Cynic is like the athlete preparing for
Olympia. But it is obviously a much more serious struggle, since it is
the struggle against evils, vices, and temptations. Epictetus expresses
this self appraisal, this taking stock of oneself before confronting tests,
in paragraph 51, when he recommends to the would-be Cynic: "Begin
by taking a mirror, look at your shoulders, examine your loins and
thighs."[12] So, the athlete taking the measure of himself.

But this self-knowledge must also be something else. It must not
only be self-appraisal, but also constant vigilance of self over self
which essentially has to focus on the movement of representations. You
remember the passage I quoted last week, in which Epictetus said: Like
the carpenter whose raw material is wood, so the Cynic is someone
whose soul is the raw material of his own work.[13] The movement of
representations must be the constant object of this vigilance. The Cynic
must be the night-watchman of his own thought. With regard to the
moral person and the use of representations, Epictetus thus says—and
here again it is easy to see the strong Stoic inflection in this text, but
no matter for the moment—: "... you will see how many eyes the Cynic
possesses, so that we could say that Argus was blind in comparison."[14]
Consequently, everyone must be like the Argus of himself.[15] All his
eyes must be focused on himself. Epictetus continues: "Would there be
in him hasty assent, thoughtless propensity, unsatisfied desire, aversion unable to avoid its object [these are the four great categories of
Stoicism; M.F.], purpose without result, disparagement, baseness of
soul, or envy? Here is where the Cynic concentrates his attention and
energy (*prosokhē kai suntasis*)."[16] Measure of self, therefore, but also vigilance over self, appraisal of one's own abilities and constant watch over
the flow of one's representations, this is what the Cynic must be.

But this relationship to the truth of oneself, of what one can do
and of the flow of one's representations, must be coupled also with
another relationship, which is that of the supervision of others. The
Cynic, Argus of himself, must direct his one thousand eyes not only on
himself, but also on others. He must watch what others do, what they
think, and he must be in a position of constant inspection with regard
to them. Hence the importance of the verb *episkopein*, which Epictetus
repeats several times when he is defining Cynic activities. Cynics are

the episcopes* of others. You recall the passage from Epictetus which I quoted last week in which he evaluates the fine father who brings two or three ugly-snouted children into the world.[17] As opposed to him, the Cynics have a much greater task, responsibility, and merit with regard to the whole of humanity since, to the best of their ability, they exercise supervision (*episkopountes*) over all men, observing what they do, how they spend their life, what they care for, and what they neglect contrary to their duties. Inspection, supervision of others, keeping an eye on others. This is again another modality of implementing the practice of the truth.

But it is important to understand that when Cynics are inspecting others, overseeing what they are doing, and keeping an eye on how they spend their lives, they are not those people—of whom the Greeks had such fear moreover, and criticized so often—who meddle in other people's affairs. In Greek vocabulary there is a word which always has a negative connotation, *polupragmosunē*, which means being concerned about many things, about everything, being interested in other people's affairs, meddling in their affairs, poking one's nose in everywhere. The Cynic must get rid of this defect, this attitude, constantly criticized by the Greeks, while concerning himself properly with other people's affairs.[18] When taking an interest in others, the Cynic must in fact attend to what in them is a matter of humankind in general. Consequently, insofar as the Cynic is concerned about others in this way, avoiding that *polupragmosunē* which meddles in the affairs of everyone and anyone, insofar as he considers only what belongs to humankind in what they do, you can see that he is at the same time concerned with himself, since he too is part of humankind. And thus it is his own solidarity with humankind which is questioned, which is the object of his care, concern, and supervision when he looks at how men act and spend their lives, and when he inquires into what they take care of. The Cynic is someone, consequently, who, caring for others in order to know what these others care about, at the same time and thereby cares for himself.

---

* [An episcope (*épiscope*) is an instrument for projecting enlarged images of opaque objects onto a screen by means of reflection, or an optical instrument employing mirrors used for observation in armored vehicles. In English, episcope is also the pastoral supervision exercised by a bishop. Foucault seems here to be giving the word the meaning of inspector, supervisor, overseer; G.B.]

Thus, in paragraphs 96 and 97, you have this passage: Why "should he (the Cynic) not have the courage to speak with complete freedom to his own brothers [here we are at the heart of *parrhēsia*: M.F.], to his children, in a word, to everyone of his race?"[19] *Suggeneis*: this, of course, designates the whole of humankind. In such a frame of mind, the Cynic is "neither a busybody [*polupragmōn*: someone who pries into other people's affairs; M.F.] nor a meddler. For he is not meddling in other people's affairs when he inspects human matters; they are his own."[20] Otherwise, if we were to have to call someone like the Cynic *polupragmōn*, someone who is concerned about human matters, then we should also have to consider the general to be *polupragmōn* (prying) when he "inspects (*episkopē*) the soldiers," reviews (*exetazē*) them, supervises them, and punishes those who breach discipline.[21] A general should not be thought to be prying when he concerns himself with his soldiers, when he reviews them and supervises them. He is not prying, since it is not as if the soldier's individual life is being questioned by the general's gaze; it is all that makes the soldier part of the army. So, just as when the general concerns himself with his solders he is concerning himself with the whole army, and therefore with himself as part of the army and with responsibility for it, so too the Cynic is not a *polupragmōn* when he concerns himself with the whole of humankind, like a soldier making his inspection. He is not a busybody prying into everybody's private life. The care of others thus coincides exactly with the care of self.

Now—and this is the new aspect of the work of the truth—the aim of this supervision of self which is also the supervision of others, or of this supervision of others which is also supervision of self, is a change, and there are two aspects to this change as it appears in Epictetus: a change in the conduct of individuals, and a change also in the general configuration of the world.

Change in conduct first of all. The Cynic's discourses, criticisms, and scandals must show others that they are completely mistaken on the subject of good and evil, and that they are looking for the nature of good and evil in the wrong place. The Cynic must thus address the people around him and tell them: "What are you doing, wretches? Like the blind, you totter about; you are following a foreign path [an other path (*une route autre*): *allēn hodon*; M.F.] after having left the true one [*tēn ousan*]; you are looking for peace and happiness elsewhere than where they exist, and when someone else shows them to you, you do not believe them."[22] This passage is interesting because, on the one hand, it reveals the true object of the Cynic's discourse, of his verbal intervention, his "diatribe," to use that particularly characteristic Cynic form of expression. The target of this intervention is to show men that they are mistaken, that they are looking for the truth elsewhere (*ailleurs*), that they are looking for the principle of good and evil elsewhere, that they are looking for peace and happiness elsewhere, and that they will not find them where they are actually looking.

You see the importance of the elsewhere, the other, in this game: you are looking for peace and happiness *elsewhere* (*ailleurs*); you are following a path which is an *other* path (*une route autre*). Now, you remember, the principle of Cynicism is quite precisely to say that the true life is an other life. One of the essential points of Cynic practice consists precisely in this, that taking up the most traditional themes of classical philosophy—we saw this last week—the Cynic changes the value of this currency and reveals that the true life can only be an other life, in relation to the traditional life of men, including philosophers. There can only be true life as other life, and it is from the point of view of this other life that the usual life of ordinary people will be revealed as precisely other than the true. I live in an other way, and by the very otherness of my life, I show you that what you are looking for is somewhere other than where you are looking for it, that the path you are taking is other than the one you should be taking. And the function of the true life—as at the same time, form of existence, manifestation of self, and physical model of the truth, but also enterprise of demonstration, conviction, and persuasion through discourse—is showing, while being wholly other, that it is others who are in otherness, mistaken, that they are where they should not be. And the task of Cynic veridiction is therefore to remind all men who do not lead the Cynic life of the form of existence which will be the true existence. Not the other, which takes the wrong path, but the same, the one which is faithful to the truth.

In this way Epictetus refers to a form of life which would not just reform individuals, but would completely reform a world. In fact, we should not think that the Cynic addresses a handful of individuals in order to convince them that they should lead a different life than the one they are leading. The Cynic addresses all men. He shows all men that they are leading a life other than the one they should be leading. And thereby it is a whole other world which has to emerge, or at any rate be on the horizon, be the objective of this Cynic practice.*

Metaphysical experience of the world, historico-critical experience of life: these are two fundamental cores in the genesis of European or Western philosophical experience. Anyway, it seems to me that what we see emerging through Cynicism is the matrix of what has been a significant form of life throughout the Christian and modern tradition, that is to say, the matrix of a life dedicated to the truth, dedicated to the manifestation of the truth in fact (*ergō*) and, at the same time, to veridiction, truth-telling, the manifestation of the truth through discourse (*logō*). And the aim of this practice of the truth characterizing the Cynic life is not just to say and show what the world is in its truth. Its aim, its final aim, is to show that the world will be able to get back to its truth, will be able to transfigure itself and become other in order to get back to what it is in its truth, only at the price of a change, a complete alteration, the complete change and alteration in the relation one has to self. And the source of the transition to that other world promised by Cynicism is found in this return of self to self, in this care of self.

This is roughly what I would have liked to tell you about Cynicism. My project—and here I move on to the second part of what I wanted to tell you today—was not to dwell on Cynicism, but to show you how

---

* The manuscript gives some clarifications here which are not taken up in the lecture.
"Epictetus refers also, at least in this passage, to the true life as to another world. This other world should not be understood in the Platonic sense, as a world promised to souls after their deliverance from the body. It is a matter of another state of the world, another "catastasis" of the world, a city of sages in which there would no longer be any need for Cynic militancy. Now the condition for arriving at this true life is that every individual form a vigilant relationship to self. The source of the true life is not to be sought in the body, in the exercise of power, or in the possession of wealth, but in oneself. In all this, many things come from Stoicism, but the most important historical core of Cynicism is clearly expressed: namely, that the true life will be the life of truth, which manifests the truth, which practices the truth in the relation to self and others. So that the objective of this life of veridiction is the transformation of humankind and of the world. No doubt Cynicism has contributed very little to philosophical doctrine: it has done little more than borrow the most traditional and standard formulae. But it has given such a singular form to the philosophical life, it has insisted so strongly on the existence of an other life (*une vie autre*), that it has marked the question of the philosophical life [for] centuries. Little importance in the history of doctrines. Considerable importance in the history of arts of living and the history of philosophy as mode of life."

Cynicism could and actually did lead to another form, another definition of the relations between the true life, the other life and *parrhēsia*,
the discourse of truth. It is clear—once again, I don't want to return to
this—that the portrait of the Cynic outlined by Epictetus is in no way
an exact historical representation of the Cynic life. It absolutely cannot be considered as the clear and coherent exposition of the general
principles of the Cynic life. It is a mixture, a doctrinal and practical
mixture.

But if I have taken the analysis of Cynicism to this point, if I have
taken this, as it were, impure and mixed text by Epictetus concerning
Cynicism as my last reference, it has been to show how certain themes
borrowed from other philosophies, and in particular from Stoicism,
gravitated around Cynicism, and how the effect of this combination
was that it was able to take a certain, no doubt impure and mixed form
in relation to what we may suspect was the true Cynic doctrine in its
purity, simplicity, and crudity. But in this somewhat mixed, rather
enigmatic character depicted by Epictetus in discourse 22 of Book III,
you will have been able to sense the presence already of certain elements which will be found again later, and in particular in Christian
experience.

In fact, the idea of a missionary of the truth coming to give men the
ascetic example of the true life, recalling them to themselves, putting
them back on the right path, and announcing to them another catastasis of the world, this personage is, of course, up to a point, part of the
modified Socratic heritage, but you can see that, up to a point, it also
comes close to the Christian model.

Maybe I will try to explore these themes a little next year—but I
cannot guarantee it, I confess that I still don't know and have not yet
decided. Maybe I will try to pursue this history of the arts of living,
of philosophy as form of life, of asceticism in its relation to the truth,
precisely, after ancient philosophy, in Christianity.

In any case, today I would just like to offer you a very brief sketch,
a sort of point of departure for analyses of this kind. A point of departure for me, if I continue them; an encouragement for you, if you take
them up in turn. So what I am going to say to you is completely provisional, uncertain, and floating. These are ideas I have had, that I have
tried to back up with some texts and references (with the reservation,

of course, that it may have to be completely reworked, re-examined from every angle, and begun again quite differently). Anyway, this is how I would see things. If I were to analyze the change from pagan asceticism to Christian asceticism, at the moment it seems to me that I would go in more or less the following direction.

First—and this is obvious—one would have to try to reconstruct something of the already fairly well known and marked out continuity between the practices of ascesis, the forms of endurance, and the modes of exercise in Cynicism, and those in Christianity. Actually, it seems to me, subject again to further clarification, that there are a number of points which are common to the, let's say, militant, aggressive Cynic, hard on himself and others, and the Christian ascetic. For example, we could try to follow the very important history, much more important than that of sexuality, of relations to food, fasting, and dietary ascesis, which once again was crucial in Antiquity and early Christianity. It is only later that sexual ascesis prevails over the problems of dietary ascesis. To start with at any rate, the problem of dietary ascesis is very important. You remember how important it was [for] the Cynics. You find it again in the Christians expressed in fairly similar ways, apart, however, from the fact that in the history of their asceticism Christians seem to have taken it infinitely further and, at least for a time, tried to radicalize even Cynic renunciation. You know that through con-tinual work of self on self Cynicism sought to reach a point where the satisfaction of needs would be fulfilled exactly, with nothing granted to pleasure. Or rather, the Cynic practiced a form of reduced diet so as to obtain maximum pleasure with minimum means. What Cynicism sought, in short, was to reduce one's diet, to reduce what one eats and drinks to the basic food and drink that gives maximum pleasure at least cost, with least dependence. With Christianity we have, however, something different. We have the same idea that one must seek the limit, but this limit is in no way a point of equilibrium between maxi-mum pleasure and minimum means. Instead, it will be the reduction of all pleasure so that neither food nor drink ever gives rise in itself to any form of pleasure. There is therefore at the same time continuity and a movement to the extreme limit.

We could also think of Christian asceticism, both as it develops with great intensity in the third and fourth centuries, and then limited, regulated, integrated, and almost socialized within cenobite forms. But in its unrestrained and free aspect, as it were, before this asceticism took these cenobite forms, we find again the themes of scandal, of indifference to the opinion of others and to the structures of power and its representatives that are found in Cynicism. I will quote you a text from the *Sayings of the Fathers* which refers to the abbot Theodore de Pherme, who one day received a visit from a powerful figure. When this man came to visit him, another ascetic noticed that Theodore had his shoulder uncovered and his chest bare. He remarked on this to the abbot, who replied: Are we the slaves of men? I meet men as I am. If someone comes to see me, do not answer him with anything human (*anthrōpinon*). If I am eating, tell him: he is eating, if I am sleeping, tell him: he is sleeping.[23] With the term "humanity" the text was referring to humanity in its materiality, but its materiality linked to conventions by which it was softened and socialized in the form of what is acceptable for the whole of humankind. When one eats, one eats. When one sleeps, one sleeps. It is this brutality of material existence which must be affirmed against all the values of humanity.

You also find a sort of point of bestiality quite openly asserted in some texts of Christian asceticism. For example, Gregory the Great recounts that some shepherds discovered the cave in which Saint Benedict was hiding, and when they saw him in the undergrowth dressed in an animal skin, they thought at first that he was a wild animal.[24] The animality of the Christian ascetic recurs frequently in the history of eremitism. Again, there is this story, [taken from those of the] holy anchorites, translated by Festugière in Volume III of the *Moines d'Orient*.[25] It involves a hermit who lived completely naked and who, the text says, ate grass like a wild animal. He could not bear even the odor of men. We are dealing with here with the affirmation of animality, and the reputation of this hermit is such that a Christian, very ascetic himself, but less advanced in asceticism, wants to meet him, and he follows him. The Christian who follows him is so poor and has seen to his poverty to the extent of wearing only a linen sack. The hermit, however, is naked. The hermit flees this man, who tries to follow him and catch up with him. The other Christian runs behind the hermit, and as he does so he loses his clothing. So he is now naked, like the hermit he is following. At this point the hermit notices that his pursuer has lost his clothing, stops, and says to him: I have halted because you have now rejected the mire of the world. We would need to go back over all this, but it does seem to me that in these practices of the ascetic life we would find some elements in continuity with Cynic asceticism, sometimes in conformity with them, and sometimes also surpassing them.

Only, in relation to the Cynic tradition, Christian asceticism contributed some different elements. And, here again, if I were to undertake this history of the movement from Cynic to Christian asceticism, at present I would tend to emphasize two things which seem significant to me.

First, in Christian asceticism there is of course a relation to the other world (*l'autre monde*), and not to the world which is other. That is to say, even if in a whole movement of Christianity—this will obviously be one of the major problems, as we can see in Origen—there is the theme of a certain catastasis of the world (Origen would have said, "apocatastasis"), by which the world returns to its original state, nevertheless it is a fairly common idea in Christianity that the aim of the other life (*la vie autre*) to which the ascetic must dedicate himself and which he has chosen, is not simply to transform this world—again, notwithstanding the theme of the catastasis or apocatastasis—but is also and above all to give individuals, possibly all Christians, the entire Christian community, access to an other world (*un monde autre*). To that extent, I think we can say that one of the master strokes of Christianity, its philosophical significance, consists in it having linked together the theme of an other life (*une vie autre*) as true life and the idea of access to the other world (*l'autre monde*) as access to the truth. [On the one hand], a true life, which is an other life in this world, [on the other] access to the other world as access to the truth and to that which, consequently, founds the truth of that true life which one leads in this world here: it seems to me that this structure is the combination, the meeting point, the junction between an originally Cynic asceticism and an originally Platonic metaphysics. This is very schematic, but it seems to me that there is in this one of the first major differences between Christian and Cynic asceticism. Through historical processes which would obviously need to be examined more closely, Christian asceticism managed to join Platonic metaphysics to that vision, that historical-critical experience of the world.

The second major difference is of a completely different order. This concerns the importance that Christianity, and only Christianity gives to something which is not found in either Cynicism or Platonism. This is the principle of obedience, in the broad sense of the term. Obedience to God conceived of as the master (the *despotēs*) whose slave, whose servant one is; obedience to His will which has, at the same time, the form of the law; obedience finally to those who represent the *despotēs* (the lord and master) and who receive an authority from Him to which one must submit completely. So it seems to me that the other point of inflection in this long history of asceticism recounted in counterpoint, facing this relation to the other world (*l'autre monde*), is the principle of an obedience to the other, in this world, starting from this world, and in order to have access to the true life. There is true life only through obedience to the other, and there is true life only for access to the other world. This way of pinning the principle of the other life (*la vie autre*) as true life to obedience to the other in this world and to access to the other world in another life (*l'autre monde dans une autre vie*), this way of pinning together a Platonic element and another specifically Christian or Judeo-Christian element, this connection is what introduces the two major inflections of Cynic asceticism and brings about the change from the Cynic to the Christian form of asceticism. The difference between paganism and Christianity should not be characterized therefore as a difference between a Christian ascetic morality and a non-ascetic morality of Antiquity. You know that this is an utter fantasy. Asceticism was an invention of pagan Antiquity, of Greek and Roman antiquity. So the non-ascetic morality of Antiquity should not be set against the ascetic morality of Christianity. Nor, I think, should we follow Nietzsche, if you like, and contrast an ancient asceticism of a violent and aristocratic Greece, with a different form of asceticism which would separate the soul from the body. The difference between Christian asceticism and other forms of asceticism which may have prepared the way for and preceded it should be situated in this double relation: the relation to the other world to which one will have access thanks to this asceticism, and the principle of obedience to the other (obedience to the other in this world, obedience to the other which is at the same time obedience to God and to those who represent him). Thus we see the emergence of a new style of relation to self, a new type of power relations, and a different regime of truth.

I think these fundamental changes, which are extremely complex and which I am only outlining very schematically now, can certainly be followed on the surface through the evolution of the notion of *parrhēsia* as mode of relation to self and relation to others, through the exercise of truth-telling in Christian experience. This notion of *parrhēsia* in Christian experience, as relation to the other world and to God, as relationship of obedience to others and to God, is what I would now like to set out for you briefly. We will take five minutes rest, and we will talk about *parrhēsia* in the first Christian texts.

1. Epictetus, III, xxii, 95, Fr. p. 84; Eng. p. 165.

2. Ibid.

3. Ibid., III, xxii, 48-49, Fr. p. 77; Eng. p. 147: "Yet what do I lack? Am I not free from pain and fear, am I not free? ... Has anyone among you seen me with a gloomy face? ... Who, when he lays eyes upon me, does not feel that he is seeing his king and his master?"

4. Ibid., III, xxii, 60, Fr. p. 79; Eng. p. 153: "How did he habitually compare his happiness with that of the Great King?"

5. Ibid., III, xxii, 60-61, Fr. p. 79; Eng. p. 153: "Or rather, he thought there was no comparison between them. For where there are disturbances, and griefs, and fears, and ineffectual desires, and unsuccessful avoidances, and envies, and jealousies—where is there in the midst of all this a place for happiness to enter?"

6. Ibid., III, xxii, 96, Fr. p. 84; Eng. p. 165: "courage to speak freely."

7. Ibid., III, xxii, 24-25, Fr. p. 73: "In reality, the Cynic is for men truly a scout (*kataskopos*) of what is favorable to them and what is hostile. And he must first explore exactly and then return to announce the truth (*apaggeilai talēthē*) without being paralyzed by fear"; Eng. p. 139: "For the Cynic is truly a scout, to find out what things are friendly to men and what hostile; and he must first do his scouting accurately, and on returning must tell the truth, not driven by fear to designate as enemies those who are not such, nor in any other fashion be distraught or confused by his external impressions."

8. Plato, *Laches*, 188c-189a, Fr. pp. 103-104; Eng. p. 132.

9. Epictetus, III, xxii, 98, Fr. p. 84; Eng. p. 165.

10. Ibid., III, xxii, 87-88, Fr. p. 83; Eng. p. 161: "For he must not merely, by exhibiting the qualities of his soul, prove to the layman that it is possible, without the help of the things which they admire, to be a good and excellent man, but he must also show, by the state of his body, that his plain and simple style of life in the open air does not injure even his body."

11. Ibid., III, xxii, 88, Fr. p. 83; Eng. p. 161: "This was the way of Diogenes, for he used to go about with a radiant complexion, and would attract the attention of the common people by the very appearance of his body."

12. Ibid., III, xxii, 51, Fr. p. 71; Eng. p. 149: "First take a mirror, look at your shoulders, find out what kind of loins and thighs you have."

13. Ibid., III, xxii, 21-22, Fr. p. 72; Eng. p. 137.

14. Ibid., III, xxii, 103, Fr. p. 85; Eng. p. 167: "you will see he has so many eyes that you will say Argus was blind in comparison with him."

15. The son of Arestor and Myceneus, Argus had one hundred eyes distributed over the whole of his head. Alternately, fifty eyes were closed while the other fifty kept watch.

16. Epictetus, III. xxii, 104-105, Fr. p. 85; Eng. p. 167: "Is there anywhere rash assent, reckless choice, futile desire, unsuccessful aversion, incompleted purpose, fault-finding, self-disparagement, or envy? Here is concentrated his earnest attention and energy."

17. Ibid., III, xxii, 77, Fr. p. 81; Eng. p. 159.

18. On this criticism, mainly on the basis of Plutarch's *On Curiosity*, see *L'Herméneutique du sujet*, pp. 210-213; *The Hermeneutics of the Subject*, pp. 218-222.

19. Epictetus, III, xxii, 96, Fr. p. 84; Eng. p. 165: "why should he not have courage to speak freely to his own brothers, to his children, in a word, to his kinsmen?"

20. Ibid., III, xxii, 97, Fr. p. 84; Eng. p. 165: "the man who is in this frame of mind is neither a busybody nor a meddler; for he is not meddling in other people's affairs when he is overseeing the actions of men, but these are his proper concern."

21. Ibid., III, xxii, 98, Fr. p. 84; Eng. p. 165: "Otherwise, go call the general a meddler when he oversees and reviews and watches over his troops, and punishes those who are guilty of a breach of discipline."

22. Ibid., III, xxii, 26-27, Fr. p. 73; Eng. p. 139: "What are you doing, O wretched people? Like blind men you go tottering all around. You have left the true path and are going off upon another; you are looking for serenity and happiness in the wrong place, where it does not exist, and you do not believe when another points them out to you."

23. English translation by Benedicta Ward, *The Sayings of the Desert Fathers. The Alphabetical Collection* (London: A.R. Mowbray, 1975) p. 67.

24. *Dialogues de Grégoire le Grand*, vol. II, Book II: *Vie et miracles du vénérable abbé Benoît*, II, 1, 8, trans. P. Antin (Paris: Éd. du Cerf, 1979) p. 137; English translation by Terence G. Kardong as Pope Gregory I, *Life and Miracles of St. Benedict* (Collegeville, Minnesota: Liturgical Press, 1980) p. 7.

25. *Les Moines d'Orient*, trans. A.-J. Festugière (Paris: Éd. du Cerf, 1961-1965) III/1, III/2, and III/3: *Les Moines de Palestine*. Foucault refers to a note by Festugière (III/3, p. 15, n. 11) reporting an anecdote concerning Egyptian hermits "living completely naked, with no other clothing than their hair." Festugière cites a text from the *Peri anakōrēton hagiōn: "eiden anthrōpon boskomenon hōs ta thēria"* (he saw a man grazing on grass like a wild animal) in H. Koch, *Quellen zur Geschichte der Askese und des Mönchtums in der Alten Kirche* (Tübingen: Mohr, 1933) pp. 118-120. With regard to this example, Festugière writes: "The author adds that unable to bear the odor of man, the hermit flees. The other person follows him and in doing so throws off his tunic (*lebētona*). The hermit then stops, and seeing the visitor completely naked, welcomes him and says: 'Since you rejected the *hulē tou kosmou*, I have waited for you.'"

eighteen

28 MARCH 1984

Second hour

[
The use of the term parrhēsia *in the first pre-Christian texts: human and divine modalities.* ∽ Parrhēsia *in the New Testament: confident faith and openness of heart.* ∽ Parrhēsia *in the Fathers: insolence.* ∽ *Development of an anti-parrhesiastic pole: suspicious knowledge of self.* ∽ *The truth of life as condition of access to an other world* (un monde autre).
]

SOME INDICATIONS, AGAIN JUST in outline and as hypotheses, with regard to the very curious evolution of the meaning of the term *parrhēsia* in the first Christian texts. To tell the truth, I would like to divide these indications around three problems: first, the use of the term in pre-Christian texts (those from Judeo-Hellenistic milieus, mainly in Philo of Alexandria and in the Septuagint; second, the notion of *parrhēsia* in New Testament texts; and third, *parrhēsia* in the apostolic texts, especially the patristic texts as well as those of Christian ascetics of the first centuries.

First of all, some words on the use of the term in Judeo-Hellenistic texts. Of course, I have no competence in this area for the excellent reason that I do not know Hebrew, which would be indispensable at least for analyzing the Septuagint more closely. I refer to information which can be found in earlier studies. Among the most accessible is Schlier's article "*Parrhēsia*" in Kittel's *Wörterbuch* (translated into English, for those of you who have difficulty with German).[1] There is also an article by Stanley Marrow, "Parrhesia and the New Testament," which appeared in July 1982 in the *Catholic Biblical Quarterly*.[2] We might situate what can be said about the use of the word in the Judeo-Hellenistic texts somewhat in the following way. First, we find the word *parrhēsia* used in the fairly traditional sense of truth-telling with boldness and courage, and as a consequence of integrity of heart. You find this sense of the word in the *De specialibus legibus*, for example, in which Philo refers to and justifies the laws which condemn the Mysteries and all practices which conceal themselves. Philo condemns mystery forms of religion, and you see that he only repeats what the Cynics said against them, saying that if there is truth, then it must be told: "Nature hides nothing of her glorious works."[3] Consequently, if nature hides nothing of her glorious works, those whose actions are beneficial to all must make use of full freedom of expression. For these people let there be *parrhēsia* (*estō parrhēsia*),[4] "that they may go in broad daylight in the middle of the public square, to talk with the crowds."[5] So aptness and general usefulness are the foundation here of a *parrhēsia*, which is nothing other than the courage to say things which are useful for everyone, for these things to be said by certain people whose pure hearts, courage, and noble souls facilitate this *parrhēsia*.

This use of the word, in a sense still very close to the classical Greek and Hellenistic tradition, is modified however in some texts. In fact, in texts of Philo himself, and also in texts of the Septuagint, we find the term *parrhēsia* with a quite profoundly modified meaning.* At this point *parrhēsia* no longer simply designates the courage of the individual who, as it were, facing others on his own, has to tell them the truth and what must be done. This other *parrhēsia* we see emerging is defined as a sort of full and positive modality of the relation to God. It involves something like openness of heart, the transparency of the soul which offers itself to God's sight. And at the same time as this openness of heart, this transparency of the soul before God occurs, there is a kind of ascending impulse of this pure soul which lifts it up to the Almighty. So *parrhēsia* will no longer be situated, if you like, on the [horizontal] axis of the individual's relations to others, of the

---

* In the margin of the manuscript there are references, for Philo, to paragraphs 150, 126, and 95, and for the Septuagint, to *Proverbs*, 10, 9-11.

person with courage vis-à-vis those who are mistaken. It is now situated on the vertical axis of a relation to God in which the soul is, on the one hand, transparent and opens itself to God and, on the other, rises up to Him. Thus, in the Septuagint you find the word *parrhēsia* employed to translate a text in what for us is a sense fairly distant from the traditional sense of the term. Here is the text, just as it is given in French in Segond's translation. It is from the book of Job: "Devote yourself to God, and you shall have the prize, the Almighty shall be your gold, your silver, your wealth. Then you will find in the Almighty your delight, you will lift up your face to God, you will pray to him, he will hear you, you will fulfill your vows, your resolutions will meet with success, the light will shine on your path."[6]

What is interesting is that to translate the Hebrew text, "then you will find in the Almighty your delight" (word for word), the Septuagint uses the verb *parrhēsiazesthai*. In other words, that immediate relation of contact, delight, and enjoyment which the soul may experience when in contact with God, that bliss, enjoyment, and pleasure are translated in the Septuagint by "*parrhēsiazesthai*." So *parrhēsia*, you see, is no longer the courageous and risky truth-telling of someone who speaks boldly to those who are mistaken. It is this impulse, this openness of heart by which heart and soul are lifted up to God, may come to grasp God, to enjoy Him, as it were, and experience the principle of His bliss. We move, you see, from the truth, from *parrhēsia* as the unconcealed, to a relation in which the soul is raised up to God, borne up to His height, brought into contact with Him, and in which it may find His bliss.

There is a passage in Philo of Alexandria (*On the Special Laws*, 203) with a somewhat similar meaning, in which *parrhēsia* is linked to prayer. *Parrhēsia* in prayer is a sort of quality, or rather it is a dynamic, an impulse by which the soul is lifted up to God, provided at least that its conscience is pure enough. Thus, Philo writes: Someone capable of prayer *ek katharou tou suneidotos* (on the basis of the purity of his conscience) is capable of *parrhēsia*.[7] *Parrhēsia* is still, in a sense, a truth-telling, but it is not even a "telling" any more: it is the openness of the heart which manifests itself in its truth to God and lifts up this truth to Him.

In these pre-Christian, Judeo-Hellenistic texts, we find a third sense, which is no longer either the traditional sense found in Greece, or that of the soul's movement towards God, that openness and impulse towards God of the Septuagint, examples of which were given by Philo of Alexandria. *Parrhēsia* appears in a set of texts as a property, a quality, or let's say more exactly, a gift of God. It is God Himself who is endowed with *parrhēsia*. And when God is endowed with *parrhēsia*, it is insofar as He speaks the truth, but also insofar as He manifests Himself and His love, His power, and possibly His anger. It is God's being itself in its manifestation which is called *parrhēsia*.

Two texts on this accepted meaning of the word. In *Proverbs* (Septuagint version), the text is the following: "Wisdom cries out in the streets, She raises her voice in public squares: She cries out at the entrance of thoroughfares; at the gates, in the town, she makes her words heard."[8] It is the cry of wisdom in the streets that is called *parrhēsia*. And, you see, at this point *parrhēsia* is the *parrhēsia* of wisdom itself. It is God's *parrhēsia*, His overflowing presence, His overabundant presence, as it were, which is designated by *parrhēsia*. It is in fact the verbal articulation of the voice of wisdom which characterizes this *parrhēsia*.

But *parrhēsia* may also be—this at least appears in another text—the presence of God, who is hidden and withdrawn, His presence or power to which man appeals and must appeal when he is prey to misfortune or suffers injustice. I'm sorry, I have not brought the reference, and I cannot say I will give it next week since there won't be a next week; in a text it says: "God of vengeance, Eternal! God of vengeance, appear [the Hebrew text says, show yourself; M.F.]! Rise up, judge of the earth! Give the proud their just deserts! How long will the wicked, O Eternal, how long will the wicked triumph?"[9] This "appear," this "show yourself," are translated in Greek, in the Septuagint, by *parrhēsiazesthai*. So the term *parrhēsia* is employed here to designate something which is obviously quite foreign to Greek thought: the omnipotence of the Almighty who manifests Himself, who has to manifest Himself in His kindness and wisdom, and also in His anger against the unjust, the arrogant, and the proud. You see that, in this set of texts, generally speaking the term *parrhēsia* increasingly tends to designate the one-to-one encounter between the Almighty and His creature, their dissymmetry, but also their relationship. It is the movement by which man goes towards God, but inversely it is the movement by which God manifests His being as power and wisdom, as force and truth. It is within this ontological one-to-one, vis-à-vis relationship of man and God that *parrhēsia*, up to a certain point, tends to move. It is no longer the courage of the solitary man facing others who are mistaken; it is beatitude, the bliss of the man raised up to God. And, to this movement of man towards Him, God replies through the expression, the manifestation of His goodness or His power.

Second, in the New Testament literature now, the term *parrhēsia* appears a number of times, and with a meaning different from the one we have just been looking at in the Judeo-Hellenistic tradition, as also, of course, from the meaning we found in Greek usage. There are two important changes. The first is that henceforth, in this New Testament literature, *parrhēsia* no longer ever appears as a modality of divine manifestation. God is no longer the parrhesiast he was in the Septuagint and, to some extent, in Philo of Alexandria. *Parrhēsia* is simply a mode of being, a mode of human activity. Second change: this mode of human activity does include, to some extent, in a certain context, and in certain circumstances, the connotation of courage, of speaking boldly, but it is also an attitude of the heart, a way of being, which does not need to manifest itself in discourse and speech.

Some examples. The term *parrhēsia* is employed in essentially two contexts to designate a certain virtue which characterizes, or should characterize either men, or at least all Christians, or the apostles and those responsible for teaching the truth to men. For men in general, or at least for Christians, *parrhēsia* is not at all a verbal activity. It is trust in God, that confidence which every Christian can and should have in God's love, in His affection for men, in the link that binds and ties God and men. It is that parrhesiastic trust which makes prayer possible and by which man can enter into relationship with God. For example, in the *First Epistle of John* it is said: "I have written these things to you, who believe in the name of the Son of God, so that you may know that you have eternal life."[10] So, you see, it is emphasized here that John is addressing those who believe in the name of the Son of God. They are believers, Christians, and as such they know that, henceforth, they have eternal life. "We have in Him this confidence, that if we ask anything in accordance with His will, He hears us."[11] It is the term *parrhēsia* which is translated here. We have this confidence (*parrhēsia*) that if we ask anything in accordance with His will, He hears us. *Parrhēsia*, therefore, is situated in the following context. On the one hand, the Christian, as such, who believes in the name of the Son of God, knows that he has eternal life. Second, he addresses God to ask for what? Nothing other than what God wills. To that extent, man's prayer or will is nothing other than the reduplication or return to God of His own will. Principle of obedience. *Parrhēsia* is anchored in this circularity of, on the one hand, belief in God and certainty of eternal life, and, on the other, a request which is addressed to God and which is itself nothing other than God's will. *Parrhēsia* is the confidence that God will hear those who are Christians and who, as such, having faith in Him, ask of Him nothing other than what is in accordance with His will. It is this parrhesiastic attitude which makes possible the eschatological confidence in the Day of Judgment, the day which one can await, which one must await with complete confidence (*meta parrhēsias*) because of God's love. It is this eschatological confidence, this confidence in what will happen on the Day of Judgment which is expressed in the *First Epistle of John*: "God is love; and whoever remains in love remains in God, and God in him. As He is, so we are also in this world; it is in this that love is perfect in us, so that we have confidence (*parrhēsia*) on the Day of Judgment."[12] On the side of men, of Christians, *parrhēsia* is therefore this confidence in God's love, the love that He manifests when He hears the prayers addressed to Him and which He will manifest on the Day of Judgment.

But in these New Testament texts, *parrhēsia* is also the sign of the courageous attitude of whoever preaches the Gospel. Here, *parrhēsia* is the apostolic virtue par excellence. And here we find again a meaning and use of the word which is fairly close to the classical Greek or Hellenistic conception. Thus, in the *Acts of the Apostles*, where the issue is Paul's vocation and the disciples', the apostles' initial mistrust of him. He is not taken to be a disciple of Christ. And then Barnabas recounts how he saw Paul at Damascus, and how he had seen him preach "frankly" in the name of Jesus:[13] at Jerusalem, in the same way as at Damascus, Paul will now go around with the disciples, expressing himself with full assurance (*meta parrhēsias*) in the name of the Lord. He argued in this way with the Greeks and "they sought to take his life."[14] Here, you can see, oral, verbal preaching, the fact of speaking out, of arguing with the Greeks, and arguing with them at the risk of one's life, is characterized as *parrhēsia*. The apostolic virtue of *parrhēsia* is thus quite close to what the Greek [virtue] had been. In the same way, in *The Epistle of Paul to the Ephesians*, Paul asks the Ephesians to pray for him so that, he says, "when I open my mouth, I may boldly and freely make known the mystery of the Gospel, for which I am an ambassador in chains, and that I speak of it with assurance (*meta parrhēsias*) as I ought to speak."[15] So, there are some reference points for the New Testament literature: *parrhēsia* as apostolic virtue, very close in its meaning to what we saw in the Greeks; and then *parrhēsia* as a form of the general Christian confidence in God.

Now we come to the ascetics of the first centuries, and even after, and this is where things no doubt become more complicated, at any rate more interesting. *Parrhēsia* then begins to acquire an ambiguous value. To some extent this ambiguity of the values of the notion of *parrhēsia* takes up and amplifies the ambiguity we have already noted in the Greeks, when it appeared as the virtuous individual's courage to address others and try to bring them back from error to the truth, as well as the freedom of speech, disorder, and anarchy of everyone being able to say everything and anything. To some extent we find this ambiguity again, but very profoundly transposed.

First, in its positive value, *parrhēsia* appears as a sort of hinge virtue, which characterizes both the attitude of the Christian, of the good Christian, towards men, and his way of being with regard to God. With regard to men, *parrhēsia* will be the courage to assert the truth one knows and to which one wishes to bear witness regardless of every danger. And here we are close to the value and meanings of *parrhēsia* we encountered in Greek antiquity. Thus, in John Chrysostom, for example (*On the Providence of God*), there is this: In the midst of persecutions, the sheep perform the office of shepherds, soldiers perform that of leaders, thanks to their *parrhēsia* and their courage (*andreia*).[16] Here we are in the familiar context of persecution and martyrs. In the face of persecution, some people have the courage to assert the truth in which they believe. They demonstrate this courage: soldiers take on the role of leaders, and they do so because they are able to adopt an attitude of courage and *parrhēsia*. In the same way, John Chrysostom (*On the Providence of God*) says: "Think what profit watchful men have undoubtedly drawn from these examples, seeing an invincible soul, a wisdom which refuses to be enslaved, a tongue full of courageous boldness."[17] "Courageous boldness" is the translation here of the word *parrhēsia*. The idea is that *parrhēsia*, by which some individuals managed to oppose persecution and accept martyrdom, was profitable and useful. "Think what profit watchful men have undoubtedly drawn from these examples." There are watchful men to be persuaded, convinced, or at any rate called back to the truth of the evangelical lesson by the courage of these parrhesiasts, the martyrs. The martyr is the parrhesiast par excellence. And, to that extent, you see that the word *parrhēsia* refers to one's courage in the face of persecutors, a courage one exercises for oneself, but also for others, and those one wishes to persuade, convince, or strengthen in their faith.

But this *parrhēsia*, a relationship to others, is also a virtue with regard to God. *Parrhēsia* is not just the courage one demonstrates in the face of persecution in order to convince others, [but also a] courage [which] is confidence in God, and this confidence cannot be separated from one's courageous stance towards others.* What distinguishes the courage of someone like Socrates, or Diogenes, for example, from the martyr's courage—I think it is Saint Jerome who says this—is precisely that the former is only the courage of man addressing other men, whereas the courage of the Christian martyrs rests on this other aspect, this other dimension of the same *parrhēsia*, which is trust in God; confidence in salvation, in God's goodness, and also in His listening. And here a whole set of texts show that the theme of *parrhēsia* joins up with the theme of faith and trust in God.

For example, in Gregory of Nyssa (*On Virginity*, chapter XII) there is a very interesting passage on this *parrhēsia*, because to some extent it matches up with some Cynic themes. The subject of this text is the becoming again and returning to the first man in his first life by turning in on oneself, by self-examination, and all the work by which one tries to decipher the original form of the soul behind all that has clouded and soiled it. And Gregory of Nyssa asks: Who then was this first man? "He was naked ... he looked on God's face with free assurance (*en parrhēsia*) and did not judge yet according to taste and sight, but 'found delight in the Lord alone.' "[18] This passage matches up with the Cynic idea of an original life which is at the same time a true life

---

* The manuscript refers here to letter 139 of Theodoret of Cyrus.

to which one should return, a life of destitution and nakedness. You find again the idea of a *parrhēsia* as *parrhēsia* of vis-à-vis, of face-to-face with God. In this original state of the relationship of humanity to God, men have full confidence. They are in *parrhēsia* with God: openness of heart, immediate presence, and direct communication of the soul and God. There are some other texts like this, but in the end maybe less significant. You see that the term *parrhēsia* appears therefore with this positive value of a relationship to others inasmuch as one can demonstrate the courage of truth, even to the point of martyrdom. One can have this courage of truth only insofar as one embeds it, roots it in a relationship of trust in God which brings us closest to Him, in a sort of face-to-face encounter which recalls, up to a point at least, the first face-to-face encounter of man with his Creator. That is the positive core of this term *parrhēsia*.

Yet, with the increasing stress on obedience in Christian life, in Christian practice and institutions, in relation to oneself as well as in relation to truth, this relationship of confidence, in which *parrhēsia* consists, of man in himself, sustained by a relationship of confidence in God, this confidence (in salvation, in being heard by God, in being close to God, in the soul being open to God), will become obscured, as it were, and wavers in relation to its own principle and its first axis, becoming as if clouded over. And this theme of *parrhēsia*-confidence will be replaced by the principle of a trembling obedience, in which the Christian will have to fear God and recognize the necessity of submitting to His will, and to the will of those who represent Him. We will see the development of the theme of mistrust of oneself, as well as the rule of silence. As a result of this, *parrhēsia*, [as] that openness of heart, that relationship of confidence which brought man and God face-to-face, closest to each other, is increasingly in danger of appearing as a sort of arrogance and presumption.

All of this, of course, would have to be developed further, but from, let's say, the fourth century, but increasingly clearly in the fifth and sixth centuries, you see the development of structures of authority in Christianity which, as it were, embed individual asceticism within institutional structures, like those, [on the one hand,] of the coenoby and collective monasticism, and those, on the other hand, of the pastorate, which entrust the conduct of souls to pastors, priests, or bishops.

As these structures develop, the theme of a relationship to God having to be mediated by obedience brings with it, as condition and consequence, the idea that the individual is unable to bring about his salvation by himself, that he is not capable of finding by himself that vis-à-vis, that face-to-face encounter with God which characterized man's first existence. And if he cannot have that relation to God on his own, through the impulse of his soul and the openness of his heart, if he can have it only through the intermediary of these structures of authority, then this is in fact the sign that he must mistrust himself. He must not believe, imagine, or be so arrogant as to think that he can secure his own salvation and find the way of opening to God by himself. He must be the object of his mistrust. He must be the object of an attentive, scrupulous, and suspicious vigilance. By himself and in himself he can find nothing but evil, and only by renunciation of self and putting this general principle of obedience into practice will man be able to secure his salvation.

That *parrhēsia* that had become a relationship of confidence and openness of heart that could bind man to God will disappear, or rather, it will reappear as a confidence which is seen as a fault, a danger, a vice. *Parrhēsia* as confidence is foreign to the principle of the fear of God. It is contrary to the necessary feeling of a distance with regard to the world and things of the world. *Parrhēsia* appears incompatible with the severe gaze that one must now focus on oneself. The person who can bring about his salvation—that is to say, who fears God, who feels himself to be a stranger in the world, who keeps a watch on himself, and must constantly keep a watch on himself—cannot have that *parrhēsia*, that jubilant confidence by which he was bound to God, borne up to grasp Him in a direct face-to-face encounter. So *parrhēsia* now appears as a blameworthy behavior of presumption, familiarity, and arrogant self-confidence.

There are a number of texts along these lines, in the ascetic literature in particular, and in the *Sayings of the Fathers*. There is, for example, this saying: Be not the intimate of the hegumenos (the superior of the community), do not associate with him too much, for you will acquire thereby a certain *parrhēsia*, and end up desiring to be superior in turn.[19] And the most famous, most fundamental text in this new criticism of *parrhēsia* is the saying of Agathon (the first in the alphabetic list).

A young monk comes to Agathon and says: "I want to live with the brethren; tell me how to remain with them." Agathon's reply is: "Every day of your life retain the stranger's mentality you had the first day you came to them, so that you do not become too free with them."[20] And he continues: What is there worse than *parrhēsia*? Nothing, he says. "It is like a great scorching wind which, when it gets up, drives everyone before it and destroys the fruit of the trees."[21] The context of this saying is interesting and can be reconstructed very schematically in the following way. What is at issue, as you can see, is community life. It involves a young monk who has come to practice asceticism, but with the brethren. Now in this new life, with the brethren then, under the authority of a hegumenos, and with a common rule, there is a danger. The danger is that the monk, linked in this way with the others, will lead the life of the world in full confidence, mistrusting neither himself nor the others, and that he will practice *parrhēsia*, a *parrhēsia* which we have seen is confidence in self, in others, and in what can be done together, thereby forgetting that in a true ascetic life one must always be working at the elaboration of self, the decipherment of self, which involves mistrust of oneself, fear for one's salvation, and trembling before God's will.

Agathon's text from the *Sayings* will be taken up later by Dorotheos of Gaza, in Book IV of his *Instructions*. He takes up this saying to comment on it in the following way in which I think we find the elements of this developing anti-*parrhēsia*: "We drive the fear of God far from ourselves ... by not thinking of death or punishment, by not taking care of ourselves, by not examining our conduct, by living anyhow and associating with anyone. In short, by giving ourselves up to *parrhēsia*, which is the worst of all and absolute ruin."[22] If we look at the different elements characterizing this *parrhēsia*, we see that it consists in driving the fear of God far from oneself, by thinking neither of death nor of punishment. In that confidence that one claims to have [in] God, one turns around and away from the fear of God, from the fear of what will happen when one dies, from the fear of Judgment and its punishments. The second characteristic of this *parrhēsia*, which has now become a fault and a vice, is that not only does one not fear God, but one does not take care of oneself. "We drive the fear of God far from ourselves ... by not thinking of death or punishment, by not taking care of ourselves, by not examining our conduct."[23] You see that *parrhēsia* is now negligence with regard to self, whereas previously it was care of self. One does not care about self; one lacks the proper mistrust of self. Third, "living anyhow and associating with anyone."[24] This time, it is confidence in the world. Familiarity with the world, the habit of living with others, accepting what they do and say, are all hostile bonds, contrary to the necessary strangeness one should have with regard to the world.

This is what characterizes *parrhēsia*: non-fear of God, non-mistrust of self, and non-mistrust of the world. It is arrogant confidence. Dorotheos goes on to say, and this is also interesting: "*Parrhēsia* is multiform, moreover: it manifests itself through speaking, touching, and looking. It is *parrhēsia* which encourages idle speech and talk about worldly things."[25] In this communal, coenobitic life, *parrhēsia* encourages idle speech and talk about worldly things. "Again, *parrhēsia* is touching someone needlessly, putting a hand on a brother for fun."[26] So, insofar as one mistrusts self, mistrusts others, and fears God, one must turn one's back on all that familiarity, on the physical, bodily familiarity which may exist in community life. And finally, *parrhēsia* consists in looking at a brother without shame (*anaidōs*).[27] "Without respect one cannot even honor God, nor obey a single commandment just once, whatever it may be."[28] You see that, quite strangely, *parrhēsia* appears here as an absence of respect. It is not impossible that there is an explicit reference in this to all that which, in the Greek conception, connected the problem of *parrhēsia* to the Stoic and Cynic problem of *aidōs* or *anaideia* (shame and shamelessness). But even without this explicit reference, we find again here the problem of *parrhēsia* as self-confidence which ignores the necessary respect due to others. Consequently: elimination of *parrhēsia* as arrogance and self-confidence; necessity of respect, whose first form and essential manifestation must be obedience. Where there is obedience there cannot be *parrhēsia*. We find again what I was just saying to you, namely that the problem of obedience is at the heart of this reversal of the values of *parrhēsia*.

It seems to me, and I will stop there, that, through this split in the notion of *parrhēsia*, we see the opposition between two major frameworks, two major cores of Christian experience being marked out. I told you that *parrhēsia* is not a universally, uniformly, and continually negative notion in these patristic texts. There is a positive and a negative conception of *parrhēsia*. The positive conception makes *parrhēsia* a confidence in God, a confidence as the element which enables an apostle or a martyr to speak the truth with which he has been entrusted. *Parrhēsia* is also the confidence one has in God's love and in how one will be received by Him on the Day of Judgment. Around this conception of *parrhēsia* crystallized what could be called the parrhesiastic pole of Christianity, in which the relation to the truth is established in the form of a face-to-face relationship with God and in a human confidence which corresponds to the effusion of divine love. It seems to me that this parrhesiastic pole was a source of what could be called the great mystical tradition of Christianity. To whoever has sufficient confidence in God, to whoever has a heart pure enough to open itself to God, God will respond with a movement which will assure that person's salvation and allow them access to an eternal face-to-face relationship with [Him]. Such is the positive function of *parrhēsia*.

And then you have another, anti-parrhesiastic pole in Christianity, which founds, not the mystical, but the ascetic tradition. Here the relation to the truth can be established only in a relationship of fearful and reverential obedience to God, and in the form of a suspicious decipherment of self, through temptations and trials. This ascetic, anti-parrhesiastic pole without confidence, this pole of mistrust of oneself and fear of God, is no less important than the parrhesiastic pole. I would even say that historically and institutionally it has been much more important, since it was ultimately around this pole that all the pastoral institutions of Christianity developed. And it seems to me that the long and difficult persistence of mysticism, of mystical experience in Christianity, is nothing other than the survival of the parrhesiastic pole of confidence in God, which, not without difficulty, has subsisted in the margins against the great enterprise of anti-parrhesiastic suspicion that man is called upon to manifest and practice with regard to himself and others, through obedience to God, and in fear and trembling before this same God.

Henceforth, with the development of this ascetic, anti-parrhesiastic, non parrhesiastic pole, the truth of self, or again the problem of the relations between knowledge of the truth and truth of self, will no longer be able to take, as it were, the full and complete form of an *other* existence (*une existence autre*) which would be at once existence of truth and existence capable of knowing the truth of self. Henceforth, knowledge of self (knowledge regarding self, about oneself) will be one of the fundamental conditions, and even the prior condition of the soul's purification, and consequently for the moment when one will finally be able to arrive at the relationship of confidence with God. One will attain the true life only on the prior condition of having practiced on oneself this decipherment of the truth.

Only by deciphering the truth of self in this world, deciphering oneself with mistrust of oneself and the world, and in fear and trembling before God, will enable us to have access to the true life. It was by this reversal, which put the truth of life before the true life that Christian asceticism fundamentally modified an ancient asceticism which always aspired to lead both the true life and the life of truth at the same time, and which, in Cynicism at least, affirmed the possibility of leading this true life of truth.

There you are, listen, I had things to say to you about the general framework of these analyses.* But, well, it is too late. So, thank you.

---

* M.F. is referring here to the following argument, which ends the 1984 manuscript:
"Relations between subject and truth

A. Studying them in Antiquity: more precisely over that long period which goes from Classical Greece to what we call Late Antiquity or the start of Christianity; it is a question here of the other side of the event that historians of philosophy are familiar with, in which the relations of being and truth are defined in the mode of metaphysics.
B. I tried to study these relations in their relative autonomy with regard to the latter (= an independence which implies also a presence of relations); I tried to study them from the point of view of the practice of self.
a: that is to say, by keeping the analyses as much as possible this side of the definition of the subject as soul and focusing on the problem of the self, of the relation to self; of course, this relation to self often takes the form of the relation to the soul, but it would clearly be somewhat reductive to leave it at that, and the diversity of meanings given to the term *psukhē* is comprehensible, or at least becomes clearer, if we understand in fact that the relation to the soul is part of a set: relation to the *bios*, to the body, to the passions, to events.
b. and I have tried to analyze these relations as themes of practices, that is to say: objects of elaboration by technical processes which one thinks about, modifies, and perfects; which one teaches or passes on through examples; which one implements throughout one's existence, either at certain privileged and select moments, or regularly and continually; these practices are rooted in a fundamental attitude which is concern about oneself, the care of self; and their aim is to constitute an *ēthos*, a way of being and doing things, a way of conducting oneself corresponding to rational principles and founding the exercise of freedom understood as independence; the study of practices of self is therefore the study of concrete forms, prescriptions, and techniques taken by the care of self in its ethopoetic role.
C. I thought that we could pose the question of the games of truth to which these relations to self appeal, on which they are supported, and from which they expect certain specific

effects; and there are several responses to that question: the ethical constitution of oneself presupposes the acquisition of more or less numerous and complex bodies of knowledge which concern more or less extensive domains which are more or less close to or distant from the subject himself: fundamental truth about the world, life, the human being, etcetera; practical truths about what it is appropriate to do in such and such circumstances; in short, a whole set of things to be learned: the *mathēmata*.

But the constitution of oneself as ethical subject also implies another game of truth: no longer that of the apprenticeship, the acquisition of true propositions with which one arms oneself, equips oneself for life and its events, but that of the attention focused on oneself, on what one is able to do, on the degree of independence one has attained, on the progress one has to make and remains to be made; and these games of truth do not come under the *mathēmata*, they are not things that are taught and learned, but exercises one performs on oneself: self-examination; tests of endurance, and other checks of representations; the dimension of *askēsis*.

That is not all: this exercise of the truth about oneself is not enough. It is possible, it finds a foundation only on the basis of that attitude of the courage of truth: having the courage to tell the truth without concealing anything and regardless of the dangers this involves.

And it is here that we encounter the notion of *parrhēsia*: originally a political notion which, without losing this meaning, is inflected by joining up with the principle of the care of self.

Parrhēsia, or rather the parrhesiastic game, appears in two aspects:

- the courage to tell the truth to the person one wants to help and direct in the ethical formation of himself

- the courage to manifest the truth about oneself, to show oneself as one is, in the face of all opposition.

It is on this point that the Cynic appears: he has the insolent courage to show himself as he is; he has the boldness to tell the truth; and in his criticism of rules, conventions, customs, and habits, addressing himself off-handedly and aggressively to sovereigns and the powerful, he reverses the functions of political *parrhēsia* and dramatizes also the philosophical life.

I am well aware that by presenting things in this way I give the impression of according Cynicism a crucial place in ancient ethics and of making it an absolutely central figure, whereas it remains, at least from a certain point of view, marginal and borderline.

In fact, with Cynicism, I wanted solely to explore a boundary, one of two boundaries between which the themes of care of self and courage of truth are deployed.

It would be better to present things in this way.

Ancient philosophy linked the principle of the care of self (duty to take care of oneself) and the requirement of the courage to tell the truth, to manifest the truth.

Actually, there were many different ways of linking together care of self and courage of truth, and we can no doubt recognize two extreme forms, two opposed modalities, both of which, each in their own way, have taken up Socratic *epimeleia* and *parrhēsia*:

- the Platonic modality. In a very significant way it accentuates the importance and extent of the *mathēmata*; it gives knowledge of self the form of the contemplation of self by self and the ontological recognition of what the soul is in its own being; it tends to establish a double division: of the soul and the body; of the true world and the world of appearances; in short its considerable importance is due to it having been able to link that form of the care of self to the foundation of metaphysics, while the distinction between esoteric teaching and the lessons given to all limited its political impact.

- the Cynic modality. It reduces as strictly as possible the domain of the *mathēmata*, it gives knowledge of self the privileged form of exercise, test, and practices of endurance; it seeks to manifest the human being in its stripped down animal truth, and if it held itself back in relation to metaphysics and remained foreign to its great historical posterity, it left a certain mode of life in the history of the West, a certain *bios*, which, in its different modalities, has played a crucial role.

1. H. Schlier, "Parrēsia, parrēsiazomai" in G. Kittel, ed., *Theologisches Wörterbuch zum Neuen Testament* (Stuttgart: Kohlammer Verlag, 1932-1979) pp. 869-884; English translation as *Theological Dictionary of the New Testament* (Grand Rapids, MI: William B. Eerdmans Publishing Company, 2006 [1964]).

2. S.B. Marrow, S.J., "Parrhesia and the New Testament," *Catholic Biblical Quarterly*, 44, 1982, pp. 431-436.

3. Philon d'Alexandrie, *De specialibus legibus*, I, §322, trans. S. Daniel (Paris: Éd. du Cerf, coll. "Œuvres de Philon d'Alexandrie" 24, 1975) p. 205. And §320, p. 203: "If these things are actually good and advantageous, why then, initiates, do you shut yourselves up in a deep darkness?"; English translation by F.H. Colson, as Philo, "On the Special Laws," Book One, in *Philo. Volume VII* (Cambridge, Mass.: Harvard University Press, Loeb Classical Library, 1937) p. 287: "nature also does not conceal any of her glorious and admirable works" and p. 285: "For tell me, ye mystics, if these things are good and profitable, why do you shut yourselves up in profound darkness?"

4. Ibid., §321, Fr. p. 203: "Let those whose actions are beneficial to all make use of a full freedom of speech"; Eng. p. 287: "But let those whose actions serve the common weal use freedom of speech."

5. Ibid.; Eng.: "and walk in daylight through the midst of the market-place, ready to converse with crowded gatherings."

6. *Job*, 22, 21-28 (French translation by L. Segond, 1910). [The English translation by Claude E. Fox in *A New English Translation of the Septuagint* (London: Oxford University Press, 2009), pp. 683-684 is significantly different: "And if you turn and humble yourself before the Lord,/you have put what is unjust far from your dwelling./ ... /Therefore the Almighty will be your help from your enemies,/for he will render you pure as silver tried by fire./ Then you will speak frankly before the Lord, looking up to heaven cheerfully./And when you pray to him, he will listen to you/and give to you to pay your vows./Yes, he will restore you to a righteous way of life,/and there will be light on your ways"; G.B.]

7. Philo, *On the Special Laws*, I, §203, Fr. p. 131: "The Law wishes first of all that the mind of the person who sacrifices has been made holy by good thoughts...so that at the same time as he imposes his hands, he may utter words in all frankness (*parrhēsiasamenon*), in the purity of his conscience (*ek katharou tou suneidotos*)"; Eng. p. 215: "For the law desires, first, that the mind of the worshipper should be sanctified by exercise in good and profitable thoughts and judgments...so that as he lays his hands on the victim, he can boldly and with a pure conscience speak in this wise."

8. *Proverbs*, I, 20-21 (Segond); English translation by Johann Cook, in *A New English Translation*, p. 624: "Wisdom sings hymns in the streets,/and in the squares she leads frankly,/and on the top of the walls she proclaims,/and at the gates of the powerful she waits,/and at the gates of the city she speaks boldly."

9. *Psalms*, 94, 1-3 (Segond); English translation by Albert Pietersma, in *A New English Translation*, p. 594: "The Lord is God of vengeance;/the God of vengeance spoke openly!/Be exalted, O you who judge the earth;/give to the proud what they deserve!/How long shall sinners, O Lord,/how long shall sinners boast."

10. *The First Epistle of John*, 5, 13; King James version: "These things have I written unto you that believe on the name of the Son of God; that ye may know that ye have eternal life."

11. Ibid., 5, 14; King James: "And this is the confidence that we have in him, that if we ask anything according to his will, he heareth us."

By raising the question of the relations between care of self and courage of truth, Platonism and Cynicism seem in fact to represent two major forms which face each other and each of which has given rise to a different genealogy: on one side the *psukhē*, knowledge of self, work of purification, access to the other world; on the other side, the *bios*, putting oneself to the test, reduction to animality, battle in this world against the world.

But what I would like to stress in conclusion is this: there is no establishment of the truth without an essential position of otherness; the truth is never the same; there can be truth only in the form of the other world and the other life (*l'autre monde et de la vie autre*).

12. Ibid., 4, 16-17; King James: "God is love; and he that dwelleth in love dwelleth in God, and God in him. Herein is our love made perfect, that we may have boldness in the day of judgment: because as he is, so are we in this world."

13. *Acts of the Apostles*, 9, 26-27: "When he got to Jerusalem, Saul tried to join them; but they all feared him, not believing that he was a disciple. Then Barnabas took him, and led him to the Apostles, and told them how Saul had seen the Lord on the road, how He had spoken to him, and how at Damascus he had preached frankly in the name of Jesus"; King James: "And when Saul was come to Jerusalem, he assayed to join himself to the disciples: but they were all afraid of him, and believed not that he was a disciple. But Barnabas took him, and brought him to the apostles, and declared unto them how he had seen the Lord in the way, and that he had spoken to him, and how he had preached boldly at Damascus in the name of Jesus."

14. Ibid., 9, 28-29: "He went around with them in Jerusalem, and expressed himself with full assurance in the name of the Lord. He spoke also and argued with the Hellenists; but they sought to take his life"; King James: "And he was with them coming in and going out at Jerusalem. And he spake boldly in the name of the Lord Jesus, and disputed against the Grecians: but they went about to slay him."

15. *Epistle of Paul to the Ephesians*, 6, 19-20; King James: "that utterance may be given unto me, that I may open my mouth boldly, to make known the mystery of the gospel, For which I am an ambassador in bonds: that therein I may speak boldly, as I ought to speak."

16. Jean Chrysostome, *Sur le providence de Dieu*, XIX, 11, trans. A.-M. Malingrey (Paris: Éd. du Cerf, 1961) p. 241: "While no one is there to guide the flock, the sheep themselves perform the office of shepherds, soldiers the office of leader, thanks to their bold confidence (*parrhēsias*) and courage (*andreias*), and you, with appropriate fervor, zeal, and self-control, are you not struck with amazement and full of admiration for the acts of virtue caused by the events?"

17. Ibid., XXII, 5, p. 259.

18. Grégoire de Nysse, *Traité de la virginité*, 302c, XII, 4, trans. M. Aubineau (Paris: Éd. du Cerf, 1966) pp. 417-418; English translation by Virginia Woods Callahan as "On Virginity" in Saint Gregory of Nyssa, *Ascetical Works* (Washington, D.C.: The Catholic University of America Press, "The Fathers of the Church," 1967) p. 46: "But what was he? Liberated from the threat of death, looking freely upon the face of God, not yet judging the beautiful by taste and sight, but only enjoying the Lord."

19. *Les Apophtegmes des Pères*, vol. II, §XV, no. 107, trans. A. Guy (Paris: Éd. du Cerf, "Sources chrétiennes," 2003): "An old man says: 'Be not intimate with the hegumenos and do not associate with him too much, for you will acquire thereby assurance (*kai parrhēsian hexeis*) and desire to command others (*hēgeisthai allōn*).'"

20. Ibid., p. 31; *The Sayings of the Desert Fathers*, p. 17: "'I want to live with the brethren; tell me how to dwell with them.'"; "'All the days of your life keep the frame of mind of the stranger which you have on the first day you join them so as not to become too familiar with them.'"

21. Foucault here quotes Agathon in the text of Dorotheos of Gaza. Dorothée de Gaza, *Œuvres spirituelles, Instructions*, IV, 52, 16651 (Paris: Éd. du Cerf, 1963) p. 233; English translation by Eric P. Wheeler, "On the Fear of God" in Dorotheos of Gaza, *Discourses and Sayings* (Kalamazoo, Michigan: Cistercian Publications, 1977) p. 114: "it is like a great conflagration from which, when it burns up, men flee and the fruit of the trees around it is utterly destroyed."

22. Ibid.; Eng. pp. 113-114: "We chase away from us the fear of the Lord by the fact that...we do not keep before us the thought of death, or punishment, nor do we attend to our own condition, or examine how we spend our time, but we live differently and are occupied with different things, pandering to our liberty, giving way to ourselves, self-indulgence-this is the worst of all, this is perfect ruin."

23. Ibid.

24. Ibid.

25. Ibid., §53, p. 235; Eng. p. 114: "Self-indulgence takes many forms. A man may be self-indulgent in speech, in touch, in sight. From self-indulgence a man comes to idle speech and worldly talk."

26. Ibid.; Eng.: "There is self-indulgence in touching without necessity, making mocking signs with the hands."
27. Ibid.: "It is again *parrhēsia*...to look at him without reserve (*anaidōs*)"; Eng.: "approaching someone shamelessly."
28. Ibid.; Eng.: "For without mutual respect, God himself is not honored, nor is it possible to fulfill a single commandment."

COURSE CONTEXT

Frédéric Gros*

THE 1984 COURSE WAS the last Foucault gave at the Collège de France. He was very weak at the beginning of the year and did not start the lectures until February, ending them at the end of March. His last public words at the Collège were: "It is too late. So, thank you." His death the following June threw a rather particular light on the lectures, with the obvious temptation to read into them something like a philosophical testament. The course lends itself to this moreover, since Foucault decides to situate the whole of his critical work in this return to Socrates and the very roots of philosophy.

1. THE GENERAL METHODOLOGICAL FRAMEWORK: THE ONTOLOGY OF TRUE DISCOURSES

As usual, Foucault devoted a good part of the first lectures to methodological considerations, trying once again to define the specificity of his approach. Returning to a problematic of *The Archeology of Knowledge*,[1] Foucault constructs the distinctive character of his approach around the concept of truth. Archeology consisted in bringing to light a discursive organization which structures constituted knowledge. This discursive stratum possessed neither the systematic nor the demonstrative character of science, but represented a constraining code of

* Frédéric Gros is Professor of Political Philosophy at the University of Paris-XII. He also teaches at the Paris Institute of Political Studies (Master "Political History and Theory"). His most recent book is *États de violence. Essai sur la fin de la guerre* (Paris: Gallimard, Les Essais, 2006).

organization for discourses.[2] By situating his object of analysis at that level, Foucault escaped from the canons of both epistemology and the history of science: what was involved was no longer the question of the formal conditions of the possibility and progressive revelation of true discourses, but that of their historical-cultural conditions of existence. In 1984, Foucault now constructs the distinction between an analysis of epistemological structures, on the one hand, and a study of "alethurgic" forms, on the other.[3] The former addresses the question of what makes a true knowledge possible, the latter that of the ethical transformations of the subject, as it makes the subject's relation to self and others dependent on a particular kind of truth-telling. What Foucault calls "alethurgy" presupposes a principle of irreducibility to any epistemology.

Throughout 1984 he sets out a resolutely original concept of truth which, according to him, had a major presence in ancient philosophy which has been largely hidden by the modern regime of discourse and knowledge. Moreover, as in the previous year, in the first lectures Foucault sets out again the triptych of his critical work: a study of modes of veridiction (rather than an epistemology of Truth); an analysis of forms of governmentality (rather than a theory of Power); a description of techniques of subjectivation (rather than a deduction of the Subject)—the stake consisting in taking a determinate cultural nucleus (confession, care of self, etcetera) as the object to be studied, which acquires its volume precisely from the intersection of these three dimensions.[4]

The analysis of the notion of *parrhēsia*, begun in 1982 and continued in 1983, should be placed in this general theoretical framework. More precisely, it finds its place in what Foucault, in 1983, called an "ontology of true discourses."[5] This should be understood as a study which does not look for the intrinsic forms which confer validity on true discourses, but examines the modes of being which true discourses entail for the subject who uses them. By considering the type of relation to self and others entailed by an assertion of truth, Foucault is able to propose a unique typology of styles of veridiction in ancient culture, far removed from that of the tradition known since Aristotle (the ranking of discourses according to their logical form). Thus, the truth-telling of *parrhēsia* is distinguished from the truth-telling of teaching, prophecy, and wisdom inasmuch as it aims for the transformation of the *ēthos* of its interlocutor, involves a risk for its speaker, and belongs to a temporality of present reality.[6]

2. THE GREEK SECRET OF POLITICS: ETHICAL DIFFERENCE

Foucault devoted a good part of 1983 to the study of the notion of *parrhēsia* in its political dimension. It involved eliciting a non-formal condition of Athenian democracy: the courage of a truth-telling practiced in the form of a public exposition. Courage of truth was defined as what made the democratic game effective and authentic.[7]

In the first lectures of 1984,[8] Foucault claims to be doing no more than taking stock of the previous year, but we realize that what is presented as a simple restatement is actually a radicalization of the stakes. In fact, now meaning to get to the nodal point of Greek political philosophy, Foucault discovers it in what he calls a principle of ethical differentiation.

It has always been said that the political philosophy of the Ancients was obsessed with the search for the "best regime." This was usually seen as the effect of a somewhat naive and insipid moralism, in contrast with the tragic pessimism of the Moderns. Foucault attempts here a different reading: to show that the search for the "best constitution" does not confirm a moral quest, but constitutes the insertion of a principle of ethical differentiation within the problem of the government of men. In fact, it is not a matter of defining an ideal form or an optimal mechanics of the distribution of powers, but of pointing out that political excellence depends on the way in which the political actors have formed themselves as ethical subjects. It is difficult to grasp the difference, however, since in the end it always amounts to saying that a good politics will depend on virtuous leaders. But Foucault's contribution is crucial in that he points out that this ethical differentiation is not in fact the moral quality of a leader, or even the singularity of a stylization of existence which would mark out an exceptional individual from the anonymous mass. Rather, it presupposes bringing the difference of the truth into play in the construction of the relation to self, or rather the truth as difference, as distance taken from public opinion and common certainties. Hence the structural fragility of democracy,[9] for if it is possible to think of an individual or small group managing to carry out this ethically differentiating work on themselves, it seems improbable that an entire people will succeed in doing so. It remains that ethical difference, which allows the best *politeia* to exist, is only the effect of the difference of truth itself in a subject.

This revaluation of Greek political thought at the same time allows Foucault's approach to follow in its wake.[10] He arrives in fact at the following result: ancient philosophy makes the problem of the government of men (*politeia*) dependent upon an ethical elaboration of the subject (*ēthos*) that is able to bring out in him and in front of others the difference of a discourse of truth (*alētheia*). The three dimensions of Knowledge, Power, and the Subject (or rather, of veridiction, governmentality, and subjectivation), by which Foucault had characterized his undertaking, are thus present here. But these three dimensions are not like three distinct parts to be studied in turn, like three separate domains. Foucault insists on the idea that the identity of the discourse of philosophy since its Socratic-Platonic foundation consists precisely in a structure of reciprocal correlation: never studying discourses of truth without at the same time describing their effect on the government of self and others; never analyzing structures of power without at the same time showing the knowledge and forms of subjectivation they rely on; never identifying modes of subjectivation without including their political extensions and the relations they have to the truth. And we should not hope for one of these dimensions to be consecrated as the fundamental dimension: political violence or moral postures will never disappear in a general logic; the demands of knowledge or ethical constructions will never be reduced to forms of domination; and finally, it will never be possible to found forms of veridiction and modes of government on subjective structures. These two principles of necessary correlation and definitive irreducibility suffice to define the identity of philosophy since the Greeks, and this is where Foucault situates his project.

Finally, this is why, to those who might say (we have heard this, and will do so again) that a "true" philosophy of knowledge or a "true" political or moral philosophy cannot be found in Foucault, he means to reply: thank goodness, for to claim that epistemology, morality, and politics could ever constitute autonomous, juxtaposed domains, that each of them must be worked out methodically and separately, would mean leaving behind philosophy in its original inspiration.

3. THE LIGHT OF DEATH

Foucault died of AIDS on 25 June 1984. In January of the same year he was treated with antibiotics.[11] He wrote to Maurice Pinguet: "I thought I had AIDS, but energetic treatment has put me back on my feet."[12] He recovered and was once again able to give his lectures, starting in February, although at the beginning of March he complained of a bad attack of influenza.[13]

It is difficult to know precisely what knowledge Foucault had and wanted to have of the illness which was weakening him. In his *Chronologie*, Daniel Defert points out that in March, regularly treated at the Tarnier hospital, "he did not ask for or receive any diagnosis," and that the only question he seemed to ask the doctors was: "How much time have I got?"[14] This is a question of the personal relationship each individual has with his or her body, illness, and death. It remains that some of the readings put forward in 1984 of great texts from the history of philosophy are situated precisely in this horizon of illness and death.[15] We could cite here especially, since it is a matter of founding texts, Plato's the *Apology* and the *Phaedo*.

With regard to the fate of Socrates, it is striking to see that Foucault's demonstration focuses on his relation to death, and even more precisely on the problem of the fear of dying.[16] The general theme is that of the transformation of a *parrhēsia* practiced in the political arena (Pericles or Solon facing the Athenians) into a *parrhēsia* (Socratic examination) practiced on the public square within the framework of an inter-individual relationship. To the possible reproach that he had not got involved in politics, Socrates replied: If I had done so I would have long been dead. However, Foucault shows that this answer does not signify a fear of dying, but rather the attempt to preserve for as long as possible a mission given to him by the gods; the care of others: that insistent and perpetual vigilance aimed at checking whether everyone is taking proper care of himself. Incidentally, we see the binding together of the themes of *parrhēsia* and *epimeleia* (care of self) carried out around the figure of Socrates, and the philosophical enterprise redefined as that courageous truth-telling which aims to transform the mode of being of its interlocutor in order that he learns to take care of himself correctly. It is in order to be able to safeguard this task that Socrates refuses to engage in politics. It is not out of fear of dying; it is the fear of his crucial mission being compromised by his disappearance. Similarly, it could be said that a serious illness frightens us, not because it arouses the hideous specter of nothingness, but because it would prevent us from completing our research or work. The best proof of this is that Socrates (the whole of the *Apology* recounts this) finally prefers death to the betrayal of his essential mission.

If the whole of Foucault's reading of the *Apology* does in fact revolve around the problem of the fear of death, that of the *Phaedo* investigates the essential relation between philosophy and illness.[17] The problem raised is that of Socrates' last words, that enigmatic injunction: "Crito, we owe a cock to Asclepius; take care of it" (118a). Traditionally, these last words have always been given a nihilistic interpretation. As if Socrates had said: The god of medicine must be thanked, for by the death which saves, I am cured of the illness of living. To give this famous phrase a different reading, Foucault calls on Dumézil:[18] if Socrates thanks Asclepius in his last moments, it is indeed because he has been cured, but cured by philosophy of the disease of false discourse, of the contagion of common and dominant opinions, of the epidemic of prejudices.

Thus the two statements Foucault arrives at in 1984, and which we cannot separate from his struggle against disease and his death in June, would be: it is not death that frightens me, but the interruption of my task; of all diseases, the one which is genuinely mortal is the disease of discourses (false clarity and deceptive self-evidence), and right to the end philosophy cures me of it. Finally we should note that the whole of Socrates' last words (take care of it, don't neglect my request: *mē amelēsēte*) refers to the *epimeleia* dear to Foucault. This care of self, which Foucault wanted to place at the heart of ancient ethics, will have been in fact the last word on Socrates' lips.

But it still remains to show, and this is the whole stake of the 1984 lectures, that this care of self, which in 1982[19] was understood simply as a specific structuring of the subject irreducible to the Christian or transcendental model (neither the subject of confession nor the transcendental ego), is also a care for truth-telling, which calls for courage, and especially a care for the world and for others, demanding the adoption of a "true life" as continuous criticism of the world.

4. THE *LACHES* AND RADICALIZATION OF THE STAKES

In a course entitled "The courage of the truth" it was virtually imperative that Foucault read Plato's *Laches*, since it is one of the rare texts of philosophy devoted entirely to the problem of courage. But if the choice of the work is not surprising, the perspective of the reading is more so. In fact, whereas the great majority of commentators endeavor to study the central body of the text (the dialectical moment of the aborted attempts of Nicias and Laches to define the virtue of courage), Foucault is interested exclusively in the beginning and end of the dialogue, that is to say, in what many have considered to be part of its anecdotal staging.[20] With the emphasis once again on *parrhēsia*, this division of the text permits him to envisage as courageous only someone who maintains a truth-telling and especially a style of existence.

In continuity with the commentary on the *Apology*, Socrates is always presented as someone who in his approach to individuals practices a courageous truth-telling in order to correct their *ēthos*. But the reading of the *Laches* puts forward a new dimension: Socrates is also the person with the courage to assert this requirement of truth in the visible fabric of his existence. This second element is decisive for the overall logic of the lectures, since it will make it possible to pose the problem of the "true life" and hence to provide a general theoretical framework for the study of ancient Cynicism. Moreover, this revaluation is decisive at this point in that it immediately leads to Foucault putting the history of philosophy into an overall perspective which, while modifying its content, takes up the binary structure of derivation which had served to describe modern thought since Kant.[21] From the end of the seventies, on several occasions Foucault had in fact distinguished two Kantian legacies: the transcendental legacy (with the question: what can I know?) and the critical legacy (with the question: how are we governed?). In the eighties he enriched that distinction, adding the ethical dimension to the study of power relations, the question becoming: what modes of subjectivation are articulated with forms of the government of men, either in order to resist them or to inhabit them?

In 1984 Foucault takes things well upstream, since he now derives two major spiritual directions of philosophy from Plato: on one side, drawing inspiration from the *Alcibiades*, a metaphysics of the soul which, in discourse and by theoretical contemplation, endeavors to found the original bond of the immortal *psukhē* and transcendent truth; on the other, problematized in the *Laches*, an aesthetics of existence pursuing the task of giving a visible, harmonious, beautiful form to life (to the *bios*). The alternative derived from Plato is strongly distinguished from the Kantian alternative. With Kant it was a matter of distinguishing two domains of research: defining either the formal conditions of truth or the conditions of the governmentality of men. This time it will be a question of contrasting, on the one hand, a spiritual task which is fulfilled in a *logos*, in the formation of a system of knowledge with, on the other, a different task embodied in the effectiveness of concrete existence and ascesis. One gets the impression in fact that in 1984 Foucault put in the balance philosophy as discursive domain, as constituted knowledge, and philosophy as test and attitude, rather than two possible types of study (transcendental or historical-critical).

5. THE CYNIC GESTURE

A large part of the 1984 course is devoted to a highly original and one might even say abrasive presentation of ancient Cynicism. Cynicism has always been the poor relation in the history of ancient philosophy. The studies which have been devoted to it remain ridiculously few when compared with those dealing with Epicureanism, Stoicism, and even Skepticism. Foucault was therefore one of the first to renew interest in France for this ever marginal movement.[22] It is also true that very little has survived of the representatives of Cynicism since, on the one hand, the doctrinal content was relatively crude and, on the other, following the example of Socrates, who left us no book, generally speaking they neglected the art of writing. Cynicism has basically come down to us through anecdotes, little stories, witty remarks, or other cutting replies. It is precisely this theoretical poverty that Foucault takes up in order to make Cynicism the pure moment of a radical revaluation of philosophical truth, placed in the context of *praxis*, test of life, and transformation of the world.

The Cynics were recognized by their *parrhēsia* (free-spokenness) and so this notion again serves as the introductory framework for this new study. Until now, Foucault had studied two major sides of the notion: first of all, the political side, which developed from a highly ambivalent democratic moment—*parrhēsia* designating both the courageous speech of the citizen addressing unpleasant truths to his peers, thereby risking their wrath, and the demagogic right of anyone to say anything—towards an autocratic moment which sees the philosopher come on the scene as counselor to a Prince to whom he lectures courageously, raising himself above the hubbub of court flatterers; and then the ethical side, represented by Socrates stopping each person to ask them if they are taking proper care of themselves.

Cynic *parrhēsia* is a third major form of the courage of truth, although to start with it may be understood as the simple continuation of Socratic truth-telling. For after all, Diogenes and Crates are also described as haranguing the crowds in public, denouncing everyone's compromises and forcing each individual to question their way of life. But this demand takes place in an incomparably more aggressive, brutal, and radical way than with Socrates. Moreover, the difference is not only one of intensity or style. It is already no longer just a matter, as after all was the case with Socrates, of setting out to disturb the good (or false) conscience that everyone has with regard to their certainties, of denouncing false knowledge, or even of ironically underlining the dissonances between someone's discourses and actions. One feels in fact that with the Cynics the challenges are more radical, more extensive: the whole of everyday practices and accepted values in ancient culture are attacked and affected. Socrates is no doubt an odd character, but apart from his mania for interminable discussions, he adopts a rather orderly and traditional way of life. In some aspects he even presents the form of a model citizen. While being out of line, he is not a complete marginal. The Cynic, on the other hand, is noted for a way of life at odds with society. As we have said, he is recognized first of all by his frankness (*parrhēsia*: his language is rough, his verbal attacks virulent, and his harangues violent), but also by his external appearance: rather grubby, he goes about in an old cloak which also serves as a blanket, carrying a simple beggar's pouch, with bare feet or just sandals, and holding his walking and imprecator's staff. Now, for Foucault, this absolutely brutish way of life, this wandering destitution is the manifest expression of a testing of existence by the truth.[23] This theme is crucial, for it allows the sudden appearance of a dimension which has largely been unnoticed by classical Western philosophy: the elementary (*l'élémentaire*). When the question of the truth is put to thought it raises the dimension of the essential as that which *always remains*, transcends mental variations, and knows no temporal decomposition. The Cynics will put the question of the truth to life in its materiality, permitting that which *resists absolutely* to be brought to light: do I need feasts to feed myself, palaces to sleep? What really is necessary to live? Then, after ascetic reduction, the elementary rises to the surface, like a nappe of absolute necessity. There remains the earth for living, the starry sky as roof, and streams from which to drink. Like the Platonists trying to discern the essential knowledge through the thick fog of received opinions, the Cynics track down the elementary in the undergrowth of conventions and social artifice: that which absolutely resists in the concreteness of existence. By asking for what is true in each desire and each need, Cynic *parrhēsia* produces a scouring of existence as a result of which our lives appear overburdened with contingencies and futile vanities.[24] This close weave of life and truth, this commitment to manifesting the true in the visible body of existence will be the essential characterization of Cynicism, whose descendants are to be sought in religion (the mendicant orders of Christianity), politics (the nineteenth century revolutionary), or modern and contemporary art.[25]

The idea of a life wrought in the thickness of its materiality by the truth is again pursued by Foucault in the framework of a reinterpretation of the famous Cynic motto: *parakharaxon to nomisma* ("Falsify the currency"). Foucault begins by noting what has often been noted, that the idea of *nomos* (law, custom) should be heard behind the word *nomisma*, and that the values to be overturned are not only monetary. But above what must be stressed is that the *parakharaxis* means again the fact of effacing the effigy used on a coin so that it recovers its genuine value. The Cynic injunction can then be understood as a reversal of the values of truth.

So the question arises of the "meanings" or "values" of the truth[26] (he does not speak of criteria). Foucault distinguishes four: non-concealment, purity, conformity to nature, and sovereignty. In the Cynics *parakharaxon to nomisma* will then mean: assert the true, stripped down meanings of the truth by making them the guiding principles of existence. To lead a "true life" will thus mean: to lead an entirely public and exposed life (the unhidden), an existence of destitution and complete poverty (the pure), a radically wild and animal life (the straight [*droit*]), and manifesting an unlimited sovereignty (the immutable). The Cynic transvaluation is the work which consists in living the principles of truth *to the letter*. The truth, definitively, is that which is unbearable, as soon as it leaves the domain of discourse to be embodied in existence. The "true life" can only manifest itself as "other life (*vie autre*)."

6. THE TRUE LIFE AS CALL FOR THE CRITICISM AND TRANSFORMATION OF THE WORLD

At the end of his study of ancient Cynicism, Foucault is able to redeploy an overall view and recontextualize the relationship between Greco-Latin thought and Christianity. Since the 1980 lectures, this relationship had taken on the features of an opposition between, on the one hand, an ancient mode of subjectivation involving a construction of self, a shaping of its existence, the continuous application of a care of self as practice of freedom, and, on the other, a mode of subjectivation leading to self-renunciation through the application of knowledge and a permanent obligation to obey.[27] In 1984 he modifies this overall perspective.

The analysis of the "reversal" of the meanings of truth had already enabled the concept of "an other life (*une vie autre*)" to be established. By setting to work in the very substance of his life the values of truth which were traditionally referred to discourse, the Cynic actually produces the scandal of a "true life" which breaks with all the usual forms of existence. The true life is no longer represented as that accomplished existence which carries to perfection the qualities or virtues that ordinary lives bring out only in a weak light. With the Cynics, it becomes a scandalous, disturbing, immediately rejected and marginalized "other" life.

In the last lectures, by pushing the reading of Epictetus' discourse III-22 (the great portrait of the Cynic) as far as possible,[28] Foucault shows how this other life is at the same time the criticism of the existing world and supports the call for "an other world (*monde autre*)." The true life thus manifests itself as an other life giving rise to the demand for a different world. The ascesis by which the Cynic forces his life to permanent exposure, radical destitution, unrestrained animality, and unlimited sovereignty (the four reversed meanings of truth) is hardly designed (as could be the case for Epicureans, Stoics, and Skeptics) merely to guarantee inner tranquility as an end in itself, albeit edifying at the same time. The Cynic strives for the "true life" so as to get others to see that they are mistaken and have lost the way, and to explode the hypocrisy of accepted values. Through this dissonant irruption of the "true life" in the midst of the chorus of lies and pretences, of accepted injustice and concealed iniquities, the Cynic makes "an other world" loom up on the horizon, the advent of which would presuppose the transformation of the present world. This critique, presupposing a continuous work on self and an instruction to others, should be interpreted as a political task. And this "philosophical militancy," as Foucault calls it, is even the noblest and highest politics: it is the great *politeuesthai* of Epictetus.[29]

We understand thereby how the study of the Cynic movement enabled him to resolve the risk represented by the position of the "care of self" at the heart of ancient ethics. Certainly the virtue of this reorientation was first of all polemical, since it involved deposing the classical privilege of the *gnōthi seaton* (self knowledge) and contrasting Christian ascesis, entailing self-renunciation and obedience to the other, with an ancient ascesis leading to a self-construction.[30] However, Foucault was insistent on showing that this care was not a solitary exercise, but a social practice, and even an invitation to good government (correctly caring for self in order to care correctly for others). It remains that this care of self, basically presented in its Stoic and Epicurean version, revealed a game of freedom in which internal construction took precedence over the political transformation of the world. The introduction of the concept of *parrhēsia*, in its Socratic and Cynic version, had to bring a decisive shift of balance to this presentation of ancient ethics. In all their aggressiveness, the Cynics represent in fact the moment at which the value of ascesis consists in it being addressed as a provocation to others, since it involves constituting oneself as a spectacle which confronts each individual with his own contradictions, so that the care of self becomes precisely a care of the world, the "true life" calling for the advent of an "other world."

For Foucault, facing the Cynic articulation "other life (*vie autre*)"/"other world (*monde autre*)" stands Platonism. In Platonism, it is a matter rather of getting "the other world (*l'autre monde*)" and "the other life (*l'autre vie*)" to function together. The other world is the realm of pure Forms, of eternal Truths, transcending that of perceptible, changing, corruptible realities. The other life is that promised to the soul when, after being separated from the body, it will discover its native homeland in the other world, for a transparent, luminous, and eternal life. We understand then the style that the care of self must take in the Platonist tradition: preserving and purifying one's soul for the beyond, looking forward to its authentic destiny. According to Foucault, the originality of Christianity is precisely its having blended the Platonic aim of "another world (*autre monde*)" and the Cynic demand for an "other life (*vie autre*)": faith and hope in a heavenly homeland will have to be authenticated by an existence which transgresses temporal customs. The meaning of the break represented by Luther and the Reformation consists in refusing to make access to the other world depend on an other life: henceforth one will be able to ensure one's salvation by fulfilling one's daily task, one's immanent vocation.[31]

7. THE TRUE AND THE OTHER

The interplays between *"autre vie"*/*"vie autre"* and *"autre monde"*/*"monde autre"* presuppose a philosophy of otherness in Foucault which, while not stated systematically, gives thought its élan. This notion of otherness enables him in fact to philosophically anchor his concept of truth.[32] Already in 1983, in order to disturb the idea of a happy marriage between democracy and truth, Foucault had called on the *Republic*. The virtue of true discourse, according to Plato, was that of introducing a difference and hierarchies into the soul, shattering consensual logics and establishing orders of precedence between desires. In 1984 Foucault again makes use of this dimension of otherness as sign of the true, but this time with regard to life (the *bios*). The "true life," the life which puts itself to the test of the truth, cannot fail to appear to the common people as a transgressive other life which marks a break.

We can see why, when he had compiled the different "meanings" and "values" of the truth, Foucault, after having established the themes of the unconcealed, the pure, the straight, and the sovereign, abandons, crossing it out in the manuscript, the theme of the "identical" or "same" that he had first recorded as one of the major traditional meanings of the truth—and which is in fact at the heart of our philosophical culture. But precisely in 1984 he wants to emphasize that the hallmark of the true is otherness: that which makes a difference in the world and in people's opinions, that which forces one to transform one's mode of being, that whose difference opens up the perspective of an other world to be constructed, to be imagined. The philosopher thus becomes someone who, through the courage of his truth-telling, makes the lightning flash of an otherness vibrate through his life and speech.

Foucault can thus write these words, which he will not have time to utter, but which are the last he wrote on the last page of the manuscript of his final lecture: *"What I would like to stress in conclusion is this: there is no establishment of the truth without an essential position of otherness; the truth is never the same; there can be truth only in the form of the other world and the other life (l'autre monde et de la vie autre)."*

1. *L'Archéologie du savoir* (Paris: Gallimard, 1969); English translation by Alan Sheridan, *The Archeology of Knowledge* (London: Tavistock, and New York: Pantheon, 1972).
2. Ibid., Fr. pp. 232-255; Eng. pp. 178-195 (Chapter 6: Science and Knowledge).
3. See above, lecture of 1 February 1984, first hour. (Foucault first formed the concept of "alethurgy" in 1980, and he explained it in the Collège de France course, "On The Government of the Living," in the lectures of 23 and 30 January 1980).
4. Ibid.
5. *Le Gouvernement de soi et autres. Cours au Collège de France, 1982-1983*, ed. F. Gros (Paris: Gallimard-Le Seuil, "Hautes Études," 2008) pp. 285-286; English translation by Graham Burchell, *The Government of Self and Others. Lectures at the Collège de France, 1982-1983*, English series ed., Arnold I. Davidson (Basingstoke and New York: Palgrave Macmillan, 2010) pp. 309-310.
6. See above, lecture of 1 February 1984, first and second hour.
7. *Le Gouvernement de soi et des autres*, pp. 145-147; *The Government of Self and Others*, pp. 158-159.
8. See above, lecture of 1 February 1984, first and second hour.
9. See above, in the lecture of 8 February, first hour, the conclusion of the analysis of the enigmatic passage in Aristotle's *Politics* (III, 7, 1279a-b), pp. 49-50.
10. See above, lecture of 8 February, conclusion of the second hour.
11. D. Defert, "Chronologie," in *Dits et Écrits, 1954-1988*, vol. I, ed. D. Defert and F. Ewald, collab. J. Lagrange (Paris: Gallimard, 1994) p. 63.
12. Ibid.
13. See above, the first words of the lecture of 21 March, first hour.
14. D. Defert, "Chronologie," p. 63.
15. Moreover, Foucault's existence in the Winter of 1984 seemed to bear the stamp of that radical asceticism which he was describing at that time in the Cynics.
16. See above, lecture of 15 February, first hour.
17. See above, lecture of 15 February, second hour.
18. G. Dumézil, *"Le Moyne noir en gris dedans Varennes." Sotie nostradamique suivie d'un Divertissement sur les dernières paroles de Socrate* (Paris: Gallimard, 1984); English translation by Betsy Wing as *The Riddle of Nostradamus. A Critical Dialogue* (Baltimore and London: The Johns Hopkins University Press, 1999).
19. *L'Herméneutique du sujet. Cours au Collège de France, 1981-1982*, ed. F. Gros (Paris: Gallimard-Le Seuil, 2001); English translation by Graham Burchell, *The Hermeneutics of the Subject. Lectures at the Collège de France, 1981-1982*, English series editor Arnold I. Davidson (New York and Basingstoke: Palgrave Macmillan, 2004).
20. See above, lecture of 22 February.
21. On this point, see already in 1978, the lecture "Qu'est-ce que la critique?" given to the Société française de Philosophie on 27 May 1978; English translation by Kevin Paul Geiman as "What is Critique?" in James Schmidt, ed., *What is Enlightenment? Eighteenth-Century Answers and Twentieth-Century Questions* (Berkeley, Los Angeles, and London: University of California Press, 1996), and in 1983, the lecture of 5 January, *Le gouvernement de soi et des autres*, pp. 21-22; *The Government of Self and Others*, pp. 19-21.
22. Studies of the Cynics have however been widely carried on from the end of the 1980s, notably in France around M.-O. Goulet-Cazé. See M.-O. Goulet-Cazé, *L'Ascèse cynique. Un commentaire de Diogène Laërce VI 70-71* (Paris: Vrin, 1986); M.-O. Goulet-Cazé and R. Goulet, eds., *Le Cynisme ancien et se prolongements. Actes du colloque international du CNRS (Paris, 22-25 juillet 1991)* (Paris: Presses universitaires de France, 1993); and M.-O. Goulet-Cazé and R. Bracht Branham, eds., *The Cynics. The Movement in Antiquity and its Legacy* (Berkeley: University of California Press, 1996). We note also the appearance, contemporary with the lectures, of: P. Sloterdijk, *Kritik der zynischen Vernunft* (Frankfurt/Main: Suhrkamp, 1983); English translation by Michael Eldred as *Critique of Cynical Reason* (London: Verso, 1988), and A. Glucksmann, *Cynisme et Passion* (Paris: Grasset, 1981); English translation as *Cynicism and Passion* (Stanford French and Italian Studies, vol. 76, September 1995).
23. See above, lecture of 29 February, first hour.
24. Ibid.

25. See above, lecture of 29 February, second hour.

26. See above, lecture of 7 March, first hour.

27. See the lectures of 12, 19, and 26 March 1980 of the 1979-1980 lectures at the Collège de France ("The Government of the Living").

28. See above, lecture of 21 March, first hour.

29. It will be noted that in the last months, even when he was living a rarefied existence and focused entirely on the work of preparing his lectures as well as reading and correcting the proofs of volumes 2 and 3 of his *History of Sexuality—L'Usage des plaisirs* and *Le Souci de soi* (Paris: Gallimard, 1984); English translations by R. Hurley as, *The Usage of Pleasure* (New York: Random House, 1985) and *The Care of Self* (New York: Random House, 1986)—Foucault still found time in March to meet Claude Mauriac accompanied by Senegalese and Malian workers, evicted by the police from their homes, in order to write letters supporting them (on this point, see D. Defert, "Chronologie" in *Dits et Écrits*, vol. I).

30. See in *L'Herméneutique du sujet*; *The Hermeneutics of the Subject*.

31. See above, lecture of 14 March, first hour.

32. This work of the notion of truth based on Greek philosophy had already begun in the first course given at the Collège de France in 1971 ("The Will to Knowledge"), which focused on the techniques of truth in archaic Greece and thereby initiated a secret dialogue with Heidegger's thought concerning the Greek idea of truth, which is therefore brought to a close in 1984.

INDEX OF CONCEPTS AND NOTIONS

Compiled by Sue Carlton

INDEX OF NAMES

Compiled by Sue Carlton

Page numbers followed by n refer to the chapter notes

Printed by Printforce, the Netherlands